T0207490

Lecture Notes of the Institute for Computer Sciences, Social Informatics and Telecommunications Engineering   452

More information about this series at https://link.springer.com/bookseries/8197

Adilson Luiz Pinto ·
Ricardo Arencibia-Jorge (Eds.)

Data and Information in Online Environments

Third EAI International Conference, DIONE 2022
Virtual Event, July 28–29, 2022
Proceedings

 Springer

Editors
Adilson Luiz Pinto ⓘ
Federal University of Santa Catarina (UFSC)
Florianópolis, Brazil

Ricardo Arencibia-Jorge ⓘ
National Autonomous University of Mexico
(UNAM)
Mexico City, Mexico

ISSN 1867-8211   ISSN 1867-822X (electronic)
Lecture Notes of the Institute for Computer Sciences, Social Informatics
and Telecommunications Engineering
ISBN 978-3-031-22323-5   ISBN 978-3-031-22324-2 (eBook)
https://doi.org/10.1007/978-3-031-22324-2

This Springer imprint is published by the registered company Springer Nature Switzerland AG
The registered company address is: Gewerbestrasse 11, 6330 Cham, Switzerland

Preface

Two decades of the 21st century have passed. At the height of the fourth industrial revolution, and after a period of social distancing caused by the COVID-19 pandemic, online social environments have become essential spaces for human interaction. The constant generation of data and information in these environments, and the development of tools for its processing and analysis, is now a critical task for information professionals and data scientists. In this context, we are happy to present the proceedings of the 3rd EAI International Conference on Data and Information in Online Environments (DIONE 2022), which took place during July 28–29, 2022.

The conference was initially conceived to be onsite in Florianopolis, Brazil, but it was held online given the COVID-19 pandemic. DIONE aims to bring together academicians and practitioners willing to discuss topics around the intersection of computer science, information science, and communication science. The attractiveness of the scope and topics has brought relevant research results. This proceeding consists of chapters covering deep learning, data management, software design, social networks, natural language processing, and data processing in various contexts like scholarly publishing, health and medicine, higher education, innovation and research, energy and transportation, and business organizations.

DIONE 2022 brought together doctoral and post-doctoral students, researchers, professors, and scholars from Brazil, China, Peru, Switzerland, and Vietnam. Brazil was the most represented country since 75% of submissions were from Brazilian researchers. The conference consisted of 20 papers (18 full papers and two short papers), which were selected from 56 submissions. Each submission was reviewed by at least three members of the Program Committee in an double blind process. In addition to the paper presentations, a core topic was covered during the keynote speech "Infodemic as a contemporary informational challenge", presented by Carlos Alberto Ávila Araújo (Department of Information Science, Federal University of Minas Gerais, Brazil).

We appreciate the continuous support of the Organizing Committee, the members of the Technical Program Committee, and the external reviewers who were committed to delivering their evaluations on time. We also acknowledge once again all the support received from the EAI office. Last but not least, we thank all the attendees for being part of this project.

We hope that the proceedings of DIONE 2022 are of interest to the scientific community devoted to the topics covered herein and help to bring more research discussions to our future editions.

Adilson Luiz Pinto
Ricardo Arencibia-Jorge

Organization

Steering Committee

Imrich Chlamtac — University of Trento, Italy
Adilson Luiz Pinto — Federal University of Santa Catarina (UFSC), Brazil

Organizing Committee

General Chair

Adilson Luiz Pinto — Federal University of Santa Catarina (UFSC), Brazil

TPC Chair

Ricardo Arencibia Jorge — Universidad Nacional Autónoma de México, Mexico

Local Chair

Márcio Matias — Federal University of Santa Catarina (UFSC), Brazil

Publicity and Social Media Chair

Enrique Muriel Torrado — Federal University of Santa Catarina (UFSC), Brazil

Publications Chair

Genilson Geraldo — Federal University of Santa Catarina (UFSC), Brazil

Posters and PhD Track Chair

David Caldevilla — Universidad Complutense de Madrid, Spain

Panels Chair

María Josefa Peralta González — Central University of Las Villas, Cuba

Demos Chair

Almudena Barrientos Báez   Universidad Europea de Madrid, Spain

Tutorials Chair

Orlando Gregorio Chaviano   Javeriana University of Colombia, Colombia

Technical Program Committee

Alessandra de Benedictis	Università di Napoli Federico II, Italy
Alexandre Ribas Semeler	Universidade Federal do Rio Grande do Sul, Brazil
Caio Coneglian Saraiva	UNIVEM, Brazil
Claudio Silvestri	Università Ca' Foscari Venezia, Italy
Denysson Axel Ribeiro Mota	Universidade de São Paulo, Brazil
Joaquin Garcia-Alfaro	Institut Polytechnique de Paris, France
Joe Tekli	Lebanese American University, Lebanon
Laercio Pioli	FUSC, Brazil
Lakshmish Ramaswamy	University of Georgia, USA
Li Xiong	Emory University, USA
Lucas Wanner	UNICAMP, Brazil
Manuel Paulino Linares Herrera	Cuban Academy of Sciences, Cuba
Marcio Sembay	Centro Universitário Unifacvest, Brazil
Marcos Yuzuru de Oliveira Camada	IFBaiano, Campus Catu, Brazil
María Josefa Peralta González	Central University of Las Villas, Cuba
Mariana Matulovic	UNESP, Brazil
Mirelys Puerta Diaz	UNESP, Brazil
Nancy Sánchez Tarragó	Universidade Federal de Rio Grande do Norte, Brazil
Rafael Lima	UNIMONTES, Brazil
Rahul Katarya	Delhi Technological University, India
Ricardo Arencibia Jorge	UNAM, Mexico
Ulises Orozco Rosa	CETYS Universidad, Mexico
Vinicius Faria Culmant Ramos	FUSC, Brazil

Contents

Advances in Artificial Intelligence for Data Processing and Analysis in Online Social Environments

Informational Challenges for the Study of Science, Technology and Society Relationships

Disinformation as a Social Phenomenon

Fabiano Couto Corrêa da Silva[(✉)]

Universidade Federal do Rio Grande do Sul, Porto Alegre, Brasil
fabianocc@gmail.com

Abstract. Disinformation has created a new global disorder, where the new conditions of production, circulation and consumption of information have made disinformation an important geostrategic tool that, associated with hybrid techniques, requires a reformulation of the action of communication media. **Methodology:** We analyzed the way the media disseminate information based on five filters indicated by Chomsky and Herman [1]: Filter 1: Importance, ownership and orientation of the benefits of the media; Filter 2: Advertising as the main source of income; Filter 3: The provision of news to the media; Filter 4: The corrective measures as a method to discipline the media; Filter 5: Anticommunism as a control mechanism. **Results:** The analysis carried out shows that, in addition to false news, real news are manipulated and oriented to polarize, requiring an adaptation of society in the construction of a new cognitive muscle. And social networks cannot counteract the global highways of disinformation that cross countries, continents and languages.

Keywords: Disinformation · Fake news · Communication · Public manipulation · News

1 Introduction

We spend our lives accumulating knowledge and experiences in order to build a personal identity and an individual worldview, through which we observe and understand new information and knowledge. The construction of this lens is ongoing and subconscious for most of us most of the time. Often, when we receive new cognitive information that "feels right" for the lens we have constructed, we continue without making many adjustments. We may reach a point where something shakes us up enough to require us to change focus or find a new pair of lenses altogether. No matter how individual events or messages may shape our internal understanding and external perception, we are likely to benefit most from seeing as much of the picture as possible from as many points as possible. That is, our understanding and accuracy of vision are more guaranteed by understanding the context and seeing enough to make our own choices of where and how to "pick out" the information that makes sense of our reality.

Thus, if the role of worldview in the construction of a viable society depends on the information we receive, we must ask ourselves: what happens when the information we are receiving is false and manipulated; moreover, it is not readily visible?

© ICST Institute for Computer Sciences, Social Informatics and Telecommunications Engineering 2022
Published by Springer Nature Switzerland AG 2022. All Rights Reserved
A. L. Pinto and R. Arencibia-Jorge (Eds.): DIONE 2022, LNICST 452, pp. 3–15, 2022.
https://doi.org/10.1007/978-3-031-22324-2_1

Misinformation, lies, hoaxes, false advertising and "fake news" have been updated under the name "fake news". So this is not a new phenomenon. Although the use of the term fake news is relatively recent - popularized during and by the US campaign between Hillary Clinton and Donald Trump - the phenomenon of disinformation is much older than recent history suggests.

As early as the sixth century B.C., the Chinese general and strategist Sun Tzu explained in the famous book Art of War the importance of deception in the conduct of conflict. In particular, he insisted on the need to find a compromise between truth and falsehood in order to make fake news as credible and effective as possible. To do this, it was necessary to properly calibrate its purpose and, in particular, the target people, by playing a combination between real data and the purpose of the interlocutor [2].

This method was also used in the 1st century to justify the Roman persecutions against Christians. Marriage between "brothers and sisters" meant eating "the body of Christ". Those who committed this offense were accused of incest and cannibalism. The Roman authorities manipulated the emotions of the multitudes to arouse a feeling of indignation and rejection that legitimized political condemnation, itself based on moral disapproval.

Since the 1880s and during the sixty years in which contemporary anti-Semitism was relentlessly anchored in Europe, fake news directed at Jews increased and grew, from the Protocol of the Elders of Zion, a false plan to conquer the world by Jews and Masons, to the debates over the entry into Canadian territory of tens of thousands of European Jewish refugees in 1943–44 [3].

In the Middle Ages and in modern times, the same mechanisms are at work in societies where rumor circulates quickly and where the powers that be do not hesitate to instrumentalize multiple and unfounded noises in a public space in which they shape. In recent years, this fight against misinformation - or "fakenews" - has become a cornerstone of contemporary political debate. It serves as a support for politicians who wish to defend their public action or to be exempted from any behavior harmful to their career, or even for states seeking to destabilize an opponent [4].

The phenomenon of false information has been multiplied by a new model that is based on a triad: creating a rumor, strengthening it through lies, and disseminating it in publicly accessible information sources. These resources enable and diversify the dissemination of false information. The mechanisms used in this triad are essentially aimed at capturing the attention of Internet users, generating an impact and convincing the user to share and amplify its acceptance. The goal is simple: to manipulate the reality of the facts. This mechanism involves, for example, discrediting a public figure, destabilizing him, or undermining his reputation. Once the rumor is shared by the largest number of people, it becomes credible. The same "scheme" works to alter reality about any concept or reality that differs from the belief of the spreader of a fake news story. In contemporary times, the qualitative and quantitative change in the dissemination of information is a turning point in the way we receive content of all kinds, expanding the reach and power of information, centralized in large media centers.

This paper analyzes a theory about the manipulation created by mass media companies, which are responsible for much of today's information and entertainment "content".

We will describe this framing process in light of current media trends, including additional theories about the influences and driving forces behind the production/distribution of information to the general public. Finally, we will discuss some ways and suggestions for preserving the balance by increasing awareness of "framing" and alternative views (those outside of the mainstream mass/multimedia media we have access to).

2   How is Information Selected?

Every day, hundreds of news stories arrive in the newsrooms of major newspapers and media conglomerates. How do the editors decide what they will inform us about each region of the world? Why do contradictory news stories sometimes appear, and at other times they are all repeated synchronously?

The selection and construction of the news, from the discursive-argumentative point of view, signals to us that there is no informative neutrality or impartiality. The very defense of this type of argument from the editorial point of view, is, above all, an ideological position in relation to the discourses that the newspapers construct.

When a newspaper chooses a cover with the denunciation of an act of corruption or the educational methodology of the Ministry of Education, no matter how apparently objective its presentation may be, it is assuming a certain position, tied to the ideological positions defended by the newspaper. Therefore, our first mission must be to discover the mechanism of news selection.

An analysis in this respect comes from the American linguist Noam Chomsky and the economist and media analyst Edward S. Herman, in the book The Manipulation of the Public [1]. In their analysis, they present us with what they call "Filters," that is, the verdicts by which money and power filter the news until it is ready for publication, marginalize discrepancies, and allow government and dominant private interests to find a suitable message for the public. These are structures of power and ideology that are often ignored by information professionals. This is because the current model is absolutely internalized. Let's take an example: In April 2008, the purchase of a DVD, television, or cell phone was allowed in Cuba [5]. All journalists and also citizens interpreted it as an advance of Cubans' freedoms; they reported about freedom not in the economic sense, but in the political sense. They forgot that this criterion of freedom ignores one detail: the availability of money to access the products that carry the news. In our model, we call everything we can do freedom if we have the money for it; therefore, it is not freedom. Cubans who did not have money could not buy these products.

With this example we don't intend to question the Cuban government's measure, we only want to highlight the imperceptible ideological bias that the media and the citizens apply in the interpretation of reality. When it is said that a sign of Cuban repression is that lobster fishermen are forbidden to keep, consume or trade them, we forget that not even the waiters of seafood restaurants in Porto Alegre can afford to go to that restaurant to have dinner with their friends. Not even the mason who builds luxury villas on the beach can spend a single summer day in one of them, i.e., there is at the foundation of discursive constructions, their historicity, ideology, social class struggles, and the action of economic, political and social power.

But let's go back to the filters, the mechanisms by which it is determined what is news and what is not, what we should be interested in and what we will talk about in the cafeteria when we have breakfast with our co-workers, what the experts call agenda setting[1]. It is not so much that they set our ideology, to the point of selecting which topics should interest us, which is more than imposing an ideology, because it means replacing reality, even more so in a world where social relations have greatly diminished to the detriment of our role as media consumers.

3 Methodology

In this paper we analyze how the media disseminate information based on the five filter theory of researchers Chomsky and Herman [1]. The definition of each filter is:

Filter 1: Importance, ownership and benefit orientation of media;
Filter 2: Advertising as the main source of income;
Filter 3: The supply of news to the media;
Filter 4: The corrective measures as a method to discipline the media;
Filter 5: Anti-communism as a control mechanism.

4 Results

According to Chomsky and Herman's [1] model, the media operates through 5 filters. These are:

Filter 1: Importance, ownership, and benefit orientation of the media
In the 19th century, the workers' press in the UK had a key role with the workers, their cultural problems and the potential to foster organization and awareness [7]. As much as it bothered the government, they could not try to stifle it because they risked popular revolts. It was in the late 19th and early 20th centuries that the industrialization of the press came, so that the investments needed to start a newspaper went from 1,000 lb in 1837 to 50,000 in 1867. The Sunday Press, which appeared in 1918, needed two million pounds. For industrial development to achieve what no government had ever achieved: to extinguish all the informational projects that did not have a large investment [8]. The most humble people lost the right to co-administer a means of communication as a result of the big fortunes that started to dominate the publishing market. This is a phenomenon caused by globalization. It is enough to observe the current panorama to realize that behind the media there are powerful business groups that disseminate international information through local media, which simply replicate the content of large agencies. Currently, 80% of the news that circulates around the world comes from four international news agencies: Associated Press, United Press International, Reuters, and Agence France Press. These agencies are the ones that set the agenda and provide most of the international news [9]. In the Brazilian case, the newspapers of large circulation are controlled by five families, which seek to meet their own interests and those of the political groups they represent. We would like to recall an episode reported by Fernando Morais [10] in his biography of

---

[1] The agenda setting hypothesis is a type of media social effect that comprises the selection, arrangement, and incidence of news about topics of public interest [6].

the journalist Assis Chateaubriand, Rubem Braga opposed to the censorship promoted by Chateaubriand in a chronicle that would be published in Diários Associados, protested to the owner of the newspaper, the latter would have replied as follows "If you want to have full freedom, Rubem, buy a newspaper to write everything you want". We believe that this anecdote portrays the reality of media conglomerates, that is, opinion in the newspaper only exists in the spectrum of the conglomerate's own performance.

Until recently, the main threat to information plurality was the concentration of media in a few media companies. These companies have managed to make their work more profitable by offering the same information product to feed the newspaper, radio, and television of the same media group. As media owners have ceased to be pure communication groups, they are now simply colossal economic groups that need not have communication as their core business. The progressive accusation that they have turned information into business has also been left behind. With most of the mechanisms of domination by violence eliminated in developed countries, the value of shaping public opinion is now so high that it is worth spending money on lost funds. Therefore, many media have become mere image departments of the business sectors. Thus, we have in our press, radio and television shareholders who are banks, financial companies, insurance companies, telecommunications companies, or even guns. Bankers and business executives who have no relation to information sit on the boards of these media companies.

The financial engineering is such that we can't even tell if they make a profit. If they want to improve the newspaper's income statement, all they have to do is inject shareholder advertising (Vale, Petrobras, etc.).

Filter 2: Advertising as the main source of income

Obviously, in the case of the British press in the 19th century the selling price of the newspaper had to cover all production costs. In this way, income depended only on the number of citizens who bought it. The addition of advertising began to serve as extra income for the media that catered to the public's preferences. Newspapers that got it could even reduce their selling price. On the other hand, those that did not attract advertisements had more expensive prices, reduced their sales, suffered losses or less benefits to reinvest and improve their sales possibilities (color, attractive format, etc.). As Chomsky and Herman [1] say, with advertising, the free market does not offer a neutral system in which the buyer finally decides. The advertisers' choices are those that influence the prosperity and survival of the media. Just look at how the calls for boycott are not directed at the public, but at the advertisers. Currently, what we pay for a newspaper is equivalent to 50% of its cost and the advertisers pay the rest. The newspaper that does not have the advertisers' approval must cost twice as much, even assuming that the same number of people buy it; if fewer people buy it - which would be logical if it costs twice as much - the price per copy increases much more. This thesis about the distortion factor of advertising is neutralized when one tries to argue that advertisers do not condition the content, and that if the media has a large audience, advertisers will be left without considering what kind of information is offered. Let's look at the fallacy of this theory: for starters, not all citizens are equal for advertising: the one with greater spending power is more valuable than the one without it. A newspaper read by a thousand executives is not the same as by a thousand homeless people. While a financial newspaper presents a promotional ad to attract advertisers, remembering that it is the most read by executives and businessmen; a syndicalist newspaper is not expected to capture many advertisers, although it is the most read by the Metalurgists who demand better working conditions and salary. That's why Petrobrás is advertised in the press and Casas Bahia distributes leaflets in the mailboxes. For the lawyers' association monthly magazine there will be no lack of advertisers, but the magazine aimed at Venezuelan refugees will cost much more to get publicity and certainly the rates will be lower. The current advertising system, in terms of electoral democracy, would be like living with a weighted voting system.

Advertising also triggers a decrease in the cultural level of the content and causes the audience to be recruited, even appealing to the most miserable elements of human nature. If we look closely, we will see that what the media sell is not good informational content, but the audience: they sell us to advertising agencies. One television network offers 30-s ads that are more expensive than the other, because the first one puts as its main value the fact that it has three million viewers watching, and the second ad a much smaller audience. We believe that the media offers us content, but in reality what it is offering are viewers for the advertising companies. This is why a weekly magazine offers cosmetic products with a higher value than the magazine, because in this way it achieves high circulation numbers to offer to advertisers. Put your advertising here: I have half a million readers to advertise a leaflet in the magazine.

But the claim that advertisers have no ideology is false. In 2019 the card operator Mastercard decided to suspend its advertising campaigns that would run during the Copa America with Neymar due to the rape accusation against the player. On occasion, the advertiser's budget serves not only to advertise, but also to ensure that they do not appear negative news of their company. It is easy to understand that ads cannot coexist with the image of bad behavior, at least in theory, so that the sponsor is not seen as supporting bad behavior.

In Brazil, cable television stations function by selling programming space, and each producer must find sponsors to finance his or her program. Therefore, we can't find a company sponsoring a program that denounces the violations by multinationals in Africa, the corruption in Brasilia or that defends the decrease of consumption in the search for a sustainable development model. If there is a supplement about cars in the written press, it is because there has been potential publicity from car companies. Following the same logic about market demand, the Obituaries section was created when it was seen that there was a market for the publication of paid advertisements.

Filter 3: The supply of news to the media
The market demands cost reduction, the media must make the most of its resources, it cannot have journalists and cameras everywhere. The economy forces them to focus on those where important news is produced, in which press conferences are held, and there are influential people whose decisions have great relevance.

According to data from IBGE [11], the percentage of households using the Internet rose from 69.3% to 74.9% from 2016 to 2017 and 96.7% of the country's 70.4 million households had a television set, of which 79.8% had a converter to receive the open television digital signal. Therefore, the maxim that what someone does not want to be known is news, to be only what someone wants to be known is left behind. In journalism, we know that sources who are "anxious" to tell the press something are not offered the same guarantee, nor can they be treated in the same way as those who wish to conceal it. Nor can the source who is part of or has a position affected by the news that those who are not interested in the report be given the same consideration. Among the television news programs of the major Brazilian networks, most are prepared with content provided by an informant whose interests are directly related to what the news says. This model is already so consolidated that even politicians divulge comments for journalists to comply with the "rules of the game", that is, they only spread what politicians ask them to spread. On the other hand, according to Souza [12], most sources are the result of declarative acts that consist of providing a version that confirms a fact or event. Television comments in an empirical way, not about what happens. There are no facts. Noise reigns. That is the main menu. Every day, in the hours before the Brazilian networks broadcast the news, thousands of journalists are willing not to lose their positions. It is the informational dominance of organized sources on what Tarso Genro [13] called "genetically modified journalism."

For the media, it is very expensive to have a journalist for weeks at a time investigating a subject compared to the ease of rewriting press releases, transcribing public statements, or copying news. The regional press is the clearest example, and any local journalist knows what their work routine is: The editor-in-chief or section chief analyzes the press releases or press conferences, chooses the sources that best fit their editorial line, and sends the editors on a tape recorder tour. Then they return to the newsroom and dedicate themselves to transcribing the news from each of the sources. For national and international information, the news is analyzed, chosen and reproduced according to the audience profile before being published. Similarly, political and social life fits the following model perfectly: doctors issue press releases, with medical reports on the status of celebrities when they are sick, politicians transfer their positions to the press rooms more than in institutions, and offer more explanations and details to the media than to judges. So newspapers become bulletin boards, but with content filtered by managers.

But there are also different types of "news" when it comes to selling. For a news outlet, it will always be more credible and comfortable to reproduce a beautiful color print dossier with bar and pie charts from a major company (perhaps advertiser or shareholder) that can be delivered to the public, than a precariously written press release by a workers' assembly where they denounce non-payment of overtime. Neighbors in a neighborhood who will be evicted from their homes will not have a good media schedule and e-mails to send an unseemly note inviting them to a press conference in a carpeted and lighted room where to install television cameras. They will need to face the police for the media to remember them.

On the other hand, the official media always has an aura of truthfulness and neutrality that seduces the newspapers, which for Pecheux and Fuchs [14], we will know as the action of ideology in such a way that the erasure of its (ideological) formulation occurs. A statement by a guerrilla raises more questions about the authenticity of its content than a press conference by the Minister of Defense, because there is in his discourse a defined and institutionalized authorship. Although, in the end, we cannot help but see that the greatest untruths about the reality of Amazon deforestation were announced by the federal government and would eventually be disproved by the National Institute for

Space Research [15]. Finance capital and ideological influences have the potential to disseminate their beliefs and business interests, hire journalists, prepare archival footage that they provide to television stations, and induce committed journalists to tell their version. Our police invite journalists to accompany them in their patrol car, but they are also accused of apologizing for crime when they show the reality of police violence.

Filter 4: Corrective measures as a method to discipline the media
Lobbies, foundations and political or business power groups have enough organizational, financial and political capacity to organize pressure campaigns against media or journalists who leave the dominant line. This is what the 2019 edition of the World Press Freedom Ranking, published by Repórteres sem Fronteiras [16], shows. Threats, insults and assaults are now part of the "occupational risks" of the profession in many countries, including Brazil, which has dropped three places in the ranking and is in 105th place, ever closer to the red zone of the ranking (which indicates the level of difficulty for press professionals).

In countries where there is repression against the press, there are foundations created for the sole purpose of engaging in pressure campaigns against the rebel media. There are oil-related companies acting as a lobby against information about global warming, industry lobbying to increase the limits of glyphosate, the most widely used poison in Brazil, tobacco companies against accusations of illnesses linked to cigarette smoking, or pharmaceutical products pressuring the media that releases news about the side effects of drugs [17]. or lack of therapeutic value. For most media, it is more profitable and less problematic to accept these pressures than to confront these lobbies. The result is that information from human social organizations, precariously organized labor groups, or low-budget human rights groups do not meet the demands of these filters and are excluded from the media.

Filter 5: Anticommunism as a control mechanism
The final filter is the ideology of anti-communism. Communism as the ultimate evil has always been the specter that haunts landlords, because it threatens the very root of their class position and superior status. This ideology has the potential to mobilize society against an enemy. It can draw on a confusing concept to be used against anyone who advocates policies that threaten property interests or supports accommodation with communist states and radicalism. Therefore, it helps fragment the left and labor movements and serves as a mechanism of political control. If the triumph of communism is the worst imaginable outcome, the support of fascism abroad is justified as a lesser evil. Opposition to Social Democrats being too soft on Communists and "playing into their hands" is rationalized in similar terms.

Liberals at home, often accused of being pro-communist or insufficiently anti-communist, are continually kept on the defensive in a cultural environment where anti-communism is the dominant religion. If they allow communism, or something that can be labeled communism, to triumph in the provinces while they are in office, the political costs are heavy. Most of them have completely internalized the religion anyway, but all are under great pressure to demonstrate their anti-communist credentials. This makes them behave very much like reactionaries. Their occasional support for the Social Democrats usually deteriorates when the latter are insufficiently tough on their own indigenous radicals or on popular groups that are organizing among generally marginalized sectors.

It should be noted that when anti-communist fervor is aroused, the demand for serious evidence in support of claims of "communist" abuses is suspended, and charlatans can thrive as sources of evidence. The defectors, informants, and various other opportunists move to center stage as "experts," and remain there even after exposure as highly unreliable liars, if not completely so.

5 Discussion

In recent years, in the face of various conflicts imposed by politics and ideologies of all kinds, as well as competition for new technologies, markets, energy, biological resources, and virtually the entire mass production chain, the threat of deliberate dissemination of false information (disinformation) on the Internet has greatly increased. It is known that through disinformation one can mislead people and impose an inappropriate public opinion. It is also possible, to some extent, to manipulate the consciousness and behavior of individuals and groups of people. Attackers can strengthen or weaken people's views about various events, life values, work done, behavior in current situations, etc. The fact that the Internet is one of the channels for spreading false information is due to the features of the information infrastructure, which include the simplicity and low cost of access, extensive possibilities for manipulating information and its perception, and a high level of anonymity regarding the sharing of information on the net.

It is possible to find websites with objectively false information relatively easily. Fake news about supposedly resonant events (terrorist attacks, death of famous people, financial turmoil) is disseminated in large numbers. Often attention-grabbing techniques are used that distort information about events that have occurred.

To protect the public from false information on the Internet, an effective system is needed to combat it. In general terms, such a system is understood as a set of interrelated organizational, technical, legal and other measures that ensure: timely prevention, detection, blocking, deletion of false information on the Internet, elimination of consequences, liability of attackers for illegal actions. To ensure the functioning of such a system, adequate scientific and methodological support is required.

The problem of protection against false information has existed for a long time, but with the advent and active development of the Internet, the situation has changed dramatically. The volume of information disseminated and the possibilities of its use for the purpose of misleading people have increased substantially. As the international events of recent years have shown, large-scale informational impacts on people for various terrorist, political, religious, economic, and other purposes are possible with the use of robots and artificial intelligence via the Internet. At the same time, the tasks of operational detection, recognizing information impacts, identifying the sources of generation, and predicting such threats have become more complicated. Traditional protection methods under these conditions are not effective enough. They require the active participation of a person in the analysis of information on the subject of its destructiveness and danger to Internet users. This requires a significant expenditure of human and material resources.

The media world constantly feeds back on itself. The obsession with competitiveness is such that on many occasions they forget reality in order to devote themselves to everything at once, to compete for the same news. This is something like the counter-programming that television networks do on non-news issues. Everyone wants to exploit the same supposed news convinced that anyone who doesn't show up will be taken out of the pack. So even if at a given time several events are happening in the world, all the media will be directed to the same focus. This is why for one week the burning in the Amazon occupies the front page of the newspapers and opens the television news, and the following week it disappears from the present, as if the devastation in the jungle had also disappeared.

A striking example around the world is that one of the major conflicts silenced by the media is that of the indigenous peoples anywhere in the world (Latin America, Asia or Africa are clear examples). The conflicts in the so-called "First World" also suffer a clear distortion, mainly because what they raise are structural changes that affect the foundations of the system. Through the media they fully exploit their potential to discredit or hide the demands of these movements.

The need to monetize human resources causes the decrease of stable and knowledgeable correspondents in the country; the mobility of special envoys is enormous to increase their productivity. Even in some cases, journalists are not displaced to report news from the region that may be thousands of miles away. Invaded countries suffer daily the ferocity and barbarism of the modern obsession with control, while invasion and war are consumed as a spectacle, as a fusion of image and reality, with a hyper-reality in which the image no longer represents reality. In it, war is consumed as something electronic, pre-programmed, something that is conducted according to the interests of those who produce and consume the information.

Actually, the problem is a bit of distortion of the rules with the wrong mechanism. So far, by making people confused there are no stationary points that can be used to determine which ones should not be. The words good, morality, ethics and justice all get caught when prevented from access. Even the word logically is distorted bit by bit until it is warped. We all have reasons for different versions, along with societal issues that must be seen together.

There are new rules that give rise to reason in a strange logic: it is reproduced on many levels until people do it on their own. The acquisition of the rules is repeatedly wrong, until people are confused and confused by being "right". Every time this is done, the structure is being distorted. Finally, all sides can think of their own rules. Combined with the spreading of news on the Internet with the intention of being consumed by the international community, the process of universalizing truths becomes faster and more consensual. It establishes content that was quickly presented to be self-interpreted. The "truth" can be presented in parts so that some issues are seen as presented: separate. Then the media or the individual can choose one of the parts of this truth to sustain themselves.

Elections, which should be a tool to reset this mechanics, do not work. Thus, information continues to be constantly distorted. Since society moves at a slower speed than the individual, most people seek to be thought leaders and ideologists because they move faster than the speed of society. When society does not move according to what we believe, we get upset as individuals, because what we express does not transform the reality around us. This is why we seek the networks, a cluster to create ripples in harmony with what we think, feel and express.

The problem is also not limited only to information with wrong content, but also to its legacy. The quality of news, advertising information, and societal commentary are dependent. In the past, the top news stories were often found in the published content. Now, when they are published they begin to develop with hyperconnections; an extension of the truth itself, where social networks play the role of verdict makers on right and wrong, truth and lies.

In fact, we all know less than we expect. This applies to ideas about the total amount of our knowledge. The only thing we are sure about is that after so much scientific effort people still think little, don't like to think, and don't particularly appreciate those who do think. It is likely that one of the main causes of the widespread power of fake news is the inertia of our thinking, because we hardly agree to trigger critical thinking mechanisms. We often follow the lead of our desires, believing what is simple and understandable. We do not want to criticize the information that meets our expectations. In the media space of professional channels and social networks people get unlimited access to series of contents mostly in the world and absorb information in a food compulsion mode. Fake news in this situation is gracious only to those who feel satisfaction or interest in spreading false information. Sociologists, health professionals and even virologists see their object of study being manipulated in fake news.

Spreading misinformation is not unlike spreading a viral infection: first from person to person, then from group to group, and finally the population from one country or entire continent to another. Along with the distribution of fake news by the media comes a process of sharing by large groups of people. The role of social networks in the distribution of fake messages, including Facebook, Twitter or Instagram, are capable of launching an "epidemic model", while traditional media can incur, by mistake, or to strengthen a lie, amplify the coverage of fake news.

Recent history has recorded many examples of the use of fake news for various purposes, competing with verified publications by media that value their reputation. The 21st century has become the digital age of communication, where there are no authorities. In mainstream media outlets the content provided is able to compete with the audience itself. The New York Times or Folha de São Paulo no longer compete for their opinions or investigative quality in front of their readers. The main prize is the number of views. Based on Orlandi [18], we are talking about authorship and its meanings, that is, as the social networks give voice to deinstitutionalized discourses, the sense of authorship, as attributed to a minister, a doctor or a professor is substituted by the authorship constructed in networks.

Disinformation is structured in such a way that it inspires confidence in the consumer and affects his or her opinion, decisions, or general behavior according to the intended goals of the disinformation creators. It is important to remember that disinformation can serve as a special case of propaganda. In particular the military intelligence service that uses disinformation is part of a game in which the media are involved. It is a space that uses a tremendously dangerous psychological weapon of manipulation, the effect of which on mass consciousness can be unpredictable in terms of influence and extremely negative consequences.

6 Conclusions

The current "social online era" in which we live causes people's behavior to change on the Internet. The use of information, once restricted to television and newspapers, can now be followed and studied on sites or posts on Social Networks and content posts on a variety of platforms, with textual, audio, visual, etc. content. On the one hand, the possibility of everyone being a producer of information is an advance in the context of individual freedoms. On the other, when there are more ways to access information without guidance, the problem that emerges is the credibility of that information.

When there are news sources for us to access more easily, the convenience of following the communication channels that we have more identification with our personal interests can become a well-designed trap, as demonstrated in Chomsky and Herman's [1] 5 filters. We need to distinguish the reliability of the information, and it is necessary to use some analytical skills. Many people do not understand these manipulation mechanisms; it becomes easier to believe this information and share it again, making a continuous cycle of sharing and feedback of low-quality information. The problem has worsened because false information has become widely shared due to people's lack of analysis of sources or judgment. In this context, state intervention is necessary in order to criminalize the dissemination of false news. In relation to their textual content, as well as imagery and sound, they also receive comments that misrepresent or lie, in the sequence they are published. To increase visibility, many media companies sell their credibility along with the spaces in their communication channels. The reader looks at the provider, who broadcasts, before getting to the content.Media companies know that their abuse, when discovered, makes them lose their credibility and very difficult to regain it. So they not only try to tell us what is important and how it happened, but also to convince us that they are right in their selection and not lying, so they take a big risk if the falsehood is discovered.

Historian and media analyst Michael Parenti [19] believes that the most effective propaganda is based on reality rather than focusing on falsehood. Weaving truth rather than violating it. By using emphases and auxiliary sources, communicators can create the desired impression without resorting to explicit pronouncements and without straying too far from the appearance of objectivity. Framing is achieved through the way news is "packaged," the length of the exposition, its location (front page or within some secondary section, lead article, or back page), the tone of the presentation (open or disparaging), headlines and photographs, and, in the case of audiovisual media, picture and sound effects.

The filters presented by Chomsky and Herman [1] show that media manipulation leads us to a conclusion as obvious as it is natural: we live in an amorphous society. We are amorphous because there is a huge incompatibility between what we think we know about things and what we really know. There is no daring worse than that which emerges from ignorance.

Everything is a sublime paradox. We have the most sophisticated tools, channels, and access to information in human history. Yet we are more vulnerable than ever to intellectual neglect and memory. If the diagnosis of what we read, see - and especially what we seek - is performed through the lens of media discourses, we will recognize filters that precede the news, the facts themselves. The information we want does not always match the information we need. And when it is combined, it is not always available. The problem behind many of the waves of lies are the people who do not want the truth, but agree with it. They are the terraplaners of the networks, proving that in the information society misinformation predominates.

References

1. Chomsky, N., Herman, E.S.: A manipulação do público. S.l., Futura (2003)
2. Clavell, J., Tzu, S.: A arte da guerra, 31st edn, p. 111. Record, Rio de Janeiro (2003)
3. Sorj, B.: Anti-semitismo na Europa hoje. Novos estud., CEBRAP, 79, São Paulo (2007). https://www.scielo.br/scielo.php?script=sci_arttext&pid=S0101-33002007000300005
4. Brandão, S.S.: Perseguições e martírios na história eclesiástica: análise dos escritos de eusébio de cesareia. Revista História e Cultura 2(3) (Especial), 268–279 (2013)
5. Voss, M.: Cuba libera venda de computadores residenciais. https://www.bbc.com/portuguese/reporterbbc/story/2008/05/080503_cubacomputadores_fp.shtml
6. de Brum, J.: A Hipótese do Agenda Setting: Estudos e Perspectivas. Razón y palabra, 35, out (2003). http://www.razonypalabra.org.mx/anteriores/n35/jbrum.html
7. Maciel, L.A.: Imprensa, esfera pública e memória operária. Rev. Hist. **175**, 415–448 (2016). https://doi.org/10.11606/issn.2316-9141.rh.2016.109940
8. Laigner, R., Fortes, R.: Introdução à história da comunicação. E-papers, Rio de Janeiro (2009)
9. Costa, S.D.: A presença das agências internacionais hegemônicas no jornalismo online brasileiro. In: 41 th, Congresso Brasileiro de Ciências da Comunicação. Intercom, Sociedade Brasileira de Estudos Interdisciplinares da Comunicação.Joinville (2018)
10. Morais, F.: Chatô: o rei do Brasil. Companhia das Letras, São Paulo (1994)
11. IBGE. Agência de notícias. PNAD Contínua TIC 2017: Internet chega a três em cada quatro domicílios do país. https://agenciadenoticias.ibge.gov.br/agencia-sala-de-imprensa/2013-agencia-de-noticias/releases/23445-pnad-continua-tic-2017-internet-chega-a-tres-em-cada-quatro-domicilios-do-pais
12. Souza, E.: Fontes jornalísticas e pluralidade: o que dizem os Manuais de Redação? In: 7th Encontro Regional Sul de História da Mídia, Alcar Sul (2018)
13. Genro, T.: Jornalismo geneticamente modificado: na semana que findou a imprensa tradicional lotou de notícias positivas seus surrados jornalões e noticiários. Carta Maior (2017). https://www.cartamaior.com.br/?/Editoria/Midia/Jornalismo-geneticamente-modificado/12/38819
14. Pecheux, M., Fuchs, C.: A propósito da Análise Automática do Discurso: atualização e perspectivas. Tradução de Péricles Cunha. In: Gadet, F., Hak, T. (Orgs.) Por uma análise automática do discurso: uma introdução à obra de Michel Pêcheux, 3rd edn. Campinas, Unicamp, pp. 163–252 (1975) (1997)
15. INPE. Ministério da Ciência, Tecnologia, Inovações e Comunicações. A estimativa da taxa de desmatamento por corte raso para a Amazônia Legal em 2019 é de 9.762 km^2. http://www.inpe.br/noticias/noticia.php?Cod_Noticia=5294
16. Repórteres sem Fronteiras: Classificação Mundial da Liberdade de Imprensa (2019). https://rsf.org/pt/classificacao%20
17. BBC News. Glifosato: Por que a Anvisa propõe manter liberada a venda do agrotóxico mais usado no Brasil. https://www.bbc.com/portuguese/geral-47374656
18. Orlandi, E.P.: Autoria, leitura e efeitos do trabalho simbólico. 5th edn. Campinas, Pontes Editores (2007)
19. Parenti, M.: Monopoly Media Manipulation, maio (2001). http://www.michaelparenti.org/MonopolyMedia.html

Overview of Citizen Science Projects Contemplated in the Civis Platform

Amanda Santos Witt[✉] and Fabiano Couto Corrêa da Silva

Universidade Federal do Rio Grande do Sul, Porto Alegre, Brasil
santos.amanda@ufrgs.br

Abstract. The idea of Citizen Science in the context of Open Science stems from the implicit recognition of the importance between science and democracy. This connection implies that knowledge is shared among evebody and that science is its institutional form. However, running counter to this idea of democratically shared knowledge is the historical process of institutionalization that has almost always assumed the exclusion of the lay citizen. This is the fundamental tension that historically underlies all the polarities between science and curious and literate citizens, novices and experts, laymen and professionals. **Proposal:** In the present research we will deal with the possibilities and analysis of participatory science, represented by Civis Portal: Citizen Science Platform, desenvolvida pelo Instituto Brasileiro de Informação em Ciência e Tecnologia (Ibict). **Methodology:** The study presents a qualitative approach, with the use of documental research and with a descriptive character, in order to verify the projects in Citizen Science developed in Brazil. The research includes consulting the website of the Civis platform, in the topic Initiatives, in order to retrieve the registered projects. The next step was to verify the models of citizen participation, defined as contributive, collaborative and co-created and establish a categorization for analysis of the projects from the elements area data collection, social participation, open data and scope. **Results:** As results of the research, it is understood that most of the projects are collaborative, developed in the area of Biological Sciences, use mobile data collection, encourage social participation, are national in scope, and do not specify the issue of open data within the projects.

Keyword: Citizen science · Open science · Citizen participation · Engagement of volunteers · Biological sciences

1 Introduction

Within the framework of the European project Socientize, in 2013 the Green Paper on Citizen Science [1] was prepared, which refers to the participation of the general public in scientific research activities in where citizens actively contribute, is supported by their intellectual effort or knowledge of their environment or by contributing their own tools and resources" [1]. These types of projects, in which citizens and experts (researchers,

A. L. Pinto and R. Arencibia-Jorge (Eds.): DIONE 2022, LNICST 452, pp. 16–28, 2022.
https://doi.org/10.1007/978-3-031-22324-2_2

scientists, etc.) are connected and interact, are open, cross-cutting, networked, inter-disciplinary and participatory, and enhance the correlation between science, society and policy, which enables research and the "collaborative construction of knowledge", which is why Citizen Science is also known as "Collaborative Science".

In this context, a new "scientific culture" is created as participants levels of collabora-tion vary: they collect data, offer new perspectives through their expertise, and add value to research. In addition, these volunteers develop skills and acquire knowledge about the scientific method. In turn, scientists contribute with methodologies to perform data processing and subsequent analysis, favoring the increase of collective creativity and the potential for scientific innovation, as a consequence of the greater number and variety of collaborators, and the adoption of values typical of responsible research. Along the same lines, Civis: Plataforma de Ciência Cidadã [2], developed by the Instituto Brasileiro de Informação em Ciência e Tecnologia (IBICT) states that its goal is to offer an infras-tructure and content aimed at understanding Citizen Science, disseminating its use and providing the basis for the development of initiatives and methodologies in this area. It is an initiative to increase visibility and citizen participation in scientific research, enabling greater engagement of volunteers. It is worth mentioning that the Brazilian Civis plat-form was developed in open source from the EU-Citizen.Science platform [3], which was funded by the European Commission's Horizon 2020 program, in the "Science with and for Society" work program.

For all these reasons, it is convenient to take into account both the ten key principles necessary for good practices in Citizen Science published by the European Citizen Science Association (ECSA) [4], and the benefits for science, society and citizenship. The objective of this research is to examine the Citizen Science initiatives registered in the Brazilian platform Civis in order to understand this scenario in contemporary Brazil. It is known that Citizen Science is still relatively recent in the country, so it is important to verify the participation models adopted by the projects and the main characteristics inherent to each one of them.

2   Citizen Science

The open science movement mirrors new ways of thinking about and practicing scientific research, resonating directly with traditional institutional guidelines and norms for doing research. This interferes with the process of doing science and how it relates to society at large. Open development is guided by open models and knowledge production in which collaboration is a crucial element, made possible by available and constantly evolving technologies and alternative license regimes, different from traditional ones.

In the context of the Foster Project [5], citizen science is both a goal and an enabling tool for open science. Therefore, it can refer to a) the active and open participation of citizens in the research process itself, through crowdsourcing-type activities, encom-passing data collection and analysis, voluntary monitoring, and distributed computing, and b) the increasing public understanding of science, facilitated by better access to information about the research process, notably by the possibility of using open data and having access to open publications.

The Societize Consortium [1] points out a set of factors that characterize experiences in citizen science: public participation in scientific research with their intellectual effort, local knowledge or tools and resources. According to Parra [6], with citizen science we have the reinvention of science, changing more than the relations between amateurs and professionals, as well as the dynamics of production, validation, dissemination and appropriation of the knowledge created. Its initiatives enable the participation in formal research activities carried out in large research centers, boosting a greater engagement with science, which later converts into benefits for the whole society in general [6].

The broad spectrum of meanings that encompass citizen science initiatives can be classified into two strands, according to Albagli's study [7]. The first is the pragmatic or instrumental one, in which there is not necessarily openness of data or participation of volunteers in the design and results of the research. The second is the democratic aspect, which incorporates the opening and conformation of new spaces and existing institutional mechanisms, giving rise to greater participation, intervention and empowerment of citizens, towards democratization and appropriation of science and technology aimed at social innovation.

In Brazil, studies in the field of citizen science are still relatively recent and the projects in the Biological Sciences area stand out, covering subjects such as biodiversity and environmental conservation. One of the oldest known is the Atlas of Brazilian Bird Records (ARA) [8], an interactive portal that gathers data on the occurrence of wild birds. A milestone in Citizen Science in Brazil was the creation, in March 2022, of the Rede Brasileira de Ciência Cidadã (RBCC) [9], uniting a group of scientists and science stakeholders, enthusiasts and practitioners of citizen science, result of the debates following the I Workshop Rede Brasileira de Ciência Cidadã; another one was the creation and dissemination of the Plataforma Civis in this year 2022.

2.1 Models of Citizen Participation

The literature review on Citizen Science presents several typologies to understand which activities and under which conditions should be considered citizen science. We will highlight three main categories [10]:

- Contributing projects: citizens often provide data for research created by scientists.
- Collaborative projects: collaboration between scientists and participants in more than one stage of the project.
- Co-created projects: joint proposition between scientists and citizens, where citizens act in the directions and definitions of a project and in various stages.

The document "Ten principles of citizen science" published in 2015 by the European Citizen Science Association (ECSA) [4], sets out the key principles necessary for good practice in Citizen Science. In it, it advocates a partnership relationship between citizens and professional scientists, in which the basic assumptions of science are guaranteed, because according to the European Citizen Science Association Citizen Science configures a research approach like any other, with its limitations and biases that must be considered and controlled during research. Moreover, citizen science programs are evaluated by several aspects: scientific results, data quality, experience for participants, and scope of social and political impacts [4].

3 Methodology

The diversity and multiplicity of national and international projects launched in the context of Citizen Science make it difficult to choose models. However, we will analyze how the selection of projects available on the portal Civis: Citizen Science Platform provides information about the contemplated projects and natural phenomena in different major areas of knowledge, such as Astronomy, Biological Sciences, and Education. Initially we conducted a survey of all the projects gathered in the portal. Then we analyzed the set of information for each project, subdivided into 5 main axis:

Area: description of the Great Areas of Knowledge according to the typology of the Table of Knowledge areas elaborated by the Conselho Nacional de Desenvolvimento Científico e Tecnológico (CNPq) [11] of Brazil for the framing of the projects and the main disciplines contemplated
Data Collection: procedure for uploading or making data available
Social Participation: broad description of the project scope to promote volunteer engagement
Open Data: levels of openness and access to data
Scope: territorial space of the data

The establishment of the axes occurred because they are relevant aspects to verify the initiatives. The grouping by area of knowledge provides a general picture of the most important areas in Citizen Science. The issue of scientific data is another important element in citizen science. According to the document "Ten Principles in Citizen Science" [4], data collection is one form of citizen participation in projects, but not the only one, i.e. citizens can participate in several stages of research. In this sense, it is worth investigating how this collection can be done and if the projects mention other forms of participation besides data collection. Moreover, it is necessary to consider that citizens' participation is voluntary. Therefore, this question seeks to verify the ways in which the projects seek the participation of society in general in their research. The scope of territorial coverage of these projects allows a better understanding of the conjuncture of Citizen Science in Brazil.

4 Results

The Civis Platform, object of this study, is still under development (Beta version). Users are called to contribute with observations and suggestions. The figure shows the user interface of the platform (see Fig. 1):

Fig. 1. Visualization of the civis platform interface. 2022

In the topic "Initiatives" in the Civic Platform, 20 projects in Citizen Science were located, which are presented in the table below (Table 1):

Table 1. Citizen science initiatives in Brazil. Source: authors based on Plataforma Civis. 2022

Project	Description
MIND.Funga - Ciência Cidadã	Registration of macrofungi through images collected by citizen volunteers. The project seeks to capture photos of fungi in high-altitude environments in order to improve the digital database of the UFSC [12]
Ciência Cidadã para a Amazônia	This is a network of organizations that work towards the empowerment of citizens and the generation of knowledge about the fish and aquatic ecosystems of the Amazon Basin [13]
Projeto Budiões	It aims to elaborate a database that will help map and monitor the presence of the Buddion fish species along the Brazilian coast [14]
Portal de Zoologia de Pernambuco	It uses Internet and cartography tools, allowing inhabitants, students, teachers, researchers, and university students to contribute with information about the wild animal species found in the State of Pernambuco [15]
SISS-Geo - Sistema de Informação em Saúde Silvestre	Available on smartphones and on the web, it allows monitoring the health of wild animals in various environments: natural, rural, and urban. It acts in the prevention and control of zoonoses, aiming at the conservation of the Brazilian biodiversity [16]

(continued)

Table 1. (*continued*)

Project	Description
Rede Brasileira de Observação de Meteoros (Bramon)	It is a non-profit, open and collaborative organization, maintained by volunteers and supporters. Its mission is to develop and operate a network for monitoring meteors [17]
OIAA Onça - Observatório de Imprensa Avistamentos e Ataques de Onças	It aims at checking data and information on jaguar occurrences from the Friends of the Jaguar university extension action and collaborative research in citizen science [18]
LabJaca - Favela gerando dados	It is a laboratory for research, training, and production of data and narratives about the favelas and the peripheries, and is made up 100% of young black people. It uses the audiovisual media to disseminate scientific data and make research accessible to the population, in addition to outlining representative actions of the demands of the territory [19]
Eu vi uma ave usando pulseiras!?	It is based on promoting the monitoring of birds with the participation of the general population. Brazilian ornithologists mark birds with colored rings in their research, and afterwards these birds can eventually be observed from a distance by anyone [20]
Do Pasto ao Prato	Through an application it has the purpose of revealing where meat products come from, aiming to improve the transparency of the supply chains in Brazil and worldwide. It makes it possible to clarify to the consumer the negative impacts of these products [21]
BioTiba - Projetos de Biodiversidade	It proposes to make the population aware of the relevance of knowing and preserving biodiversity, promoting the engagement in bioblitz actions - a short duration event that allows recording as many species as possible in a certain area [22]
BeeKeep	It is a citizen science project for participatory bee research. It covers flight activity monitoring in stingless bees and meliponiculture [23]
Cemaden Educação	It works with a network of schools and communities for disaster risk prevention. The goal is to contribute to the development of a culture of disaster risk perception within the scope of Environmental Education, contributing to the sustainability and resilience of society [24]
EXOSS	It works in partnership with scientific institutions, oriented towards the analysis of meteors and bolides, aiming to unveil their origins, natures, and characterization of their orbits. The acronym EXOSS is pronounced [ézus] ɛzʊs) and the slogan means "Exploring the Southern Sky" [25]

(*continued*)

Table 1. (*continued*)

Project	Description
Blue Change - Ciência Cidadã em ambientes marinhos e costeiros	Initiative focused on the development of Citizen Science projects in Brazil associated with the conservation of marine and coastal environments. It develops the project within the framework of Citizen Science and carries out the management of the entire project, publicizing the projects and results obtained [26]
Brydes do Brasil	A network of voluntary studies on Bryde's whale in Brazilian jurisdictional waters with the purpose of gathering the largest possible number of records of these individuals by means of photos. The objective is to create a database to gather records that will allow us to understand the movements of the species along the Brazilian coast [27]
Projeto Cidadão Cientista - Save Brasil	This is a SAVE Brasil project that aims to carry out participatory monitoring of birds in Conservation Units and urban parks. It develops regular activities, which are open to people of all ages and levels of knowledge about birds [28]
Guardiões da Chapada	The project model is based on the voluntary and conscious participation of citizens, aiming to produce scientific knowledge and raise awareness among the general public about the relevance of the services provided by pollinators with regard to the conservation of the natural heritage of the Chapada Diamantina [29]
Onde estão as Baleias e Golfinhos?	It aims to collaborate with research and the maintenance of cetaceans and their respective habitats through photos and videos of cetaceans - whales, porpoises, and dolphins - in coastal waters of Rio de Janeiro. Its premise is to form a database with the records of sightings [30]
WikiAves	It is a site with interactive content, aimed at the Brazilian community of birdwatchers with voluntary financial contribution from collaborators. It aims to support, publicize and promote the activity of birdwatching. It provides free advanced tools for controlling photos, sounds, texts, species identification, and allowing communication among birdwatchers [31]

Based on the analyses of the website of each project mentioned above, the data collected was analyzed according to the proposed axis:

Area: We identified a predominance of projects in the area of Biological Sciences (80%), with emphasis on the subjects extracted from the keywords associated with each initiative on the platform: biodiversity, ecology, conservation, aquatic ecosystems, marine and coastal environments, oceans, zoology, zoonoses, health, jaguar, participatory monitoring, ornithology, birds, bees, meliponiculture, animals, climate and weather, meat consumption and food; followed by the areas of Astronomy and Education with 10%

each, whose emphasis falls on the subjects space, meteors, bolides, periphery, slum and education (see Fig. 2).

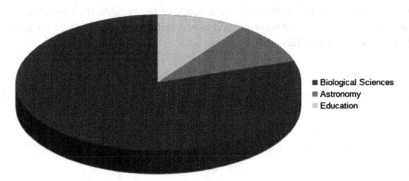

Fig. 2. Great areas of knowledge. 2022.

In the early days of humanity, what was known as the Universe was restricted to a few planets, stars, the Sun, and the Moon. The evolution of human thought over time, and the development and improvement of astronomical instruments, allowed astronomy to reach higher levels. Nowadays, satellites and space probes allow the collection of a massive amount of data and information about the Universe [32]. Astronomy is a multidisciplinary field that involves the study of celestial bodies and phenomena occurring outside the Earth. In this field, research covers the universe and its constituent elements, such as planets, stars, galaxies, among others. For purposes of understanding an area, divisions are made into subareas, as is the case of the Table of Knowledge Areas of CNPq [11], which subdivides Astronomy into: Position Astronomy and Celestial Mechanics; Stellar Astrophysics; Extragalactic Astrophysics; Solar System Astrophysics and Astronomical Instrumentation.

Education can be divided into topics, such as educational administration, planning and evaluation, as well as teaching-learning aspects, curriculum, guidance and counseling, and specific topics of Education [11]. Education, in terms of training and learning, is an activity that takes place in all spheres of life, which as a policy or strategy, cannot be limited to a formal education system. Therefore, it must be based on actions that aim at the development of a nation and its citizens [33].

Biological Sciences have a singularity as an area of knowledge and its own characteristics that distinguish it from other sciences. Until the beginning of the last century it remained more connected to the traditions of Natural History and its organization consisted of branches, more descriptive, such as zoology and botany, and experimental, such as cytology, embryology and human physiology [34, 35]. Added to this is its strengthening as a science with the emergence of genetics, among other factors [34, 35]. Biological Sciences cover subjects of biology in general: genetics, botany, zoology, ecology, morphology, physiology, biochemistry, biophysics, pharmacology, immunology, microbiology and parasitology [11]. The field of Biological Sciences is developed in Brazil. In the Diretório de Grupos de Pesquisa do CNPq [36], for example, in the field "parametrized query" one can see 20 research groups registered in the area of Biological Sciences in Brazil, besides 34 registers of research lines and the occurrence of 17 registers of the term in keywords of the research lines.

Data collection: We verified that within the scope of the projects the uploading of collected data is done in different ways, as well as we verified a diversity of types of collected documents, according to Table 2:

Table 2. Data upload.

Upload	Projects
Site	9
Application	8
Application and Website	1
Social Networks (Facebook and Instagram)	2

We found that two projects do not have a website or application, and the social networks Facebook and Instagram are the most used form of communication with volunteers. Regarding the documentary typology, photos predominate, and are mentioned in 14 projects. The other types of documents produced were categorized into: video;photo and video; photo and sound, and finally, barcode - all with one occurrence. Another interesting aspect is that three of the analyzed projects promote face-to-face activities to collect materials, as is the case of a project that collects plastic materials on the beach, with the purpose of promoting greater environmental awareness.

Social Participation: Regarding the question about how the engagement of participants is promoted and if they are informed about their possibilities of acting in the project, we obtained as a result that the vast majority of projects practice actions in this direction: 17 of them.

It is noteworthy that four projects mention the possibility of individualized face-to-face or remote service. One of the projects has on its website a topic of orientation for volunteers with clarifications on how to make a good photo, but there is no content, as the site is still under construction. The practices developed by ECSA [4] reveal that Citizen Science initiatives need to actively involve citizens in the activities, providing the generation of new knowledge and understanding about a certain object of investigation. In this sense, it is crucial that the participants are educated so that they can actively participate in the initiatives.

Open Data: Of the twenty projects described, it can be seen that:

Nine mention the issue of open data, with one project showing concern about the data that will be released and stressing the need for constant reflection about what will be shared, when and how; another points out that the data will be open to the public without identifying those responsible for collecting it;

One asserts that the data authors will inform the types of data that can be made available online. The rest, which are eleven projects, make no mention about open data and their level of openness.

Project owners need to keep in mind the ethical and legal issues involved, and the data and metadata resulting from the projects should be made publicly available in open access mode whenever possible ([4]).

Scope: Regarding the scope of the territory in which the data is collected, we infer that seven projects have local data collection scope; twelve are national and one is international.

In the current globalized scenario characterized by an economic, social and technological gap between nations, there is a growing need to take advantage of the maximum possible resources for the creation of solutions, encompassing various types of knowledge, resources, means of participation as well as collaboration, enabling the achievement of positive results with long-term sustainability. Society in general reaps the benefits of Citizen Science, because the initiatives allow the resolution of local, regional, national, or even international problems through agreements and partnerships. In the case of the citizen scientists, they can acquire skills related to the scientific process, professionalization in the area of the project, and satisfaction in acting to solve issues that are tangential to their reality. These are initiatives that do not aim at unilateralism, demonstrating the reciprocal character that Citizen Science is based on [4].

5 Discussion

In our analysis we have seen that the initiatives in citizen science published in the Civic Platform reveal a scenario where there is still no consensus on the use and availability of open data, despite the fact that citizen science has developed in the context of open science. The participation of volunteers, amateur scientists and those interested in general in the themes contemplated by the projects in Citizen Science is beneficial to all. It allows the exchange of knowledge and experiences between academia and society, enriches and improves the volunteers' skills in scientific research, and contributes to the optimization of the time and resources of a research project. However, one must keep in mind that it is necessary to provide volunteers with the opportunity to participate in all phases of the research, without limiting them only to data collection.

Most of the project initiatives come from Research Institutions and Centers, and are predominantly grouped in the axis of Contributive and Collaborative projects. The initiative Do Pasto ao Prato, according to the analysis models used, is not a Citizen Science project, but a tool, because it is an application. Regarding the participation models, it can be seen that most of the projects adopt the contributive perspective, in which citizens act in the collection of data for the research, but without involvement in other stages of the projects. Initiatives such as the Rede Brasileira de Observação de Meteoros (Bramon) and CEMADEN seem to adopt the collaborative model, because in the former it is possible to act as an operator of one or more stations or to collaborate in several important activities for the maintenance of the project, such as training, dissemination, documentation, support, among others; in the latter, students from the schools that are members of the project can, besides collecting data, guide the community to make a participatory diagnosis of the place where they live, based on a "learning by doing" methodology. Therefore, we can see a collaborative bias in these initiatives.

Projects such as Ciência Cidadã para a Amazônia and LabJaca - Favela gerando dados, present characteristics of co-created models. The latter is a project created in a Brazilian slum, by local residents, to deal with the difficulties caused by the Covid-19 pandemic, in which experts, institutions and citizens act together to solve problems that afflict them as well as to engender public policies; the former offers the possibility of implementing research proposals based on citizens' interests, with the aim of strengthening citizenship and environmental culture in the Amazon of Puno, Peru.

6   Preliminary Conclusions

The platform was recently launched and is still in the testing phase. Moreover, the registration of projects is voluntary and a wide dissemination of the tool is necessary to promote the registration of projects. This will enable a broad and deep knowledge about what is being done in terms of Citizen Science in Brazil, following the example of other countries that use similar platforms. It is suggested to expand the analysis to international Citizen Science platforms from a comparative view, looking for similarities and divergences that enrich the debate in this field and broaden the understanding why some areas arouse greater public interest, both from researchers and society in general.

In general, anyone has knowledge, tools, and resources that can contribute to the advancement of science. Under this paradigm, Civis aims to strengthen the development of a multidisciplinary platform to promote Citizen Science and collective learning based on experience and good practices.

References

1. Socientize Consortium: Green Paper on Citizen Science. European Commission (2013). https://ciencia-ciudadana.es//wp-content/uploads/2018/09/GreenPaperOnCitizenScience2013.pdf
2. Instituto Brasileiro de Informação em Ciência e Tecnologia: Civis Plataforma de Ciência Cidadã. https://civis.ibict.br/
3. EU-citizen.science: Plataforma. https://eu-citizen.science/
4. European Citizen Science Association: Ten Principles of Citizen Science, Berlin (2015). https://doi.org/10.17605/OSF.IO/XPR2N
5. Bezjak, S.: Open Science Training Handbook (1.0) [Computer software]. Zenodo (2018). https://doi.org/10.5281/zenodo.1212496
6. Parra, H.Z.M.: Ciência Cidadã: modos de participação e ativismo informacional. In: Albagli, S., Maciel, M.L., Abdo, A.H. (orgs.) Ciência aberta, questões abertas. IBICT, Brasília; UNIRIO, Rio de Janeiro, pp. 121–141 (2015). https://livroaberto.ibict.br/bitstream/1/1060/1/Ciencia%20aberta_questoes%20abertas_PORTUGUES_DIGITAL%20(5).pdf
7. Albagli, S.: Ciência aberta em questão. In: Albagli, S., Maciel, M.L.M., Abdo, A.H. (Org.) Ciência aberta, questões abertas. IIBICT, Brasília; UNIRIO, Rio de Janeiro, pp. 9–25 (2015). https://livroaberto.ibict.br/bitstream/1/1060/1/Ciencia%20aberta_questoes%20abertas_PORTUGUES_DIGITAL%20(5).pdf

8. Centro Nacional de Pesquisa e Conservação de Aves Silvestres: Atlas de Registro de Aves. http://ara.cemave.gov.br/sobre

9. Rede Brasileira de Ciência Cidadã: Grupos de trabalho. https://sites.usp.br/rbcienciacidada/grupos-de-trabalho/

10. Bonney, R., et al.: Public participation in scientific research. Center for Advancement of Informal Science Education (CAISE), Washington, D.C. (2009)

11. Conselho Nacional de Desenvolvimento Científico e Tecnológico: Tabela de áreas do conhecimento. http://lattes.cnpq.br/documents/11871/24930/TabeladeAreasdoConhecimento.pdf/d192ff6b-3e0a-4074-a74d-c280521bd5f7

12. MIND.Funga - Monitoring and Inventarying Neotropical Diversity of Fungi: Programa: Ciência Cidadã. https://mindfunga.ufsc.br/mind-funga-ciencia-cidada/

13. Ciência Cidadã para a Amazônia: Rede Ciência Cidadã para a Amazônia. https://amazoniacienciaciudadana.org/pt/home-pt/

14. Projeto Budiões: Ciência Cidadã. https://budioes.org/participe/

15. Portal de Zoologia de Pernambuco: Portal de Zoologia de Pernambuco ... e do Mundo! Fotografe, localize, compartilhe!. http://www.portal.zoo.bio.br/

16. SISS - Geo - Sistema de Informação em Saúde Silvestre: Conheça o SISS-Geo, Sistema de Informação em Saúde. https://sissgeo.lncc.br/

17. Rede Brasileira de Observação de Meteoros (Bramon): Bramon: brazilian meteor observation network. http://www.bramonmeteor.org/bramon/

18. OIAA Onça - Observatório de Imprensa Avistamentos e Ataques de Onças: OIAA Onça. https://oiaaonca.ufam.edu.br/

19. Labjaca: favela gerando dados: Labjaca. https://www.labjaca.com/

20. Eu vi uma ave usando pulseiras!?: Projeto Eu vi uma ave usando pulseiras!? https://www.sibbr.gov.br/cienciacidada/pulseira.html?lang=pt_BR

21. Do Pasto ao Prato: Um aplicativo criado para aumentar a transparência na cadeia da carne e apoiar o consumo consciente no Brasil. https://dopastoaoprato.com.br/

22. Projeto biotiba - Projetos de Biodiversidade: @ Projeto biotiba. https://linktr.ee/projeto.biotiba

23. BeeKeep: @BeeKeep. https://bio.abelha.io/beekeep/

24. Cemaden Educação: Rede de escolas e comunidades na prevenção de riscos de desastres. http://educacao.cemaden.gov.br/site/project/

25. Exploring the Southern Sky: EXOSS Citizen Science Project. https://press.exoss.org/

26. Blue Change - Ciência Cidadã em ambientes marinhos e costeiros: Blue Change - mudança azul. https://bluechangeinitiative.wordpress.com/inicio/

27. Brydes do Brasil: O que é? http://brydesdobrasil.com.br/rede/oque

28. Projeto Cidadão Cientista - Save Brasil: Cidadão cientista. http://savebrasil.org.br/cidadao-cientista-1

29. Guardiões da Chapada: Projeto Guardiões da Chapada. https://www.sibbr.gov.br/cienciacidada/guardioesdachapada.html?lang=pt_BR

30. Onde estão as Baleias e Golfinhos? Rede social Facebook. https://www.facebook.com/groups/216660765162076

31. Wikiaves: Wikiaves - observação de aves e ciência cidadã para todos. https://www.wikiaves.com.br/

32. Borges, C.L.S., Rodrigues, C.G.: Astronomia: breve história, principais conceitos e campos de atuação. Braz. Appl. Sci. Rev. 6(2), 545–577 (2022). https://www.researchgate.net/profile/Cloves-Rodrigues/publication/359878964_Astronomia_breve_historia_principais_concei tos_e_campos_de_atuacao/links/62548201cf60536e2354f755/Astronomia-breve-historia-principais-conceitos-e-campos-de-atuacao.pdf

33. Ireland, T.D.: Educação ao longo da vida: aprendendo a viver melhor. Sisyphus: J. Educ. 7(2), 48–64 (2019). https://www.redalyc.org/jatsRepo/5757/575763749004/html/index.html

34. Marandino, M., Selles, S.E., Ferreira, M.S.: Ensino de Biologia: histórias e práticas em diferentes espaços educativos. Cortez, São Paulo (2009)
35. de Campos, R.S.P.: As ciências biológicas, a biologia escolar e o humano. Arquivos do MUDI **22**(2), 21–32 (2018). file:///C:/Users/00142627/Downloads/42938-Texto%20do%20artigo-751375151570-1-10-20181031.pdf
36. Conselho Nacional de Desenvolvimento Científico e Tecnológico. Diretório de Grupos de Pesquisa. Consulta parametrizada. http://dgp.cnpq.br/dgp/faces/consulta/consulta_parametrizada.jsf

National Registry of Scientific Data Management Plans by IBICT

Fabiano Couto Corrêa da Silva[1] ⓘ,
Elizabete Cristina de Souza de Aguiar Monteiro[2](✉) ⓘ,
Marcello Mundim Rodrigues[3] ⓘ, Miguel Ángel Márdero Arellano[4] ⓘ,
and Alexandre Faria de Oliveira[4] ⓘ

[1] Federal University of Rio Grande do Sul, Av. Ramiro Barcelos, Porto Alegre 2275, Brazil
[2] São Paulo State University (UNESP), Av. Hygino Muzzi Filho, Marília 737, Brazil
ecsamonteiro@gmail.com
[3] Federal University of Minas Gerais, Av. Pres. Antônio Carlos, Belo Horizonte 6627, Brazil
[4] Instituto Brasileiro de Informação em Ciência e Tecnologia (IBICT), SAUS Quadra 5, Lote 6,
Bloco H, Brasília, Brazil
{miguel,alexandreoliveira}@ibict.br

Abstract. A Data Management Plan is a document where the main aspects of data management are recorded and sent to funding agencies. In addition, it is part of the data documentation and is filed together with the data in repositories or published by scientific journals. The National Registry of Scientific Data Management Plans (NRSDMP) by IBICT is a tool that seeks assisting researchers on their (meta) data planning and management. It was designed based on the FAIR Principles, which are guidelines to be followed in the search for findable, accessible, interoperable, and reusable data and metadata. The objectives were to: present the NRSDMP developed by IBICT; describe its implementation process; and demonstrate its compliance to the FAIR Principles. The study was designed in a qualitative research of exploratory and descriptive nature with use of the action-research method. The results contribute to the enrichment of theoretical discussions regarding factors that contribute to data management and its documentation, such as the data management plan, articulating the practices applied to the preparation of a FAIR DMP and with instructions that allow making data and metadata FAIR. The NRSDMP also serves as guidance to researchers for reaching FAIRness. In conclusion, the paper presents theoretical and practical contributions to: the development of FAIR compliant tools; as well as the creation of educational content (data literacy) for researchers in need of planning their data management, all in accordance with the international community.

Keywords: Data management · Data repository · FAIR Principles

1 Introduction

Data management integrates several professional and scientific systematized activities, with the application of procedures, protocols, standards or methodologies aiming to

A. L. Pinto and R. Arencibia-Jorge (Eds.): DIONE 2022, LNICST 452, pp. 29–38, 2022.
https://doi.org/10.1007/978-3-031-22324-2_3

collect, extract or generate, transform, store, treat, share, preserve and, in some cases, discard the data [1]. Such management is a prerequisite to the effectiveness in sharing data among the various scientific communities and contributes with communities that do not integrate the target group of the research, but that may have benefits with the data reuse [2].

A relevant element in the management of scientific data is to ensure that data can be understood and interpreted by other researchers over time and in divergent research from that which collected or generated the data. Data documentation serves this purpose. The Data Management Plan (DMP) - a document prepared by researchers with the initial intent of meeting the requirements of funding agencies for applying or granting funding - is part of such documentation and provides the contextualization of the research and its data, contributing to researchers who collect and manipulate datasets, to those professionals who work in scientific data repositories, and to data consumers.

Most researchers collect data with some sort of preconceived plan, but it is often incomplete or inadequately documented. In order to stimulate planning on the methods needed to preserve scientific data and make them available to other researchers, some agents in the process - such as scientific publishers, funding institutions, libraries, and repositories - have promoted the standardized use of Data Management Plans (DMPs), usually meeting specific institutional guidelines.

There are some open tools that enable the creation of DMPs, including free persistent identifiers (DMPTool, Pagoda DMPOnline and others). As a common characteristic among the available model forms for DMP description, they all constitute a formal document that describes the whole data life cycle, from its collection to the complete documentation of the research process. They record the decisions made regarding metadata standards, formats, databases, methods, security, and storage periods, as well as the costs associated with data management. Thus, a data management plan requires a documented sequence of actions designed to identify, secure resources, collect, maintain, protect, and use data archives. This includes securing funding and identifying technical and personnel resources for the complete data management cycle. Once the needs for data use are determined, the next step should be adopting a system to store and manipulate data that can be identified and developed.

The scope and amount of detail in a data management plan depends on the project itself and the audience for which it is being developed. In general, whether a researcher seeks scholarship or research funding from an agency, or seeks to organize the methods for data preservation, one might look for forms external to his institution, usually foreigner ones, making the national DMPs dispersed in random repositories. These plans have high value to national research, as they require a description of the project and the data generated, where and how they are stored, both in the short and long term, also the access provisions and legal requirements that adhere to them. Several tools are available in order to assist the elaboration of a DMP. In Brazil, the project called Cadastro Nacional de Planos de Gestão de Dados Científicos or National Registry of Scientific Data Management Plans (NRSDMP) has the intention of developing and making publicly available a tool that meets the needs of researchers. The tool has as its main characteristic meeting the FAIR Principles, guidelines to be followed in the search for findable, accessible, interoperable, and reusable data and metadata.

The FAIR Principles are intended to define a minimum set of principles and practices (related, but independent and separable), which allow machines and humans to find, access, interoperate and reuse scientific data and metadata [3] (RESEARCH DATA ALLIANCE, 2020, p. 4). This research communication presents a holistic view of the factors underlying the development of a data management plan tool that is compliant to the FAIR Principles.

The general objective of this paper was to present the nrsDMP project. The specific objective was to describe its implementation and its suitability to FAIR Principles.

The results of this study contribute to the enrichment of theoretical discussions regarding factors that contribute to data management and its documentation, such as the data management plan, articulating the practices applied to the preparation of a FAIR DMP and with instructions that allow making data and metadata FAIR. In possession of such information, researchers have an overview related to the topic and attention in preparing and publishing data on digital platforms.

Starting from the lack of a national registry of DMPs, as well as the growing demand from funding agencies that demand data management planning from sponsored researchers, the general objective of the NRSDMP by IBICT is to collaborate reducing the efforts on adapting demands for Open Science and increasing the visibility of the research carried out by Brazilian researchers. As for the specific objectives, we seek to: a) Develop of a tool a national DMP model by means of a form that gathers registries of Universities, Research Centers and Funding Agencies at a national level; b) Implement all the indicators of the FAIR Principles to the form (the DMP will receive an extract on the fulfillment of the FAIR Principles); and c) Develop a repository for the digital preservation of the DMPs, and assign individual persistent identifiers to its digital objects.

The present work also deals with the preservation of Data Management Plans due to their importance for the scientific communication process involving the necessary steps for digital preservation. During the NRSDMP development, we discovered the need for a DMP repository, where it could to preserve DMP, publish some descriptive, administrative, technical, preservation, use and reuse metadata, assign persistent identifiers to metadata, link metadata to related digital objects in the web, metadata standards, Knowledge Organization Systems (KOS), also trace data provenance, etc.

2 Methodological Procedures

The project adopted a triangulation of methods, consisting of a theoretical, bibliographic, and empirical research. We applied the content analysis method when investigating the DMPs deposited in research funding institutions' websites and repositories. There's also a continuous consultation of the scientific literature available. The empirical phase intends to directly question researchers on their demands and doubts facing the need of filling out their DMPs. The dialogue with researchers will occur after nrsDMP is launched publicly, and the suggestions will be incorporated gradually. The development is being done in partnership with the Brazilian Institute for Information in Science and Technology (IBICT), two librarians and a web developer. The goal is to make available a public tool so that anyone can register DMPs nationwide, and deposit them into a repository for their management and preservation, guaranteeing long-term access for research institutions (laboratories, universities, etc.), funding agencies (development agencies, government, etc.), and the society.

For the development of the tool, qualitative research of exploratory and descriptive nature was used, based on a bibliographic and documental search that contemplates theoretical and applied recommendations for the development, implementation, and guidance on its use.

So, the method adopted was action research, of empirical basis, applied to any process where a cycle is performed in which it is improved with systematic action between acting on the practice and investigating it. [4]. Therefore, the steps for the development of the tool were followed: diagnosis, planning, implementation, description and evaluation.

1) Diagnosis: we performed a diagnosis of the characteristics and features of the DMPTool, DMPOnline, and Data Stewardship Wizard; the application of the FAIR Principles, possible improvements and implementation of features.
2) Planning: the actions and implementations for the diagnosed framework were defined.
3) Action: application of action research with the implementation of the planned actions.
4) Evaluation: analysis of the implementation of the actions against the theoretical and practical support used as a starting point for the definition of the actions.
5) Learning: learning from the tests in the elaboration of the Data Management Plan by the group.

After the application of the action research steps, a pilot will be applied to researchers from different fields, which aims to identify their demands on the NRSDMP filling out and to indicate adjustments.

3   FAIR Data Management Plan

The Data Management Plan is a document in which the different activities and processes related to the data life cycle are described and involves [...] data design and creation, storage, security, preservation, retrieval, sharing, and reuse, all taking into account technical capabilities, ethical considerations, legal issues, and governance structures [5].

The Data Management Plan deals with the data that will be generated or collected during a given research study. Since it is a plan, it is based on future actions. Therefore, the researcher who answers the plan questionnaire is making conjectures, planning, proposing what will be done in the near future. In the data management plan, the researcher is contextualizing the research, saying what will be done before, during and after the data collection, where the data will be preserved and how it will be made publicly available. As a proposal, it is not possible to state precisely what information about the data will be collected, but it is reasonable to point out ways.

The FAIR Principles describe resources necessary to achieve archiving, preservation, maintenance, organization, retrieval, use and reuse of scientific data. Among such resources are those related to the software infrastructure that manages the platform on which the data will be available during or after the completion of a particular research project.

The FAIR Principles seek reasonableness between humans and machines, for common (universal) communication and understanding between data and metadata, systems and vocabularies. FAIR data and metadata are contained in the fourth scientific paradigm (e-Science), where the volume of scientific data expands exponentially. The FAIR transformation is linked to digital preservation, knowledge organization, and information retrieval.

Central to the realization of FAIR are FAIR Digital Objects. These objects could represent data, software, protocols or other research resources. They need to be accompanied by Persistent Identifiers (PIDs) and metadata rich enough to enable them to be reliably found, used and cited. Data should, in addition, be represented in common – and ideally open – formats, and be richly documented using metadata standards and vocabularies adopted by the related research community to enable interoperability and reuse [6].

It is important to emphasize that FAIR data is not necessarily open data, because 'fairification' provides licenses and copyright to the use and reuse of its assets. Some data can and should be embargoed or restricted from access and reuse, for various reasons.

The FAIR Principles are divided into four acronyms. Each acronym is subdivided into 3 or 4 statements that serve as valuable guidelines for managers, technicians, and experts in digital preservation, information systems, and knowledge organization. Figure 1 presents each of the 15 FAIR sub-principles. The FAIR goal is hardly ever achieved, because data and metadata are not always one hundred percent FAIR. This means that the control that one must have involves many variables, between humans and machines, with one of them being vocabulary control, since we do not have a universal language between people and systems. In this way, the FAIR ideal becomes a great challenge to contemporary society.

The import and use of metadata that describe scientific data amongst systems is a commitment of the Open Archives Initiative Protocol for Metadata Harvesting (OAI-PMH).

Still, in order to meet some of the FAIR Principles, one must have indexer expertise, in the case where one must use resources/instruments when indexing representative terms of domain content. Therefore, in order to align with the FAIR Principles, a dataset needs to be deposited in a FAIR repository, such as Dataverse; it needs to be well described; it needs to be indexed; etc.

During the NRSDMP development, we discovered the need for a DMP repository, where it could publish some descriptive, administrative, technical, preservation, use and reuse metadata, assign persistent identifiers to metadata, link metadata to related digital objects in the web, metadata standards, Knowledge Organization Systems (KOS), also trace data provenance, etc.

In that way, the DMPs will be stored in a Dataverse repository called Cariniana: Brazilian Network for Digital Preservation Services by the Brazilian Institute of Information in Science and Technology (IBICT), which aims to ensure continuous access and long-term preservation of the content stored therein [7]. The Dataverse platform is a free software architecture for the archiving, publishing, preservation, reuse, analysis and

---

The FAIR guiding principles: https://doi.org/10.1038/sdata.2016.18

To be Findable:

F1. (meta)data are assigned a globally unique and persistent identifier

F2. data are described with rich metadata (defined by R1 below)

F3. metadata clearly and explicitly include the identifier of the data it describes

F4. (meta)data are registered or indexed in a searchable resource

To be Accessible:

A1. (meta)data are retrievable by their identifier using a standardized communications protocol

A1.1. the protocol is free, open and universally implementable

A1.2. the protocol allows for an authentication and authorization procedure, where necessary

A2. metadata are accessible, even when the data are no longer available

To be Interoperable:

I1. (meta)data use a formal, accessible, shared, and broadly applicable language for knowledge representation

I2. (meta)data uses vocabularies that follow FAIR principles

I3. (meta)data include qualified references to other (meta)data

To be reusable:

R1. (meta)data are richly described with a plurality of accurate and relevant attributes

R1.1. (meta)data are released with a clear and accessible data usage license

R1.2. (meta)data are associated with data provenance

R1.3. (meta)data meet domain relevant community standards

Fig. 1. The FAIR principles

citation, analysis of digital objects [7]. Repositories implemented through Dataverse are in greater compliance with the FAIR Principles [8].

4 Results and Discussions

This section presents and discusses the results and analyses related to the phases of action research:

1) Diagnosis: the initial diagnosis highlighted the characteristics and requirements in the implementation of the tool and the steps, questions and guidelines on the preparation of the DMP available in the tools and templates according to Table 1. The functionalities, guidelines on the FAIR Principles, improvements and implementations of items not yet applied by the analyzed tools were identified. The tools evaluated are in column 1 and the templates consulted in column 2.
2) Planning: the implementations and actions of each group member were defined. With the diagnosis, the following were defined: categories with the questions to be answered, which information will be available for completion, and FAIR adaptation. The functionalities were also defined: certification and application of the institutional logo to each institution represented by its researchers, and the logo of the funding agencies. Furthermore, courses will be available on the NRSDMP website for orientation on its use, and on the management of scientific data.
3) Action: application of the action research with the starting actions of the planning stage.
4) Evaluation: evaluations are made at each action stage with verification of successes and mistakes, making the necessary adjustments.

5) Learning: learning by tests in the elaboration of the Data Management Plan. Afterwards, step 4 will be applied to researchers as a pilot stage.

Table 1. Templates evaluated for the indication of the questions in the tool

Tool	Templates
DMPTool	DMPTool Harvard University Ohio State University (OSU) Princeton University Stanford University Washington University
DMPOnline	Amsterdam University of Applied Sciences (Hogeschool van Amsterdam) Digital Curation Center (DCC) FAIRsFAIR - Fostering Fair Data Practices in Europe Imperial College London Lancaster University London School of Hygiene and Tropical Medicine (LSHTM)
Data Stewardship Wizard	Horizon 2020 Science Europe

It is recommended that the DMP be drafted early in the research workflow, as it can provide important insights into how to gather, curate, and disseminate data, building a common understanding in the data life cycle and providing the opportunity to reflect on decisions that will affect the FAIRness of the data [6]. For the DMP completion, guidance is given on how the data management planning could meet the FAIR Principles in ways users need not know their statements. In addition, it is indicated how users could meet Berners-Lee's Five Stars whilst planning (by answering the form) and/or managing their research data. Thus, upon completion of the DMP, the data and metadata must have:

- F1 A corresponding persistent identifier to ensure long-term access (The DMP will receive a Digital Object Identifier (DOI) with an IBICT prefix);
- F2 Data described by rich metadata (the questionnaire is exhaustive, and the DataCite Metadata Schema and Dublin Core metadata standards have been defined;
- F3 The persistent identifier associated with the DMP needs to be published on the landing page where the metadata is (the questionnaire has the field for inclusion);
- F4 The metadata need to be published on an accessible web page, that is, it needs to be indexed in a searchable resource, so that it is retrievable by Google search box or other search engines;
- A1 DMP metadata need to be retrievable by its identifier, using a standardized communication protocol. It has been requested to use OAI-PMH for the identifier syntax;
- A1.1 The OAI-PMH protocol is open and universally implementable;

- A1.2 The protocol must allow authentication and authorization, through user account creation and system access via login and password (CAFe/Keycloack was requested). The protocol must be processed by HMAC (hash-based message authentication code);
- A2 Metadata must be accessible, and to ensure this, persistent identifiers and a trusted server will be applied. The Cariniana federated network will be used for backup and long-term preservation (via CLOCKSS);
- I1 The metadata must be filled out in vernacular language, according to the current grammatical rules, it must be public and accessible, i.e., the record in the database must be compiled into a verifiable record at a persistent electronic address. This would be a referential base, a channel that addresses the metadata to the data (that will be published during or after the end of a given research);
- I2 The vocabularies cited are controlled vocabularies, generally responsible for the organization of information and knowledge in a specific scientific field. These vocabularies should comply with the FAIR Principles, i.e., they should be verifiable and accessible, ideally having persistent identification that leads the user to the address of the KOS in use. The data owner should choose to describe/contextualize their research formally, indexing subjects with the use of authorized terms, always citing their source;
- I3 External (meta)data sources or relationships amongst research are indicated with DOIs or electronic addresses of papers related to the research during plan completion;
- R1 Structured metadata fields, as well as well-described data, especially when using standards;
- R1.1 License options for the user, such as Creative Commons and others available;
- R1.2 Metadata fields indicating relationships between people and institutions, all involved in the research, the collection, and the composition of the datasets. That is, indication of relationships in the context of the research;
- R1.3 A list of controlled domain vocabularies. Users must choose from options available in the tool. Users must indicate metadata standards, standardized language by field of study.

Based on the understanding of the needs of each sub-principle to be met, we designed the following questions in order to guide users to the desired actions in achieving FAIR data and metadata:

- F1 When shared, will your dataset(s) have a persistent identifier (DOI, handle, etc.) assigned to it by the system?
- F2 What metadata will be provided to help others identify and discover the data? / What metadata standard will be used?
- F3 Will the deposit of your dataset(s) have its persistent identifier (DOI, handle, etc.) published along with the metadata at an accessible and retrievable electronic address (e.g. via Google)?
- F4 Will your dataset(s) be published in an accessible and retrievable electronic address (e.g., via Google)?
- A1 Does the system in which you will deposit, share and preserve your dataset(s) allow for retrieval via a persistent identifier?

- A1.1 Is the persistent identifier configured as a link, with syntax starting with HTTP or HTTPS (e.g.: https://doi.org/10.5072/FK2/O4HLLA)?
- A1.2 Does the system where you will deposit, share and preserve your dataset(s) allow access via login (username and password)?
- A2 Will the system in which you intend to deposit, share and preserve your dataset(s) keep your metadata accessible, even after the data becomes obsolete?
- I1/I2 What controlled vocabulary/thesaurus will be used to describe the research and data collected?
- I1/I2 Does the controlled vocabulary/thesaurus in use have a persistent identifier?
- R1 Which metadata standard will be used?
- R1.1 Inform the license that will be applied to the data.
- I.3/R1.2 Point out the electronic address or identifier (DOI, handle, etc.) that connects the source to the data or metadata.
- R1.2 Who owns the rights to the data?
- R1.2 Under which license? If not, who has granted the right of reuse?
- R1.3 Is the metadata standard in use specific to the research field? E.g., the Social Sciences field uses DDI (native in Dataverse).
- R1.3 Is the controlled vocabulary/thesaurus in use specific to the research field? E.g.: The field of Agricultural Sciences uses AGROVOC.

On the homepage of the NRSDMP by IBICT, there will be an educational course on data management and on the filling out of a Data Management Plan prepared/instructed by the team. It will contain videos, texts and exercises. In addition, there will be a tutorial on the use of the NRSDMP by IBICT.

5 Final Considerations

This paper presents theoretical and practical contributions for the development of a tool to elaborate a Data Management Plan that meets the FAIR Principles. The NRSDMP by IBICT presents guidelines that serve as instructions for the management of the data life cycle and orient those who are involved in it in any way. It is recommended that the DMP be prepared at the beginning of the research project and, because it is a dynamic document, it can be updated throughout the development of the project.

Open science represents a paradigm shift in the way science is conducted, which involves conducting all stages of scientific research (design, data collection, review, publication, etc.) with an "open" vision. Thus, the change is not in what is done nor in the means available to do it, but in how it is done. Therefore, it does not involve a scientific or technological breakthrough, but has a social and cultural character; it represents a new way of conducting and understanding scientific research, and also of disseminating and evaluating it.

These changes in the habits and behavior of researchers are being made official and will gradually be put on the agenda of Brazilian scientists through NRSDMP by IBICT, especially after the requirements made by the funding agencies are expanded. This will lead to the implementation and drive of a change that intends to revolutionize the way research is conducted throughout Brazil.

References

1. Monteiro, E.C.S.: A gestão de dados em seu ciclo de vida: principais aspectos. In: Sena, P., Pinheiro, M. (eds.) Profissionais da informação no contexto de inovações tecnológicas. No prelo (2022)
2. Monteiro, E.C.D.S.A., Sant'ana, R.C.G.: Plano de gerenciamento de dados em repositórios de dados de universidades. Encontros Bibli: revista eletrônica de biblioteconomia e ciência da informação, Florianópolis **23**(53), 160–173 (2018). https://periodicos.ufsc.br/index.php/eb/art icle/view/1518-2924.2018v23n53p160. Accessed 21 Sep 2020
3. Research Data Alliance. FAIR data maturity model: specification and guidelines. RDA FAIR data maturity model Working Group (2020). https://doi.org/10.15497/rda00045. https://www.rd-alliance.org/system/files/FAIR%20Data%20Maturity%20Model_%20specifi cation%20and%20guidelines_v0.90.pdf. Accessed 21 Sep 2020
4. Tripp, D.: Pesquisa-ação: uma introdução metodológica. Educ. Pesqui. **31**(3), 443–466 (2005)
5. Cox, A.M., Pinfield, S.: Research data management and libraries: current activities and future priorities. J. Librariansh. Inf. Sci. **46**(4), 299–316 (2014). http://lis.sagepub.com/content/46/4/ 299.full.pdf+html. Accessed 25 Oct 2020
6. European Commission. Turning FAIR into reality. Luxemburgo: Final Report and Action Plan from the European Commission Expert Group on FAIR Data. Publications Office of the European Union (2018). https://ec.europa.eu/info/sites/default/files/turning_fair_into_real ity_1.pdf. Accessed 25 Oct 2020
7. Araújo, L.M.S., Márdero Arellano, M.A., Ferrer, I.D.: Guia para os usuários do repositório Dataverse do Ibict. Ibict, Brasília (2018). https://cariniana.ibict.br/images/artigos/Dataverse/ Guia_Usuarios_Dataverse_Ibict.pdf. Accessed 11 Feb 2022
8. Rodrigues, M.M., Dias, G.A., de Lourenço, C.A.: Repositórios de dados científicos na América do Sul: uma análise da conformidade com os Princípios FAIR. Em Questão, Porto Alegre, Online First, e-113057 (2022)

Collection and Integration of Patent Data for Analysis and Validation of Brazilian Technical Production

Raulivan Rodrigo da Silva[1]([⊠]), Thiago Magela Rodrigues Dias[1],
and Washington Luís Ribeiro de Carvalho Segundo[2]

[1] Federal Center for Technological Education of Minas Gerais (CEFET-MG), Belo Horizonte,
Brazil
`{raulivan,thiagomagela}@cefetmg.br`
[2] Brazilian Institute of Information in Science and Technology (IBICT), Brasília, Brazil
`washingtonsegundo@ibict.br`

Abstract. The main objective of this work is to present an overview of Brazilian technical production from the analysis of patents registered in national repositories such as the National Institute of Industrial Property (INPI), as well as in international repositories such as Espacenet. Initially, all the INPI patent identifiers are collected so that later, all the data of these patents are collected in the Espacenet repository. In this way, a large local data repository is characterized, standing out for having consistent and structured data. This strategy makes it possible to analyze the entire dataset with the adoption of several metrics, making it possible to present a broad and unprecedented portrait of Brazilian technical production. With the dataset retrieved, it is still possible to validate other repositories or datasets, such as the curriculum base of the Lattes Platform, in which their curricula in general do not have all the information about the patents duly registered. However, it is concluded that the collection and integration of data extracted from patent documents and stored in local repositories, significantly enable patentometric analyzes that could not be performed in distributed repositories.

Keywords: Patents · INPI · Lattes platform · Espacenet · Patentometry

1 Introduction

The 21st century has been fertile ground for the creation of technological structures, and more than ever, the rapid evolution of these technologies has been visible. Daily, new devices, applications, digital media permeate the market, bringing better versions of resources and/or functionalities that we knew until then or presenting new solutions. As a result, organizations in this market are committed to constantly monitoring their activities and the viability of their products and services offered, being necessary to implement innovations that retain or increase the customer base [1]. A good part of the inventions and innovations generated originate from research initiated in public and

A. L. Pinto and R. Arencibia-Jorge (Eds.): DIONE 2022, LNICST 452, pp. 39–48, 2022.
https://doi.org/10.1007/978-3-031-22324-2_4

private educational institutions, which has been increasing over the years, making them a great pole of national innovation. This factor stimulated the creation of laws and norms that aim to protect the intellectual property generated in universities and also centers that aim to assist in the process of creating patents and enabling the relationship between the academic and marketing sectors, encouraging educational institutions and researchers to increasingly lean towards the filing of patents [2].

It is possible to find several surveys that are based on the number of patents filed and the number of patents granted, using them as parameters to determine the volume of technological innovation in a given country or institution. However, this is not enough to understand the whole scenario. As [3] states, it is not possible to say that all patents really contribute to the growth of science and technology, or even if they bear fruit for their holders and inventors.

Therefore, as with scientific productions, in the context of technical production, there are also repositories of patent records, such as the pePI (Industrial Property Research) maintained by the Brazilian patent management body INPI (National Institute of Intellectual Property). As in Brazil, each country has its own body responsible for managing the filing and granting of patents, as well as making them available for consultation. In addition, there are international repositories for patent registration, some of which, such as Espacenet, are of recognized relevance. Espacenet, which makes it possible to consult patents from approximately 70 countries in a single repository, stands out in view of the amount of data available.

Therefore, this work aims to broaden the understanding of nationally constructed patenting activities, seeking to evaluate the main actors, the hidden collaboration networks and the result that these inflict on the evolution of science. Therefore, this study proposes a technological tool for the collection and treatment of data from national patents available in the Espacenet repository, aiming to build a local repository that enables all the objective analyses.

2   Related Works

Studies based on information obtained through patent data have different approaches and have a quantitative, technological, innovation management, social, among others. Because it is a topic with a wide variety of works published, a small group was selected, in which the main theme is patentometry. The criteria defined for the selection of these studies were: publications that are available on the web, in Portuguese or English, published in the last 10 years and whose objective is to analyze patent documents of any nature. THE research was carried out in the year 2021 between the months of April and July, using the following search terms: in Portuguese "patentometria" and in English "patentometry". Using the following repositories: Arca (Fiocruz), Digital Library of Theses and Dissertations, Google Academic, Microsoft Academic, CAPES/MEC Journal Portal and SciELO.

The authors address the dimensions of intellectual property in their work, conceptualizing and highlighting patents as a rich source of data for research in the field of Human and Social Sciences, particularly in Information and Communication Science, as well as the importance of using them in the transfer of technology between countries and organizations, since the information contained in patent documents, in rare cases, is reapplied in other sources of information. In their work, the authors do not actually carry out a specific analysis of patent data, however, they emphasize the importance of using the information contained in patent documents and present several strategies for data analysis, presenting directions for researchers interested in the subject [4].

The authors present in their work an overview of patentometry in international information science journals. They begin their work citing bibliometrics and scientometrics as the most relevant methodologies in the studies of informatrics, as they cover a large area of study. Complementing, they emphasize that patentometry as a tool of competitive intelligence in science and innovation, providing indicators as a substantial basis for decision making. Since patentometry is characterized by establishing indicators that seek to identify innovation activities and technologies, through information extracted from patent documents. To establish an overview, the authors carried out a study at the international level, verifying the state of the art of research in patentometry in the area of information science. Per through research in journals with Qualis A1 to B2 concepts from 1998 to 2013, for terms referring to patentometry, such as: patent, industrial property, innovation patent and analysis patent. They conclude the work by stating that the analysis of patents is an important tool for competitiveness in research, which allows the identification and conversion of scientific knowledge into technological knowledge [5].

The author presents in his master's dissertation, an analysis of patents granted by Brazilian Public Universities in order to identify factors and/or characteristics that encourage the filing, and consequently, the granting of patents. The collection of patent data for analysis was performed in the database of the INPI, in which it was possible to collect patent data from 29 universities, out of the total of 106 universities surveyed, 65.2% correspond to universities in the southeastern region of parents. Based on the CIP (International Patent Classification) of the collected patents, it was possible to observe that the area of knowledge with the highest number of patents granted is "Chemistry and Metallurgy", in which the researchers who patent the most were professors with a background in Chemistry or Mechanical Engineering. The author also emphasizes that there is a strong presence of the public sector, since for the most part, co-ownership is constituted by funding and research institutions. In conclusion, the authors highlight the importance of Technological Innovation Centers (NITs) in public institutions as actors that contribute to implanting the culture of patenting in the country, which consequently, contribute in an indispensable way with the technological evolution of the country [6].

The authors propose in their work a methodology to assess the technology, through scientometric and patentometry techniques, thus serving as decision-making support tool for organizations regarding the introduction of new technologies. Through a model composed of 9 steps, (1) Definition of terms, where the words or expressions that you want to obtain greater information; (2) Validation of terms by experts, where defined terms are reviewed and approved by experts in the related field; (3) Definition of the bases to be used, through previously established criteria; (4) search for terms in the defined bases; (5) Extract the found records to form a local database, to enable the analyses; (6) Perform data cleaning, correction of possible errors typing, duplication and standardization; (7) Generate lists, graphs and tables; (8) Analyze the information generated; (9) Conclusions and results. The authors further argue that the proposal makes it possible to provide decision makers with scientific databases that will serve as a basis for decision-making, as evidence of offers of knowledge for the development of technology, as well as its demand [7].

The authors point to patentometry as an indispensable tool for the proposition of technologies for the chemical industry, since the prospection based on quantitative and qualitative methods, are in fact important to enable the conceptualization of tion of plausible proposals in the state of the art. Next, they explore some indicators presenting its process of construction of its relevance in the technological panorama. You authors conclude by mentioning that patentometry is a little explored area in Brazil despite its competitive value [8].

Several other works have used data recorded in patent documents to analyze technical production [9, 10].

3 Methodology

This article is a case study, that is, an empirical study that investigates a particular phenomenon, within a context in which there are still gaps in the literature, as stated [11].

A priori, information was collected regarding patent documents deposited at the INPI in the period from 01/01/1900 to 12/31/2020. With the data in hand, the patent data was consulted in the Espacenet repository, using the patent filing number collected at the INPI. This set of data extracted at INPI as well as at Espacenet is the set of data analyzed in this study, a study of great relevance, mainly due to the techniques implemented, as well as the breadth and consistency of the data collected.

After collecting patent data, using the LattesDataXplorer framework developed by Dias [12], data was collected from the curricula registered on the CNPq Lattes Platform, which have registration information and/or participation in the patent filing. With this data, algorithms were developed to equalize the entire database obtained from the curricula, and also to remove information from users without registered technical production or without a valid number of patent registrations. The objective of this strategy is to verify the consistency of the patent data registered in the curricula registered on the Lattes Platform, as well as to enable analyzes that can consider various information from the proponents that are not in the patent records, but informed in their CVs, such as, for example, data on academic training, areas of activity and scientific production.

3.1 Data Acquisition

The patent data acquisition process was divided into two stages, (1) initially the data collection at the INPI and processing of the patent filing numbers, and later, (2) the validation and collection of patent data from the patents extracted at the Espacenet repository. Figure 1 presents the schema created for the data collection process.

To collect patent data at the INPI, the patent search tool pePI (Research in Industrial Property) maintained by the INPI was used, where it is possible to consult patent documents by informing login and password or by anonymous access. What differs

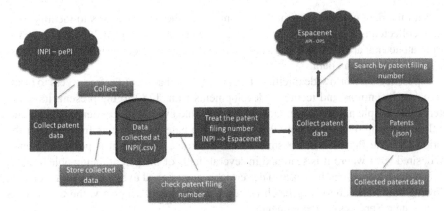

Fig. 1. Overview of the data collection process

between the two forms of identification is that choosing to inform the login and pass-word will allow access to more services, such as the availability of documents in PDF format, among others, but to achieve the objective of this work, anonymous access is the enough, therefore, the same was used.

When entering in the search field "(22) Deposit Date" the start date "01/01/1900" and end date "12/31/2020" and select the "search" option, the system returns a page with the list of 862,726 patents spread over 8,627 pages displaying 100 records per page. To optimize data collection, an algorithm was proposed to enable a computational process in order to automate the collection, consisting of 5 steps:

1. Perform anonymous login to retrieve the credentials needed to perform the search;
2. Access the advanced search, informing the credentials obtained in the previous step;
3. On the advanced search screen, enter the start date 01/01/1900 and the end date 12/31/2020 in the field "(22) Deposit Date" and trigger the search event;
4. Scroll through the entire patent listing displayed on the result page
a. For each patent, access the details page:
i. Parse the HTML (HyperText Markup Language) content of the detail page and retrieve the information: "Order number", "Deposit date", "Publication date", "Depositor Title", "Inventor" and "ICP Classification".
ii. Store the retrieved information in a CSV (Comma-separated-values) file;
iii. Back to patent listing;
5. Repeat step 4 for all search results pages.

Through web scraping and web crawler techniques, this entire strategy was coded using the Python programming language.

During the tests of the developed algorithm, it was possible to identify a limitation in this approach, due to the large volume of data, for reasons of platform security, the credentials expire after a certain time. To circumvent this limitation, monthly periods were used for the "Deposit Date" filter. Therefore, storing the data in CSV files, one file for each year, the collection was performed between the months of April and June 2020.

With the data collection at the INPI completed, the next step was to identify each patent collected at the INPI, on Espacenet, and later extract its available data. Only the set of patents that are identified on Espacenet will be considered, due to the completeness and consistency of the data.

Espacenet is a worldwide intelligent search service that provides free access to information on inventions and technical developments from 1782 to the present. Its query interface is simple and intuitive, making it accessible even to inexperienced users, currently containing data from more than 120 million patent documents from all over the world [13]. The Platform offers smart search features, in which it is possible to enter the desired term where it is searched in several fields of the patent, being able to enter up to 10 terms separated by space. The service was designed to be used by humans, not allowing automatic queries or batch retrieval, when this is necessary, the use of OPS (Open Patent Services) is recommended.

OPS is a web service that provides access to data stored in the EPO (European Patent Office) database through web services using RESTful architecture. Making use of XML (eXtensible Markup Language) and JSON (JavaScript Object Notation) standards to format the response data to requests, according to the parameterization. Consequently, the development of self-extracting applications and robots to download large volumes of data becomes viable.

The retrieval of data referring to each patent is made possible using the patent search available at OPS, using the patent application number as a selection criterion. The order number is important for patent identification both at INPI and Espacenet, as each patent has its own unique filing number. The composition of the patent filing application number at the INPI has two different formats, in which one was used for older patents and another format is currently adopted. Since January 2, 2012, the new format is assigned to new patent applications (invention and utility model), industrial design and geographical indication [14].

The format assigned to patents filed up to 12/31/2011 is composed of the following format ZZ XXXXXXX-D, where ZZ refers to the nature of the protection, XXXXXXX an annual serial number composed of 7 digits, and finally, D, which is the verifying digit.

The new format established aims to meet the INPI's international integration policy, meeting the standards internationally suggested by WIPO St133 published by WIPO (World Intellectual Property Organization). This new format has the following structure BR ZZ AAAA XXXXXX D CP, where BR is the identification of the country, ZZ is the nature of the protection, YYYY year of entry into the INPI, XXXXXX numbering that corresponds to the order of filing of applications composed of 6 digits, D the check digit and finally CP that corresponds to the publication code, the legal status of the request with the INPI.

Espacenet adopts the international standard WIPO St13 to store information about patents, which implies processing the filing application number before performing the search on Espacenet.

Based on a set of defined rules, it was developed using the Python programming language, an algorithm that goes through all the patents collected at the INPI, and applies all the defined rules, storing the results in CSV files, one file for each year of filing.

After processing the patent filing numbers, an algorithm was developed using the Python programming language, which runs through all the CSV files with the results of processing the patent filing numbers and making use of the services available in the OPS, performs the consultation of each patent, using the previously processed patent application numbers as search criteria, storing each patent located in the Espacenet repository, in a file in.json format. After 241 h of running the algorithm, it was possible to retrieve data from 722,347 patents successfully identified on Espacenet, about 83% of the 862,726 patents collected at the INPI. The collection was carried out between the months of July to December 2020 and January and February 2021.

The next step of this work was to collect CVs registered on the Lattes Platform that have patent information, such as the filing application number or the patent title, in order to validate such information with the set collected from Espacenet. The process of collecting and selecting curriculum data from the Lattes Platform was carried out using the LattesDataXplorer framework [12].

4 Results

As a result, initially, 722,347 patents were identified in the Espacenet repository, about 83% of the set of patents collected at the INPI, a hypothesis for unidentified patents is given by the fact that they have not yet been made available in the Espacenet repository, or by problems in identifying the correct format of the patent application number.

With the set of patent data retrieved from the Espacenet repository, an analysis of annual patent filings was carried out, presenting data between 1972 and 2020, with the year with the highest number of patents filed being 2012, with a total of 30,774 deposit requests (Fig. 2). It is also worth noting that there was a continuous growth in the number of deposits until 2012. And afterwards, a significant drop.

In order to evaluate the representativeness of patent records registered in the Lattes Platform curricula and duly identified in Espacenet, an analysis using a verification between the sets was carried out. Of the total of 72,256 records with patent data extracted from 29,514 curricula, after processing and cleaning the data referring to patents extracted from the Lattes Platform curricula, it was possible to identify 15,252 patents from the set extracted on Espacenet, Fig. 3 shows the distribution of patents identified in the CVs by year of filing.

The patents reported in the curricula registered on the Lattes Platform were deposited between the years 1975 to 2018, with a greater concentration between the years 2002 and 2016, highlighting an increase in the number of patent deposits between the years 2000 and 2018. It is noteworthy that the set of CVs used in the analysis were collected in 2019, which justifies the absence of patents in recent years, a sudden drop is possible in 2018, as some patents may not have been registered by their proponents.

Given this, several analyzes can be made possible for a better understanding of the retrieved dataset. Each patent, according to its nature and purpose, receives a classification according to the international patent classification system, the IPC (International Patent Classification), most of the patents produced by researchers with information extracted from their curricula, about 32%, are classified as "A-Human Needs". Figure 4 presents a graph with the patent classifications reported in the Lattes Platform curricula.

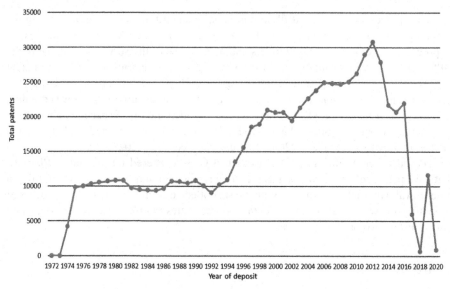

Fig. 2. Time evolution of patent filing per year

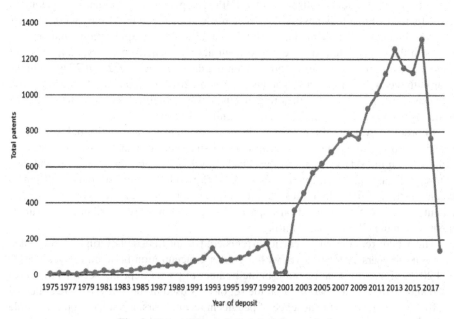

Fig. 3. Patent filing in lattes platform curricula

In a general context, most Brazilian patents receive the classifications, A - Human needs (32%); B - Processing operations, transport (14%); and C – Chemistry (23%).

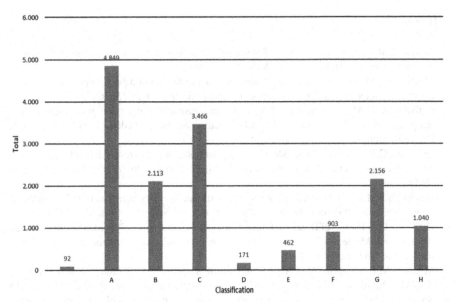

Fig. 4. Classification of registered patents in Lattes Platform curricula. A - Human needs; B - Processing operations, transport; C - Chemistry; Metallurgy; D – Textiles, Paper; E – Fixed constructions; F – Mechanical engineering, Lighting, Heating, Weapons, Explosions; G – Physics; H – Electricity.

Given the above, several new analyzes can be carried out, mainly through the integration of Espacenet data repositories and the data recorded in the Lattes Platform curricula. Such analyzes will be important to better understand how technical production has evolved in the country and the profile of researchers who have deposited patents.

5   Final Considerations

From the results obtained by the extracted data set, it was possible to verify the great viability and scientific value of adopting patent information as a source of data for analyzes about the technical production of a country, region or area of knowledge, characterizing as of paramount importance for understand the national technological scenario. The group of Brazilian patents identified in Espacenet is characterized as a significant portion of the entire set of data registered at the INPI, in view of the high complexity in identifying them in Espacenet, due to the lack of a standard for converting the deposit numbers of patents registered until the year 2011.

Assessing the representativeness of the patents registered in the Lattes Platform curricula in international repositories is presented as an important alternative, considering that such identification may even enable a validation of the data recorded in the curricula. Only 72,256 patent records were identified in the set of more than 6.8 million CVs analyzed. Few CVs present patent information, that is, only 1% of CVs have patent records, highlighting the need for a study to better understand this type of production.

References

1. Amadei, J.R.P., Torkomian, A.L.V.: Patents in universities: analysis of the deposits of public universities in São Paulo. Inf. Sci. **38**(02), 9–18 (2009)
2. Mueller, S.P.M., Perucchi, V.: Universities and the production of patents: topics of interest to the student of technological information. Perspect. Inf. Sci. **19**(2), 15–36 (2014)
3. Cativelli, A.S.: Metric indicators of patent value: construction of a value index using Brazilian green patents. Thesis (Doctorate in Information Science) - Federal University of Santa Catarina - Education Science Center (2020)
4. Quoniam, C.T.L., Kniess, M.R., Mazieri: The patent as an object of research in information and communication sciences. Encontros Bibli: electron. J. Librariansh. Inf. Sci. **19**(39), 243–268 (2014)
5. Ribeiro, S.P.M.J.C., Garcia: The state of the art of patentometry in international information science journals. Brazilian Meeting of Bibliometrics and Scientometrics, May 2014
6. Cativelli, A.S.: Patents of Brazilian Public Universities: Analysis of Concessions. Dissertation (Professional Master's Dissertation in Management of Units of Information) - University of the State of Santa Catarina (2016)
7. Mendes, M.L.S., Melo, D.R.A.: Technological assessment: a methodological proposal. ANPAD - National Association of Graduate Studies and Research in Administration (2017)
8. Speziali, M.G., Nascimento, R.S.: Patentometry: an indispensable tool in the study of technology development for the chemical industry. Kim. Nova **43**(10), 1538–1548 (2020). https://doi.org/10.21577/0100-4042.20170620
9. Stefani Cativelli, A., Pinto, A.L., Lascurain Sanchez, M.L.: Patent value index: measuring Brazilian green patents based on family size, grant, and backward citation. Iberoam. J. Sci. Measur. Commun. **1**(1), 004 (2020). https://doi.org/10.47909/ijsmc.03
10. Reymond, D.: Patents information for humanities research: could there be something? Iberoam. J. Sci. Measur. Commun. **1**(1) (2020). https://doi.org/10.47909/ijsmc.02
11. Serrano, B.P., Junior, J.A.G.: Innovation networks: mapping of patent inventors in a company in the cosmetics sector. GEPROS Mag. **09**(1), 101 (2014)
12. Dias, T.M.R.: A study of Brazilian scientific production based on data from the Lattes Platform, p. 181. Thesis (Doctorate in Mathematical and Computational Modeling) - Federal Center for Technological Education of Minas Gerais, September 2016
13. ESPECENET Espacenet patent search. https://worldwide.espacenet.com/patent/. Accessed 13 Jan 2021
14. Uece, U. F. do C. INPI - Learn more about the new numbering in DIRPA and DICIG requests. http://www.uece.br/nit/index.php?option=com_content&view=article&id=1654:inpi-saiba-mais-sobre-a-nova-numeracao-nos-pedidos-da-dirpa-e-da-dicig&catid=31:lista-de-noticias. Accessed 11 May 2021

Publications in Scientific Events as a Data Source for Scientometric Analysis

Fernanda Silva Coimbra[✉] and Thiago Magela Rodrigues Dias

Centro Federal de Educação Tecnológica de Minas Gerais (CEFET-MG), Belo Horizonte, Brazil
coimbra.sfernanda@gmail.com

Abstract. Scientific production has shown significant growth in recent years, with numerous means of communication to disseminate such production. In this context, several studies focus on exploring the behavior of scientific evolution. For this reason, one of the main means of scientific communication today are events, in which countless and valuable works are generated, also enabling rapid communication with possibilities for argumentation, as well as contributions between peers. However, most works that evaluate scientific production in scientific events usually have specific repositories as a source of data, often restricted to some areas of knowledge. This work aims to analyze the scientific production published in the annals of events of the group of doctors who have curricula registered on the Lattes Platform. The data used were extracted from the Lattes Platform so that all the selection and treatment of the data of interest could be carried out. A characterization of the articles was carried out, making it possible to understand how Brazilian scientific production occurs. Through the results, it was possible to verify that a large area of Health Sciences has a higher rate of publication in annals of events; to draw a temporal analysis, it was verified the volume of publications that use persistent identifier (DOI) and which are the 10 countries that have the highest volume of publications in events. Through the results, it is possible to present traces of how Brazilian scientific production occurs in this medium of dissemination through various characteristics outlined in this work.

Keywords: Scientific production · Events · Lattes Platform

1 Introduction

The internet has become a great repository of scientific knowledge, providing access to this valuable asset to users simply and intuitively, allowing the availability and access of scientific works, which include their analyses and their results, as well as enabling on the part of these users to disclose their personal, professional and academic information. Currently, there are several sites for recording this information and several institutional repositories that also enable scientific dissemination by groups of individuals.

There are countless studies available on the internet that use data from scientific productions and the works that carry out analyses of scientific publications have gained prominence. Scientific productions are an integral part of the individual's knowledge

A. L. Pinto and R. Arencibia-Jorge (Eds.): DIONE 2022, LNICST 452, pp. 49–59, 2022.
https://doi.org/10.1007/978-3-031-22324-2_5

production process, in which he can make available this knowledge acquired through articles in conference proceedings and journals, books, book chapters, abstracts, theses, dissertations, and monographs, among others, other means of dissemination and communication of science [1].

The volume of data currently available has its characteristics, unique patterns, quantity, and diversity of data, thus causing a complex task to carry out studies that aim to explore these data. In this context, bibliometrics appears intending to quantify the processes of written communication, through the use of methods that generate statistical analyses on the production and dissemination of knowledge applied to scientific data sources [2].

Currently, there are several quantitative techniques to assess scientific productivity such as bibliometrics, scientometrics, informatory, and webometrics. All the techniques allow different analyses. Bibliometric analysis can be used to measure the scientific production of particular individuals, research groups, institutions, geographic regions, organizations, or events [3].

Over the last few years, it is possible to verify the evolution of scientific dissemination in the various areas of knowledge, and in this context, it has been possible to verify how this increase has been driven by the increase in scientific events in the world. Being classified as one of the main means of scientific communication, the events, identified as an effective means of oral communication of knowledge, have been gaining notoriety [4].

Scientific events perform functions such as improvement of works, the reflection of the state of the art, and communication [5]. In scientific events, documents are generated with the works presented, popularly known as annals. The publications generated in the events are considered by some studies, as the most current academic productions [6].

The behavior of scientific publications in a given field of research allows new perspectives to understand it, enabling a new aspect in the evaluation of science [7]. Therefore, analyzing how publications in annals of events have been carried out presents itself as an important mechanism for understanding the evolution of scientific events in a general context or in certain areas of knowledge.

However, in general, information related to scientific production in annals of events is present in numerous data repositories, thus making it difficult to recover and analyze data, especially on a large scale. As in the study of [8], which aims to obtain a better understanding of the characteristics of academic events in four fields of science; analyze the metadata of academic events from four major fields of science; renowned academic events belonging to five sub fields; through the analysis, the authors find significant results that make it possible to observe the general evolution and success factors of academic events, thus allowing event organizers to judge the progress of their event over time and compare it with other events in the same field; analyzes are also presented that enable decision-making for researchers to choose the appropriate places for the presentation of their work.

To obtain a large set of data on scientific publications in annals of events, the CNPq Lattes Platform appears like an excellent alternative for data collection. The Lattes Platform has as one of its elements the curricula, in which it is possible to include and retrieve information inserted in the curricula by the individuals themselves, it is characterized as an open-access platform.

In this context, in Brazil, the Lattes Platform has become a standard for recording curricular data from the scientific community. The Lattes Platform is a powerful repository of Brazilian scientific data, which has high-quality data and allows access to the data of registered individuals [9]. It is the responsibility of the individual to enter and update the data. As it is a valuable repository, it is possible to find in the literature several authors who use the Lattes Platform as a source of bibliometric studies. The first work in the literature [3], since in addition to a broad study on Brazilian scientific production using as a data source all curricula registered in the Lattes Platform, the author develops a framework, implementing bibliometric techniques and metrics based on analysis of social networks, being responsible for extracting the entire data set from the curricula.

Countless works use the Lattes Platform as a data source resource, as it is a rich repository including articles published in events [10–12]. Recently, [13] presents a temporal analysis of the main keywords existing in scientific articles. Keywords from approximately 14 million scientific articles from the group of doctors referring to all major areas of activity used, the analyses presented as data characterization, and the temporal analysis of the main research topics in Brazilian science. The initial results presented from the application of bibliometric analysis and techniques based on social network analysis on the keywords of articles published in conference proceedings and in periodicals of the selected set. The results generated can serve as a basis for other studies that aim to understand the development of Brazilian science in the various areas of knowledge.

However, there is a limited amount of works that use curriculum information from the Lattes Platform as the main source of data in the context of works published in annals of events. Retrieving works published in events is a complex task, due to the range of events, formats, among other points. Using bibliometric and scientometric analyses, it is possible to perform data analysis from academic article bases, enabling measurement and quantification of scientific progress. In view of this, the present study presents itself as an analysis in order to understand the behavior of published works in annals of events registered in the curricula registered in the Lattes Platform in a global way, considering all the registered curricula, through bibliometric analyses, general characterization of the events, temporal analyses and quantitative analyses, making it possible to verify representativeness by areas of knowledge.

Several points motivate the understanding of scientific production through the annals of events, one of them is the possibility of an overview of how the different areas of knowledge have explored this means of dissemination to present the results of their research; in which periods there was a greater number of publications and which areas have the highest volume of publications. Therefore, this work has the general objective of understanding traces of Brazilian scientific production in the annals of events, using as a data source the articles registered in the Lattes Platform curricula.

2 Development

The Lattes Platform integrates the databases into a single system of Curricula, Research Groups, and Institutions. However, it is the responsibility of the individual to insert all their curricular information on the Lattes Platform, and, after inclusion, all these data are available in open access on the internet. It is a rich repository, contemplating the record of the professional, academic and scientific production trajectory, in which it allows several different analyses, thus justifying the choice of this repository as a data source for this work. However, it is not possible to retrieve all resumes at once.

The methodology used in this study was based on a bibliometric analysis concomitant with a quantitative methodology. LattesDataXplorer [3] was used, this framework allows performing the process of extracting and selecting curricular data from the Lattes Platform, which involves a set of techniques and methods, which enables the collection, selection, treatment and analysis of data. For this work, only the collection and selection modules of LattesDataXplorer were used, in order to extract and select curricular data from the Lattes Platform. Thus, the Collection module was carried out in stages, namely: collection of URLs, collection of identifiers and extraction of curriculum.

The LattesDataXplorer extractor was used in January 2021 to collect all resumes, about 7 million records. The format of the curricula is XML (eXtensible Markup Language), this format allows delimitations and is suitable for automatic processing, enabling better data handling. In order to obtain an accurate analysis of the articles published in the annals of events, it was preferred to establish a group of individuals, according to the level of academic training/title, who have completed the doctorate training level. The choice is made based on what Dias (2016) mentions in his work: doctors are responsible for 74.51% of articles published in journals and 64.67% of articles published in conference proceedings, in addition to generally having date of update their curricula recently and notably are responsible for the highest level of training. In order to help data analysis, after using the framework, it was necessary to create methods for selection, treatment, and visualization (Fig. 1).

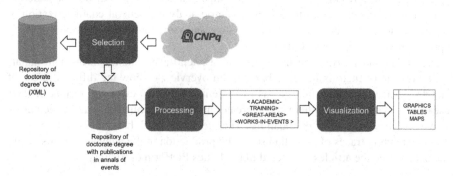

Fig. 1. Process of selection, treatment and visualization of data.

The treatment step was based on analyzing the set of XML files. For each curriculum, a file in XML format was extracted.

The XML curriculum extracted from the Lattes Platform presents its structure as the root element, called "Curriculum"; and has five child elements that have their elements and attributes. Each resume is unique and has its information; these data aggregate information on major areas, academic training, guidelines, productions, among others. At this stage of the analysis, the division of information from the curriculum is carried out, later accessing the information of interest and disregarding some information that is irrelevant for this work.

After processing the XML, the visualization step was carried out in which the data characterization is carried out, allowing the analysis of the data inserted in the Section of Works in Events, a section that contains works published in annals of events, if the individual has stated in your CV. Through the characterization of the data, it was possible to obtain general indicators such as the total number of articles published in Annals of events, year of publication of the articles, a total of individuals who have articles published in Annals of events, publications by large area, individuals without publications, publications with persistent identifiers; such indicators are presented in the Results section.

3 Results

3.1 General Characterization

The initial characterization resulted in a set of 360,888 curricula of individuals with a completed doctorate, this amount represents approximately 5% of curricula registered on the Lattes Platform (data from January 2021). Among these curricula, it was found that 57,403 curricula did not have any article reported in the section of works published in annals of events, corresponding to 16% of the group of doctors. After analyzing the data, it was possible to understand how Brazilian scientific production happens in congress proceedings, having the curricula registered in the Lattes Platform as a data source, which can be analyzed by large areas of activity and perform a temporal analysis of the publications. As the focus of this work is to characterize the articles published in the annals of events, for the next analysis, only the data set corresponding to the 11,416,655 articles published in the annals of events identified in this study will be used.

After analyzing the data, it was possible to understand how Brazilian scientific production happens in conference proceedings, having the curricula registered in the Lattes Platform as a data source, which can be analyzed by large areas of activity and perform a temporal analysis of publications. As the focus of this work is to characterize the articles published in the annals of events, for the next analyses, only the data set corresponding to the 11,416,655 articles published in the annals of events identified in this study will be used.

3.2 Temporal Analysis

The temporal analysis of articles published in Annals of events was carried out to verify the number of articles published per year, a 30-year cut-off line was drawn for better graphic representation (Fig. 2).

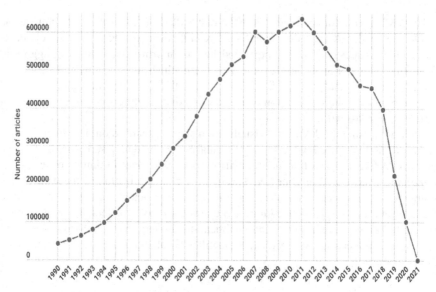

Fig. 2. Temporal analysis of articles in annals of events by year.

It is possible to observe the constant increase in the number of publications, especially from the end of the 1990s, with the peak of publications in 2011. Afterward, a significant drop in publications in events from 2011 and 2018 can be seen. An abrupt drop is displayed. However, a hypothesis for the significant drop in the number of publications in recent years may be related to the lack of updating of some curricula, which even the author has published work, may not have registered the article in his CV. of the Lattes Platform.

3.3 Articles in Annals of Events by Large Area

The Lattes Platform curricula allow the insertion of information on large areas of activity of individuals following the classification of areas of CNPq. Thus, the individual inserts his classification into nine major areas, namely: Agricultural Sciences, Biological Sciences, Health Sciences, Exact and Earth Sciences, Human Sciences, Applied Social Sciences, Engineering, Linguistics, Letters and Arts, and others. If the individual does not inform this field, it will be blank, and in the context of this work it was characterized as "Not informed".

In order to understand in which large areas the individuals considered in this study are distributed (Fig. 3). It is noteworthy that as it is possible to insert more than one large area of activity in a curriculum when this phenomenon happened, the first record was considered as the main large area.

It can be seen that the large area of Health Sciences has a higher rate of publication in annals of events (20.79%). The large area of Agricultural Sciences (17.22%) is presented with the second-highest percentage, and with a similar amount, the large area of Biological Sciences (15.51%).

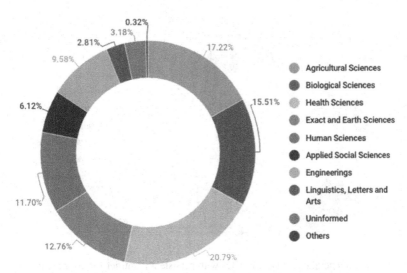

Fig. 3. General quantity of individuals with publication by large areas.

It was also possible to observe that the large area that has the highest referenced value without publications in the annals of events corresponds to Human Sciences (16.67%), followed by the large area of Applied Social Sciences (14.94%) and Exact and Earth Sciences (14.22), respectively, with similar amounts.

3.4 Persistent Identifiers

All data from works published in events are manually entered by the individuals themselves, however, there is an alternative way to enter such data partially automatically, using the persistent identifier DOI. When typing the identifier, the query is performed and the data is automatically indexed in specific fields in the curricula.

In 2007, Lattes Platform curricula started to accept the DOI, making it possible to insert it, through manual typing, allowing the Platform to make a query and fill in the publication data automatically.

When analyzing the data of the publications registered in the curricula of the doctors that have the persistent identifier (DOI), it is possible to verify that only 30,936 of the articles in the proceedings of events registered in the curricula of the selected set have a persistent identifier, represented as follows approximately 3% of the articles. Demonstrating that it is still a little used identifier, considering that its use could add a greater amount of data referring to the articles that are being registered. Thus, by retrieving the information that has DOI registered in the productions of their curricula, it was possible to distribute these over large areas (Fig. 4).

Checking the articles published in Annals of events by large area, which have this persistent identifier linked to bibliographic production, it can be seen that there is a notable difference referring to Fig. 3, being that individual from large areas of Exact and Earth Sciences (30.68%) and Engineering (25.78%) are the ones that most use

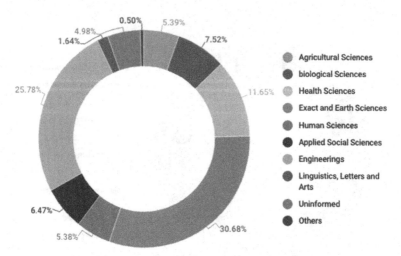

Fig. 4. General quantity of articles with persistent identifier for large areas.

persistent identifiers, and thus, provide easier access to their work, which can result in greater visibility of their studies.

Performing the temporal analysis of articles published in Annals of events that have the DOI, it is possible to verify some articles published before 1994 (DOI proposition) that informed the identifier (Fig. 5).

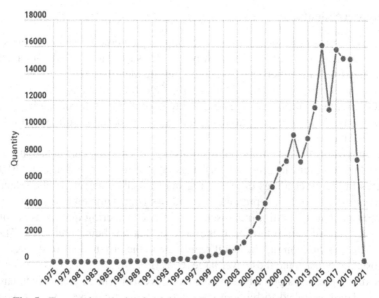

Fig. 5. Temporal analysis of articles with persistent identifier by large areas.

It is observed that there is a significant temporal variation in the use of the identifier. This variation has as one of the hypotheses the volume of events in that year, in which the number of publications may have influenced the quantitative. Or rather, how these proceedings were published, considering that some events, under the responsibility of some organizers, value the incorporation of the DOI in the proceedings of their publications.

3.5 Analysis by Countries

The UN (United Nations), one of the main references in the recognition of countries internationally, currently recognizes 193 countries. Through the analyzes carried out here, it was possible to verify that the Lattes Platform has works published in annals of events in 185 countries. These data demonstrate that Brazilian scientific production is published in international events, enabling greater visibility of these works. For better visualization, the ranking of the ten countries with the highest number of published works performed, presented in shades of blue on the world map (Fig. 6).

Fig. 6. Ranking - 10 countries with the highest number of publications in events

It can be seen that Brazil is the country that has the highest number of publications, since these data were extracted from a Brazilian Platform it is understandable. However, the difference between the other countries in the ranking is large, a hypothesis due to this large difference in values or due to the lack of investment for the participation of the authors in international scientific events. The investments of higher education institutions to send their professors to international events have been decreasing rapidly, the criteria for participation between national and international congresses are of paramount importance for the improvement of academic production, and should be seen as an investment and not as a cost [14].

4 Final Considerations

With the accomplishment of this work, it observed that the data extracted from the Lattes Platform are an excellent source to understand how Brazilian scientific production happens in congress proceedings. Studies that focus on analyzing articles published in annals of events in general are relevant and capable of providing several analyzes in the context of understanding the behavior of individuals participating in the events, as well as the publications that are being carried out.

Through the analyses carried out, some general characteristics of the data can be observed, such as: participation in events by large area, making it possible in the future to understand why certain large areas present a greater volume of publications in annals of events; seasonality of publications presenting as a hypothesis the lack of updating of curricula on the Lattes Platform, generating a drop in publications from 2018; the scarce use of a persistent identifier, thus evidencing the difficulty of finding certain publications; and, countries with the highest number of participation in events, generating inputs to analyze the viability of publications outside Brazil.

This study aims to contribute to the generation of national scientific indicators, as well as the management of information in the scientific and technological area, allowing analysis of ideas for new events for the scientific community.

References

1. Domingues, I.: O sistema de comunicação da ciência e o taylorismo acadêmico: questionamentos e alternativas. Estudos avançados **28**, 225–250 (2014)
2. Araújo, C.A.: Bibliometria: evolução histórica e questões atuais. **12**, 11–32 (2006)
3. Dias, T.M.R.: Um Estudo da Produção Científica Brasileira a partir de Dados da Plataforma Lattes. Centro Federal de Educação Tecnológica de Minas Gerais, Doutorado em Modelagem Matemática e Computacional (2016)
4. Mello, L.: Os anais de encontros científicos como fonte de informação: relato de pesquisa. **20**, 53–68 (1996)
5. Campello, B.S., Cendón, B.V., Kremer, J.M.: Fontes de informação para pesquisadores e profissionais (2007)
6. Carmona, I.V., Pereira, M.V.: Ciência, tecnologia e sociedade e educação ambiental: uma revisão bibliográfica em anais de eventos científicos da área de ensino de ciências. **8**, 94–14 (2018)
7. Araújo, R.F, Alvarenga, L.: A bibliometria na pesquisa científica da pós-graduação brasileira de 1987 a 2007. **16**, 51–70 (2011)
8. Fathalla, S., Vahdati, S., Lange, C., Auer, S.: Scholarly event characteristics in four fields of science: a metrics-based analysis. Scientometrics **123**, 77–705 (2020). https://doi.org/10.1007/s11192-020-03391-y
9. Lane, J.: Let's make science metrics more scientific. Nature **464**, 488–489 (2010)
10. Coimbra, F.S., Dias, T.M.R.: Use of open data to analyze the publication of articles in scientific events. Iberoam. J. Sci. Meas. Commun. **1**(3) (2021). https://doi.org/10.47909/ijsmc.123
11. Mascarenhas, H., Dias, T.M.R., Dias, P.: Academic mobility of doctoral students in Brazil: an analysis based on Lattes Platform. Iberoam. J. Sci. Meas. Commun. **1**(3), 1–15 (2021). https://doi.org/10.47909/ijsmc.53

12. Justino, T.S., Amaral, R.M., Faria, L.I.L., Brito, A.G.C.: Scientific collaboration analysis of Brazilian postgraduate programs in information science. AWARI (2, n1), e024 (2021). https://doi.org/10.47909/awari.85

13. Gomes, J.O.: Uma análise temporal dos principais tópicos de pesquisa da ciência brasileira a partir das palavras-chave de publicações científicas. Centro Federal de Educação Tecnológica de Minas Gerais, Doutorado em Modelagem Matemática e Computacional (2018)

14. Serra, F.A.R., Fiates, G.G., Ferreira, M.P.: Publicar é difícil ou faltam competências? **9**, 32–55 (2008)

Publications in Open Access Journals: A Bibliometric Analysis

Patrícia Mascarenhas Dias(✉) , Thiago Magela Rodrigues Dias ,
and Gray Farias Moita

Federal Center for Technological Education of Minas Gerais, Belo Horizonte, Brazil
patriciamdias@gmail.com

Abstract. The results of scientific activities and consequently their dissemination, mainly through scientific articles, make it possible to publish the techniques and indicators used, as well as the results obtained during development, to various interested parties in the investigated themes. Therefore, identifying how the results of scientific research are being published allows us to understand how scientific communication has been used to disseminate the studies carried out. In this context, the publication of articles in open access journals emerges as an interesting mechanism for the dissemination of scientific research, as it facilitates and enables access to them, since there are no barriers, especially financial ones, for access to content. of this type of publication. Therefore, this study aims to analyze, with the help of different indicators, the entire set of publications in open access journals, registered in the Lattes Platform curricula. In view of the extraction and treatment of curricular data, and with the validation with data extracted from the DOAJ, it was possible to verify the impact of the scientific journals in which the articles are being published, as well as the average of citations of the publications over the years and considering the different areas of knowledge.

Keywords: Open access · Qualitative analysis · Lattes platform

1 Introduction

According to several studies, journals – especially those available in electronic format – have been on the rise since the last decade. It can be said that journals, in all areas of knowledge, have the role of being a filter for the recognition of works that have been accepted. For [1], publication in a journal recognized by the area is the most accepted way to register the originality of the work and to confirm that the works were reliable enough to overcome the skepticism of the scientific community.

In view of the above, the Open Access Movement emerged in the early years of the 21st century, aiming to make the full text of publications available, for use without financial, legal or technical barriers that are not inseparable from access to an Internet connection [2].

A. L. Pinto and R. Arencibia-Jorge (Eds.): DIONE 2022, LNICST 452, pp. 60–69, 2022.
https://doi.org/10.1007/978-3-031-22324-2_6

In [3] presents figures that justify and are great motivators for publication in open access journals. For the author, open access articles have 336% more citations than articles that are available in print, with a median equal to 158%.

Therefore, access to scientific information has been a major challenge for developing countries such as Brazil. With the crisis of journals, which arose as a result of the high costs of maintaining subscriptions to scientific journals, access to this type of information was quite limited. Although this crisis began in the mid-1980s, there is still no definitive solution. With information and communication technologies, the open files initiative appears, which defines a model of interoperability between libraries and digital repositories, enabling alternatives for scientific communication [4].

It is also possible to notice that in most cases public resources are present in the stages of formation of a researcher. As a student, the researcher is generally supported by public schools and universities or receives public subsidies to assist in their training, such as scholarships to encourage research. As a researcher, he receives public funding to develop his research and support for participation in national and international scientific events to present research results. Finally, once published, the research results depend on the use of public resources to acquire the journals in which these researches are found. As they are scientific journals that bring together several articles in a single volume, it is necessary to acquire the set of articles published in those journals, which does not always reflect the needs of the researcher or funded research institutions [5].

In Brazil, the CAPES Periodicals Portal is one of the main sources of access to data from scientific publications. In it, it is possible to access a collection containing more than 45 thousand titles with full text, 130 reference bases and 12 bases dedicated exclusively to patents, in addition to books, encyclopedias and reference works, technical standards, statistics and audiovisual content [6].

However, the CAPES Periodicals Portal is not characterized as an open access initiative, since the government agency pays for subscriptions to periodicals made available free of charge to member institutions. In 2018 alone, the cost was BRL 402 million [7].

Investment in the CAPES Periodicals Portal has been increasing. In 2014, there was a decrease of approximately 3.3% compared to the previous year. During the years 2017 and 2018, the investment was practically the same, and according to CAPES the forecast for investing in the year 2020 in the portal was approximately 347 million reais. When considering the period between 2004 and 2019, the investment already made by CAPES to maintain the portal reaches approximately 3.1 billion reais.

Therefore, this work uses curriculum data from the Lattes Platform as a source of information for analysis using metrics such as Impact Factor and number of citations in order to better understand the set of articles published in open access journals by Brazilian researchers.

This type of study is characterized as an important mechanism to evaluate the evolution of publications in open access journals by Brazilian researchers with the adoption of qualitative indicators, making it possible to verify whether the incentive policies for the publication of research in this communication format have achieved results satisfactory.

2 Methodology

For the analysis of Brazilian scientific production in open access journals, the set of all individuals with CVs registered on the Lattes Platform was considered. The selection of this data set for the analysis is motivated by the fact that most Brazilian researchers have registered CVs and even researchers at the beginning of their careers are encouraged to register and keep their CVs up to date. Thus, the group of individuals analyzed in this work comprises a large part of the researchers working in Brazil.

In view of the difficulty in collecting and manipulating the set of curricula that make up the Lattes Platform, LattesDataXplorer [8], a framework for extracting and data processing was used (Fig. 1).

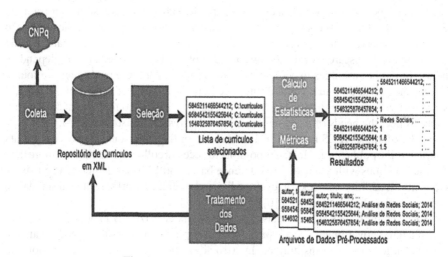

Fig. 1. LattesDataXplorer architecture [8].

A curriculum registered on the Lattes Platform can contain a lot of information capable of helping to understand the evolution of Brazilian science from different perspectives. However, for the purposes of this work, only data from articles published in open access journals, as well as their authors, were taken into account. Given the above, new components for the original framework were developed to meet the specific demand to identify for each article published in a journal (namely, 7,841,860), of each of the individuals (namely, 6,548,210) (data collected in January 2020), whether the journal in which that article had been published was open access (Fig. 2).

After collecting the entire repository of curricula using the framework initially proposed for this purpose, the new components developed were used to identify all records of open access journals from the Directory of Open Access Journals (DOAJ). As of January 2020, the DOAJ indexed 14,170 journals and 4,543,939 articles. DOAJ has been a data source and reference on open access journals for several studies [9–13].

By crossing and validating the data of each article registered in a given curriculum with the list of ISSN and eISSN of the DOAJ, it was possible to identify the publications

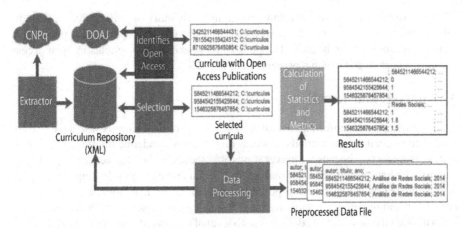

Fig. 2. LattesDataXplorer extended.

considered in this research as being an article in an open access journal. Therefore, all data from the publication, as well as from the analyzed curriculum, were included in an extract of valid data. This entire process occurs for all publications considered from all curricula initially collected.

By analyzing all article records from the collected dataset (7,841,860), 29.92% (2,090,015) was published in open access journals.

As already described, articles in open access journals have been the subject of interest for several researches in various areas of knowledge. Such interest is evident when analyzing the growing volume of publications over the years (Fig. 3).

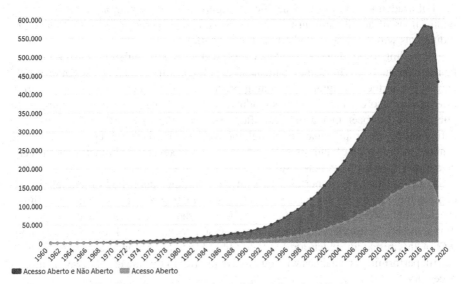

Fig. 3. Temporal comparison of the analyzed publications.

It is possible to observe a constant growth in the quantity of publications in periodicals, where in the year 2000, the percentage of publications in open access periodicals represented approximately 24%. The peak of representation of articles in open access journals occurs in 2017 with a percentage of 29.02%.

3 Analysis and Results

An important piece of information to understand the profile of authors who have already published in open access journals concerns their level of academic training. Such information is important because it makes it possible to understand the academic profile of authors who have published in journals of this format in the country. In a curriculum registered on the Lattes Platform, it is possible to record the entire history of an individual's completed and ongoing academic training, from elementary school to doctorate.

Although the postdoctoral degree is not a level of training, the authors who did it were separated from the group of doctors for statistical purposes and better understanding. It can be seen that most authors have a completed doctorate (47.62%). In second place, there are authors with a master's degree (22.51%), followed by those who completed post-doctoral studies (18.12%), so that only these three groups account for 88.25% of the analyzed group. In addition, it is observed that only 0.14% of the authors did not report completed training levels in their curricula, and that 4.56% only have completed graduation. The absence and low representation of authors at the lowest levels of academic training can be explained by the fact that scientific publications, especially those carried out in journals, are, in general, the result of research carried out in postgraduate studies.

In view of this, it is evident that most of the set of authors identified for having already published works in open access journals is composed of individuals with a high level of academic training. This justifies its significant representation in the total set of publications of articles in journals, even if it is a small percentage of the total set of individuals with CVs registered on the Lattes Platform.

According to [8], there is a tendency for researchers with higher levels of training to be more productive. This is due to the need to publicize their research, which is usually carried out in their postgraduate training process or in collaborations originated from orientations also carried out in postgraduate studies. Considering that the number of publications has been increasing year after year, driven mainly by the ease of dissemination and access to information through the web, and by the high degree of academic training of the group of authors analyzed in this work, several bibliometric metrics can be applied in order to get new results.

In this context, the importance of analysis of articles published in journals is evident, as they are one of the main means of disseminating research results. In addition, articles published in journals are also frequently used as indicators for the evaluation of researchers, research institutions and even graduate programs. Therefore, in the context of this research, which aims to analyze publications in open access journals in Brazil, performing an analysis with qualitative metrics in this means of dissemination is necessary.

The Impact Factor (IF) proposed by Garfield in 1955 is considered very valuable information for qualitative analyses. Currently, the IF is published annually by the Journal of Citation Report – JCR, as calculated by Thomson Reuters. To calculate the IF of a particular journal in a given year, the number of citations received in that year by articles published in the journal in the two preceding years is taken into account, divided by the number of articles published by the journal in the same period. It is worth mentioning that several researchers use the IF of the journal as a selection criterion for publication of their articles so that their work has greater visibility, hence the importance of the IF to qualify the journal.

Evaluating the IF of the open access journals analyzed in this work, Fig. 4 shows the medians in which the articles were published over the years. As can be seen, the apex of the medians occurred in the year 2000 with a value equal to 0.5340. After the year 2000, for three consecutive years, there was a decrease, and later, there was a growth for two years, after, from 2006 onwards, there were several drops until reaching the median equal to 0 in 2010, which remains until the year 2000. Last year analyzed in this work (2019). For better visualization of the results, Fig. 5 presents the distribution of the medians without the outliers, considering that some journals have IF much above the average.

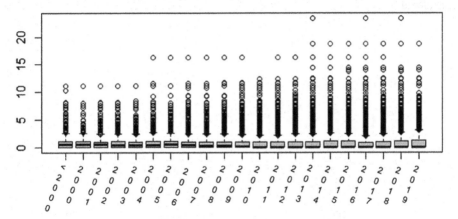

Fig. 4. Distribution of median impact factor over years.

Therefore, it is possible to perceive by the behavior of the medians, that from 2010 onwards, the publication of articles in open access journals analyzed in this work happened mostly in journals with IF equal to 0. It is worth mentioning that, even the publications of articles in open access journals being on the rise, most works are being published in journals with low IF. This fact does not necessarily indicate that publications in good journals are no longer happening, but that a large number of articles are being published in journals with low IF value.

In addition to the IF, which is often used as an indicator to qualify a journal, another indicator widely used to assess the quality of a given work refers to the number of citations that the work receives. To analyze the individual quality of the works considered in this work, the number of citations of each of the works published in open access journals was extracted from the Web of Science (WOS), Scielo and Scopus. Figure 6 shows

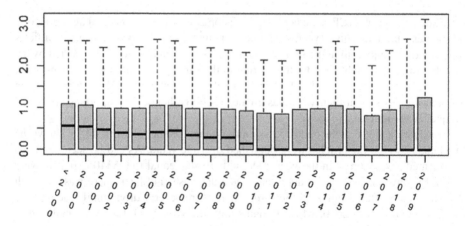

Fig. 5. Distribution of median impact factor excluding outliers.

the average citations of articles published in each of the years in the three directories considered.

■ Média de WoS   ■ Média de Scielo   ■ Média de Scopus

Fig. 6. Average citations of analyzed articles.

As can be seen, the analysis begins in 1960, the year of the first publication of the selected set and, in general, the average of citations of the articles has a variability in the following years in the three directories of citations consulted. A constant increase in the average of citations of articles can be seen from the end of the 1970s onwards. From 1996 onwards, the growth of the average of citations of Scielo becomes much more representative than that of the other directories, with the average of WoS being keeping with more modest growth than the other directories. It is noteworthy that in the articles published in the last years of the analysis, the average of citations tends to suffer a significant drop, starting to have average values very close to zero from 2017 onwards in the three directories, considering that recently published works tend to not have received many citations.

It is important to highlight that the quality of the scientific production of a given researcher cannot be measured simply by the number of citations that their work has received. This is due to several factors, such as, for example, his career time or the collaboration network in which he is inserted [8]. The number of references per article can be quite different in each of the different areas of knowledge. For example, articles in the Exact Sciences generally have a lower citation density than those related to the Health Sciences, which explains, in part, why the IFs of journals in this area are, on average, much higher compared to those of the Exact Sciences, as in the case of Mathematics [14].

The large discrepancy in the number of citations received by articles published in open access journals in different areas of knowledge makes a more detailed analysis necessary to make it possible to understand this distinction.

4 Conclusions

Currently, several studies have used data from scientific publications as a source for different types of analysis [15–17]. The publication of articles in open access journals has attracted the interest of the entire scientific community, in view of the growth in the number of journals in this format, as well as the recognized relevance that works in this publication medium have acquired. Allied to this, there is the interest of the scientific community in verifying the efforts made to boost the publication of articles in this publication medium, mainly due to the financial costs involved in accessing research that is usually financed with public resources. For these reasons, it is important to understand how publications in this dissemination format are evolving.

When carrying out an analysis that considered traditional quality metrics, articles published in open access journals registered in the Lattes Platform curricula were analyzed, considering their citations in WoS, Scielo and Scopus, as well as the IF of the periodicals. The IF is considered valuable information for qualitative analyses. Therefore, evaluating the IF of open access journals, a great distinction was observed in their values, ranging between 0 and 23.333. Therefore, when performing a temporal analysis of the articles, considering the median of the IF's of all journals, it was identified that the apex occurred in the year 2000, with a median value equal to 0.5340. It is noteworthy that in 2010 the median value was equal to zero, a value that remains until the last year analyzed in this work (2019). A hypothesis for this median value equal to zero, from the year 2010, may be related to the large number of articles, registered in the curricula from this year, in which, in most publications, the journal has null IF, or that is, with a value of zero. Of the total set of journals analyzed, approximately 82% have an IF equal to zero.

Regarding the citations received by the analyzed articles, an increase in the average of citations of the works published from the end of the 1970s can be seen, and this growth intensified in the late 1990s. Subsequently, a significant drop in the average of citations from 2008, in all considered directories. It is also important to note that as of 2017, in all directories, the average values of citations are close to zero, considering that recently published works may not have received significant amounts of citations.

The analysis of the average of citations is directly influenced by highly cited articles, which ends up raising such averages, especially in some areas, since even with many articles without citations, these highly cited works end up influencing the results.

In addition, it was possible to observe that articles published in journals with higher IF value tend to receive a greater number of citations, as a result of the credibility and visibility that such journals provide. In general, when published in journals with significant IF value, the work tends to have greater repercussion, to the detriment of most publications that are published in journals with null IF.

References

1. Rodrigues, R.S., Oliveira, A.B.: Periódicos científicos na america latina: títulos em acesso aberto indexados no ISI e SCOPUS. Perspectiv. Ciênc. Inf. **17**(4), 76–99 (2012)
2. BOAI (Budapest Open Access Initiative): Dez anos da Iniciativa de Budapeste em Acesso Aberto: a abertura como caminho a seguir. http://www.budapestopenaccessinitiative.org/boai-10-translations/portuguese-brazilian-translation (2012). Accessed: Jan 2022
3. Lawrence, S.: Free online availability substantially increases a paper's impact. Nature **411**(6837), 521 (2001). https://doi.org/10.1038/35079151
4. Kuramoto, H.: Informação científica: proposta de um novo modelo para o Brasil. Ciência da Informação **35**(2), 91–102 (2006)
5. Freire, J.D.: CNPq e o acesso aberto à informação científica. 2011. 275 f. Thesis – Curso de Programa de Pós-graduação, Faculdade de Ciência da Informação, Universidade de Brasília, Brasília (2011)
6. CAPES: O Portal de Periódicos da Capes. www.periodicos.capes.gov.br/index.php?option=com_pcontent&view=pcontent&alias=missao-objetivos&Itemid=109. Accessed 2022
7. CAPES: Orçamento – Evolução em reais. https://www.capes.gov.br/orcamento-evolucao-em-reais#A. Accessed 2020
8. Dias, T.M.R.: Um Estudo Sobre a Produção Científica Brasileira a partir de dados da Plataforma Lattes. 2016. 181 f. Thesis – Curso de Programa de Pós-graduação, Modelagem Matemática e Computacional, Centro Federal de Educação Tecnológica de Minas Gerais, Belo Horizonte (2016)
9. Lone, F., Rather, R., Shah, G.J.: Indian contribution to open access literature: a case study of DOAJ & OpenDOAR. Chin. Librarianship: an Int. Electron. J. **26**, 1–10 (2008)
10. Swan, A.: Why open access for Brazil? | Por que acesso livre no Brasil. Liinc em Revista **1**(1), 158–171 (2008). https://doi.org/10.18617/liinc.v4i2.279
11. Björk, B.-C., Solomon, D.: Article processing charges in OA journals: relationship between price and quality. Scientometrics **103**(2), 373–385 (2015). https://doi.org/10.1007/s11192-015-1556-z
12. dos Santos Costa, E.H.: Periódicos de acesso aberto: um canal de disseminação dos pesquisadores bolsistas PQ1A do CNPq? 2018. 127 f. Thesis – Curso de Programa de Pós-graduação em Ciência da Informação, Escola de Comunicação, Universidade Federal do Rio de Janeiro, Rio de Janeiro (2018)
13. Sarvo, D.D.O.: Avaliação da Plataforma Lattes como fonte de coleta de metadados para povoamento automatizado em repositórios institucionais. 2018. 96 f. Thesis (Master's degree) - Curso de Programa de Pós-graduação em Ciência, Tecnologia e Sociedade, Centro de Educação e Ciências Humanas, Universidade Federal de São Carlos, São Carlos (2018)

14. Garfield, E.: The use of JCR and JPI in measuring short and long term journal impact. In: Council of Scientific Editors Annual Meeting (2000)
15. Jorge, R.A., González, M.J.P.: Recommendations on the use of Scopus for the study of Information Sciences in Latin America. Iberoamerican J. Sci. Meas. Commun. 1(1), 8 (2020). https://doi.org/10.47909/ijsmc.07
16. Mascarenhas, H., Dias, T.M.R., Dias, P.: Academic mobility of doctoral students in Brazil: An analysis based on Lattes Platform. Iberoamerican J. Sci. Meas. Commun. 1(3), 1–15 (2021). https://doi.org/10.47909/ijsmc.53
17. Hernandez-Cruz, N.: Mapping the thematic evolution in Communication over the first two decades from the 21st century: a longitudinal approach. Iberoamerican J. Sci. Meas. Commun. 1(3), 1–10 (2021). https://doi.org/10.47909/ijsmc.88

Scientific Divulgation Before the Post-truth and the Crisis of Credibility of Science in the Context of Digital Humanities

Dheyvid Adriano do Livramento Chaves[✉] and Edgar Bisset Alvarez

PGCIN, Universidade Federal de Santa Catarina, Florianópolis, SC, Brazil
chavesdheyvid@gmail.com, edgar.bisset@ufsc.br

Abstract. This article proposes to reflect, in the light of Digital Humanities, on the influence of post-truth on the credibility crisis of science. The objective is to identify the role of scientific divulgation in the recovery of science's credibility and combat post-truth and the possibilities of using social networks for scientific divulgation by public universities. When defining itself as descriptive, the research seeks to accomplish an analysis of the benefits and contributions that can result in the contextualization of the problem with the field of knowledge regarding the Digital Humanities. The results showed that scientific divulgation through social networks contributes to combating the effects of post-truth culture and recovering the credibility of science. Finally, it was concluded that the fundamental actors in the promotion of scientific divulgation strategies are public universities, due to their social function.

Keywords: Digital humanities · Scientific divulgation · Credibility of science · Post-truth · Social networks

1 Introduction

To separate science from the digital context has become an impractical job in recent years. The primary information of the scientific means is, practically, all digital (Russel, 2011). Web 2.0 has solved a problem but has replaced it with another: the contemporary challenge is no longer the access to information but the quality of information available in the digital medium. To disseminate untruthful information has become a fad. According to the Massachusetts Institute of Technology research, fake news spreads 70% quicker than accurate news, gaining space over the Internet faster and more profound than what is indeed the truth (Vosoughi et al., 2018).

Social networks on the Internet are potential instruments to propagate disinformation, given their significant volume of users, with different profiles and the most diverse intentions. At the same time, it is on the possibility of having resources and particular tools from social networks that a solution can be proposed: the scientific divulgation. It is spoken here about digitalizing the print media of divulgation and democratizing the scientific knowledge produced in public educational institutions, which stays enclosed in

A. L. Pinto and R. Arencibia-Jorge (Eds.): DIONE 2022, LNICST 452, pp. 70–83, 2022.
https://doi.org/10.1007/978-3-031-22324-2_7

the academic community most of the time. Moreover, in the Brazilian model, there is an understanding that it is of competence of the public university to organize institutional politics to divulge science since these are responsible for over 95% of the national scientific production (Moura, 2019). There is an ethical and moral obligation to give back to society on the financing made by the citizens that compose it.

Based on the above, this article proposes to reflect, in the light of Digital Humanities, on the influence of post-truth on the credibility crisis of science. With this, the objective is to identify the role of scientific divulgation in the recovery of science's credibility and combat post-truth and the possibilities of using social networks for scientific divulgation by public universities.

2 Methodology

From the multidisciplinary methodological perspective, the research seeks to enter the knowledge domains and discourse about the themes that other areas of knowledge have approached. Defining this article as descriptive research, were performed comparative studies that allowed to know the depth of the existing experiences in implementing projects and initiatives aimed at the inclusion of Digital Humanities as a way of developing societies. Thus, it was possible to establish a group of strategies for better taking advantage of its advantages.

Successively, when defining itself as descriptive, the research seeks to accomplish an analysis of the benefits and contributions that can result in the contextualization of the problem with the field of knowledge regarding the Digital Humanities, define the scientific divulgation, and comprehend its state of emergency as derived from the ascension of post-truth culture and the crisis of credibility of science.

The next section will discuss the conceptualization of the Digital Humanities and its approaches in the scientific environment. The fourth section will define scientific divulgation by differentiating it from scientific communication. The fifth section inserts the post-truth phenomenon and its relation to the credibility of science. Finally, in the penultimate section of this article, the results are presented.

3 Digital Humanities and the Scientific Environment

The literature points to the origin of Digital Humanities in the Italian priest Roberto Busa project, from the compilation of the work of Saint Thomas Aquinas. Initiated in 1949 and having its first volumes published in 1974, this was the first example of informatics in the studies of Humanities (Russel, 2011). However, it was only from the start of the twenty-first century that the Digital Humanities began to contrast in the worldwide academic context, and from 2010 that reached a high degree of relevance at the Brazilian academy.

The concept of Digital Humanities, in turn, is broad. Among the many meanings, researchers who study it understand the concept as a field of study, area of knowledge, academic discipline, or phenomenon. In every case, it is a consensus that, in scientific research, Digital Humanities have an interdisciplinary character (Almeida and Damian 2015; Russel, 2011; Führ and Alvarez, 2022; Silveira et al., 2022).

There is no exact definition but a series of reflections about how Human and Social Sciences intersect with digital technology. This interdisciplinary field aims to comprehend the relation and impact of technology and digital fools in the research and education of Humanities. In other words, can be understood it as a set of methods and theories of Humanities that, along with computational procedures of data collection, manipulation, structuring, documentation, analysis, presentation, and divulgation, tend to the final goal of generating knowledge and research questions in the Humanities (Russel, 2011; Silva, 2022; Fernández-de-Castro et al., 2022; Rio Riande, 2015).

A plurality of other definitions can be found in research on Digital Humanities. Piscitelli related the emergence of Digital Humanities with the emergence of digital culture. On the same line, Ramos considers that the Digital Humanities, being the union of technology and Humanities fields, refer to a single form of understanding the humanistic discipline, giving origin to a connected culture. Rio Riande points out that the main news of Digital Humanities is to reconnect the Science of Humanities and the real world of the academia. Leturio emphasizes that the Digital Humanities revel new means to investigate old questions in the Humanities and open them in new dimensions (Rio Riande, 2015).

Besides the acknowledged interdisciplinarity of the Digital Humanities, some authors declare it transdisciplinary. For the signatories of the *Manifeste des Digital Humanities*, for example, *"the Digital Humanities designate a transdisciplinary, bearer of the methods, devices, and heuristics perspectives connected to the digital domain of Human and Social Sciences"* (Dacos, 2011, our translation). There are some distinctions to be considered between the interdisciplinarity and the transdisciplinarity of Digital Humanities regarding the disciplinary horizontality of the first and the disciplinary verticality of the second:

> We can understand the interdisciplinary approach as a "horizontal" study among disciplines; however, the simple addition does not cross the disciplinarians' limits that allow a better comprehension of said object of research due to its complexity presented, and this can be attached to the traditional methods of research, preventing to go beyond the disciplines, which characterizes the transdisciplinarity. Some researchers consider this approach unsatisfactory because adopting a method of a discipline can make this attempt reductionist by linking it to one of the disciplines in the interdisciplinary approach. That way, they opt for the transdisciplinary approach, which considers that the disciplines operate inside stable boundaries and have their methods and materials. Furthermore, the origin of a unitary horizon that integrates them in a higher environment, inside a common axiomatic to a group of disciplines, makes integration somewhat "vertical" in this group of disciplines. (Mucheroni et al., 2019, p.5, our translation).

However, in the academic environment, where does the problem of scientific divulgation in the field of the Digital Humanities study fit? According to Darcos (2011), *"the option of society for the digital alters and questions the conditions of production and divulgations of knowledge"*(n.p.). Thus, can be understand that the study of the application of computational tools in the search to selves a common research problem to some areas of knowledge from Human and Social Sciences Applied is inserted in the field of study of Digital Humanities. The investigation of the impact of digital technologies in the process of scientific divulgation to democratize access to science and expand the widespread credibility in science mobilizes research among several areas of research that will be explore in the following sections of this article.

4   Scientific Divulgation and Scientific Communication: Necessary Distinctions

Scientific communication and scientific divulgation are terms commonly used as synonyms. That equivalence, nonetheless, is wrong. Although both concepts have similar characteristics because they refer to the diffusion of information in Science, Technology and Innovation, the processes involved have important distinctions (Bueno, 2010). From the aspects that differ between scientific communication and scientific divulgation, Bueno (2010) separates them into: the audience profile, the level of discourse, the nature of utilized channels for broadcasting, and each process's intent. Figure 1 summarizes the singularities of these four aspects:

Aspects	Scientific communication	Scientific divulgation
Audience profile	Specialists; people with technical-scientific training, familiar with concepts	Lay public; people who cannot understand specialized information
Level of discourse	Specialized discourse, with technical terms	Discourse translated for those who are not scientifically literate
Nature of channels for broadcasting	Restricted circuits; formal channels; limited audience	Public and accessible spaces; informal channels
Process's intent	Disseminate information among peers	Democratization of science; scientific literacy

Fig. 1. Distinctions between scientific communication and scientific divulgation. Prepared by the authors based on Bueno (2010)

From another perspective, Mata Marín et al. (2015) understand the scientific divulgation - synonym of scientific dissemination, generalization of science, public communication of science, or public comprehension of scientific knowledge - as part of a subdivision of the process of scientific communication, asking the scientific diffusion. The authors (2015) embraced a classification that distinguishes scientific diffusion and divulgation by the public to which they are addressed, bringing the first directed to the scientific community in a broader sense and the second directed to society in general.

From the sharp distinctions, it is possible to recognize the social part of scientific divulgation:

> *Although it is essential to comprehend that the diffusion of science is a complex activity in itself and constitutive of the research process, to enrich its debate and discussion, the research team must recognize, reflects, and participate in new communication alternatives that provide not only recognition in the specialists' communities, but also acknowledgment and value in the social tissue, which undoubtedly contributes to the progressivity of scientific knowledge* (Mata Marín et al., 2015, p.7, our translation).

Valeiro and Pinheiro (2008) accordingly the necessity of strengthening this connection of scientific knowledge with the social tissue through communication. The authors (2008) highlight the convergence trend of audiences between the scientific community and society in general provided through the digital means that compose a new audience for science. That enhanced the visibility of science *"favors the scientific awareness of society about the bigger participation in the formulation of public policies for science and technology for development"* (Valeiro and Pinheiro, 2008, p.3, our translation). Thus, the scientific divulgation can be interpreted as inclusive since it allows the approximation of the lay citizen to scientific knowledge. This insertion of society in science, if revealed on a large scale, contributes to strengthening the credibility of science.

5   The Post-truth Phenomenon and the Crises of Science Credibility: The Problem

The context of the world health crisis and the outcome of the Covid-19 pandemic manifested on a large scale some phenomena that were present in the daily lives of society in the last decades. Nevertheless, when this article is written, it appears to have come to normality and naturality that are tragic and worrisome, considering the impact they cause. These phenomena are that explosion of disinformation and the popularization of the post-truth culture when allied to scientific denialism and the crises of science credibility that it derives from, contribute to the aggravation of the world health crisis — beyond the political, economic, and social crisis, which will be discussed later in the text.

Giordani et al. (2021) define the current time, in this context of informational distortion, as a time when parallel realities are manufactured that legitimize discourses within opinion bubbles in a process of delegitimization of institutions and science. It is possible to observe cause and effect relationships between the diffusion of negationist or false discourses, the trust crisis in official production systems and vehiculation of news and knowledge, and the valuing of knowledge from alternative sources (Giordani et al., 2021).

It is necessary to approximate the definitions of such phenomena, making it simpler to understand the relations of phenomena that are intended to be investigated. Post-truth, which is "post" in the hierarchical sense, and not of succession, is a growing term in academic research these last years, mainly after being elected, in 2016, as the word of the year by the Oxford Dictionaries. It is defined as *"relating to or denoting circumstances in which objective facts are less influential in shaping public opinion than appeals to emotion and personal belief"* (Oxford Dictionaries, 2016).

Nonetheless, if phenomena such as spreading lies, untruthful information, and fact distortion are ancient, why has the post-truth become perceptible in recent years? McIntyre (2018) has dedicated himself to explaining factors that, manifested in parallel, created an environment conducive to the post-truth: the scientific denialism, a phenomenon where the public starts to question the authority of science in a process guided by the economic interests of elitists groups; the human cognitive bias, meaning, the human tendency to not form its opinions based in reason and evidence in an attempt to avoid psychic discontent; the disinterest by traditional means of communication, explained, first, by the preference of the following news through social media, secondly, by the expansion of the far-right party media uncompromised with the facts, and, lastly, by the attempt of ideological neutrality from traditional media that hides the side that's closer to the truth; the rise of social networks, controlled by algorithms that direct, massively, information according to the public interests, creating a "bubble effect"; and, the post-modernism, that has as characteristic the revitalization of truth (Mcintyre, 2018).

Araujo (2021) argues that the post-truth should be understood while in a context, a condition, that means, due to conditions that arise in the relationship of people with information and the truth, such conditions are established by technological, social, and cultural dimensions. The author goes beyond when interpreting the phenomenon of post-truth both as a transformation of informational dynamics and as a culture:

> There is a process of acceptance and replication of concepts that normalize the disdain for the truth. Moreover, that dimension means that, essentially, the problem of post-truth is a human problem, a problem related to mentalities, attitudes, ethos, a culture. (Araújo, 2021, p.6, our translation).

Even though the disdain for facts in the formation of opinion is a historical social behavior, the ascension of post-truth has become viable from the explosion of fake news and disinformation through social networks and online social media, which allows the massive sharing of instant information with the absence of quality regulation or veracity of information.

Based on the Council of Europe Report, Silva (2019) classifies fake news into three categories: the first is "disinformation", which *"consists of fake news created and spread deliberately to harm a person, social group, organization, or country"* (p.53). The second, "misinformation", *"also consists in a fake news shared by an unwarned person that, at first, does not have the intention to hurt anybody"* (ibid). Finally, "malinformation" *"consists in the news that, even though they have a real basis, are manipulated and disseminated to cause damage"* (ibid.). Although the translation of these words to Portuguese is the same word, *"desinformação"*, it is the context in which can be differentiated. In other words, it can be clarified in the existence of an intention to harm something or someone. All these words, however, are related to the post-truth.

When it comes to disinformation, the popularization of this phenomenon has a known mark in the presidential election of the United States in 2016 and the famous Brexit case, a plebiscite accomplished in 2016 in the United Kingdom that resulted in the country leaving the European Union. In both events, fake news with political means spread on social media (Martins and Furnival, 2020; Gutiérrez and Larrosa, 2020). In Brazil, disinformation for political-ideological manipulation is highlighted in the process that culminated in the impeachment of President-elect Dilma Rousseff, also in 2016 and the presidential election in 2018.

With the discussion till this point, the interdisciplinary dimension of the problem in question has become evident. Post-truth and the credibility of science cannot be reduced to a simple conflict of opinions, beliefs, and ideologies where each reserves the freedom to "pick a side". Nor can the question be resumed in a dualism of "right versus wrong" or "good versus evil". These are phenomena with complex roots that cannot be limited to a single cause. They require comprehending the entire economic, social, political, technological, and cultural context they manifest. They require the investigation of ideological, religious, or moral motivations of whom share naive fake news and the political and economic structure behind who stimulates its sharing. They require an interdisciplinary and even transdisciplinary reflection, if one considers that research interests and approaches from different disciplines coincide — the competence to explore the problem encompasses Human Sciences and Social Sciences disciplines, as Information Science, Communication, Economy, Psychology, Sociology, Philosophy and Education.

After all, the post-truth united with disinformation, denialism, unscientific fad, pseudoscience, clickbaits, fallacies, conspiration theories, and others that promote the delegitimization of science? Or is it the lack of trust in science that feeds these several manifestations of misalignment with the truth? The answer can be both. The culture of accepting, stimulating, and disseminating truths and the scientific invalidation are conditions between themselves. Does this mean that weakening one side can strengthen the other, and vice versa? An outline of the answer is made in the following section, which explores the possibility of fighting the post-truth culture and soon, enabling a public comprehension of scientific knowledge, pointing out the actors, actions, and mechanisms involved.

6 Results

Propositions arise in several areas of knowledge to fight disinformation and recuperate the credibility of science. The discussions are common, for example, of propositions in the legal field, such as the regulation policies of content posted on social platforms. However, in this article, the proposition is to explore a different path from regulation and punishment: the path of institutional public policy of scientific divulgation through social networks. It is a process with well-defined parts that will be justified during this section:

- The actors are the public universities.
- The strategies are the public policies of communication.

– The actions referred to scientific divulgation.
– The mechanisms are social networks.

The solutions to soften the problem of the post-truth phenomenon can also come from individual actions and collective intelligence for the development and adoption of social and informational control mechanisms. The digital self-criticism of users can be named, as well as the analysis and verification of the authenticity of facts in reliable sources and the habit of critical reading. This attitude would transform the digital channel from a source of collective disinformation into an environment knowledge generator (Tobias and Corrêa, 2019).

Despite being important that individuals rethink how to manipulate information to which they are daily exposed in digital technologies, that is a more significant challenge than organizing an institutional policy. It would take a revolution in collective rationality, which would involve many methods to be accomplished, starting from a profound critique of the structure of the educational system that encompasses society and institutions.

It is worth standing out the importance of developing research that points out the guidelines for efficient combat to the post-truth and promoting institutional scientific divulgation. The relevance of Information Science in the development of study on this theme is well-known. Araújo (2020) and Araújo (2021) argue that given these phenomena related to the production, circulation, and appropriation of fake information, the Information Science has relevant categories to understand them and *"puts itself in an urgent way for Information Science: [...] develop methodologies, products, and services to fight its harmful effects"* (Araújo, 2020, p.4, our translation). Following that reasoning, Tobias and Corrêa (2019) argue it is necessary for studies in Information Science *"that search for ways to soften the consequences of post-truth in the digital environment, demonstrating to the citizen how important it is for society to participate in information management"* (p.15, our translation).

As it aims to democratize access to scientific knowledge, the scientific divulgation becomes an unequivocal proposition to combat disinformation and consequent recovery of popular trust in science. Addressing this relationship, Ramalho (2020) highlights that the popularization of science is a way for the academy to fulfill its social and emancipatory function and can, in the long term, help people comprehend the importance of rational thinking and make unfeasible future waves of post-truth. For Caldas (2010), the scientific knowledge must be disseminated, contextualized and critical, assuming the educational character and enabling democracy. Thus *"the scientific knowledge is an integral part of full citizenship and the process of social inclusion, once it allows the individual to have access to the minimum information essential to an active and transforming citizenship"* (Caldas, 2010, p.9, our translation).

The scientific divulgation, beyond the function of confrontation with the culture of disinformation, post-truth, and denialism, can exert other functions, some of which were already revealed in this article, and they are: informational function, which allows citizens to find out about scientific advances; educational function, to approach the citizens to scientific knowledge; social function, critical stance towards science; cultural function, work for the enhancement of national culture and preservation of its values; economic function, which encourages the exchange between research producers and the productive sector; and the political-ideological function, which forms a public opinion about the importance of science and the possible interests involved (Bueno, 1984, *apud* Mendes and Maricato, 2020).

Among the prominent Brazilian examples of scientific divulgation in the media — a list that includes newspapers, journals, magazines, websites, and television — the web stands out for presenting some peculiarities, such as the constant content updating, broad contextualization, non-linear navigation, historical information, link to related materials, the interactivity that reveals new forms of participation, the types of media file that provide multiple languages and the possibility of personalizing searches or pages (Mendes and Maricato, 2020). According to the authors (2020), online media has the potential to attract the most diverse audiences, providing opportunities for researchers to dialogue with society through interactions on social networks such as Instagram, Facebook, Twitter, Linkedin, YouTube, and ResearchGate — it is also pertinent to include WhatsApp in this list.

Scientific divulgation uses informal channels to democratize access to scientific research and discoveries and include society in the debate on scientific topics. Social networks on the Internet, in turn, it makes it possible to amplify this divulgation because it has the potential to collaborate, mobilize and transform society (Vicente et al., 2015). It is a challenging process because, as Menegusse et al. (2022) point out, the daily use of social networks and the use to reach a specific audience are distinct, which demands divulgation strategies, "*such as interaction with the public, the perception of which type of content the public would most identify with, use of images aimed at that age group as well as the translation of technical terms that varies according to age*" (p.15, our translation).

A new model to produce and divulge science is rethought from Information and Communication Technologies,

> *leading to much more dynamic, interactive, and hypertextual information models. These characteristics, allied to interactive forms of presenting data, news, and knowledge (online), are typical of this modality of communication in cyberspace [...] These new forms and range manage to aggregate multiple subjects from different places and knowledge, characterizing a space for collective construction and allowing interaction of different cultures, guaranteeing the conciliation of the scientific knowledge of different subjects and institutions that produce knowledge* (Dias et al., 2020b, p.7, our translation).

Social networks are spaces that require linguistic informality to attract public attention, in addition to the use of more dynamic resources that facilitate the understanding of the lay reader, as in the examples of Dias et al. (2020b): animated graphics, gifs, slang, audios, catchphrases/jargon, videos, emojis and memes. These tools, coupled with interactions such as likes, comments, and shares on social media posts, are some of which public universities, primarily responsible for maintaining scientific communication channels, are responsible for adopting in the scientific divulgation process, aiming to promote interaction with society and not leave knowledge restricted to peers (Dias et al., 2020b; Dias et al., 2020a).

In the way it is designed, academic logic can be interpreted as a disincentive for researchers to experiment with new means of disseminating their scientific production since their careers are reduced mainly to publishing articles for recognition (Barros, 2015). However, Kunsch (2022) argues that the university should be the protagonist of scientific divulgation, which would have repercussions on the production of research that would focus on intervention in society and would no longer be just instruments for growth in the academic career. Then, it is understood that the university's responsibility to democratize its scientific and technological achievements, creating conditions for scientific production to reach the general public and being a bridge between the media and recipients (Kunsch, 2022). The author (n.d.) points out the guidelines for a university characterized as an open, borderless, globalized organization that promotes dialogue with society:

> To fulfill its mission, the university will have to have communication guided by a global policy that guides the divulgation of its scientific production. A firm and courageous decision must be taken concerning concrete actions. Isolated, palliative, and transitory measures are no longer conceived in this field. It is necessary to create adequate conditions for something systematized in this sense, such as a center, agency, or department dedicated explicitly to scientific communication. (p.1, our translation).

Mata Marín et al. (2015) highlight the social commitment of the public university to divulgate science:

> Public universities are called upon to carry out this work [of scientific divulgation] with zeal. They are institutions financed by citizens, which must seek social positioning and accountability to public opinion for the resources allocated. Scientific communication processes should seek only the divulgation or divulgation of results, but also promote citizens' interest and participation in knowledge management processes. Moreover, their applications, scope, risks, and uncertainties eventually promote literacy in scientific technologies but mainly the acquisition of a solid scientific culture. In this way, the social commitment to communicate science is also linked to the establishment of ethical and transparent processes in academic research. (p.7-8, our translation).

A set of institutional mechanisms is available to public universities to enforce their social function. Daehn and Tosta (2018) attach importance to the use of technological tools for the circulation of information to contribute to the transformation of science and the university's role as a social institution. Rossetto et al. (2009) highlight the role of extension through events aimed at exchanging experiences between university and community. Valério (2006) emphasizes the indispensability of institutional policies that help to consolidate a culture of scientific divulgation as a social function of public universities. Zucolo (2012, *apud* Dias, 2017) reinforces the challenge imposed on universities to carry out scientific divulgation to fulfill the social function of promoting public understanding of science.

7 Final Considerations

Is the relationship between institutional scientific divulgation through social networks, post-truth culture, and the credibility crisis of science among the research problems of interest to the Digital Humanities? The article proposed to direct the reflection on these phenomena towards a positive answer. The issue is understood as a human problem, investigated in the various fields of knowledge of the Human and Social Sciences. However, digital tools provide opportunities for understanding and solving problems like these, in addition to being directly related to the manifestation of the phenomenon, they also have skills for use in research and practical actions to face the problem.

Social networks have great potential for education and science, but, at the same time, they are favorable environments for the repercussion of false information, and this side has reached enormous proportions, revealing the emergence of scientific divulgation (Santos et al., 2019). However, actions such as scientific divulgation in wide-ranging social networks contribute to a society walking side-by-side with science and, therefore, weakening the harmful effects of post-truth, disinformation, and fake news proliferated by these same networks (Santos et al., 2019; Teixeira et al., 2021).

Public universities are key actors in promoting scientific divulgation strategies through social networks. These institutions have the human and technological resources necessary to implement scientific divulgation policies. In addition, the democratization of access to knowledge is a social commitment of the Brazilian public university.

There are several possibilities for research on this issue. The Digital Humanities perspective allows to support propositions about the practical inversion of the role of digital technologies: from allies of collective disinformation and scientific illiteracy to allies of the popularization of scientific knowledge and promotion of national social development.

In the initial stage of such a transition, science must be thought critically, understanding the importance of each informational process related to it, from creating knowledge to its forms of textualization, circulation, and divulgation. Alves-Brito et al. (2020, p.20, our translation) corroborate this final reflection, that *"we must not only trust science but also teach it, without being uncritical. A posture of critical surveillance of science and its social impacts through technology is also fundamental"*.

References

Almeida, M.A., Damian, I.P.M.: Humanidades digitais: um campo praxiológico para mediações e políticas culturais? Anais. João Pessoa: ANCIB (2015). Available at: https://repositorio.usp.br/single.php?_id=002749636 Accessed 31 January 2022

Alves-Brito, A., Massoni, N.T., Guimarães, R.R.: Subjetividades da comunicação científica: a educação e a divulgação científicas no Brasil têm sido estremecidas em tempos de pós-verdade? Caderno brasileiro de ensino de física. Florianópolis **37**(3), p. 1598–1627 (dez. 2020). Available at: https://www.lume.ufrgs.br/handle/10183/217946 Accessed 31 January 2022

Araújo, C.A.Á.: A pós-verdade como desafio para a ciência da informação contemporânea. Em Questão, Porto Alegre **27**(1), 13–29 (2021). https://doi.org/10.19132/1808-5245271.13-29 Available at: https://www.seer.ufrgs.br/EmQuestao/article/view/101666/59067 Accessed 31 January 31

Araújo, C.A.Á.: O fenômeno da pós-verdade e suas implicações para a agenda de pesquisa na Ciência da Informação. Encontros Bibli: revista eletrônica de biblioteconomia e ciência da informação [en linea]. **25**, 1–17 (2020). Available at: https://www.redalyc.org/articulo.oa?id= 14763386016 Accessed 31 January 31

Barros, M.: Altmetrics: métricas alternativas de impacto científico com base em redes sociais. Perspectivas em Ciência da Informação [S.l.] **20**(2), 19–37 (jun. 2015). ISSN 19815344. Available at: http://portaldeperiodicos.eci.ufmg.br/index.php/pci/article/view/1782 Accessed 31 January 2022

Bueno, W.C.: Comunicação científica e divulgação científica: aproximações e rupturas conceituaiss. Informação & Informação [S.l.] **15**(1esp), 1–12 (dez. 2010). ISSN 1981–8920. https://doi.org/10.5433/1981-8920.2010v15n1espp1. Available at: https://www.uel.br/revistas/uel/index.php/informacao/article/view/6585 Accessed 01 February 2022

Caldas, G.: Divulgaçao científica e relações de poder. Informação & Informação [S.l.] **15**(1esp), 31–42 (dez. 2010). ISSN 1981–8920. https://doi.org/10.5433/1981-8920.2010v15n1 espp31. Available at: https://www.uel.br/revistas/uel/index.php/informacao/article/view/5583 Accessed 01 February 2022.

Dacos, M.: Manifesto das digital humanities. That Camp Paris. 26 mars 2011. Available at: https://tcp.hypotheses.org/497 Accessed 31 January 2022

Daehn, C.M., Tosta, K.C.B.T.: Desafios da gestão universitária no contexto das universidades públicas federais. XVIII Colóquio Internacional de Gestão Universitária (2018). UTPL. Available at: https://repositorio.ufsc.br/handle/123456789/190506 Accessed 31 January 2022

Dias, C.C., Dias, R.G., Santa Anna, J.: Potencialidade das redes sociais e de recursos imagéticos para a divulgação científica em periódicos da área de ciência da informação. BIBLOS [S. l.] **34**(1), 109–126 (2020a). https://doi.org/10.14295/biblos.v34i1.11241. Available at: https://periodicos.furg.br/biblos/article/view/11241 Accessed 01 February 2022

Dias, P.R.M.: O papel da Assessoria de Comunicação na divulgação da produção científica e tecnológica da Universidade Federal do Maranhão. Dissertação (mestrado) – Universidade Federal da Bahia, Escola de Administração, Salvador (2017). Available at: https://repositorio.ufba.br/ri/handle/ri/22957 Accessed 31 January 2022

Dias, P.R.M., Morais, O.J., Gomes, R.F.L.: Divulgação Científica por Instituições de Ensino Superior: estratégias e práticas discursivas em redes sociais digitais. XIV Congresso Brasileiro Científico de Comunicação Organizacional e de Relações Públicas - Bauru/SP - 18 a 21/05/2020 (2020b). Available at: https://www.researchgate.net/profile/Pablo-Dias-3/publication/351779 049_Divulgacao_cientifica_por_Instituicoes_de_Ensino_Superior_estrategias_e_praticas_d iscursivas_em_redes_sociais_digitais/links/60a94426299bf1031fc1325d/Divulgacao-cienti fica-por-Instituicoes-de-Ensino-Superior-estrategias-e-praticas-discursivas-em-redes-sociais-digitais.pdf Accessed 31 January 2022

Fernández-de-Castro, P., Bretones, E., Solé, J., Sampedro, V.: Digital Social Education: An Exploration of the Training and Digital Competencies of Social Education Professionals. TECHNO REVIEW. International Technology, Science and Society Review /Revista Internacional De Tecnología, Ciencia Y Sociedad 11(1), 13–27 (2022). https://doi.org/10.37467/gkarevtechno.v11.3113

Führ, F., Alvarez, E.B.: Humanidades digitais e criatividade: intersecções. In: Veria, E.H. (ed.) Advanced Notes in Information Science, vol. 1, pp. 15–30. Tallinn, Estonia, ColNes Publishing (2022). https://doi.org/10.47909/anis.978-9916-9760-0-5.95

Giordani, R.C.F., et al.: A ciência entre a infodemia e outras narrativas da pós-verdade: desafios em tempos de pandemia Ciênc. Saúde Colet. **26**(07) (Jul 2021). https://doi.org/10.1590/1413-81232021267.05892021 Acesso em jan/2022. Available at: https://www.scielo.br/j/csc/a/MWf cvZ797BYyNSJBQTpNP8K/?lang=pt Accessed 31 January 2022

Gutiérrez, E.M., Larrosa, J.M.C.: Popularity in Facebook Pages: What role network structural variables play?. AWARI **1**(1), e005 (2020). https://doi.org/10.47909/awari.68

Kunsch, M.M.K.: Divulgação científica: missão inadiável da universidade. Available at: http://www.e-publicacoes.uerj.br/index.php/logos/article/viewFile/13176/10094 Accessed 31 January 2022

Martins, Furnival, A.: Desinformação E As Fake News: Apontamentos Sobre Seu Surgimento, Detecção E Formas De Combate (2020). Available at: https://www.researchgate.net/public ation/342134682 Accessed 31 January 2022

Mata Marín, C., Álvarez, B., Castillo Vargas, T., Montenegro Montenegro, A., Diálogo, E.: Ecos y recovecos: la comunicación científica en el ámbito académico. Revista de Ciencias Sociales (Cr) [Internet]. III(149), 59–70 (2015). Retrieved from https://www.redalyc.org/articulo.oa?id=15343488005 Accessed 31 January 2022

Mcintyre, L.: Posverdad. Cátedra, Madrid (2018)

Mendes, M.M., Maricato, J. de M.: Das apresentações públicas às redes sociais: apontamentos sobre divulgação científica na mídia brasileira. Comunicação & Informação, Goiânia, Goiás 23 (2020). https://doi.org/10.5216/ci.v23i.49959. Available at: https://www.revistas.ufg.br/ci/article/view/49959. Accessed 01 February 2022

Menegusse, R.B., Da Silva, T.R.C., Gomes, F.T.: Divulgação Científica: o uso de redes sociais para divulgação de trabalhos acadêmicos. ANALECTA-Centro Universitário Academia 7(2) (2022). Available at: https://seer.uniacademia.edu.br/index.php/ANL/article/view/3086 Accessed 31 January 2022

Moura, M.: Universidades públicas realizam mais de 95% da ciência no Brasil. In: Ciência na Rua. (16 Abril 2019). Available at: https://www.unifesp.br/noticias-anteriores/item/3799-uni versidades-publicas-realizam-mais-de-95-da-ciencia-no-brasil Accessed 01 February 2022

Mucheroni, M.L., Paletta, F.C., Silva, J.F.M.: Transdisciplinaridade nas ciências sociais e tecnologia: a questão das humanidades digitais. VIII Seminário Hispano-Brasileiro de Pesquisa em Informação, Documentação e Sociedade (8shb) (2019). Available at: https://seminariohispano-brasileiro.org.es/ocs/index.php/viishb/viiishbusp/paper/view/548 Accessed 31 January 2022

Oxford Dictionaries. Word of the Year 2016 is... (Nov 2016). Available at: https://en.oxforddic tionaries.com/word-of-the-year/word-of-the-year-2016 Accessed 31 January 2022

Ramalho, V.G.: O Brasil do negacionismo Uma análise da disputa entre pós-verdade e ciência. In: O Manguezal, Revista de Filosofia, vol. 1 no. 5 (2020). Crise da verdade e crítica da pós-verdade. Disponível em https://seer.ufs.br/index.php/omanguezal Accessed 31 January 2022

Rio Riande, G.: qué son las humanidades digitales? In: María Gimena del Rio Riande (2015). La realidad de las Humanidades Digitales en España y América Latina. Available at: https://www.aacademica.org/gimena.delrio.riande/65.pdf Accessed 31 January 2022

Rossetto, A., Jerônimo, V., Souza, I.: SEPEX – semana de ensino, pesquisa e extensão: exemplo de comunicação científica na Universidade Federal De Santa Catarina. 2009 [Preprint]. Available at: http://eprints.rclis.org/14468/ Accessed 31 January 2022

Russell, I.G.: Qué son las Humanidades Digitales? Revista Digital Universitaria [en línea]. 1 de julio de 12(7) (2011). ISSN: 1607-6079. Available at: http://www.revista.unam.mx/vol.12/num7/art68/index.html Accessed 31 January 2022

Santos, L.S.A., Chagas, A.M., Porto, C.M.: Isso não é fake news: a divulgação científica como instrumento para conhecer e compreender a ciência. In: Educiber: dilemas e práticas contemporâneas / organização [de] Cristiane Porto, Kaio Eduardo de Jesus Oliveira, Alexandre Meneses Chagas Aracaju: EDUNIT, 2019. Volume 2 - E-book 2º Ediçã0 244 p. il. ; 22 cm. Inclui bibliografia. ISBN – 978-85-68102-51-0. https://doi.org/10.17564/2019.68102.51.0 Available at: https://editoratiradentes.com.br/e-book/educiber2.pdf#page=33 Accessed 31 January 2022

Silva, E.A.: Transformação digital e a gestão do conhecimento: relações na produção científica. In: Dias, R.T.M. (ed.), Informação, Dados e Tecnologia. Advanced Notes in Information Science, vol. 2, pp. 43–52. Tallinn, Estonia: ColNes Publishing (2022). https://doi.org/10.47909/anis.978-9916-9760-3-6.107

Silva, F.B.: O regime de verdade das redes sociais on-line: pós-verdade e desinformação nas eleições presidenciais de 2018. Orientador: Prof. Dr. Paulo César Castro de Sousa. 2019. 157 f. Dissertação (Mestrado em Ciência da Informação) – Escola de Comunicação, Universidade Federal do Rio de Janeiro; Instituto Brasileiro de Informação em Ciência e Tecnologia, Rio de Janeiro, RJ (2019). Available at: http://ridi.ibict.br/handle/123456789/1027 Accessed 31 January 2022

da Silveira, L., Méndez-Solano, A., Mora Campos, A.: La ciencia abierta desde la perspectiva de expertos: una propuesta de taxonomía brasileños. Encontros Bibli: Revista eletrônica De Biblioteconomia E Ciência Da informação **27**(1), 1–31 (2022). https://doi.org/10.5007/1518-2924.2022.e86251

Teixeira, A.L.C.S.B., et al.: O tempo da ciência e o tempo das fake news: um estudo de produção e recepção de mídias de divulgação científica em tempos de pós-verdade. Anais do XIII Encontro Nacional de Pesquisa em Educação em Ciências... Campina Grande: Realize Editora (2021). Available at: https://www.editorarealize.com.br/index.php/artigo/visualizar/76603. Accessed 01 February 2022

Tobias, M.S., Delfini Corrêa, E.C.: O paradigma social da Ciência da Informação: o fenômeno da pós-verdade e as fake news nas mídias sociais. Revista ACB [S.l.] **24**(3), 560–579 (dez. 2019). ISSN 1414-0594. Available at: https://revista.acbsc.org.br/racb/article/view/1529. Accessed 01 February 2022

Valeiro, P.M., Pinheiro, L.V.R.: Da comunicação científica à divulgação. Transinformação **20**(2), 159–169 (2008). https://doi.org/10.1590/S0103-37862008000200004 Accessed 01 February 2022

Valério, M.: Ações de divulgação científica na Universidade Federal de Santa Catarina: extensão como compromisso social com a educação em ciência e tecnologia. Florianópolis, 2006. 1 v. Dissertação (Mestrado) - Universidade Federal de Santa Catarina. Programa de Pós-Graduação em Educação Científica e Tecnológica. Available at: http://www.tede.ufsc.br/teses/PECT0036. pdf Accessed 31 January 2022

Vicente, N.I., Corrêa, E.C.D., Sena, T.: A divulgação científica em redes sociais na internet: proposta de metodologia de análise netnográfica. XVI Encontro Nacional de Pesquisa em Pós-Graduação em Ciência da Informação (2015). Available at: http://www.ufpb.br/evento/index. php/enancib2015/enancib2015/paper/viewFile/2853/1160 Accessed 31 January 2022

Vosoughi, S., Roy, D., Aral, S.: The spread of true and false news online. Science **359**(6380), 1146–51 (Mar. 2018). Available at: https://science.sciencemag.org/content/sci/359/6380/1146. full.pdf. Accessed 31 January 2022

Workflow with Emphasis in Technologies for the Construction of an Aggregator and a Dashboard of Brazilian Museums Digital Collections

Joyce Siqueira[1]([✉]) [iD], Dalton Lopes Martins[1] [iD], and Vinícius Nunes Medeiros[2] [iD]

[1] Universidade de Brasília, Brasília, DF, Brazil
joycitta@gmail.com, daltonmartins@unb.br
[2] Tainacan.Org, Brasília, DF, Brazil
vnicius.nm.ba@gmail.com

Abstract. The Brazilian Institute of Museums - Ibram, began the process of disseminating its museum collections on the web, through the Tainacan software, a result of the Collection Platform Project, carried out in partnership with the Federal University of Goiás and the University of Brasília. With the project's developments, a new information service is under study, the creation of Brasiliana Museums, an aggregator of cultural digital objects from museums managed by Ibram, which aims to offer a single search and data retrieval interface. Beyond that aggregator it is possible developed another new service, a dashboard for Ibram's managers, very important for an analytical thinking through graphical interfaces. This research this is configured as a case study, because is aimed at solving Ibram's data aggregation problem, in addition to being a qualitative, exploratory and descriptive research. This paper aims to present the development process of Brasiliana Museums and a dashboard, highlighting the technological tools used: 1, mapping origin museums; 2, automated collection of items the collections; 3, aggregation of collections and data transformation; 4, submission of items to Tainacan; 5, data integrate storage; 6, dashboard development and; 7, publication of the aggregated collections for the search and recovery of Brazilian museum items. The main technologies used in the prototype was the Elastic Stack, the new plugin, developed in Ruby programing language, and the Tainacan repository software. This result is the aggregation than more 17 thousand objects from 20 Ibram's museums, that allow in single interface to search and retrieve digital Brazilian museum items. The prototyping of the service reveals itself, therefore, as an efficient solution, both from the point of view of socialization and dissemination of digital objects and in the monitoring and monitoring of information from the collections through analytical panels. In addition to presenting a cheap and viable technological solution to be implemented.

Keywords: Aggregator · Elastic stack · Tainacan · Museums · Technologies

A. L. Pinto and R. Arencibia-Jorge (Eds.): DIONE 2022, LNICST 452, pp. 84–97, 2022.
https://doi.org/10.1007/978-3-031-22324-2_8

1 Introduction

The Brazilian Institute of Museums - Ibram is an autarchy of the Brazilian Federal Government, responsible for the National Policy on Museums and for the improvement of services in the sector, for example, increase in museums visitation, promotion of policies for the acquisition and preservation of collections, enable access to culture to a part of the population that would not be able to enjoy it, in addition, of administration of 30 museums (Gov.br 2022b).

In 2014, Ibram, in partnership with the Federal University of Goiás, through the Participatory Public Policy Laboratory, started the development of the project "Platform Collections: inventory, management and dissemination of museum heritage", to promote the fundamentals of a policy for digital collections, which resulted, in 2016, in the first version of Tainacan, a software free and open-source for the management and publication of digital collections. In 2018, the project, now entitled Tainacan Project, is being developed in partnership with the University of Brasília - UnB, through the Networks Intelligence Laboratory.

In 2022, 20 Ibram's museums they had already migrated the documentation of their collection to Tainacan and are available for access via the web (Gov.br 2022a). With this panorama and the growing number of migrated museums, the Laboratory has been carrying out several studies with the aim of creating a new information service, Brasiliana Museums, an aggregator of cultural digital objects from the collections of different museums, which aims to offer an interface unique search and retrieval of information using Tainacan both in the origin museums, that is, in the data providers, and in the own aggregator, as the final repository. Beyond that, with digital items from all museums integrated went too possible a dashboard was built for Ibram's managers.

In this paper, we present the workflow for data aggregation and dashboard construction, however, with emphasis on the technologies used to implement a pilot and experimental service for Ibram.

The steps taken to develop the prototypes of the aggregation service are presented. The main technological solutions used are the Elastic Stack (Beats, Logstash, Elasticsearch and Kibana) and the Tainacan digital repository, as well as the aggregation workflow, which has seven steps, the know: step 1, mapping origin museums, in Tainacan; step 2, automated collection of items the collections, with Beats - Filebeat; step 3, aggregation of collections and data transformation, with Logstash; step 4, submission of items to Tainacan, with Logstash plugin development in Ruby; step 5, data integrate storage, in Elasticsearch; step 6, dashboard development, with Kibana and; step 7, publication of the aggregated collections for the search and recovery of Brazilian museum items, with Tainacan.

The paper is organized as follows: Sect. 2 describes the methodological procedures; Sect. 3 presents the results of the study, Brasiliana Museum's aggregation process; Sect. 4 discusses the results; and finally, Sect. 5 identifies important aspects for further research.

2 Methodology

Qualitative research, with an exploratory and descriptive nature, which addresses the process of aggregating Ibram's digital museum collections and dashboard creation, configuring the research as a case study. As a technical procedure, bibliographic, exploratory (Siqueira and Martins 2020) and systematic review literature - SRL (Siqueira and Martins 2021) research was used in order to provide theoretical sustainability to the study.

In the studies mentioned above, 20 different international projects for the aggregation of cultural data were found, many of which deal with the aggregation for the Europeana Foundation, that is, different projects that use similar processes and technologies. In both studies were found some data aggregators, Table 1.

Table 1. Data aggregators

Data aggregator	Link	Current
Ariadne	https://ariadne-infrastructure.eu/	Yes
CHO repository	https://github.com/psu-libraries/cho	No
D-NET	https://github.com/dnet-team/dnet-basic-aggregator	No
META-SHARE	https://github.com/metashare/META-SHARE	No
MINT	https://github.com/mint-ntua/Mint	No
MoRe	http://more.dcu.gr/	No
Repox	https://doi.org/10.1007/978-3-642-04346-8_65	No
Supplejack	https://digitalnz.org/developers/supplejack	Yes

Siqueira and Martins (2021, 2020)

Not all articles Siqueira and Martins (2021, 2020) indicated which technologies are used. From the articles that did it, we found that there were several different technologies in use and not a more used one. In order to complement the answer, we verified whether it is current or not. For the purpose of this survey, we considered the updates that have occurred in the last two years. In general, it was not clear how these technologies are used or how they are integrated. Concomitantly, the documentation proved to be rather lacking in detail and with lengthy discussions on the subject. We identified the D-NET technology as more frequently; however, in the GitHub we observed that the last update repository was conducted four years ago, which makes it more difficult to adopt in new projects. We can observe that the tools developed specifically for aggregation are mostly outdated.

This is the international scenario. In Brazil, although there are initiatives that aim to integrate cultural collections, these are limited, isolated and require technical support and scalable governance models for the Brazilian territory (Martins et al. 2022). We could see that the simple replication of international solutions would not be possible, because, they are diversified and deal with the specificities of each location; there is not enough documentation available to try to implement something and there is no consensus on better solutions and/or technologies. That is, even if it were possible to replicate, it would probably not be effective in the Brazilian context, since they are different realities, considering infrastructure, investment, specialized labor, among others (Siqueira and Martins 2021; Siqueira et al. 2021).

Looking for modern, free tools with an active community that would scalability to the process, but that were also relatively simple to deploy, we selected to carry out the aggregation of the data with the Elastic Stack[1], in addition to a plugin for Logstash developed by the authors, using the Ruby[2] programming language and the Tainacan[3].

We emphasize that this tool was chosen because it meets the minimum criteria we are looking for and there is no intention here to define it as the best, but rather as the most appropriate for the context of Brazilian museums.

With the development of the prototype, it was possible to prove that the Elastic Stack with Tainacan achieves excellent results, as it allows extremely fast queries, text search, horizontal scalability, is capable of handling petabytes of data and the model with the Elastic Stack proved to be of medium complexity and customization for a viable possibility of use and analysis of data or models of learning configurations.

Tainacan is a technological solution for creating digital collections on the Internet. It was designed to meet the reality of cultural institutions, allowing the management and publication of collections in an easy and intuitive way. It is a plugin and a theme from WordPress[4], which offers an administrative panel for, for example, the creation of user profiles, with different levels of access to the collections, as well as web pages for the communication of the collections (Tainacan.org 2021b).

The Elastic Stack is composed by four technologies tools: Beats, Logstash[5], Elasticsearch[6] and Kibana[7] for "get data from any source, in any format, to search, analyze and visualize everything in real time" (Elastic 2021a). The Filebeat[8] is an Elastic Beat, is a lightweight shipper for forwarding and centralizing log data. Installed as an agent on your servers, monitors locations that you specify, collects log events, and forwards them either to Elasticsearch or Logstash for indexing (Elastic 2021b). The Logstash is data collection engine with real-time can dynamically unify data from disparate sources and normalize the data into destinations of your choice. Cleanse and democratize all your data for diverse advanced downstream analytics and visualization use cases (Elastic 2021i). Elasticsearch is a distributed search and data analysis engine that stores data centrally for fast search. Finally, Kibana is a user interface for viewing Elasticsearch data and navigating the Elastic Stack (Elastic 2021d).

It is possible to develop new plugins for Logstash: add your own input, codec, filter, or output plugins to Logstash following the guidelines and best practices can help you build a better plugin (Elastic 2021c). The filter developed for Logstash, tainacan_submission,

---

[1] https://www.elastic.co/elastic-stack/.

[2] https://www.ruby-lang.org/about/.

[3] https://tainacan.org/.

[4] https://wordpress.org/.

[5] https://www.elastic.co/logstash/.

[6] https://www.elastic.co/elasticsearch/.

[7] https://www.elastic.co/kibana/.

[8] https://www.elastic.co/beats/Filebeat.

aims to retrieve the data processed by Logstash and send them to a new Tainacan installation, through its submission API.

The aggregation service and the dashboard, in principle, consists of digital collections from 20 museums, with 22 collections, resulting in 17,315 digital objects, Table 2.

Table 2. Digital museums and their respective numbers of digital objects online

N.	Online digital collections	Digital objects number
1	Museu Casa da Hera	1220
	Museu Casa da Hera (Indumentaria)	67
2	Museu Casa da Princesa	799
3	Museu Casa de Benjamin Constant	983
4	Museu Casa Histórica de Alcântara	631
5	Museu da Abolição	301
6	Museu da Inconfidência	4625
7	Museu das Bandeiras	401
8	Museu das Missões	90
9	Museu de Arqueologia de Itaipu	1040
10	Museu de Arte Religiosa e Tradicional	132
11	Museu de Arte Sacra da Boa Morte	783
12	Museu do Diamante	895
13	Museu do Ouro	126
14	Museu Histórico Nacional	847
	Museu Histórico Nacional (Moedas de Ouro)	1215
15	Museu Regional Casa dos Ottoni	463
16	Museu Regional do Caeté	243
17	Museu Regional São João Del Rey	328
18	Museu Solar Monjardim	77
19	Museu Victor Meirelles	237
20	Museu Villa Lobos	1812
Total items		**17315**

For this research, were used the Tainacan version 0.15 or higher. Aggregation Tainacan uses the latest version. Elastic Stack use version 7.9. For the entire process to work correctly, Tainacan must have a minimum version 0.15 and Elastic Stack, version 7.9.

3   Technologies Workflow or the Construction of an Aggregator and a Dashboard

Although it uses the same technologies, there are two different workflow paths, each for its own purpose. The path 1 refers to the creation of the dashboard and the path 2 to the creation of Brasiliana Museums. The Fig. 1 presents the architecture.

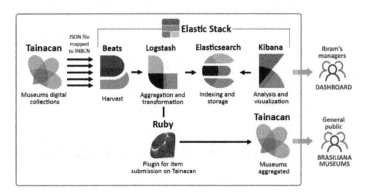

Fig. 1. Brasiliana museums workflow. Prepared by the authors (2022)

The paths are described below.

3.1   Tainacan: Mapping Origin Museums

By default, Tainacan offers alternative URLs for viewing data in Application Programming Interface: JavaScript Object Notation - JSON API formats; HyperText Markup Language - HTML and CSV files (Tainacan.org 2021a), enabling new applications to benefit from the data.

In Tainacan, from version 0.15 onwards, allows, through a plugin developed for Ibram, to map the metadata to the Ibram's standard entitled 'National Inventory of Museum Cultural Assets" – INBCM (BRASIL 2021).

The plugin titled "Tainacan Mappers IBRAM INBCM" was developed using the Hypertext Preprocessor - PHP[9] programming language, and is available on GitHub[10] under the GPLv3 license[11].

It is also available for installation on WordPress and offers a simplified interface for mapping a collection's metadata, in a one-to-one degree of equivalence, that is, a metadata from the originating museum can be mapped to an INBCM metadata. In elements where there is no exact equivalence, the metadata is disregarded. Regarding semantic mapping, it is performed by specialized personnel.

Beyond the INBCM's metadata are includes in JSON file: the pagination information (the items are presents in pages on Tainacan), the collection's identification number (id),

---

[9] https://www.php.net/.

[10] https://github.com/tainacan/tainacan-mappers-ibram-inbcm.

[11] https://www.gnu.org/licenses/gpl-3.0.pt-br.html.

Item URL in the museum of origin and the thumbnail URL, Fig. 2. All are important metadata for museums identification after aggregation.

Fig. 2. Mapped JSON file. National Historic Museum (2022)

After the mapping, Tainacan makes available the JSON API, "Simple JSON: inbcm-ibram mapper"[12], which will be collected by Filebeat.

3.2 Beats - Filebeat: Automated Collection of Items from Museums

In the case of aggregation, only the metadata is collected, that is, documents or attachments are not considered. In the moment, ways are being studied to collect thumbnails of documents to provide users with a preview of them.

We emphasize that the interest is for the user to visit the museum of origin, through the access link to the item, and not just use the aggregator, so collection efforts are focused on metadata. The idea is to allow the search and retrieval of information, to lead the user to the museum of origin of that item.

To harvest the JSON file of each museum, we use the Filebeat, from two configuration files. The first is the configuration necessary for each collection, for each museum, which will have its data collected. This file basically contains the URL of the JSON API, information about the pagination and the inclusion of four new metadata: museum: the name of the museum, the name of the collection and its location, with city and state. All Ibram's files are available in GitHub[13]. The second is a general configuration file, which orchestrates access to individual files (.yml) and sends their results to Logstash. This file too is available in GitHub[14].

---

[12] National Historic Museum JSON file example: https://mhn.acervos.museus.gov.br/wp-json/tai nacan/v2/collection/24/items/?perpage=96&order=ASC&orderby=date&exposer=json-flat& mapper=inbcm-ibram&paged=1.

[13] https://github.com/tainacan/tainacan-elk/tree/master/Filebeat/inputs.d.

[14] https://github.com/tainacan/tainacan-elk/blob/master/Filebeat/Filebeat.yml.

3.3 Logstash: Aggregation of Collections and Data Transformation

After the collection of data sources made by Filebeat, Logstash receives hem, aggregates them and performs transformations on the data, when necessary.

A Logstash pipeline has two required elements, input and output, and one optional element, filter. The input plugins consume data from a source, the filter plugins modify the data as you specify, and the output plugins write the data to a destination (Elastic 2021h).

In the input plugin, data is received from Filebeat. Afterwards, the filters are executed. "A filter plugin performs intermediary processing on an event. Filters are often applied conditionally depending on the characteristics of the event" (Elastic 2021d). There are three standard Logstash filters: prune, mutate and fingerprint, and one, tainacan_submission, developed by the authors using the Ruby programming language, in order to submit items to a Tainacan installation. In the output plugin the data is sent to Elasticsearch storage. Figure 3 shows the pipeline with the main steps.

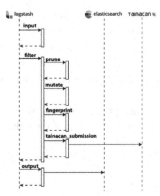

Fig. 3. Logstash pipeline. Prepared by the authors (2021).

The prune filter removes fields from events based on whitelists or blacklist. This can be useful for a json filter that creates fields with names that you don't know the names of beforehand, and you only want to keep a subset of them (Elastic 2021g). The prune filter performs the cleaning of received data, delivering the relevant data, configured in Logstash, removing any others sent by Filebeat.

The mutate filter allows you to perform general mutations on fields. You can rename, remove, replace, and modify fields in your events (Elastic 2021f). In Ibram, the following mutate filters were used: capitalize[15], lowercase[16], remove_field[17], rename[18], strip[19] and split[20].

Subsequently, the Fingerprint filter:

> Create consistent hashes (fingerprints) of one or more fields and store the result in a new field. You can use this plugin to create consistent document ids when events are inserted into Elasticsearch. This approach means that existing documents can be updated instead of creating new documents (Elastic 2021e).

To create the unique code, a hash was created using three fields: the installation, that is, the museum's name, the item's id and registration number, collected from the museums of origin.

The last filter, tainacan_submission, was developed by the authors to perform the submission of items collected in Tainacan, for Brasiliana Museums.

In output, the data is sent to Elasticsearch and used by Kibana to build the dashboard.

3.4   Ruby Plugin in Logstash: Item Submission in Tainacan

For the best performance of submissions, a queue of processes, Fig. 4, that organize and forward them to the Tainacan API was implemented, since Logstash sends a high number of items simultaneously. All processed items are included at the end of the queue, while a set of threads (four, by default, in Fig. 4) are responsible for processing the output of items from that queue, effecting the items submission in Tainacan. The Ruby code is available in GitHub[21].

After all items in the queue are processed, they will be available for access in the Tainacan installation. It is important to note that after this step, the items will also be sent to Elasticsearch.

3.5   Elasticsearch: Data Storage

All items are stored in Elasticsearch, where you can perform various data search and retrieval operations. The Fig. 5 show the Elasticsearch interface.

---

[15] https://www.elastic.co/guide/en/logstash/current/plugins-filters-mutate.html#plugins-filters-mutate-capitalize.

[16] https://www.elastic.co/guide/en/logstash/current/plugins-filters-mutate.html#plugins-filters-mutate-lowercase.

[17] https://www.elastic.co/guide/en/logstash/current/plugins-filters-mutate.html#plugins-filters-mutate-remove_field.

[18] https://www.elastic.co/guide/en/logstash/current/plugins-filters-mutate.html#plugins-filters-mutate-rename.

[19] https://www.elastic.co/guide/en/logstash/current/plugins-filters-mutate.html#plugins-filters-mutate-strip.

[20] https://www.elastic.co/guide/en/logstash/current/plugins-filters-mutate.html#plugins-filters-mutate-split.

[21] https://github.com/tainacan/tainacan-elk/tree/master/logstash/plugins/src/filters/logstash-filter-tainacan_submission.

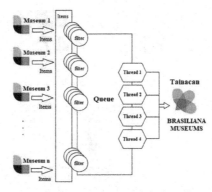

Fig. 4. Submission queue scheme. Prepared by the authors (2022)

Fig. 5. Elasticsearch interface. Prepared by authors (2022)

In the case of the aggregator, the data will be used to feed the dashboard developed in Kibana.

3.6 Kibana: Dashboard

The Kibana tool accesses the integrated data stored in Elasticsearch, enabling the creation of interactive panels, composed of visualization elements, such as graphs, titles, metrics and maps.

The panels, which can be easily created and/or edited, offer managers different views of the collections, in a single, fully interactive interface that reacts to each new search. As it is directly related to the data aggregation process, the updates carried out in the museums of origin are also carried out in the panels.

We emphasize that the panels are designed to bring information considered important by managers, however, Kibana offers numerous and agile forms of research. We cite an example, if you want to find all items typed "chair" (cadeira, in Portuguese). As shown in Fig. 6 from a simple search, all your panel shapes the result, showing, for example, which museums have chairs, in addition to listing the links that direct to the objects in the museums of origin.

The prototype is available for access at: http://200.137.217.144:6601/goto/613663 b72fc306a908e86a6233e5219c.

Fig. 6. Search example in Ibram's dashboard. Prepared by authors (2022)

3.7 Tainacan: Final Repository

The aggregated data is sent to a new Tainacan installation via the plugin, and this installation is set up to provide efficient searching and browsing. Figure 7, shows part of the interface.

Fig. 7. Brasiliana Museums. Prepared by authors (2022)

As it is a prototype, the Brasiliana Museums can be seen at http://integracaoibram.tainacan.org/, in which 20 museums are integrated, resulting in 17,315 digital objects.

4 Discussions

Different countries offer the cultural data aggregation service, providing search and retrieval portals, such as the Europeana Portal, of Europe, and the Portal of the Digital Public Library of America - DPLA, of the United States of America, which bring together millions of digital objects from countless different data sources.

In Brazil, although there are initiatives of this type, they are still limited, isolated practices that need technical support and scalable governance models for the Brazilian territory. Thus, the aggregation process exposed in this article was designed to meet the reality of Brazilian institutions managed by Ibram, both budgetary and specialized technical support, in a scalable way, and it is a simple and efficient solution to integrate the collections in an automated way, using only free software.

The research demonstrates the viability of the technologies and, therefore, validates the technological model and the flow of information circulation. It is noteworthy that the combination of Tainacan and Elastic Stack proved to be of medium complexity, becoming a viable learning and customization option.

We emphasize that important goals are achieved, such as allowing users to search for museum objects in a simplified way without the need for more advanced knowledge about museums.

The aggregator can bring other relevant benefits, such as offering resources to improve the management of museum documentation, as it presents, in a unified and interactive way, a macro view of museums; demonstrate syntactic or semantic inconsistencies, enabling museums to improve their information at the base; compare different institutions, making it possible to find patterns and connections of interest, finding indicators that can ensure better strategic planning, greater productivity and agility in accessing data, generating effects in administrative, cultural and educational dimensions and enriching the data source for research.

Another important topic is the financial return that aggregators can bring. Two leading institutions, the British Library and Europeana, carried out studies, both published in 2013, indicating that the British Library's online services are valued at £19.5 million a year, generating benefits for UK students, researchers and citizens. Europeana concluded that the economic impact for the European continent would be approximately 78.8 million euros in a baseline scenario, 59.6 million euros in a pessimistic scenario and 97.7 million euros in an optimistic scenario (Martins et al. 2018).

As it is something new at the national level, in addition to the aggregator of cultural data, it is necessary to provide institutions with best practices to maintain their collections on the web, in order to provide better results related to integrated search and, consequently, to improve the national collections as a whole.

It is important to highlight that to retrieve content in the aggregator it is important to establish quality parameters to be applied to the source data, which requires the creation of guidelines for better data quality, such as Europeana and DPLA, enabling museums to improve their data continuously. These guidelines are also under study by the Network Intelligence Laboratory.

For Ibram, as an institution that manages museums, aggregation also brings advantages related to the management and monitoring of collections, which makes it possible to carry out more accurate diagnoses of the status of collections and information about them, in addition to the generation of reports broader and more reliable analytics.

5 Conclusions

Technological evolution has enabled the reinvention of the museum space, opening up potential paths for the dissemination and socialization of memory and culture. Thus, international and national institutions have invested in making their digital collections available, resulting in countless museum data distributed on the web, generating different possibilities for searching and retrieving information.

This scenario, although very rich, brought challenges to the discovery of cultural heritage resources. To this end, in order to optimize the location of digital objects present in different museum sites across the internet, several institutions around the world have become data providers for services specialized in the aggregation of cultural collections of cultural heritage, as is the case of Europeana and of the DPLA. In this sense, aggregation makes the search and retrieval of information about collections a more efficient information retrieval operation for the users of these collections.

For example, to find a specific digital object, it is necessary to know the collection in which it belongs and some of its characteristics, which for a lay user would be practically impossible, greatly limiting the actual dissemination of the collection. In this perspective, providing museums and users with aggregation services for efficient search and retrieval becomes an essential theme.

The study and prototyping of the service for the aggregation of digital museum collections, Brasiliana Museums, reveals itself, therefore, as an efficient solution, both from the point of view of socialization and dissemination of digital objects and in the monitoring and monitoring of information from the collections through analytical panels, which can change the way managers, researchers and users interact with cultural data, bringing countless benefits to society. In addition to presenting a cheap and viable technological solution to be implemented.

As future works, research continues and improvements will be carried out during the studies, with the next step being the collection of thumbnails of images of digital objects from the museums of origin for the aggregator.

References

BRASIL. Instituto Brasileiro de Museus, Resolução Normativa nº 2, 2014. Diário Oficial. https://www.in.gov.br/web/dou/-/resolucao-normativa-ibram-n-6-de-31-de-agosto-de-2021-342359740. Accessed 03 Mar 2022

Elastic: Elastic stack (2021a), https://www.elastic.co/elastic-stack/. Accessed 10 July 2021a

Elastic: Filebeat reference [7.13]. Filebeat overview (2021b). https://www.elastic.co/guide/en/beats/Filebeat/current/Filebeat-overview.html. Accessed 10 July 2021

Elastic: Logstash reference [7.13]. Contributing to Logstash (2021c). https://www.elastic.co/guide/en/logstash/current/contributing-to-logstash.html. Accessed 10 July 2021

Elastic: Logstash reference [7.13]. Filter plugins (2021d). https://www.elastic.co/guide/en/logstash/current/filter-plugins.html. Accessed 09 July 2021

Elastic: Logstash reference [7.13]. Filter plugins. Fingerprint filter plugin (2021e). https://www.elastic.co/guide/en/logstash/current/plugins-filters-fingerprint.html. Accessed 09 July 2021

Elastic: Logstash reference [7.13]. Filter plugins. Mutate filter plugin (2021f). https://www.elastic.co/guide/en/logstash/current/plugins-filters-mutate.html. Accessed 09 July 2021f

Elastic: Logstash reference [7.13]. Filter plugins. Prune filter plugin (2021g). https://www.elastic.co/guide/en/logstash/current/plugins-filters-prune.html4. Accessed 09 July 2021

Elastic: Logstash reference [7.13]. Getting started with Logstash. Stashing your first event (2021h). https://www.elastic.co/guide/en/logstash/current/first-event.html. Accessed 09 July 2021h

Elastic: Logstash reference [7.13]. Logstash introduction (2021i). https://www.elastic.co/guide/en/logstash/current/introduction.htm. Accessed 10 July 2021

Gov.br: Museus Ibram (2022a). https://www.gov.br/museus/pt-br/museus-ibram. Accessed 02 Dec 2022

Gov.br: Sobre o órgão (2022b). https://www.gov.br/museus/pt-br/acesso-a-informacao/institucional/sobre-o-orgao. Accessed 02 Dec 2022

Martins, D.L., Silva, M.F., do Carmo, D.: Acervos em rede: perspectivas para as instituições culturais em tempos de cultura digital. Em Questão **24**(1), 194–216 (2018). https://doi.org/10.19132/1808-5245241.194-216

Martins, D.L., Carmo, D.do., Silva, M.F.S.: Modelos de governança em serviços de acervos digitais em rede: elementos para a produção de uma política pública nacional para objetos culturais digitais. Perspectivas Em Ciência Da Informação, **27**(1) (2022). https://periodicos.ufmg.br/index.php/pci/article/view/39044

Siqueira, J., Martins, D.L.: Recuperação de informação: descoberta e análise de workflows para agregação de dados do patrimônio cultural. Ciência Inf. **49**(3) (2020). http://revista.ibict.br/ciinf/article/view/539910

Siqueira, J., Martins, D.L.: Workflow models for aggregating cultural heritage data on the web: a systematic literature review. J. Assoc. Inf. Sci. Technol. 1–21 (2021). https://doi.org/10.1002/asi.24498

Tainacan.org: Páginas do Tainacan (2021a). https://tainacan.github.io/tainacan-wiki//tainacan-pages?id=as-páginas-especiais-do-tainacan. Accessed 09 July 2021

Tainacan.org: Tainacan. Home (2021b). https://tainacan.org/en/. Accessed 10 July 2021

Concept Maps as a Support for Learning:
A Proposal from the Consent for the Processing of Personal Data in Private Organizations

Herbert Alcântara Ferreira[1]([✉]) [iD] and Rodrigo de Sales[2] [iD]

[1] Universidade Estadual de Montes Claros, Montes Claros, Brazil
`Herbert.ferreira@unimontes.br`
[2] Universidade Federal de Santa Catarina, Florianópolis, Brazil
`rodrigo.sales@ufsc.br`

Abstract. Knowledge Organization has Knowledge Organization Systems (KOS) to represent, organize and retrieve information. Among these systems are the concept maps, which represent ideas from the illustration of concepts that are linked together. Originating from pedagogy, concept maps began to be used in several areas as learning methods, including in the context of private institutions. Therefore, the demand to implement the rules of the Brazilian General Law for Personal Data Protection (LGPD in Portuguese) requires learning from agents involved in the treatment of this type of data, especially in corporations. The general objective of this article is to prepare a concept map that represents the main rules of the LGPD regarding personal data processed based on the consent of its data subjects. As specific objectives, it seeks to investigate the main characteristics and typologies of concept maps, in addition to analyzing the aspects and fundamental rules of the LGPD. The purpose of the proposal is to use the map to study the aforementioned law. The methodology of construction of input and output concept maps was used, in addition to Data Life Cycle, which interprets the "life" of data in four phases: collection, storage, retrieval and disposal. As a result, a simplified map was arrived at, but with a broad view of personal data management from collection to disposal. The constructed map serves as a representative model of the treatment addressed and can be adjusted according to the needs of each institution.

Keywords: Knowledge organization · Concept maps · General law for personal data protection

1 Introduction

Information Science, as a discipline that studies information and the reality that surrounds it [1], has the Knowledge Organization (KO) as one of its fields of theoretical studies and practical solutions for activities that have the information as object. Within the KO, Knowledge Organization Systems (KOS) are the instruments responsible for organizing information in order to represent and retrieve it [2]. Among these systems are the concept maps, which are alternatives created by the education researcher Joseph

© ICST Institute for Computer Sciences, Social Informatics and Telecommunications Engineering 2022
Published by Springer Nature Switzerland AG 2022. All Rights Reserved
A. L. Pinto and R. Arencibia-Jorge (Eds.): DIONE 2022, LNICST 452, pp. 98–110, 2022.
https://doi.org/10.1007/978-3-031-22324-2_9

Novak to improve the learning process from the visual representation of concepts that are interconnected and generate propositions among themselves [3]. From this perspective, concept maps were added to the list of KO systems as an alternative to support people and institutions in the process of representing and organizing ideas in graphic supports. Thus, given the various demands in current organizations, which require the learning of employees involved, concept maps are interesting systems to represent information and build knowledge on various possible subjects.

In the Brazilian context, the General Law for Personal Data Protection (LGPD in Portuguese), which establishes rights and duties in relation to the processing of data referring to natural persons, is one of the emerging demands in organizations. Adapting to the requirements of this law requires knowledge on the part of organizational directors and professionals specialized in the area of information management and the legal sector, as well as all employees of an institution.

Therefore, using the Data Life Cycle as a theoretical support to understand the existence of data, the main objective of this work is to develop a concept map that addresses the main rules of LGPD influential in the four phases of this model: collection, storage, retrieval and disposal [4, 5]. In order to achieve this proposal, two specific objectives are outlined: a) to investigate the main aspects of concept maps and their best-known typologies; b) analyze the main characteristics and rules involving the LGPD. Given the extent of the law and the various possible treatment scenarios, the construction of the map only observed the rules referring to the hypothesis of treatment based on the consent of the data subject to collect data in private organizations.

After this introduction (Sect. 1), Sect. 2 turns to the literature review on concept maps (concept, purposes and construction method), while Sect. 3 studies the basic aspects of the LGPD. In Sect. 4, the Data Life Cycle is presented. Finally, in Sect. 5, the desired concept map is presented, accompanied by a brief explanation of its representation. As a result, it is understood that the illustrative structure of the concept map serves as a support for the learning of people involved and interested in the use of personal data.

2 Concept Maps

In the scope of Information Science, Knowledge Organization (KO) is the discipline responsible for ordering information so that it can be represented and retrieved [6–8]. In addition to its theoretical corpus, the practice of KO involves actions such as listing terms, controlling synonyms and ambiguities, defining hierarchies and associations between concepts, classifications, among other activities [9]. Knowledge Organization Systems (KOS) are responsible for operationalizing such procedures. For Hodge [10, p. 1], "the term knowledge organization systems is intended to encompass all types of schemes for organizing and promoting knowledge management". Souza, Tudhope and Almeida [2] associate the definition of KOS with models of information representation, so that they can be organized and retrieved. Among the KOS, we can mention classification schemes, taxonomies, ontologies, folksonomies, thesauri, indexing languages, among others.

From this perspective, it is noteworthy that the purpose of representing information in KO involves several tools that serve as support for the learning process, such as the organization of concepts in facets, arrangements and maps [11]. The latter constitute themselves as their own KOS called a concept map. Concept maps are systems that use visual resources to present ideas and, despite not being good KOS for information retrieval, they are useful for representing knowledge [7].

Interestingly, concept maps do not originate from KO as a discipline, but arise in the context of pedagogy. They were created by Joseph Novak in the 1970s during studies on the learning process among children. Novak's research was influenced by David Ausubel's theory of meaningful learning, which considers the mental construction of knowledge as a result of the encounter between new information and pre-existing concepts in individual consciousness. Since then, concept maps have been used to consolidate knowledge through the visual organization of concepts [3, 12, 13]. According to Lima [14, p. 135], "[…] concept map is a representation that describes the relationship of ideas of thought […]".

Within the structure of a concept map, fundamental elements for its construction and understanding are mentioned. The most basic entity is the concept, defined as follows: "[…] the perceived regularity in events or objects, or records of events or objects, designated by a label" [3, p. 1]. The label, which represents the concept, can be a word, a short sentence or a symbol. In turn, labels are connected by linking words or phrases that imply propositions (statements) that state something about concepts [3]. In this system, labels are found in icons, usually frames, which can be differentiated in color and format, for example. Linking words or phrases are accompanied by arrows. For example, to state that a cat is a species of mammal, one label has "cat", another has the concept "mammal", and both are connected by the phrase "is a species of". The connections between concepts can express relationships of different kinds, whether temporal, logical, hierarchical, etc. [12]. In this sense, Tavares [13, p. 72] states that "the concept map is a schematic structure to represent a set of concepts immersed in a network of propositions" (Fig. 1).

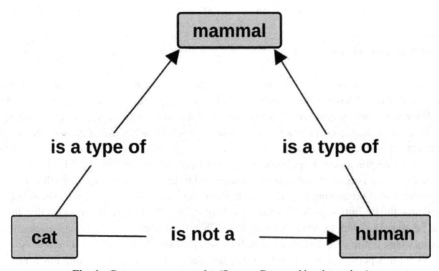

Fig. 1. Concept map example. (Source: Prepared by the author)

According to Dahlberg [15, p. 86], "our knowledge condenses itself in concepts by their informative content. Concepts are therefore knowledge units and form the elements of systems of knowledge". Thus, relationships between concepts, evidenced in the map, allow the human mind to assimilate information to generate knowledge. In this perspective, with the organization of concepts in icons, both those who build the concept map and those who read it can better learn the information worked (developing the "iconic memory") and, thus, build their knowledge about the topic covered in the map [3]. Because of this capacity, concept maps were instrumentalized by the Knowledge Organization [7] and started to be used in several areas, from the traditional pedagogical purpose to scientific research and in the administration sector [14]. Despite its advantages for representing information, the fact that its labels are summarized in a few words stands out as a major problem with this KOS, which can limit the reader's understanding [14]. However, it is understood that its image organization still makes its use viable for learning purposes, especially if there is prior knowledge (albeit superficial) on the topic addressed or other support materials that delve into the concepts presented in the labels. Tavares [13] presents some of the different types of existing concept maps:

- "Spider's Web" type map: Organized from a central concept that connects with other concepts, which orbit around it. It focuses on this concept, called "generator", and the relationships formed from it, to the detriment of other types of propositions (such as hierarchical ones, for example).
- "Flowchart" type map: Its focus is the representation of processes, having start and end points.
- "Input and output" type map: It has a basic format similar to the flowchart, but has a greater richness in the number of relationships, as it imposes greater possibilities of inputs and outputs.
- "Hierarchical" type map: Organizes information in a hierarchical manner, with broader concepts at the top and more specific ones at the bottom.

Despite these typologies, Novak and Cañas [3] understand that a good concept map must be surrounded by a hierarchical structure (in the sense that specific concepts must come from broader concepts within the graphical representation of the system). Thus, observing this orientation, it is understood that, regardless of the type of concept map, the organization of concepts from the most generic to the most specific allows a better construction and understanding of the map, within the fundamental intentions of those who build it.

Novak and Cañas [3] present a concept map construction methodology, which is used for the purpose of this work. According to the authors, it is first necessary to define the area of knowledge that will be worked on (domain) and which fundamental question will be answered by the map (focal question). Afterwards, the key concepts of the map must be chosen and listed. From this list of concepts, these can be ordered from broadest to most specific (to serve as support for the organization). Once these initial steps have been taken, you can create a preliminary map. Soon, it can be revised (even more than once). New concepts and connections can be added or modified, until a desirable version of this system is reached. Also, you are advised to avoid large phrases in the icons. In the end, the map must undergo a final revision until it reaches its definitive version.

Finally, it is observed that, according to Tavares [13], what makes a map good or bad is its author's ability to create rich relationships between concepts.

3   General Law for Personal Data Protection

In the environment of an organization, there are several types of demands, whether constant or intermittent: organizational management, customer service, budget planning, logistics, institutional relations, definition and fulfillment of goals or commitments, etc. Any of these needs, undoubtedly, require knowledge for their execution, either from specialized collaborators or from the entire community involved. Within an organized society, laws are also demands that must be observed by institutions, when they are addressed to them. In this sense, it is important that organizations know the legal norms that must be observed and complied with within their scope.

In Brazil, the General Law for Personal Data Protection (Law n. 13.709/2018), known by the acronym LGPD, stands out. It defines rights and duties in relation to the handling of personal information, so that it obliges public and private institutions to implement security measures to guarantee the privacy of data concerning individuals. As a contextualization of this norm, it is observed that the current world is immersed in information whose traffic is potentiated by the performance of modern technologies [16]. Thus, personal data have become active in the present context of the digital economy [17], both for the private sector (commerce, industry, service provision, marketing, etc.) and for the public sector. Faced with the need to protect this type of data from possible abuses and violations (for example, leaks) and guarantee citizens' privacy and autonomy over their own data [18], the LGPD was enacted in 2018. Inspired by the European standard General Data Protection Regulation (GDPR), the LGPD is also a general law and therefore gives guidelines on how personal data must be protected in Brazilian law. People and institutions that comply with this standard must know it and know how its determinations influence their personal data management activities.

From this premise, it is understood the possibility of using concept maps as a support for learning the rules present in this regulation. Unlike other KOS, such as classification schemes (aimed at ordering concepts), thesauri (which perform vocabulary control) and indexing languages (aimed at retrieval), the focus of concept maps is to represent ideas. This representation has the ultimate purpose of building knowledge in the conscious-ness of those who have contact with its graphic structure. Thus, concept maps can be useful for learning how LGPD rules should be applied in environments that work with personal data. It would work, therefore, as a support for the study of its legal guidelines, contextualizing it with the reality of each institution.

In view of the central proposal of this work, it is necessary to present some relevant rules provided for in the LGPD, although, given the extent of the law, it is not possible to address all of them. First, some basic terms involving the matter of regulation of this law are presented. About the definition of personal data, according to its article 5, item I, it is said that they refer to "information related to an identified or identifiable natural person" [19]. It is observed that the concept of natural person is synonymous with physical person, that is, of a human individual. Still, there is a kind of this category of data called "sensitive personal data" (or just "sensitive data"), which concerns information of sensitive content, with greater potential for abusive or illegal discrimination [20]. As an example, article 5, item II, of the LGPD cites data related to "racial or ethnic origin, religious conviction, political opinion, union membership, [...] referring to health or sexual life [...]" [19] A data can be anonymized, so that it is not possible to identify who it refers to and, thus, the LGPD does not need to be applied to operations that have it as an object. The person to whom the data refers is called personal data subject [19].

The "processing of personal data" (or merely "processing") is another expression recurrent in the text of the LGPD. According to article 5, item X, of the LGPD, the treatment refers to "any operation carried out with personal data [...]" [19], whether collection, use, sharing, disposal, among other possible activities. The people responsible for these operations are called "processing agents", which can be controllers or operators. The controller is a natural or legal person who decides on the essential aspects of data processing, such as which data will be processed and what the purpose of the treatment is. If a natural person is primarily responsible for the treatment, then he is the controller. If an organization, such as a company, is responsible, then its legal entity is considered to be the controller. The processor is the person (also natural or legal) who carries out the data processing operations, in accordance with the controller's guidelines. Thus, it is a function performed by a hired person, by an outsourced company and even by the controller itself [21]. Although not a processing agent, the person in charge (or Data Protection Officer - DPO, according to the European model nomenclature) is also a mandatory actor in the processing of personal data. According to article 5, item VIII, of the LGPD, the function of the person in charge is "[...] to act as a communication channel between the controller, the data subjects and the National Data Protection Authority (ANPD in Portuguese)" [19]. Finally, according to article 5, item XIX, of the LGPD, the ANPD is a federal public body "[...] responsible for ensuring, implementing and monitoring compliance with this Law throughout the national territory" [19]. Among the powers of the ANPD, the application of administrative sanctions for those who fail to comply with LGPD rules stands out. Penalties range from warnings to fines and suspension of data processing activities [19].

As for the application of the LGPD, it is observed, firstly, that it regulates the processing of personal data in both the digital and analog contexts (such as information printed in documents, for example). Not only legal entities (public bodies, private institutions and companies) must observe the LGPD, but also natural persons when they are treatment agents. Regardless of the involvement of other countries in the processing of personal data, the LGPD should apply when [19]:

- the treatment operation takes place in Brazil;
- the processing has the purpose of offering goods or services in Brazil, or;
- the personal data is collected in Brazil (its data subject is in Brazilian territory at the time of collection) or the data subject is in the country during the treatment.

However, there are exceptions to these rules. When the processing of data has journalistic, artistic, academic, public security or State purposes, or for the purpose of investigation and repression of crimes, the application of the LGPD is waived. However, it is observed that, regarding the processing of data for academic purposes, agreement with the legal bases of articles 7 and 11, which will be addressed later on, is still required. Furthermore, the law is not applied when the data originate outside Brazil and are not communicated, transferred or shared with Brazilian processing agents [19].

As a way of protecting personal data, the LGPD establishes hypotheses that justify its treatment. These are legal circumstances that authorize operations with personal data, so that they can only be processed if the treatment agrees with any of these hypotheses [22]. These provisions of the law can also be called "legal bases" [23]. There is a list of legal bases that authorize the processing of personal data in general (in article 7) and another list especially dedicated to sensitive data (in article 11), as these require greater protection by law. Among the legal bases, it is possible to cite hypotheses of data processing for the execution of legal obligations of the controllers, for the execution of public policies by the Public Administration, for the protection of the life and physical integrity of data subject or another person, among other possibilities [19].

The hypothesis of consent for the processing of personal data, whether sensitive or not, stands out. According to article 5, item XII, of this law, consent is the "free, informed and unequivocal expression by which the data subject agrees to the processing of his personal data for a specific purpose". According to article 8, it must be "provided in writing or by another means that demonstrates the owner's expression of will". At the time of collection, the data subject must be informed about the purpose of processing the data granted. In addition, whenever the data subject wants, he can request the revocation of the processing of his data, through an express, free and simple request. Also, you have the right to request, free of charge, clear information about the treatment that has your data as object, including: purpose, identity of the controller, existence or not of data sharing, duration of treatment and way in which it is carried out. [19].

If the data subjects are children and adolescents (under 18 years of age), their parents or guardians must give consent for the use of the information [17]. Only contact data of these, for the request of consent, can be collected directly from the minors, but they must be used only once and cannot be stored, according to article 14 of that law [19].

Finally, according to article 15, the end of the processing of personal data occurs when: its purpose is achieved; operations are no longer needed; if the stipulated period for treatment has expired; or if the data subject requests the revocation of consent. However, data retention is allowed, even if one of the above requirements is met, when [19]:

- the controller needs the data to comply with any legal or regulatory obligation;
- the data are used by research bodies, preferably anonymized;
- there is a transfer to another person, provided that the requirements for data processing are respected (for example, definition of some legal basis);
- or the controller uses it, the data being anonymized and access to another person prohibited.

In addition to these rules, there are many others that could not be addressed in this work, given the scope of the LGPD. In this sense, the importance of adapting private institutions, especially companies, to the requirements of the LGPD is emphasized. Despite being a normative demand, it is understood that there are benefits caused by the implementation of the rules of the new law to the organizations submitted to it. Firstly, the very promotion of the security of personal data of customers, service users, contractors, among others, through the aforementioned rule. Adapting to the LGPD helps ensure the privacy of these people, which is of notable social importance. Secondly, as a result of the above reason, the corporation that respects the privacy of personal information will have a competitive point in the market compared to companies that remain inert in the face of this legal demand [24].

Therefore, it is understood that everyone benefits from the implementation of LGPD rules in a corporate organization. However, employees involved in the processing of personal data must be aware of the main requirements of the law, which radiate over the various phases of operations. For this reason, this article proposes a concept map model that organizes concepts related to data protection rules in the various moments of use of personal information by an organization. Knowing how this data should be managed in compliance with the LGPD is a learning need for agents in an institution. Thus, we seek to understand whether the concept map's ability to represent ideas through its graphic structure allows this KOS to be a support for private organizations. In this sense, the concept map could be used to study the LGPD, understanding its rules within the context of how personal data should be managed within an organization. As theoretical support for this objective, the Data Life Cycle proposed in [4, 5] is considered, for the management of this type of informational content.

4 Methodology

In view of the literature reviews whose objects of study were, respectively, the concept maps and the LGPD, we proceeded with the development of the construction of the concept map then proposed. It is considered that the execution of activities that have data as objects can be a real challenge, which requires knowledge of computing, Information Science and as many others as are necessary to meet the needs of this type of operation [4]. This difficulty is exacerbated by the requirement of the LGPD, which, as previously mentioned, imposes requirements aimed at protecting personal information. In this perspective, the proposal of this work passes through the observance of the phases of the Data Life Cycle as a theoretical and methodological reference for the definition of the treatment of data studied in stages.

Data Life Cycle is a theoretical tool that divides the existence of data into phases, each with its own needs. It uses the research of Sant'ana (2013; 2016), which has, among other concerns, the care with the protection of data managed in digital support, especially when present in large volume. The main characteristics of each phase of this model are presented below [4, 5]:

- Collection: It happens from the verification of the need to access or use the data for the satisfaction of some purpose. It is necessary to know, in advance, what data should be collected, its format and the way in which this collection should take place. Sant'ana [5] suggests that the data collected be described in metadata.
- Storage: If the person responsible for the data does not discard it after its first use, it is stored on a digital medium. In this circumstance, it is necessary to define which data must be stored, the physical and virtual structure for that, in addition to the definition of security measures that are necessary to avoid violations of the information. The intention is for the data to be stored so that it can later be used or made available for retrieval.

- Recovery: Occurs when there is an intention to make the data available to some public, so that it can be recovered. Sant'ana [5] advises the determination of certain guidelines, such as the definition of the recovery target audience, which data must be made available and the way to do so, period of availability, in addition to the possibility (or not) of returning to storage in banks of data.
- Disposal: Moment when it is verified that the data are no longer needed or that there is any other circumstance that imposes the deletion of the data initially collected. It must be well defined what data needs to be discarded, the ways to safely delete it and whether those responsible for the database have the right to delete it.

The map was structured based on the type of input and output, as the trajectory of the arrows represents processes (in this case, the "path" taken by the data in each phase of the Data Life Cycle) and, due to the multiple possibilities of operations with the data, there is more than one possible path to be traced. For example, as in the general Data Life Cycle model in [4], one can go from collection directly to disposal or, rather, go through the storage and retrieval phases. Furthermore, it took advantage of the guidelines for the construction of concept maps in [3]. The concepts that involve these processes were organized from the most comprehensive (which are the phases of data life) to the most specific (which are the special rules for each circumstance). As much as possible, specific rules (such as a list of requirements) were privileged at the bottom of the map and broader processes at the top. For the construction of the concept map, the CmapTools software, suggested in [3] was used.

5   Results and Discussion: Representative Concept Map of Data Life Cycle According to LGPD Rules

After studying the concept maps and the LGPD, the map built from the four phases of the Data Life Cycle and whose representative model was elaborated in the CmapTools software, reached the following resulting structure (Fig. 2):

On the map, the four phases of the Data Life Cycle (collection, storage, retrieval and disposal) are highlighted in green, different from the other labels. The map is read from the collection frame, which is the first phase of the cycle. According to the legal basis chosen to represent the treatment, data collection can only be done through consent, which is granted by the data subject or his guardians (if he is a minor). Remember that consent must be free (given at the will of the data subject or his/her responsible), unambiguous (given by means of proving such will) and informed (the data subject must be informed about the data collected and the purpose of the treatment). As with other legal bases, consent covers the data subject's right to request information about the processing of their data.

The collected data can go for disposal, after its use, or be stored. As the second phase of the Data Life Cycle, storage is the moment in which data is saved for use when necessary. According to the LGPD, it is prohibited to store contact data of a person responsible for a minor data subject. As previously stated, after using this information to contact those responsible for the minor, it must be discarded. Also, the possibility of sharing data with another person is highlighted. In this case, it is evident that sharing

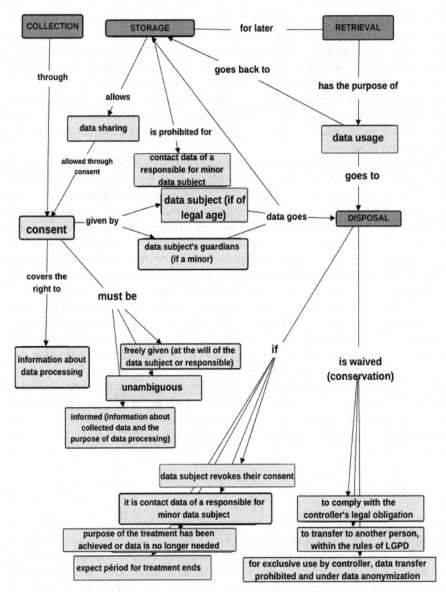

Fig. 2. Representative concept map of data life cycle according to LGPD Rules (Source: Prepared by the author)

requires the consent of the data subject, which can be granted from the moment the data were collected or through a new specific consent for this purpose.

On the left side of the "storage" label, the arrow leads to the recovery phase. In the processing of personal data presented as a model on the map, the agents themselves retrieve the data to use them. After its use, the data can be stored again or taken for disposal. The last phase of the Data Life Cycle refers to the deletion of data. Within the rules of the LGPD, as already seen, the disposal occurs in the following situations: after using the contact data of the person responsible for a minor data subject; if the data subject requests the revocation of consent; whether the purpose of the treatment is achieved; if the data is no longer needed or the predetermined period of treatment has expired. On the other hand, the data can be kept: to fulfill the controller's legal obligation; for transfer to another person (among the legal requirements, for example, if it is allowed by law or by the data subject to keep it through consent); or even for the exclusive use of the controller, under anonymization of this data, being forbidden the transfer to another person in this case.

In view of the analysis of the map, it is noticeable that its graphic structure is capable of representing the "life" of personal data according to the rules of the LGPD, from its collection for treatment to its disposal. A concept map structured in this way serves as a model for the organization to understand how this type of informational content should be managed so that it is adequate to legal requirements. His way of presenting concepts, in an accessible way, can be useful to all employees who need to know the rules for protecting personal information in an organization. Specifically, people in senior management, data management and legal sectors can benefit even more, as they decide on the purposes and directions for handling personal information in an institution.

Furthermore, although this general model is useful in demonstrating a panoramic view of the processing of personal data under the legal basis of consent in private organizations, it can be adjusted according to the needs of each specific corporation. For example, if the institution does not collect data on minors, there is no need to explain how this type of information should be treated in its concept map. Likewise, also by way of example, the concepts involving the sharing and use of data can be adjusted, in case there is an international transfer of them (which was not addressed in this work). Also, depending on the treatment to be performed, it is more advisable to build a new map than to use this model – for example, if the institution observes another legal basis, other than consent.

6   Conclusions

KO, as a discipline of Information Science, has its Systems (KOS) as tools for the representation, organization and retrieval of information in several areas. As for the possibility of image representation of organized information, concept maps stand out, linking concepts illustrated by labels and, thus, formulating propositions about a certain domain. As a result, concept map writers and readers are able to build knowledge about the area covered from the information represented.

In the Brazilian organizational context, LGPD has become a legal demand that requires knowledge from all employees of an institution, especially directors and those directly involved in the legal and information management sectors. Based on this assumption, the present work intended to build a concept map that would present the main rules involving the aforementioned law within a private organization (companies and other private institutions). Data Life Cycle, proposed by Sant'ana [4, 5], was used as a reference for the description of the "life" of the data (from collection to disposal), contextualizing it with the contents that bring information personal (referring to a natural person). For the delimitation of the subject, more specific rules of the law were omitted and only the processing of data collected through the consent of the subject was worked (since there are other "legal bases" that do not require such consent).

The result was a concept map whose format is "input and output", representing a process that can occur in different ways depending on the operations that involve the treatment and the nature of each data collected. Thus, while some data can be stored and retrieved, others must be disposed of immediately after being used (such as contact data of those responsible for a minor used to request consent to collect information from that child or adolescent).

Finally, it is understood that the concept map prepared can serve as a learning model about the aforementioned rules of the LGPD. It presents an overview (albeit simplified) of the main requirements that influence the life cycle of personal data. Still, it can be used as a basic model, so that adjustments are possible according to the reality of the organization (such as the existence of international transfer of these data, which was not addressed in this work). The guidelines given by Sant'ana in relation to each phase of the Data Life Cycle can also be used in the management of personal information. Furthermore, it is emphasized that other legal bases, which are not covered by the proposed map, can change the dynamics of how personal information is treated. In this case, the construction of a new concept map is more viable, although the guidelines indicated in this work can be used. Finally, it is understood that it is feasible to use this type of KOS, not only for the representation of the Data Life Cycle in the scope of this article, but also to support the learning of processing personal data influenced by other rules of the LGPD. There is no way to adjust the processing of personal data to the rules of this law without knowing how the management of this type of information should work, and this can be inferred through concept maps.

References

1. Borko, H.: Information science: what is it? Am. Doc. **19**(1), 3–5 (1968)
2. Souza, R.R., Tudhope, D., Almeida, M.B.: Towards a taxonomy of KOS: dimensions for classifying knowledge organization systems. Knowl. Org. **39**(3), 179–2012 (2012)
3. Novak, J.D., Cañas, A.J.: The theory underlying concept maps and how to construct and use them. Thecnical Report IHMC CmapTools, pp. 1–36 (2008)
4. Sant'ana, R.C.G.: Ciclo de vida de dados e o papel da Ciência da Informação. In: 14° Encontro Nacional de Pesquisa em Ciência da Informação, n. Universidade Federal de Santa Catarina, Florianópolis (2013)
5. Sant'ana, R.C.G.: Ciclo de Vida dos Dados: uma perspectiva a partir da Ciência da Informação. Inf. Inf. **21**(2), 116–142 (2016)
6. Smiraglia, R.P.: The Elements of Knowledge Organization. Springer, Heidelberg (2014)
7. Barité, M.: Sistemas de organización del conocimiento: una tipologia actualizada. Inf. Inf. **16**(3), 122–139 (2011)
8. Pontes, F.V., Lima, G.A.B.L.: A organização do conhecimento em ambientes digitais: aplicação da teoria da classificação facetada. Perspect. Ciênc. Inf. **17**(4), 18–40 (2012)
9. Zeng, M.L.: Knowledge organization systems (KOS). Knowl. Org. **35**(2), 160–182 (2008)
10. Hodge, G.: Systems of Knowledge Organization for Digital Libraries: Beyond Traditional Authority Files, 1st edn. The Digital Library Federation, Washington (2000)
11. Soergel, D.: Knowledge organization for learning. Adv. Knowl. Organ. **14**(5), 22–32 (2014)

12. Suenaga, C.M.K., Rodrigues, M.R., Santos, J.C.F., Cervantes, B.M.N.: Sistemas de organização do conhecimento: taxonomia e mapa conceitual. In: 5° Seminário em Ciência da Informação, pp. 501–520. Universidade Estadual de Londrina, Londrina (2013)
13. Tavares, R.: Construindo mapas conceituais. Ciências Cognição **12**, 72–85 (2007)
14. Lima, G.A.B.L.: Mapa conceitual como ferramenta para organização do conhecimento em sistema de hipertextos e seus aspectos cognitivos. Perspect. Ciênc. Inf. **9**(2), 134–145 (2004)
15. Dahlberg, I.: What is knowledge organization? Knowl. Org. **41**(1), 85–91 (2014)
16. Currás, E.: The nature of information and its influence in human cultures. Knowl. Org. **41**(1), 92–96 (2014)
17. Pinheiro, P.P.: Proteção de dados pessoais: comentários à Lei n. 13.709/2018 (2018). 2nd edn. Saraiva Educação, São Paulo (2020)
18. Ruaro, R.L., Rodríguez, D.P.: O direito à proteção de dados pessoais na sociedade da informação. Direito Estado Sociedade **36**(1), 178–199 (2010)
19. Lei n° 13.709, de 14 de agosto de 2018. http://www.planalto.gov.br/ccivil_03/_ato2015-2018/2018/lei/L13709.htm. Accessed 19 Jan 2022
20. Mulholland, C.S.: Dados pessoais sensíveis e a tutela de direitos fundamentais: uma análise à luz da Lei Geral de Proteção de Dados (Lei 13.709/18). Rev. Direitos Garantias Fundam. **19**(3), 159–180 (2018)
21. Autoridade Nacional de Proteção de Dados [ANPD]: Guia Orientativo para definições dos agentes de tratamento de dados pessoais e do encarregado. 1st edn. Presidência da República, Brasília (2021)
22. Ferreira, H.A., Lima, R.A.G.: LGPD comentada artigo por artigo. 1st edn. Fontenele Publicações, São Paulo (2021)
23. Teffé, C.S., Viola, M.: Tratamento de dados pessoais na LGPD: estudo sobre as bases legais. Civilistica.com **9**(1), 1–38 (2020)
24. Cavoukian, A.: Privacy by design: the 7 foundational principles. Inf. Priv. Commissioner Ontario **5**(12), 1–2 (2009)

Effect of Network Embedding on the Performance of Chinese Venture Capital Institutions: Mediatory Role of Organizational Learning

Yanxia Ni[1]([⊠]) and Jianqiang Li[2]

[1] Jianghan University Business School, Wuhan 430056, China
wangyi163ni@163.com
[2] Genaral Construction Company of CCTEB Group Co. LTD., Wuhan 430064, China

Abstract. By combining organizational learning and social network theories, we used 2,935 investment dealings of 942 investment institutions in 2,345 enterprises from 1999 to 2014 as a sample to explore the mechanism of heterogeneous knowledge learning in network embedding and investment performance. Empirical results show that structural and relationship embedding remarkably improve investment performance. Heterogeneous knowledge learning plays a mediatory role between structural embedding and investment performance, as well as between relational embedding and investment performance.

Keywords: Network embedding · Heterogeneous knowledge learning · Investment performance

1 Introduction

High-risk and high-yield characteristics of investment institutions has caused network embedding to become an important feature of investment institutions. The influence of network embedding on the investment performance of investment institutions is also receiving extensive research attention. Substantial literature has discussed the impact of different network embedding features on performance involving strong connections, weak links, relationship quality, network size, network location, and structural holes. However, the necessary research and analysis of the internal mechanisms of network embedding and its influence on investment performance are still lacking. The organizational learning theory can explain the interoperability between the two because it provides a target channel for the expansion and deepening of network embedding and enables process interpretation for the improvement of organizational performance by network resources. Whether external knowledge and information brought by network embedding

Fund project: 2021 Jianghan University high-level talent research start-up funding project (2021003).

A. L. Pinto and R. Arencibia-Jorge (Eds.): DIONE 2022, LNICST 452, pp. 111–130, 2022.
https://doi.org/10.1007/978-3-031-22324-2_10

can be effectively transformed into investment performance depends on organizational learning. Organizational learning enables organizations to receive and integrate information and knowledge obtained from the network selectively and enhances the competitive advantage and business ability of organizations. Therefore, this study explores and analyzes the mechanism of organizational learning on network embedding and investment performance.

How investment institutions obtain different attribute knowledge from different embedded mechanisms and how different attribute knowledge affects investment performance is not well explained in theory. One view is that network embedding allows investment institutions to acquire heterogeneous resources, information, and knowledge and thus improve investment performance. This view is mainly based on the theory of resource complementarity. The network embedding of investment institutions enables organizations to obtain the professional and complementary knowledge of their partners better, greatly reducing the cost of organizational learning and improving investment performance and exit success rate. By acquiring the heterogeneous knowledge of partners, investment institutions can focus on deepening their specialized knowledge and effectively combine, integrate, and apply internal and external knowledge (Grant & Baden-Fuller, 2004) [1]. In the context of venture capital with high risk characteristics, co-investment through network embedding provides an effective way for investment institutions to apply heterogeneous knowledge (Rodan & Galunic, 2004) [2]. Some scholars have pointed out that diversified investment is a typical feature of the venture capital industry, which requires investment institutions with different resources and skills that can be satisfied through alliances with other venture capital institutions (Hochberg et al., 2011) [3]. Additionally, accessing these resources and skills from familiar, close-knit, and strong relationships is easier for investment institutions. Alexy et al. (2012) [4] believe that the diversification of network partners enables investment institutions to obtain heterogeneous social capital, including complementary resources, knowledge and strategic information, which greatly reduce the uncertainty of venture capital and effectively improve investment performance. Another view is that network embedding renders homogenization knowledge more accessible to investment institutions. Investors can only obtain their specialized knowledge based on the trust of their partners, and the premise of trust is that partners have similar resource attributes to themselves (Meuleman et al., 2009) [5]. The third view is that the knowledge that network embedding brings to investment institutions should be analyzed from different dimensional attributes but not as generalized as heterogeneity and homogenization. Bubna et al. (2013) argued that the network embedding of investment institutions tends to be homogenized in terms of size, impact, and geographical distribution while tending to be heterogeneous in the investment industry and investment stage [6]. In summary, limited studies have uncovered the impact of network embedding on investment performance by analyzing investment institutions' knowledge of different attributes (heterogenization and homogenization) from different network embedding dimensions.

Hansen (1999) pointed out that the learning of knowledge among alliance organizations includes two stages: knowledge search and knowledge transfer [7]. Grant & Baden-Fuller (2004) indicated that knowledge learning among organizations in the alliance includes two aspects: access and acquisition [1]. According to previous studies, structural embedding provides a channel for the circulation of non-redundant information, and relationship embedding is the key to knowledge transfer and sharing (Moran, 2005) [8]. Especially in the Chinese context characterized by relationship governance, strong relationships make it easier to access resources (Bian, 1997) [9]. In view of the intractability and quantification of "knowledge search" and "knowledge transfer," the learning effect of knowledge in the network can be reflected in the investment industry. On the basis of the network and organizational learning theories, this study examines the impact of network embedding (structure embedding and relationship embedding) of venture capital institutions on investment performance and explores the role path and impact mechanism of heterogeneous knowledge learning.

2   Theory and Research Hypothesis

2.1   Relationship of Network Embedding and Investment Performance

Network location is the result of the direct and indirect relationship between actors. The difference in network location represents the difference in the opportunities for actors to acquire knowledge, information, and resources in the network. Organizations that occupy a good network position are more dominant (Zaheer & Bell, 2005) [10]. Some scholars believe that the resources acquired by enterprises can be interpreted as a function of the location of the enterprise network (Wasserman & Faust, 1994) [11]. However, most scholars believe that the variables that best reflect and measure the location of the network are centrality and structural holes (Powell et al., 1996) [12].

Centrality is a variable that characterizes whether an investment institution is close to the core of the network and represents the position of the investment institution in the cooperative network. Investment institutions with a higher centrality performs better than others due to the following aspects: First, investment institutions in the central position have more sources of information. Centrality represents the possibility of investment institutions to acquire and control resources. More sources of information increase the selectivity of the organization's available knowledge and the possibility that institutions will receive valuable and complementary information that competitors do not have, thereby giving them a competitive advantage. Second, the central position of the institution is higher, and the reputation and privileges that it enjoys are greater. Centrality is an important indicator for evaluating the importance of investment institutions in the network and for measuring the superiority, privilege, identity, and reputation of investment institutions. The higher the centrality of the investment institution, the higher the status, the more opportunities for accessing information and resources, and the greater the positive effect on investment performance. Finally, investment institutions with higher centrality are more likely to increase their learning ability. According to the theory of organizational learning, investment institutions in the central position have more opportunities to access new information, have a broader vision, and have a higher possibility of organizational learning. Promoting the exchange and integration of knowledge inside and outside the organization is easier, thereby developing new knowledge, enhancing capabilities (Brown & Duguid, 2001) [13], and improving investment performance.

Structure hole refers to the phenomenon of non-redundant connections among actors in the network. The reasons for the higher performance of investment institutions occupying more structural holes are as follows: First, structural holes can bring more non-redundant heterogeneous connections to investment institutions, and the information and knowledge fields that can be accessed are wider, which is beneficial to the integration of internal and external knowledge (McEvily & Zaheer, 1999) [14]. Second, the more number of structural holes that investment institutions have in a cooperative network, the more non-redundant information is obtained, the more the investment institution has the advantage of maintaining and controlling knowledge, information, and resources (Burt, 1992) [15]. And the more the investment institution can obtain scarce resources that can generate competitive advantages and promote investment performance. Finally, the occupation of structural holes with non-redundant connection features can effectively reduce the transaction costs between investment institutions and other institutions, thus excellent cost and energy invested in the core business of investment institutions improve investment performance (Gnyawali & Madhavan, 2001; Soda et al., 2004) [16, 17]. Based on these ideas, this study proposes the following assumptions:

H1a: The centrality of venture capital institutions has a positive impact on investment performance.

H1b: The structural holes of venture capital institutions have a positive impact on investment performance.

Relationship embedding focuses on the dual transaction problem of direct linkage, that is, the degree of mutual understanding, trust, and commitment between the parties of direct transactions (Granovetter, 1992; Uzzi, 1997) [18, 19]. Uzzi (1997) divided relationship embedding into three dimensions: trust, information sharing, and joint problem solving. The reasons for the relationship embedding of investment institutions for the effective improvement of investment performance are as follows: First, the high degree of inter-institutional relationship embedding means a high degree of trust between the two parties, which promotes sharing, communication, and exchange of complex knowledge and information between them (Rindfleisch & Moorman, 2001) [20] and increases the probability of a successful exit of investment institutions. Second, as the degree of embeddedness of investment institutions deepens, the degree of information sharing between the two partners increases, which is more conducive to the transfer of resources, information, and knowledge between each other, especially tacit and complex knowledge (Moran, 2005) [8]. Moreover, encouraging and promoting investment activities are more likely to improve investment performance. Finally, when the investment institutions have strong connections, they are more likely to solve problems through repeated communication and negotiation, thus having a common understanding of the investment process and results (Halinen & Tornroos, 1998) [21]. Besides, they may have a common coding and cognition for complex and tacit knowledge, which is more conducive to mining and utilizing valuable knowledge that can gain strategic advantages, thereby improving investment performance. Additionally, relationship embedding greatly reduces the occurrence of opportunistic behavior. Rowley et al. (2000) argue that in a close network, the threat of reputational loss can effectively prevent opportunistic behavior among partners, thereby promoting performance improvement [22]. McFayden (2009) [23] pointed out that the strong connection of network individuals is conducive to the development of technical activities. Based on these ideas, this study proposes the following assumptions:

H1c: The relationship embedding of venture capital institutions has a positive impact on investment performance.

2.2 Mediatory Role of Organizational Learning

Similar to previous studies, the professionalization of the investment industry represents the professionalization of the knowledge acquired. Therefore, this study uses the heterogeneity of the investment industry to represent the learning of heterogeneous knowledge of investment institutions in network embedding. Hansen (1999) pointed out that knowledge learning among alliance organizations includes two stages: knowledge search and knowledge transfer [7]. Knowledge search refers to the process of finding and determining. The knowledge in this process is generally explicit, simple, independent, and easy to code. The migration of knowledge is the process of movement and integration. In this process, knowledge is generally invisible, complex, dependent, and hard to code. If an organization wants to improve its performance by learning knowledge through network embedding, knowledge search and knowledge migration are indispensable. Grant & Baden-Fuller (2004) pointed out that knowledge learning among organizations in the alliance includes two aspects: access and acquisition [1]. Access of knowledge refers to the channels and opportunities for obtaining information resources in the alliance network, whereas acquisition of knowledge refers to the absorption, transfer, and application of information resources in the alliance network. The effect of knowledge learning among venture capital institutions is ultimately reflected in the investment industry and its performance. Heterogeneous knowledge brings diverse information and resources to the organization and expands the scope and possibilities of investment. Homogenization of knowledge enables organizations to improve investment efficiency through repeated learning of knowledge. Therefore, how different will network embedding affect the learning of various attribute knowledge? What is the internal knowledge learning mechanism that influences investment performance by network embedding?

Centrality measures the characteristics of direct contact with the organization. Investment institutions in the center of the network have more direct access to information and are more likely to be exposed to a variety of new knowledge and information, which are conducive to the improvement of investment performance. Koka & Prescott (2008) pointed out that individuals in the center of the network have more direct contact with other individuals, which improves the efficiency of the organization's search information, thus, they can quickly and easily access valuable and differentiated information and obtain more opportunity for competition and strategic advantage [24]. Hoskisson et al. (1993) believe that organizations with network-centric locations gain more opportunities for knowledge and information exchange, thus, the organization's product differentiation is more pronounced [25]. Polidoro et al. (2011) pointed out that organizations in the center of the network are more likely to have the opportunity to cooperate and become partners of other network individuals [26]. The diversity of partner attributes directly leads to the benefits of information diversification, which improves organizational performance (Koka & Prescott, 2002) [27].

Structural holes pay more attention to the relationship model between organizations, emphasizing the characteristics of indirect organizational connections. According to Burt's network structure hole theory (2004), investment institutions occupying network structure holes can gain more opportunities to access non-redundant information, knowledge, and resources [28]. Hans (2008) pointed out that the maximization of network structure holes means the minimization of redundant connections between partners, which promotes the diversification, heterogeneity, and non-redundancy of knowledge and information in the network, improve the effectiveness of information circulation, and promote performance improvement [29]. Mors (2010) showed that the biggest advantage that an organization's structural holes bring to an organization is the novelty and diversity of information, which is conducive to the development of technological innovation activities [30]. Zaheer & Soda (2009) indicated that the network structure hole enables organizations to reach more bilateral non-connected partners and is more accessible to diverse information, knowledge, ideas, and resources, thus enabling access to diverse information flows, which in turn enhances the organization performance [31]. Based on these ideas, this paper proposes the following assumptions:

H2a: Heterogeneous knowledge learning plays a mediatory role between centrality and investment performance.

H2b: Heterogeneous knowledge learning plays a mediatory role between structural holes and investment performance.

Structural embedding represents the network location of an investment institution and represents the "pipeline" of access and exchange of information and resources (Cartwright, 2002) [32], affecting the search for heterogeneous knowledge. However, the difference in investment performance also depends on the migration of network knowledge, which is inseparable from the relationship between investment institutions. Structure embedding provides an opportunity for organizations to access heterogeneous knowledge, whereas relationship embedding determines whether an organization takes advantage of these opportunities to achieve the migration of the sought heterogeneous knowledge. Burt (1992) pointed out that weakly coupled and non-redundant knowledge (heterogeneous knowledge) is related rather than causal. Hansen (1999) suggested that according to Burt (1992), strong ties may still produce heterogeneous, non-redundant knowledge, and empirical studies have shown that strong linkage can considerably promote the transfer of heterogeneous and non-coding knowledge. Kohli & Jaworski (1990) indicated that the internalization of knowledge learned between partners is an important factor in the effective improvement of performance through relationship embedding, that is, only the profound understanding and absorption of information with other network members, which can be transformed into a competitive advantage to improve organizational performance effectively [33]. Although Granovetter (1992) argued that weak relationships can bring non-redundant, non-repetitive information, knowledge, and resources to the enterprise, strong relationships are the opposite. However, in the Chinese context, the knowledge brought by weak relationships has only quantitative advantages and lacks qualitative advantages. The process of knowledge learning involves the search for and migration of knowledge. The search for knowledge is the only channel for information acquisition. The transformation of information into performance also requires the transfer of knowledge, which means improvement of knowledge. Studies have shown that in a relationship governance environment, only organizations with frequent, close relationships and high trust can provide and share important information (Bian, 1997) [9]. Therefore, as mentioned above, structural embedding only means searching for heterogeneous knowledge, and relational embedding is the basis for realizing the transfer of these heterogeneous knowledge. Rindfleisch & Moorman (2001) suggested that early relationship embedding is the intensity of relationship between individual actors and is an excessive simplification of interorganizational relationships. Organizations are multiple roles at the same time. Organizational structure is complex and changeable. Through empirical research in the context of organization, strong relationships will bring more differentiated knowledge [20]. Therefore, this paper argues that relationship embedding provides conditions for implicit, non-coding, heterogeneous knowledge between investment organizations and organizational networks.

Uzzi (1997) pointed out that relational embedding includes three dimensions of trust, information sharing, and common problem solving and suggested that the trust dimension in relationship embedding is an important factor to promote knowledge transfer. Spekman et al. (1998) indicated that the number of alliances grow rapidly, but the performance of the alliance is low. One of the most important reasons is the lack of trust [34]. Trust is an important foundation for the formation of a cooperative network and an important social capital, which can reduce the incidence of speculation between organizations and reduce transaction costs (Hoang & Rothaermel, 2005) [35]. Moreover, trust can effectively promote the exchange and integration of knowledge among network members (Uzzi, 1997) and promote the transfer of knowledge. Oliver (2007) pointed out that the role of non-redundant information brought about by structural embedding is affected by trust variables between organizations [36]. With the deepening of the relationship between the two parties, the direct benefit brought by frequent contacts and exchanges is the deepening of trust between the two sides (Capaldo, 2007) [37]. This kind of relationship will help reduce opportunistic risks and will also help investment institutions to obtain rich and diverse knowledge of partners (Shi Lin et al., 2017) [38]. Grant (1996) [39] found that strong relationships between organizations remarkably improved the efficiency of organizations in discovering, acquiring, and absorbing new knowledge.

McEvily & Marcus (2005) found that the establishment of information sharing mechanisms between alliances facilitates the acquisition of heterogeneous knowledge and information [40]. The reason is that the deepening of information sharing enables organizations to share knowledge better in a timely manner and to promote the acquisition of new knowledge. Furthermore, new knowledge can be applied effectively and quickly due to the excavation and exchange of deep knowledge between organizations. A weak relationship is conducive to the search of knowledge, but it is not conducive to the sharing and transfer of knowledge, especially the use of complex knowledge (Hansen, 1999). Whereas a strong relationship is the opposite because organizations with strong relationships tend to share important, relevant, and cutting-edge knowledge and information. De Clercq (2003) pointed out that the same type of investment (investing in a certain industry) will have a "learning effect" on investment institutions. Investment institutions can improve their ability to identify, manage, and serve the invested enterprises through the knowledge and information learned in the previous investment, instead of relying only on the cooperative institutions [41]. This finding shows that the learning of heterogeneous knowledge depends more on partners.

Hansen (1999) believes that long-term and frequent contact and communication between organizations have a benefit on solving problems together. As time passes and the understanding of both parties deepens, they gradually form behavioral norms and languages suitable for cooperation between the two parties, which invisibly promote the transfer of tacit knowledge on both sides. McEvily & Marcus (2005) pointed out that an important feature of a common problem solving between organizations is feedback to the problem. By organizing feedback from both parties on the issue, the learning ability of both organizations is improved, the sensitivity to new knowledge perception and accuracy of grasping are enhanced, and the rational and effective use of new knowledge is promoted. As the mechanism for joint problem solving between organizations becomes more flawless, organizational partners will be more tacit, which can promote transfer of knowledge more efficiently, especially non-coding, implicit, non-redundant, and heterogeneous knowledge among organizations. The characteristics of the specialized knowledge acquired by venture capital institutions indicate the non-coding and complex characteristics of interagency knowledge transfer. In the case of strong links, investment institutions can spend more time and energy to gain and explain complex knowledge clearly. Granovetter (1992) also pointed out that "stronger connections with stronger motivations provide help and are generally more dependable." Therefore, strong links promote a two-way interaction between organizations (Leonard-Barton & Sinha, 2017) [42]. More opportunities and motivations are present between strong organizations to discuss, guide, and feedback. This two-way interaction promotes the migration and absorption of deep heterogeneous knowledge within directly connected organizations. Based on these concepts, this paper proposes the following assumptions:

H2c: Heterogeneous knowledge learning plays a mediatory role between relationship embedding and investment performance.

3   Research Design

3.1   Data Sample Matching

The sample from this paper comes from two major Chinese venture capital information databases: CVSource and Zero2IPO. The structure of these two databases is similar to the database of the US venture capital industry, VentureXpert of Thomson Reuters, which has been used extensively in research. The data in these two databases is available for a fee. Both CVSource database and Zero2IPO database provide basic information of VCFs, investment events and exit events of various industries over the years, so the corresponding data tables include VCFs information table, investment event table and exit event table. This study refers to the practices of predecessors (Gu & Lu, 2014), [43] matching the two databases to avoid missing information from a single database. This study uses data from venture capital investments in China from January 1, 1999 to December 31, 2014. Selecting the data from January 1, 1999 can ensure the maximum amount of sample data and minimize errors caused by missing samples. The limit for sample data collection (December 31, 2014) is based on previous studies(Gu & Lu, 2014; Matusik & Fitza, 2012), [43, 44] leaving three years to observe investment performance.

By matching the CVSourse database with the Zero2IPO data and deleting the missing data, a total of 2,942 investment dealings for 2,345 companies are obtained from 942 investment institutions.

The data in the two databases are processed as follows:

First, the corresponding raw data in the two databases are processed according to the following procedures: (1) delete the PE-PIPE sample in the investment event table (the investee in this sample is a listed start-up enterprise); (2) delete The investment event table contains samples with ambiguous information such as "undisclosed company name" and "undisclosed investor"; (3) delete duplicate records in the venture capital information table, investment event table and exit event table; (4) Relevant data of the same VCFs in the same round in the consolidated event table (some VCFs use two or more funds to invest in the invested companies, and in the original sample, the VCFs appear multiple times in the same round). Second, after preliminary processing of the original data of the two databases, the corresponding tables are matched, that is, the VCFs information table, investment event table and exit event table in the two databases are matched respectively to avoid information omission. Third, the matched VCFs information table, investment event table, and exit event table are matched to obtain the final complete sample.

3.2 Mediating Effect Test Model and Steps

The commonly used mediating estimation method is Causal Steps. According to the formula:

$$Y' = cX + e_1 \tag{1}$$

$$M = aX + e_2 \tag{2}$$

$$Y'' = c'X + bM + e_3 \tag{3}$$

In the mediating effect model of the continuous dependent variable, the regression coefficient of M to X (the scale of the continuous variable), the regression coefficient of Y to M (Logit scale), and the regression coefficient of Y to X are not on the same scale. Therefore, the existence of mediating effects cannot be tested simply via dealing with the mediating effects of continuous variables. Therefore, this study follows the proposal of MacKinnon & Dwyer (1993) [45] and MacKinnon (2008) [46] to achieve the equalization of the regression coefficients through standardized conversion. The conversion method is as follows:

$$\text{var}\left(Y'\right) = c^2\text{var}(X) + \pi^2/3 \tag{4}$$

$$\text{var}\left(Y''\right) = c'^2\text{var}(X) + b^2\text{var}(M) + 2c'b\text{cov}(X, M) + \pi^2/3 \tag{5}$$

$$b^{std} = b \cdot \frac{SD(M)}{SD(Y'')} \tag{6}$$

$$c^{std} = c \cdot \frac{SD(X)}{SD(Y')} \tag{7}$$

$$c'^{std} = c' \cdot \frac{SD(X)}{SD(Y'')} \tag{8}$$

The specific steps for the mediating effect test, in which the dependent variable is a dichotomous variable, and the independent and intermediate variables are continuous variables are as follows:

Step 1: Regression Analysis

First, according to Formula (1), the logistic regression of the dependent variable Y on the independent variable X is obtained, and the estimated value of c and the corresponding standard error SEc are obtained. Second, the regression of M to X is performed according to Formula (2), and the estimated value of a and the corresponding standard error SEa are obtained. Finally, according to Formula (3), the logistic regression of Y to X and M is calculated to obtain b and c' and the corresponding standard error SEb and SE c'.

Step 2: Standardization

We calculate the standard deviation and the variance of X, M, Y', Y'', and the covariance of X and M. The standard deviation, variance, and covariance of X and M are obtained from the original data. According to Formulas (4) and (5), we can obtain the variance of Y' and Y''. Then, the regression coefficients are normalized according to Formulas (6) to (8).

Step 3: Sobel Test

The standard error corresponding to the mediation effect is:

$$SE\left(ab^{std}\right) = \sqrt{(b^{std})^2 (SE(a^{std}))^2 + (a^{std})^2 (SE(b^{std}))^2}$$ Sobel test z $= ab^{std}/SE\left(ab^{std}\right)$. When $|z| > 1.96$, the mediating effect is significant. The ratio of mediating effects to total effects is: $ab^{std}/\left(ab^{std} + c'^{std}\right)$.

3.3 Variable Measure

Dependent Variable

The dependent variable of this study is the investment performance of China's venture capital institutions. Ideally, income indicators should be used to measure investment performance. However, by examining the samples of CVSource and Zero2IPO, commonly used variables for measuring investment performance, such as internal rate of return and multiples of returns, are found to be seriously deficient. Therefore, the successful exit of venture capital institutions is used as a proxy variable for investment performance (Cochrane, 2005; Lerner, 2000) [47, 48]. Initial public offerings, mergers and acquisitions, and equity transfers are three types of exit methods commonly used by venture capital institutions. Therefore, in the sample observation period, if the institution withdraws by any of these three exit methods, the institution is considered to have successfully exited.

Independent Variable
In the study, the social network analysis software Ucinet6 is used to calculate the relevant variables.

(1)   Structural Embedding

Most studies have shown that the size of the data window does not theoretically affect the fifinal result. According to the predecessors' practice, this study selects the data window calculated by the relevant variables for four years, which can ensure the stability of network establishment and avoid the obsolescence of the information caused by the long data window.

Centrality: This study adopts a more comprehensive degree of centrality, which refers to the ratio of the number of alliance institutions directly connected with the focused investment institutions to the total number of network nodes.

Structural holes: Structural holes refer to non-redundant connections between actors (Burt, 1992). According to Burt (1992), the four indicators that measure structural holes are effective size, efficiency, limits, and ratings. The effective scale (effsize) considers the number of structural holes and network size; thus, it can better reflect the structural hole positions of individuals in the network. Accordingly, this study uses an effective scale to measure structural holes. The effective scale is calculated by the total number of nodes directly related to node i minus the average number of connections of all nodes in the individual center network of node i.

(2)   Relationship Embedding

Relational embeddedness (relational) refers to the practice of De Clercq et al. (2008), which refers to the number of contacts in the time window [49]. For example, from January 1, 2001 to December 31, 2004, the total number of cooperative investments with each partner is the degree of embedded relationship of the investment institution in 2004.

Mediator Variable: Heterogeneous Knowledge Learning
According to the Herfidhal Index, we use the differentiation of the investment industry as a proxy variable for heterogeneous knowledge learning (Zheng & Xia, 2017) [50]. The calculation formula is: Hete $= 1 - \sum_{j=1}^{N}(T_j/T)^2$, where T_j represents the number of companies investing in a certain industry, and T represents the total number of enterprises invested by the institution. The closer the value is to 1, the more diverse the investment industry is, and the higher the knowledge heterogeneity is. On the contrary, the closer

the value is to 0, the more centralized the investment industry is, and the lower the knowledge heterogeneity is.

Control variable

Considering existing research at home and abroad, we control other factors that affect the successful exit of venture capital. (1) The age of investment institutions (vcage): The longer a venture capital institution is established, the more experience it will accumulate. (2) The size of the investment institution (vcsize): The logarithm of the investment fund is used as the proxy variable for the size of the investment institution. (3) Stage of investment: Four types of venture capital investment are used in this paper, namely seed stage, initial stage, expansion stage, and maturity stage. The stage of venture capital is the key factor that determines the successful exit of the institution. With the gradual maturity of the financing enterprise and the gradual occupation of the market, the probability of successful exit of the venture capital institution will gradually increase. (4) Geographical proximity (geop): Considering the practice of Zheng & Xia (2017), this study constructs the dummy variable of geographical proximity, that is, when the investment institution and the invested enterprise are in the same province, the geop is set to 1, and vice versa. (5) Type of investment institution (type): Two types of investment institutions are present in the sample, namely Venture Capital and Private Equity. (6) Funding sources (fund): Three sources of venture capital are present in the sample: Chinese, foreign, and joint ventures. Therefore, according to the research needs, two dummy variables are set. When it belongs to a certain resource type, it takes 1; otherwise, it takes 0. (7) Industry dummy variables (industry): This study classifies the industry of venture capital according to the constructs corresponding virtual variables. (8) Time dummy variable (year), which controls the change of risk investment in the time dimension and the change of the external macroeconomic environment.

4   Descriptive Statistics and Correlation Analysis

Table 1 is a descriptive statistic of the relevant variables and a Pearson correlation coefficient table. Table 1 shows that relationship embedding has a significant positive correlation with investment performance. The correlation coefficient is 0.121 ($p < 0.01$). Hypothesis H1c has been preliminarily verified. Centrality and heterogeneous knowledge learning have no significant positive correlation with investment performance. The correlation coefficients are 0.018 and 0.021. Structural holes and investment performance have no significant negative correlation, pending further examination. Additionally, results of the multicollinearity test show that the variance expansion factor VIF is less than the threshold of 10, indicating that no multicollinearity problem exists between variables.

The mean of investment performance is 0.244 and the standard deviation is 0.430, indicating that the performance of Chinese venture capital institutions is low. The mean value of variable heterogeneous knowledge learning is 0.530, and the standard deviation is 0.246, indicating that the knowledge learning of Chinese venture capital institutions tends to be homogeneous. The mean value of the variable structure hole is 5.168, and the variance is 8.311, indicating that the partners among Chinese venture capital institutions are relatively fixed and the alliance network is relatively sparse.

Table 1. Descriptive statistics of related variables and Pearson correlation coefficient

Variable	Success	Hete	Degree	Effsize	Mean	SD	VIF
Success	1				0.244	0.430	–
Hete	0.018	1			0.530	0.246	1.15
Degree	0.021	0.316***	1		0.007	0.009	9.61
Effsize	−0.012	0.303***	0.938***	1	5.168	8.311	8.81
Relation	0.121***	0.179***	0.403***	0.334***	2.948	2.917	1.26
Vcage	0.067***	0.095***	0.079***	0.038**	13.160	13.672	1.20
Vcsize	−0.002	0.019	−0.026	−0.021	6.374	0.922	1.01
stAge	0.234***	0.138***	0.015	0.024	2.998	0.791	1.08
Geop	−0.076***	−0.058***	−0.148***	−0.126***	0.332	0.471	1.15
Type	−0.116***	−0.053***	0.123***	0.098***	0.586	0.493	1.12
Fund	0.033*	0.021	0.134***	0.069***	1.349	0.528	1.28
Variable	relation	vcage	vcsize	stage	geop	type	fund
Relation	1						
Vcage	−0.043**	1					
Vcsize	−0.057***	0.018	1				
Stage	0.101***	0.014	0.039**	1			
Geop	−0.095***	−0.098***	0.004	−0.079***	1		
Type	0.036*	−0.018	0.011	−0.201***	0.206***	1	
Fund	0.091***	0.378***	−0.011	−0.060***	−0.245***	0.026	1

Note: *, **, *** indicate the level of significance of 10%, 5%, and 1%, respectively.

5   Regression Results

Table 2 presents the analysis results of the intrinsic influence mechanism of China's venture capital network embedding on investment performance under the mediatory role of organizational learning. The first step models 1–3 in Table 2 test whether centrality, structural hole, and relationship embedding have a significant relationship with investment performance. Then, coefficient c is obtained. In the second step model 4–6, heterogeneous knowledge learning is used as the dependent variable, and centrality, structural hole, and relationship embedding are sequentially used as independent variables to obtain coefficient a. In the third step model 7–9, investment performance is used as the dependent variable, centrality, structural hole, and relationship embedding are used as independent variables, and heterogeneous knowledge learning is used as a mediating variable. Simultaneously, the independent variables and the mediating variables are placed into the model. The first and third steps are estimated using the OLS method, and the second step is estimated using the Logit method. The Wald chi2 (F value) statistic for all models is significant at the 0.01 level, indicating that each measurement model has statistical power. Table 3 is a Sobel test of the mediating effect.

Table 2. Mediating effect results of organizational learning

	model	1	2	3	4	5	6	7	8	9
		first step			second step			third step		
	DV	performance			Hete			performance		
	vcage	0.0025	0.0026	0.0049	0.0018***	0.0018***	0.0021***	0.0029	0.0029	0.0054
		(0.00)	(0.00)	(0.00)	(0.00)	(0.00)	(0.00)	(0.00)	(0.00)	(0.00)
	vcsize	-0.0476	-0.0488	-0.0327	0.0054	0.0051	0.006	-0.0475	-0.0488	-0.0322
		(0.05)	(0.05)	(0.05)	(0.00)	(0.00)	(0.00)	(0.05)	(0.05)	(0.05)
	stage	0.7797***	0.7776***	0.7672***	0.0126**	0.0127**	0.0072	0.7808***	0.7785***	0.7673***
		(0.07)	(0.07)	(0.07)	(0.01)	(0.01)	(0.01)	(0.07)	(0.07)	(0.07)
CV	geop	-0.139	-0.1498	-0.1247	0.0006	-0.0018	-0.0092	-0.1398	-0.1508	-0.1277
		(0.11)	(0.11)	(0.11)	(0.01)	(0.01)	(0.01)	(0.11)	(0.11)	(0.11)
	type	-0.4902***	-0.4716***	-0.4913***	-0.0235***	-0.0198**	-0.0078	-0.4966***	-0.4759***	-0.4951***
		(0.10)	(0.10)	(0.10)	(0.01)	(0.01)	(0.01)	(0.10)	(0.10)	(0.10)
	fund_2	-0.1504	-0.1245	-0.1937	-0.0064	0.0019	0.0053	-0.1521	-0.1245	-0.1925
		(0.13)	(0.12)	(0.13)	(0.01)	(0.01)	(0.01)	(0.13)	(0.12)	(0.13)
	fund_3	0.1943	0.1925	0.1711	0.0126	0.0133	0.0086	0.1945	0.1928	0.1692
		(0.29)	(0.29)	(0.29)	(0.02)	(0.02)	(0.02)	(0.29)	(0.29)	(0.29)
	cons	-4.3314***	-4.2684***	-4.4868***	0.5045***	0.5136***	0.5337***	-4.1891***	-4.1565***	-4.3005***
		(0.46)	(0.46)	(0.46)	(0.05)	(0.06)	(0.06)	(0.49)	(0.49)	(0.49)
	degree	13.5515**			6.6268***			14.9704***		
		(5.51)			(0.55)			(5.61)		
IV	effsize		0.0098*			0.0062***			0.0109*	

(continued)

Table 2. (*continued*)

relation		(0.01)		(0.00)		(0.01)		(0.01)	(0.01)
MV hete	0.0092*** (0.02)		0.0922*** (0.02)		(0.00)	0.0119*** (0.00)	-0.2213 (0.22)	-0.1717 (0.22)	0.0951*** (0.02) -0.2691 (0.22)
Wald chi2/F	323.70***	322.21***	335.05***	34.37***	34.43***	44.78***	325.08***	323.18***	337.10***
Pseudo R2/R2	0.1224	0.1215	0.1312	0.2471	0.2374	0.2194	0.1228	0.1217	0.1316
Log pseudolikelihood	-1432.00	-1433.52	-1417.77				-1431.49	-1433.21	-1416.99
model	Logit	Logit	Logit	OLS	OLS	OLS	Logit	Logit	Logit
N	2935	2935	2935	2935	2935	2935	2935	2935	2935

Note: Robust standard errors are in parentheses; *, **, *** indicate the level of significance of 10%, 5%, and 1%, respectively; all models control industry-fixed effects and time-fixed effects.

Table 3. Sobel test

Hypothesis	cov(X,M)	SD(Y')	SD(Y")	ab^{std}	SE(ab^{std})*	z = ab^{std}/SE(ab^{std})
H2a	0.0007	1.6541	1.6553	−0.2179	23188.7103	9.3949
H2b	0.6200	1.6483	1.6488	−0.0002	0.0201	7905.6886
H2c	0.1287	1.6811	1.6823	−0.0005	0.0729	6417.5601

Note: SE(abstd)* is the corresponding value × 10–6.

Tables 2 indicate that model 1 in the first step test shows that a significant positive relationship exists between centrality and investment performance (c = 13.5515, P < 0.05), assuming H1a is supported; model 4 in the second step test shows that centrality has a significant positive impact on heterogeneous knowledge learning (a = 6.6268, P < 0.01); in the third step test, model 7 shows that after adding the independent and mediating variables, only the coefficient of the independent variable is significant (c = 14.9704, P < 0.01). According to the previous mediation effect process, the Sobel test in Table 4 shows that |z| = 9.3949, which is greater than 1.96, assuming that H2a is supported. Similarly, model 2 in the first step test shows that a significant positive relationship exists between structural holes and investment performance (c = 0.0098, P < 0.1), assuming H1b is supported. In the second step, model 5 shows that the structural holes have a significant positive impact on heterogeneous knowledge learning (a = 0.0062, P < 0.01). In the third step test, model 8 shows that after adding the independent variable structure hole and the mediating variable heterogeneity knowledge learning, only the coefficient of independent variable is significant (c' = 0.0109, P < 0.1). According to the previous mediation effect process, the Sobel test in Table 4 shows that |z| = 7905.6886, greater than 1.96, assuming H2b is supported. In the first step, model 3 shows that a significant positive relationship exists between relationship embedding and investment performance (c = 0.0922, P < 0.01), assuming H1c is supported. In the second step, model 6 shows that structural holes have a significant positive impact on heterogeneous knowledge learning (a = 0.0119, P < 0.01). In the third step test, model 9 shows that after adding the independent variable, relationship embedding and mediating variable, heterogeneity knowledge learning, only the coefficient of independent variable is significant (c' = 0.0951, P < 0.01). According to the previous mediation effect process, the Sobel test in Table 4 shows that |z| = 6417.5601, which is greater than 1.96, assuming that H2c is supported. At this time, the mediatory effect of heterogeneous knowledge learning on the relationship between network embedding and investment performance has been supported.

As for the control variables, the age of investment institutions has no significant positive correlation with investment performance, and the age of investment institutions has a significant positive correlation with heterogeneous knowledge learning, indicating that as the age of institutions increases, the heterogeneity of knowledge learned by investment institutions increases, leading to the diversification of investment industry. The scale of investment institutions and investment performance has no significant negative correlation, and no significant positive relationship exists with the learning performance of heterogeneous knowledge learning. The investment stage and investment performance show a significant positive correlation, indicating that in the later stage, with the increase of information and stability of investment, the probability of successful exit of investment institutions significantly improves. The learning performance of investment stage and heterogeneous knowledge shows unsteady positive correlation, which means that with the development of investment stage, the accumulation of investment institution experience, and the grasp of market sensitivity, the investment institution tends to adopt the differentiation strategy.

6 Conclusion and Enlightenment

On the basis of the organizational learning and social network theories, this study conducts theoretical analysis and empirical research on the mechanism of the impact of network embedding on the performance of China's venture capital institutions and examines the mediating effects of different knowledge attributes. The main conclusions are as follows:

(1) In the study of the relationship between network embedding and investment performance, network embedding has a positive and significant impact on investment performance. From the perspective of structural embeddedness, investment institutions located at the center of the network have more information sources and opportunities to contact new information and enjoy more superiority, privilege, identity, and reputation. Thus, centrality can remarkably improve the performance of investment. Investment institutions occupying the positions of structural holes have access to broader information and knowledge, have the right of control and priority to use information, and can effectively reduce transaction costs and improve core business, thus improving investment performance. Relational embeddedness is conducive to the establishment of mutual trust, joint problem solving, and information sharing mechanisms, improving the transfer of knowledge, as well as the common encoding of tacit knowledge. It also reduces the opportunistic behavior of network investment funding institutions, which is conducive to improve the performance of investment institutions.

(2) The study also discovers the mediating role of heterogeneous knowledge learning. The learning of knowledge undergoes two stages: access and acquisition. Structural embeddedness provides knowledge and information search channels for the institution. Located at the center position, the investment institutions have direct contact with more information channels, which may come into contact with the heterogeneity of knowledge and information. Investment institutions that occupy the location of the structure hole have the advantage of information control, with more non-redundant information channels. Relational embeddedness provides the possibility for the transfer of heterogeneous knowledge searched through structural embedding. In the context of China with relationship governance characteristics, only with a strong relationship with frequent and close contacts can investment institutions be guaranteed to acquire knowledge. Investment institutions that learn heterogeneous knowledge through network embedding can effectively cope with market fluctuations, and more diversified investment opportunities can be obtained

to adapt to market trends, which is more conducive to the improvement of investment performance and is consistent with the research conclusion of Du Qianqian (2009) [51].

The conclusions of this paper have important theoretical implications for China's venture capital institutions network practice:

(1) Investment institutions should expand their knowledge network, strengthen collaborations with other investment institutions, upgrade the center position of their networks, increase the number of structural holes, eliminate the edge of the network position, strengthen liaison with other agencies, improve trust between organizations, improve information sharing, strengthen organizational learning capability, enhance search and transfer ability, and promote investment performance.

(2) To improve investment performance effectively, investment institutions should pay more attention to heterogeneous knowledge learning. Investment institutions should use network sources rationally, improve their center position, and increase structural holes, searching for more heterogeneous knowledge opportunity. Through relationship embedding, trust relationship, information sharing and problem-solving mechanisms among investment institutions are established to improve the ability to utilize heterogeneous knowledge and promote the improvement of investment performance.

References

1. Grant, R.M., Baden-Fuller, C.: A knowledge accessing theory of strategic alliances. J. Manag. Stud. **41**(1), 61–84 (2004)
2. Rodan, S., Galunic, C.: More than network structure: how knowledge heterogeneity influences managerial performance and innovativeness. Strateg. Manag. J. **25**(6), 541–562 (2004)
3. Hochberg, Y.V., Lindsey, L.A., Westerfield, M.M.: Economic Ties: Evidence from Venture Capital Networks (2011)
4. Alexy, O.T., Block, J.H., Sandner, P., et al.: Social capital of venture capitalists and start-up funding. Small Bus. Econ. **39**(4), 835–851 (2012)
5. Meuleman, M., Wright, M., Manigart, S., et al.: Private equity syndication: agency costs, reputation and collaboration. J. Bus. Financ. Acc. **36**(5–6), 616–644 (2009)
6. Bubna, A., Das, S.R., Prabhala, N.R.: What types of syndicate partners do venture capitalists prefer? Evidence from VC communities. Indian School of Business, Leavey School of Business, Robert H. Smith School of Business (2013)
7. Hansen, M.T.: The search-transfer problem: the role of weak ties in sharing knowledge across organization subunits. Adm. Sci. Q. **44**(1), 82–111 (1999)
8. Moran, P.: Structural vs. relational embeddedness: social capital and managerial performance. Strateg. Manag. J. **26**(12), 1129–1151 (2005)
9. Bian, Y.: Bringing strong ties back in: Indirect ties, network bridges, and job searches in China. Am. Sociol. Rev. **62**(3): 366–385 (1997)
10. Zaheer, A., Bell, G.G.: Benefiting from network position: firm capabilities, structural holes, and performance. Strate. Manag. J. **26**(9), 809–825 (2005)
11. Wasserman, S., Faust, K.: Social Network Analysis: Methods and applications. Cambridge University Press, Cambridge (1994)

12. Powell, W.W., Koput, K.W., Smith-Doerr, L.: Interorganizational collaboration and the locus of innovation: networks of learning in biotechnology. Adm. Sci. Q. **41**(1), 116–145 (1996)
13. Brown, J.S., Duguid, P.: Knowledge and organization: a social-practice perspective. Organ. Sci. **12**(2), 198–213 (2001)
14. McEvily, B., Zaheer, A.: Bridging ties: a source of firm heterogeneity in competitive capabilities. Strateg. Manag. J. **20**(12), 1133–1156 (1999)
15. Burt, R.S.: Structural Holes: The Social Structure of Competition. Harvard University Press, Boston (1992)
16. Gnyawali, D.R., Madhavan, R.: Cooperative networks and competitive dynamics: a structural embeddedness perspective. Acad. Manag. Rev. **26**(3), 431–445 (2001)
17. Soda, G., Usai, A., Zaheer, A.: Network memory: the influence of past and current networks on performance. Acad. Manag. J. **47**(6), 893–906 (2004)
18. Granovetter, M.: Economic institutions as social constructions - a framework for analysis. Acta Sociol **35**(1), 3–11 (1992)
19. Uzzi, B.: Social structure and competition in interfirm networks. Adm. Sci. Q. **42**(2), 417–418 (1997)
20. Rindfleisch, A., Moorman, C.: The acquisition and utilization of information in new product alliances: a strength-of-ties perspective. J. Mark. **65**(2), 1–18 (2001)
21. Halinen, A., Tornroos, J.Å.: The role of embeddedness in the evolution of business networks.Scand. J. Manag. **14**(3), 187–205 (1998)
22. Rowley, T., Behrens, D., Krackhardt, D.: Redundant governance structures: an analysis of structural and relational embeddedness in the steel and semiconductor industries. Strateg. Manag. J. **21**(3), 369–386 (2000)
23. McFadyen, M.A., Semadeni, M., Cannella, A.A.: Value of strong ties to disconnected others: examining knowledge creation in biomedicine. Organ. Sci. **20**(3), 552–564 (2009)
24. Koka, B.R., Prescott, J.E.: designing alliance networks: the influence of network position, environmental change, and strategy on firm performance. Strateg. Manag. J. **29**(6), 639–661 (2008)
25. Hoskisson, R.E., Hitt, M.A., Hill, C.W.L.: Managerial incentives and investment in R&D in large multiproduct firms. Organ. Sci. **4**(2), 325–341 (1993)
26. Polidoro, F., Ahuja, G., Mitchell, W.: When the social structure enhances WS competitive incentives: the effects of network embeddedness on joint venture dissolution. Acad. Manag. J. **54**(1), 203-223 (2011)
27. Koka, B.R., Prescott, J.E.: Strategic alliances as social capital: a multidimensional view. Strateg. Manag. J. **23**(9), 795–816 (2002)
28. Burt, R.S.: Structural holes and good ideas. Am. J. Sociol. **110**(2), 349–399 (2004)
29. Hans, T.W.F.: Structural holes, technological resources, and innovation: a longitudinal study of an interfirm R&D network. Acad. Manag. Ann. Meet. Proc. **2008**(1), 1–6 (2008)
30. Mors, M.L.: Innovation in a global consulting firm: when the problem is too much diversity. Strateg. Manag. J. **31**(8), 841–872 (2010)
31. Zaheer, A., Soda, G.: Network evolution: the origins of structural holes. Entrep. Res. J. **54**(1), 1–31 (2009)
32. Cartwright, P.A.: Only converge: networks and connectivity in the information economy. Bus. Strateg. Rev. **13**(2), 59–64 (2002)
33. Kohli, A.K., Jaworski, B.J.: Market orientation: the construct, research propositions, and managerial implications. J. Mark. **54**(2), 1–18 (1990)
34. Spekman Forbes, III I.M.R.E.T.M.L.A.T.C.: Alliance management: a view from the past and a look to the future. J. Manag. Stud. **35**(6), 747–772 (1998)
35. Hoang, H., Rothaermel, F.T.: the effect of general and partner-specific alliance experience on joint R&D project performance. Acad. Manag. J. **48**(2), 332–345 (2005)

36. Oliver, A.L.: Reflections on "Brokerage and Closure." Social Netw. **29**(2), 330–339 (2007)
37. Capaldo, A.: Network structure and innovation: the leveraging of a dual network as a distinctive relational capability. Strateg. Manag. J. **28**(6), 585–608 (2007)
38. 石琳, 党兴华, 韩瑾. 风险投资机构关系嵌入、知识专业化对成功退出的影响:一个交互效应. 财贸研究 **28**(11), 79–87 (2017)
39. Grant, R.M.: Toward a knowledge-based theory of the fifirm. Strateg. Manag. J. **17**(S2), 109–122 (1996)
40. McEvily, B., Marcus, A.: Embedded ties and the acquisition of competitive capabilities. Strateg. Manag. J. **26**(11), 1033–1055 (2005)
41. Clercq, D.D., Sapienza, H.J., Crijns, H.: The internationalization of small and medium-sized firms: the role of organizational learning effort and entrepreneurial orientation. **24**(63), S13–S4 (2003)
42. Leonard-Barton, D., Sinha, D.K.: Developer-user interaction and user satisfaction in internal technology transfer. Acad. Manag. J. **36**(5), 1125–1139 (2017)
43. Gu, Q., Lu, X.: Unraveling the mechanisms of reputation and alliance formation: a study of venture capital syndication in China. Strateg. Manag. J. **35**(5), 739–750 (2014)
44. Matusik, S.F., Fitza, M.A.: Diversification in the venture capital industry: leveraging knowledge under uncertainty. Strateg. Manag. J. **33**(4), 407–426 (2012)
45. Mackinnon, D.P., Dwyer, J.H., MacKinnon D.P., Dwyer, J.H.: Estimating mediated effects in prevention studies. Eval. Rev. **17**(2), 144–158 (1993)
46. Mackinnon, D.: Introduction to Statistical Mediation Analysis. London Lawrence Erlbaum Associates, New York (2008)
47. Cochrane, J.H.: The risk and return of venture capital. J. Finan. Econ. **75**(1), 3–52 (2005)
48. Lerner, J.: Assessing the contribution of venture capital to innovation. RAND J. Econ. **31**(4), 674–692 (2000)
49. De Clercq, D., Dimov, D.: Internal knowledge development and external knowledge access in venture capital investment performance. J. Manag. Stud. **45**(3), 585–612 (2008)
50. Zheng, Y., Xia, J.: Resource dependence and network relations: a test of venture capital investment termination in China. J. Manag. Stud. (2017)
51. Du, Q.: Birds of a Feather or Celebrating Differences? The Formation and Impacts of Venture Capital Syndication. Social Science Electronic Publishing (2009)

Advances in Artificial Intelligence for Data Processing and Analysis in Online Social Environments

Contributions and Limitations About the Use of Deep Learning for Skin Diagnosis: A Review

Eduardo L. L. Nascimento^(⊠) (ID) and Angel Freddy Godoy Viera (ID)

Postgraduate Program in Information Science - Federal University of Santa Catarina, Florianópolis, SC 88040-900, Brazil
nascimento.lln@gmail.com

Abstract. The aim of this study is to analyze the characteristics and applicability of Deep Learning (DL) models for the diagnosis of skin diseases. This study is characterized as a bibliographic review, exploratory-descriptive, qualitative in nature. Primary data was reported in the article databases. A total of 37 articles were analyzed to characterize the use of DL for the diagnosis of skin diseases. The survey results that public datasets access is mostly used in these surveys are (86%). The data collection that stood out was ISIC - International Skin Imaging Collaboration (54%). Greater commonly used data types in these models are images. Ultimately used model is the Convolutional Neural Network (CNN) and the uttermost used pre-trained model was ResNet. The most used techniques in the articles, in addition to classification (73%), focused on data segmentation (35%) and feature extraction (24%). The evaluation indicators that stand out are accuracy (89%), sensitivity (75%), and specificity (67%). The literature indicated that the approaches of studies that use DL for classification of skin diseases are very promising, however, practically all of the applied technologies have a greater need for interaction with clinical practices. As a suggestion for different works, studies that approach the task of DL work for diagnosis of different ethnic groups and their solutions for the democratization of such technologies.

Keywords: Deep learning · Skin lesion classification · Skin lesion diagnostics · Skin disease · Dermatopathology · Image recognition

1 Introduction

Emerging technological alternatives that have the ability to impact healthcare are Deep Learning (DL) applications. With the improvement of these practices in recent years models based on DL are already presented as possible allies for the identification of diseases such as COVID-19 [1, 2], in addition to possible applications in medical areas such as: psychiatry [3], ophthalmology [4], oncology [5, 6] and dermatology [7].

The traditional task of recognizing skin lesions consists of several steps, where the automated system is typically trained on pre-processed images with a known diagnosis, which allows the prediction of new specimens in defined classes [8].

A. L. Pinto and R. Arencibia-Jorge (Eds.): DIONE 2022, LNICST 452, pp. 133–149, 2022.
https://doi.org/10.1007/978-3-031-22324-2_11

In the development of DL models some tasks are performed to increase performance, such as: Feature Extraction, Data Segmentation, Data Augmentation, Transfer Learning, etc. Feature Extraction is the process of simplifying a large dataset to make it more suitable for further processing [9–11].

Data Augmentation (DA) is another widely used approach that consists of expanding the amount of training data [12]. In this way, AD seeks to solve the problem of a small dataset for training of skin diseases, in addition to improving the generalization capacity of the model. Some tasks such as: rotation, mirroring, and adding artifacts are tricks used to increase the amount of dataset elements [13, 14].

The use of pre-trained models (Transfer learning) is another technique applied in these models where characteristics of other models are incorporated into the model under development with similar objectives [15–18].

Despite promising Deep Learning systems to aid in skin diagnosis, several challenges are proposed for the adoption of these technologies in a safe and effective way, when it comes to the health of the population [19].

Another point that deserves attention is the availability of specialized professionals in remote or rural areas is a problem faced in several countries. When we combine technologies to support medical diagnosis based on techniques such as DL and Telehealth service this combination allows us to overcome obstacles such as time, cost and distance to provide health care in a supervised way regardless of how far these health services are from the population [20].

The research question that guided this study is: How is Deep Learning used in the process of diagnosing skin diseases?

The objective of this study was to analyze and describe the scientific literature on the subject of diagnosis of skin diseases that use deep learning identified in the bases of selected articles.

As specific objectives: 1) to observe if the article presents the structural criteria for the elaboration of the scientific production, 2) to analyze if the research presents the technical aspects for the construction of the experiment, and 3) to identify if the study presents/informs the context of application, users and/or integration with clinical practices.

2 Literature Review

Computer-aided diagnostic (CAD) systems allow accurate detection, segmentation and classification of skin lesions. Thus, in clinical applications a CAD system can be a great ally to support medical decisions [21].

CAD models developed for skin diseases are often image-trained, others also use metadata and clinical data [15, 22, 23]. Models based on convolutional neural network (CNN) architectures were developed with promising results revealing good diagnostic accuracy [24].

Shoieb, Youssef and Aly [25] present an improved CAD system using a hybrid model for skin lesion identification composed of CNN (designed as a feature extractor) combined with a multiclass Support Vector Machine (SVM) based classifier model.

The results showed superior performance compared to other models identified in the literature.

However, automatic segmentation of lesions on dermoscopic images is a challenge. Some studies compare the accuracy of these models with health professionals at a specialized level, others also compare it with non-specialized professionals [26].

Esteva et al. [7] suggest a model for classifying skin lesions using CNN full connect from images and later evaluate the performance of the model comparing it to 21 dermatologists.

Automated classification of skin lesions through images is a challenging task due to the variability in the appearance of skin lesions. It is extremely difficult due to the complexities of the skin tone, color, skin hair and the presence of other artifacts contained in the images [27].

As for the applied techniques, Saker et al. [28] point out that most skin lesion segmentation approaches use models with a large number of parameters configuring a major obstacle for practical application in the clinical environment.

Majtner, Yayilgan and Hardeberg [8] addressed the effective use of the feature set extracted from pre-trained deep learning models - ImageNet. In this study the authors propose the improvement of a melanoma detection method based on the combination of linear discriminant analysis (LDA).

Saker et al. [28] presented a lightweight and efficient generative adversarial network model called MobileGAN, which basically seeks to extract relevant features with multiscale convolutional networks evaluated in two datasets ISBI 2017 [29] and ISIC 2018 [30]. In addition, the experimental results demonstrate that the proposed model provides results comparable to the state of the art of skin lesion segmentation in terms of precision and similarity coefficients.

There are studies that highlight the use of machine learning classifiers in the diagnosis of skin lesions and point to their importance in clinical practice as a promising proposal [31].

Polat and Koc [32] propose a hybrid model for automatic classification of skin diseases divided into seven classes, combining CNN with One-versus-All, using data from the HAM10000 dataset.

3 Methodology

As for the methodological procedures, this is an exploratory-descriptive bibliographic study characterized as an integrative review. Thus, this research aims to generate knowledge about the use of deep learning for the diagnosis of skin diseases as well as the identification of gaps in the scientific field and the formulation of proposals for further research.

The primary data comes from the limitations imposed by the researchers in the searches in available databases. The approach is a qualitative study, in the production of critical analysis performed at the time of selection and analysis of the set of articles. As for the technical aspects, it is classified as a bibliography research in its form of integrative literature review.

This research was divided into three stages: 1) definitions and delimitations of research strategies, 2) data collection selection and 3) data analysis. In the first stage, a research protocol was elaborated to guide the delimitations of the theme and strategies for defining the objectives and research proposal.

In the second stage, a search was carried out on the CAPES journals portal, between the 22nd and 26th of March 2021, only articles written in english and with a publication date between 01/01/2016 to 06/30/ 2021 was selected. The period of publication selected was the result of search tests with better adherence to the problem that involves this research and the feasibility of the proposal.

As a search strategy, only articles that contained the search terms in the title and abstract were selected. The bases selected for collecting the studies were: Scopus (18), Web of Science (24), PubMed (11) and IEEE Xplore (7). The selection of the bases was the one that offered the best return on the works related to the techniques addressed in this study and their relevance in the scientific field.

The search expression used: "deep learning" AND (skin lesion* OR "skin lesion classification" OR "skin lesion segmentation" OR "skin cancer" OR "skin disease" OR "dermatopathology"), which resulted in 60 preliminary articles.

Then, titles, abstracts and keywords were read. Articles that did not contain the application of models based on Deep Learning for the diagnosis of dermatitis were excluded.

Duplicate studies, articles that were not practical (experimental) and literature reviews were excluded and resulted in 37 articles that were identified at the end of each reference in the last item of this research with "[PB]".

In the third step, the systematization and analysis of data in electronic spreadsheets were carried out using MS Excel 2010.

In this way it was verified whether the abstract presents and elements of the article's structure such as: introductory section, methodological procedures results obtained sources used in the studies.

Analysis criteria: clarity, justification and consistency in the methodology used, if there is a description of the elements/procedures, statistical analysis of the data, indicators used in the study, and sample size (Table 1).

Regarding the conclusions, it was observed whether the articles present results consistent with the problem analyzed, allowing the reproduction of the experiment (Table 1).

As for the relevance of the research the approaches used and their characteristics, and the results obtained and their integration with clinical practices were analyzed. This last element seeks to understand whether there is an integration and/or understanding of these studies with the health context, also identifying the users of these technologies such as: specialized and non-specialized health professionals and the population that can use these health services.

Table 1. Article evaluation criteria:

Block 1. Evaluation of the article structure:
Is it clear about the unambiguous presentation of the problem studied?
Can the methodology used be reproduced in another experiment?
Does the work present the form of data collection?
Does the work inform the origin of the data used in the experiment? (public and/or private access)
Does the work present the size of the sample used?
Block 2. Evaluation of the technical aspects of the articles:
Does the work objectively present a justification for choosing the techniques used in the research?
What models are used in the experiments?
Which software libraries are used?
Do they present the evaluation indicators? Which?
Do you use metadata (or other types of data) in the experiment?
Block 3. Assessment of aspects of the health context:
Are the models concerned with the application of clinical practices?
Does the article inform/cite the participation of the health professional?
Does the study characterize/cite the population that gave rise to the training and testing data of the models?

Source: survey data.

4   Results and Discussion

The scientific aspects (Block 1) raised based on the structures of the articles indicate that 26 studies presented the problem studied in a clear and unambiguous way. As for the reproduction of the experiment, in 31 articles the methodology used can be reproduced in another study. The form of data collection was another criterion observed in only 25 studies and in 22 they adopted statistics to analyze the data.

Regarding the technical aspects of the articles (Block 2), 78% of the articles presented a clear justification for the choice of techniques used.

According to the bibliographic survey carried out, there are fundamental steps to build a Deep Learning model for the diagnosis of skin diseases, which are: 1) definition of the data collection (Data collections), 2) data preprocessing step (they are techniques such as: Data Segmentation, Feature Extraction, Data Augmentation and Data Aggregation), 3) training and testing steps performed in a classifier model, and 4) evaluation and results step. Visually, these steps were described in Fig. 1:

The datasets most used by the authors for training and testing were the International Skin Imaging Collaboration (ISIC) and its editions (freq. 20), followed by the dataset from the Centro de Dermatologia do Hospital Pedro Hispano (PH2) (freq. 5), both are publicly accessible (Table 2).

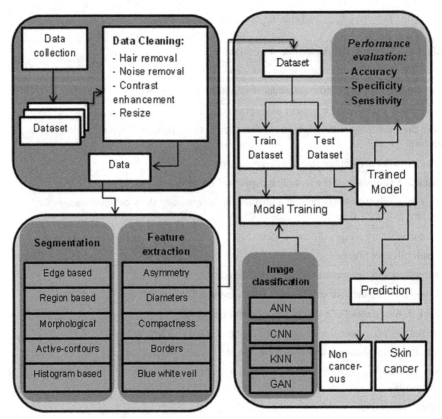

Fig. 1. The skin cancer diagnosis process. (Source: Adapted from Dildar (2021) [33]. ANN = Artificial neural network; CNN = Convolutional neural network; KNN = Kohonen self-organizing neural network; GAN = Generative adversarial neural network.)

Other data collections used by the authors were: HAM10000 (freq. 4) and with only 1 occurrence: Atlas of Dermoscopy Dataset (AtlasDerm), Dermnet Skin Disease Atlas dataset (Dermnet) and DreamQuest, all of which are publicly accessible (Table 3). The experiments that used data from public and private datasets (freq. 2) and only private (freq. 7).

As for the data collected in the studies, the research with data from the Taiwan National Health Insurance Research Database [34] stands out for the maximum amount, with 2 million images used in the experiment, while the minimum amount observed was 102 images and the average of 65,422 images. Only 2 articles did not report the amount of data collected.

As for the topics most addressed in the process of diagnosing skin diseases that use LBP, all studies had the final objective of classifying/predicting skin lesions. However, 27 studies were identified where the focus or main objective was only the classification step, aiming to promote the performance of the model.

Table 2. Studies that used the ISIC and PH2 data sources:

Authors	Article focus*	Source of data	Sample used
(Yap, Yolland, Tschand, 2018)	CLAS	ISIC	2.917
(Mohamed, Mohamed, Zekry, 2019)	CLAS	ISIC	600
(Kanani, Padole, 2019)	SEG/FEX/AUG	ISIC	10.000
(Seeja, Suresh, 2019)	SEG	ISIC	1.800
(Hekler et al., 2020)	CLAS	ISIC	1.188
(Wei, Ding, Hu, 2020)	SEG/FEX	ISIC(ISBI 2016)	1.289
(Ravikumar, Maier, 2018)	CLAS	ISIC(ISBI 2017)	2.750
(Li, Shen, 2018)	SEG/FEX/CLA	ISIC 2017	2.500
(Serte, Demirel, 2019)	CLAS/AUG	ISIC 2017	2.000
(Serte, Demirel, 2020)	CLAS/AUG	ISIC 2017	2.000
(Sherif, Mohamed, Mohra, 2019)	CLAS	ISIC 2018	700
(Almaraz-Damian et al., 2020)	FEX	ISIC 2018	10.015
(Pacheco, Krohling, 2021)	CLAS/AGG	ISIC 2019	35.867
(Molina-Molina et al., 2020)	SEG	ISIC 2019	25.331
(El-Khatib, Popescu, Ichim, 2020)	CLAS	ISIC 2019 + PH2	300
(Khan et al., 2021)	SEG/CLAS	ISIC (ISBI) + PH2	17.738
(Rodrigues et al., 2020)	FEX/CLAS	ISIC (ISBI) + PH2	6.570
(Goyal et al., 2020)	SEG	ISIC 2017 + PH2	2.950
(Tan, Zhang, Lim, 2019)	FEX	Dermofit + PH2	1.500
(Song, Lin, Wang, Wang, 2020)	CLAS/SEG	ISIC 2017 + ISBI 2016	13.750
(Abhishek, Kawahara, Hamarneh, 2021)	CLAS	ISIC (MClass-D) + Atlas	1.011
(Dascalu, David, 2019)	SEG/CLAS	ISIC + Private	5.161

Source: survey data. * Focus of articles - CLAS = Classification, SEG = Data Segmentation, FEX = Feature Extraction, AUG = Data Augmentation, AGG = Data Aggregation

Data segmentation was the subject of study in 13 articles, being also a technique widely used by the authors. The Feature Extraction task was 9 articles. In 4 studies the Data Augmentation approach was the main theme. Another technique identified Data Aggregation was also the object of study in only 1 article. All these techniques were oriented towards improving the efficiency of the models and/or the state of the art.

Other data sources that were used for training the pre-trained models cited by the authors were: 1 article used only the ImageNet dataset [24] and another study [47] that also used ImageNet with the MS COCO dataset (Microsoft Common Objects in Context).

Table 3. Studies that used other data sources

Authors	Article focus*	Source of data	Sample used
(Ameri,2020)	SEG	HAM10000	3.400
(Harangi, Baran, Hajdu, 2020)	CLAS	HAM10000	10.015
(Srinivasu et al., 2021)	CLAS	HAM10000	8.479
(Kadampur, Al Riyaee, 2020)	CLAS	HAM10000	55.043
(Olsen et al., 2018)	CLAS	Private	695
(Liu et al., 2019)	CLAS	Private	79.720
(Jinnai et al., 2020)	CLAS	Private	5.846
(Zhu et al., 2021)	CLAS	Private	13.603
(Jiang, Li, Jin, 2021)	CLAS/SEG	Private	1.167
(Wang et al., 2019)	CLAS	Private (Taiwan National Health)	2.000.000
(Thomsen et al., 2020)	CLAS /FEX /AUG	Private (AUH Dinamarca)	16.543
(Burlina et al., 2019)	CLAS	Private + Public	1.834
(Premaladha, Ravichandran, 2016)	SEG/FEX	SkinCancerAtlas + Dermnet	992
(Jafari, Mohammad et al., 2016)	SEG	Dermquest	126
(Bhavani, R. et al., 2019)	FEX	N/A	102

Source: survey data. * Focus of articles - CLAS = Classification, SEG = Data Segmentation, FEX = Feature Extraction, AUG = Data Augmentation, AGG = Data Aggregation, N/A = Not Presented by Author

CNN models are the most used and were identified in all articles in the portfolio, other models combined with CNN were also observed, such as: LSTM - Long Short Term Memory (freq. 1), Deconvolutional Network (freq. 1) and FCN - Fully Connected Network (freq. 1).

The Transfer Learning technique was observed in 25 articles (Tables 4 and 5) of which the most used models were based on ResNet [60] identified in 9 studies, followed by the Inceptions class [60] in 6 articles. The VGG [61] and U-Net [62] models are present in 3 researches each and the models that appeared in only 2 articles were FCRN [10], DenseNet [63] and MobileNet [64].

The most used software libraries are: Keras/TensorFlow (freq. 12), Pytorch (Table 4) and Caffe DL (Table 5). In 14 studies, the authors did not inform the libraries used to build the DL models. The most used development environments for implementation are: Python, followed by MatLab (freq. 8), and with only 1 article each, they used R Language and Deep Learning Studio (DLS). In 11 studies the development environment was not reported.

Table 4. Python software libraries:

Software libraries	Articles	Models
Keras and TensorFlow	(Li & Shen, 2018)	FCRN-88
	(Kanani & Padole, 2019)	CNN
	(Wei, Ding & Hu, 2020)	U-Net
	(Abhishek, Kawahara & Hamarneh, 2021)	InceptionV3
	(Liu et al., 2019)	Inception V4
	(Goyal et al., 2020)	CNN + ENC_DEC*
	(Thomsen et al., 2020)	VGG-16
	(Song et al., 2020)	ResNet50/ResNet101
	(Burlina et al., 2019)	ResNet50
	(Rodrigues et al., 2020)	VGG/Inception/ResNet/MobileNet/DenseNet
Scikit-learn and Scipy	(Hekler et al., 2020)	ResNet 50
Keras and scikit-learn	(Almaraz-Damian et al., 2020)	CNN
Chainer, ChainerCV and Cupy	(Jinnai et al., 2020)	FRCNN
OpenCV and Caffe DL	(Serte & Demirel, 2020)	ResNet 18 ResNet 50
PyTorch	(Srinivasu et al., 2021)	MobileNet V2
	(Zhu et al., 2021)	CNN
	(Pacheco & Krohling, 2021)	CNN

Source: survey data. * Model Encoder - Decoder.

In the classification step, and in addition to the Multilayer Perceptron (MLP), other most used algorithms were: Support Vector Machines (SVMs), Naïve Bayes, Extreme Learning Machine, multi-class SVM (MSVM), Random Forest (RF) and K-Nearest Neighbor. (KNN).

The evaluation indicators most used to evaluate models were: Accuracy (33), Sensitivity (28), Specificity (25), ROC Area under the curve (14). Other indicators observed in the studies with less frequency but of great importance: Dice coefficient (19%), Jaccard Index (16%), Precision (13%), F-Score (10%), MCC - Matthew Correlation Coefficient (8%), Kappa (5%), in only one F2-Score and Recall study. In two articles, the indicators of the evaluation stage were not presented.

The use of metadata and other types of data such as clinical reports for training and testing the models were used in only 7 articles, revealing that multimodal models are still approaches that are still little used by these researchers.

Regarding aspects of the health context (Block 3), almost half of the studies (18) analyzed did not have the proper concern with the improvement of techniques and assertiveness of the models, acting restricted to the experimental field without addressing the application context presenting distance from the clinical aspect (Table 6).

As for the inclusion of health professionals (specialized, residents, non-specialized) in the research and in addition to the practical application in LD, they were identified in six articles that, in the evaluation stage, compare results between man and machine.

Studies that characterize or cite the population that gave rise to training and testing data were identified in only 2 studies. Characteristics such as ethnicity/race were presented: 100% Caucasian [16] and 100% Asian [34].

This point has great relevance, due to the fact that many articles of this research revealed that the skin tone would be one of the biggest obstacles for the development of LD models for skin diagnosis by images. In this way, when analyzing the collections of images informed by the authors, it is observed the absence of images of skin color that are not Caucasian or Asian, as well as the origins of these collections are predominantly from countries in the northern hemisphere.

In order to solve this gap, only 1 study was found in the literature, proposed by Minagawa et al. [65] a Deep Learning model that, despite mentioning the effectiveness, accuracy and sensitivity of the proposed model, did not present specific results for each participating population of the study. Thus, the verification of the effectiveness of this proposal for ethnic/racial diversity in the diagnosis of skin can result in ambiguities.

5   Final Considerations

The objective of this study is to analyze the characteristics and use of Deep Learning (DL) models for the diagnosis of skin diseases and their integration with clinical practices. This research carried out a literature review of a qualitative nature. The primary data collected in the databases of scientific articles which resulted in 37 articles from the bases: Scopus, Web of Science, PubMed and IEEE Xplore.

The scientific aspects raised based on the structures of the articles indicate that 26 studies presented the problem studied in a clear and unambiguous way, in 31 experiments the methodology adopted can be replicated in another study and 29 articles presented a justification of the approaches used.

The data collection that stood out was ISIC - International Skin Imaging Collaboration. The most commonly used data types in these models are images. The most used model is the Convolutional Neural Network (CNN) and the most used pre-trained model was ResNet.

The most used techniques in the articles focused on the prediction of skin diseases, data segmentation and feature extraction. The assessment indicators that stand out are accuracy, sensitivity and specificity.

Integration with clinical practices was another theme analyzed in this research, a little less than half of the studies did not have any direction or mention the application in the

Table 5. Other software libraries used:

Software	Libraries	Articles	Models
MATLAB (MathWorks Inc.)	Caffe DL	(Jafari et al., 2016)	CNN
		(Olsen et al., 2018)	VGG
	Patternnet	(El-Khatib, Popescu & Ichim, 2020)	ResNet 101
	SGDM algorithm	(Ameri, 2020)	CNN
	N/A	(Sherif, Mohamed & Mohra, 2019)	CNN
		(Tan, Zhang & Lim, 2019)	Ensemble
		(Molina-Molina et al., 2020)	Densenet 201
		(Khan et al., 2021)	ResNet101 and DenseNet 201
R Language (3.4.4)	Keras/TensorFlow	(Wang et al., 2019)	CNN
Deep Learning Studio (DLS)	Model Driven Architecture Tool	(Kadampur & Al Riyaee, 2020)	ResNet 50, Densenet and Inception V3
N/A	N/A	(Premaladha & Ravichandran, 2016)	Ensemble
		(Ravikumar & Maier, 2018)	U-Net
		(Yap, Yolland & Tschand, 2018)	ResNet50
		(Serte & Demirel, 2019)	CNN
		(Mohamed, Mohamed & Zekry, 2019)	CNN
		(Bhavani et al., 2019)	Inception V3
		(Seeja & Suresh, 2019)	U-Net
		(Dascalu & David, 2019)	Inception V2
		(Harangi, Baran & Hajdu, 2020)	Inception V3
		(Jiang, Li & Jin, 2021)	CNN

Source: survey data. N/A - not informed by the authors.

clinical context being limited only to the development and improvement of algorithms. Only in 6 studies were health professionals participating in the experiment. Another

Table 6. Indicators for analysis of clinical practices:

Article	Was the study aimed at application in clinical practice?		Did any health professional participate in the study?		Does the study report patient characteristics?	
	YEA	NO	YEA	NO	YEA	NO
(Abhishek, Kawahara, Hamarneh, 2021)	√		√			√
(Almaraz-Damian et al., 2020)		√		√		√
(Ameri, 2020)		√		√		√
(Bhavani, R. et al., 2019)	√			√		√
(Burlina et al., 2019)	√		√			√
(Dascalu, David, 2019)	√			√	√	
(El-Khatib, Popescu, Ichim, 2020)		√		√		√
(Goyal et al., 2020)	√			√		√
(Harangi, Baran, Hajdu, 2020)		√		√		√
(Hekler et al., 2020)		√	√			√
(Jafari, Mohammad et al., 2016)		√		√		√
(Jiang, Li, Jin, 2021)	√			√		√
(Jinnai et al., 2020)	√		√			√
(Kadampur, Al Riyaee, 2020)	√			√		√
(Kanani, Padole, 2019)		√		√		√
(Khan et al., 2021)		√		√		√
(Li, Shen, 2018)		√		√		√
(Liu et al., 2019)	√		√			√
(Mohamed, Mohamed, Zekry, 2019)	√			√		√
(Molina-Molina et al., 2020)	√			√		√
(Olsen, Thomas et al., 2018)	√			√		√
(Pacheco, Krohling, 2021)		√		√		√
(Premaladha, Ravichandran, 2016)	√			√		√
(Ravikumar, Maier, 2018)		√		√		√
(Rodrigues et al., 2020)		√		√		√
(Seeja, Suresh, 2019)		√		√		√
(Serte, Demirel, 2019)		√		√		√
(Serte, Demirel, 2020)		√		√		√
(Sherif, Mohamed, Mohra, 2019)		√		√		√
(Song, Lin, Wang, Wang, 2020)		√		√		√
(Srinivasu et al., 2021)	√			√		√
(Tan, Zhang, Lim, 2019)		√		√		√
(Thomsen et al., 2020)	√			√		√
(Wang et al., 2019)	√			√	√	
(Wei, Ding, Hu, 2020)	√			√		√
(Yap, Yolland, Tschand, 2018)	√			√		√
(Zhu et al., 2021)	√		√			√
Total (37)	19	18	6	31	2	35
(%)	51,3%	48,6%	16,2%	83,7%	5,4%	94,5%

Source: survey data.

important factor, identified in only 2 articles, was the characteristics or information of the patients.

Finally, the analyzed literature indicated that approaches that use DL to classify skin diseases are very promising, however, most studies using these technologies reveal the need for greater interaction with clinical practices.

As a suggestion for future work, studies that address the effectiveness of DL models for the diagnosis of skin lesions in different ethnic groups and their limitations for the democratization of such technologies. The aspects raised for analysis of integration with clinical practices can be expanded in greater depth on the subject.

As limitations of this research, only articles in the English language were collected and the criteria raised in this study are subject to interpretation and subjectivity, which may not converge with the opinion of the authors of the studies surveyed.

References

1. Elaziz, M.A., Hosny, K.M., Salah, A., Darwish, M.M., Lu, S., Sahlol, A.T.: New machine learning method for image-based diagnosis of COVID-19. PLoS ONE 15(6), e0235187 (2020). https://doi.org/10.1371/journal.pone.0235187

2. Marques, G., Agarwal, D., de la Torre Díez, I.: Automated medical diagnosis of COVID-19 through efficientnet convolutional neural network. Appl. Soft Comput. J. 96 (2020). https://doi.org/10.1016/j.asoc.2020.106691

3. Su, C., Xu, Z., Pathak, J., et al.: Deep learning in mental health outcome research: a scoping review. Transl. Psychiatry 10, 116 (2020). https://doi.org/10.1038/s41398-020-0780-3

4. Jaiswal, A.K., Tiwari, P., Kumar, S., Al-Rakhami, M.S., Alrashoud, M., Ghoneim, A.: Deep learning-based smart iot health system for blindness detection using retina images. IEEE Access 9, 70606–70615 (2021). https://doi.org/10.1109/ACCESS.2021.3078241

5. Kuwahara, T., et al.: Usefulness of deep learning analysis for the diagnosis of malignancy in intraductal papillary mucinous neoplasms of the pancreas. Clin. Transl. Gastroenterol. 10(5) (2019). https://doi.org/10.14309/ctg.0000000000000045

6. Li, Y., Shen, L.: Deep learning based multimodal brain tumor diagnosis. In: Crimi, Alessandro, Bakas, Spyridon, Kuijf, Hugo, Menze, Bjoern, Reyes, Mauricio (eds.) BrainLes 2017. LNCS, vol. 10670, pp. 149–158. Springer, Cham (2018). https://doi.org/10.1007/978-3-319-75238-9_13

7. Esteva, A., et al.: Dermatologist-level classification of skin cancer with deep neural networks. Nature 542(7639), 115–118 (2017). https://doi.org/10.1038/nature21056

8. Majtner, T., Yildirim-Yayilgan, S., Hardeberg, J.Y.: Optimised deep learning features for improved melanoma detection. Multimed. Tools Appl. 78(9), 11883–11903 (2018). https://doi.org/10.1007/s11042-018-6734-6

9. Rodrigues, D.D.A., Ivo, R.F., Satapathy, S.C., Wang, S., Hemanth, J., Filho, P.P.R.: A new approach for classification skin lesion based on transfer learning, deep learning, and IoT system. Pattern Recogn. Lett. 136, 8–15 (2020). https://doi.org/10.1016/j.patrec.2020.05.019

10. Li, Y., Shen, L.: Skin lesion analysis towards melanoma detection using deep learning network. Sensors 18(2), 556 (2018). https://doi.org/10.3390/s18020556

11. Tan, T.Y., Zhang, L., Lim, C.P.: Intelligent skin cancer diagnosis using improved particle swarm optimization and deep learning models. Appl. Soft Comput. 84, 105725 (2019)

12. Serte, S., Demirel, H.: Gabor wavelet-based deep learning for skin lesion classification. Comput. Biol. Med. 113, 103423 (2019)

13. Pollastri, F., Bolelli, F., Paredes, R., Grana, C.: Augmenting data with GANs to segment melanoma skin lesions. Multimed. Tools Appl. **79**(21–22), 15575–15592 (2019). https://doi. org/10.1007/s11042-019-7717-y
14. Serte, S., Demirel, H.: Wavelet-based deep learning for skin lesion classification. IET Image Process. **14**(4), 720–726 (2020)
15. Abhishek, K., Kawahara, J., Hamarneh, G.: Predicting the clinical management of skin lesions using deep learning. Sci. Rep. **11**(1), 1–14 (2021). https://doaj.org/article/7db5a0869123411 895ea4b08b90c398b
16. Dascalu, A., David, E.O.: Skin cancer detection by deep learning and sound analysis algorithms: a prospective clinical study of an elementary dermoscopeResearch in context. EBioMedicine **43**, 107–113 (2019). https://doaj.org/article/ee249e1460e249f2965a73b06db 9683a
17. Khan, M.A., Sharif, M., Akram, T., Damaševičius, R., Maskeliūnas, R., Ellinger, I.: Skin lesion segmentation and multiclass classification using deep learning features and improved moth flame optimization. Diagnostics **11**(5) (2021). https://www.mdpi.com/2075-4418/11/5/ 811/htm
18. Srinivasu, P.N., Sivasai, J.G., Ijaz, M.F., Bhoi, A.K., Kim, W., Kang, J.J.: Classification of skin disease using deep learning neural networks with MobileNet V2 and LSTM. Sensors (Basel, Switzerland) **21**(8), 2852 (2021). https://doaj.org/article/4b4420e8f6dc4239a3ee2e97 ff34b3a3
19. Greenhalgh, T., et al.: Beyond adoption: a new framework for theorizing and evaluating nonadoption, abandonment, and challenges to the scale-up, spread, and sustainability of health and care. Technol. J. Med. Internet Res. **19**(11), e367 (2017). https://doi.org/10.2196/jmir. 8775
20. Coccia, M.: Deep learning technology for improving cancer care in society: new directions in cancer imaging driven by artificial intelligence. Technol. Soc. **60**, 1–11(2020). https://ssrn. com/abstract=3493655
21. Shrivastava, V.K., Londhe, N.D., Sonawane, R.S., Suri, J.S.: Computer-aided diagnosis of psoriasis skin images with HOS, texture and color features: a first comparative study of its kind. Comput. Meth. Programs Biomed. **126**, 98–109 (2016). https://doi.org/10.1016/j.cmpb. 2015.11.013
22. Liu, Y., et al.: A deep learning system for differential diagnosis of skin diseases. Nature Med. **26**(6), 900–908 (2019). https://doi.org/10.1038/s41591-020-0842-3
23. Pacheco, A.G.C., Krohling, R.: An attention-based mechanism to combine images and meta-data in deep learning models applied to skin cancer classification. IEEE J. Biomed. Health Inf. **25**(9), 3554–3563 (2021)
24. Thomsen, K., Christensen, A.L., Iversen, L., Lomholt, H.B., Winther, O.: Deep learning for diagnostic binary classification of multiple-lesion skin diseases. Front. Med. **7**(September), 1–7 (2020). https://doi.org/10.3389/fmed.2020.574329
25. Shoieb, D.A., Youssef, S.M., Aly, W.M.: Computer-aided model for skin diagnosis using deep learning. J. Image Graph. **4**(2), 122–129 (2016). https://doi.org/10.18178/joig.4.2.122-129
26. Haenssle HA, Fink C, Schneiderbauer R, Toberer F, Buhl T, Blum A, Kalloo A, Hassen ABH, … Man against machine: diagnostic performance of a deep learning convolutional neural network for dermoscopic melanoma recognition in comparison to 58 dermatologists. Ann Oncol. Aug 1,29(8):1836–1842 (2018).https://doi.org/10.1093/annonc/mdy166. PMID: 29846502
27. Patnaik, S.K., Sidhu, M.S., Gehlot, Y., Sharma, B., Muthu, P.: Automated skin disease identification using deep learning algorithm. Biomed. Pharmacol. J. **11**(3), 1429 (2018)
28. Sarker, M.M.K., et al.: MobileGAN: skin lesion segmentation using a lightweight generative adversarial network (2019)

29. Menegola, A., Tavares, J., Fornaciali, M., Li, L.T., Avila, S., Valle, E.: RECOD titans at ISIC challenge 2017. In: International Skin Imaging Collaboration (ISIC) 2017 Challenge at the International Symposium on Biomedical Imaging (ISBI) (2017). https://arxiv.org/pdf/1703.04819.pdf

30. Codella, N., et al.: Skin lesion analysis toward melanoma detection 2018: a challenge hosted by the international skin imaging collaboration (ISIC) (2018). https://arxiv.org/abs/1902.03368

31. Tschandl, P., et al.: Comparison of the accuracy of human readers versus machine-learning algorithms for pigmented skin lesion classification: an open, web-based, international, diagnostic study. Lancet Oncol. (2019).https://doi.org/10.1016/s1470-2045(19)30333-x

32. Polat, K., Koc, K.O.: Detection of skin diseases from dermoscopy image using the combination of convolutional neural network and one-versus-all. J. Artif. Intell. Syst. 2(1), 80–97 (2020). https://doi.org/10.33969/AIS.2020.21006

33. Dildar, M., et al.: Skin cancer detection: a review using deep learning techniques. Int. J. Environ. Res. Public Health 18, 5479 (2021). https://doi.org/10.3390/ijerph18105479

34. Wang, H., Wang, Y., Liang, C., Li, Y.: Assessment of deep learning using nonimaging information and sequential medical records to develop a prediction model for nonmelanoma skin cancer. JAMA Dermatol. 155(11), 1277–1283 (2019). https://doi.org/10.1001/jamadermatol.2019.2335[PB]

35. Yap, J., Yolland, W., Tschandl, P.: Multimodal skin lesion classification using deep learning. Exp. Dermatol. 27(11), 1261–1267 (2018)

36. Mohamed, A., Mohamed, W., Zekry, A.H.: Deep learning can improve early skin cancer detection. Int. J. Electron. Telecommun. 65(3), 507–513 (2019). http://ijet.pl/index.php/ijet/article/download/10.24425-ijet.2019.129806/600

37. Kanani, P., Padole, M.: Deep learning to detect skin cancer using google colab. Int. J. Eng. Adv. Technol. 8(6), 2176–2183 (2019). https://www.ijeat.org/wp-content/uploads/papers/v8i6/F8587088619.pdf

38. Seeja, R.D., Suresh, A.: Deep learning based skin lesion segmentation and classification of melanoma using support vector machine (SVM). Asian Pac. J. Cancer Prev. 20(5), 1555–1561 (2019). https://www.ncbi.nlm.nih.gov/pmc/articles/PMC6857898/pdf/APJCP-20-1555.pdf

39. Hekler, A., et al.: Effects of label noise on deep learning-based skin cancer classification. Front. Med. 7, 117 (2020). https://doaj.org/article/7c8a3d919b4d4e7da94887fa5381fe8d

40. Wei, L., Ding, K., Hu, H.: Automatic skin cancer detection in dermoscopy images based on ensemble lightweight deep learning network. IEEE Access 8, 99633–99647 (2020). https://doi.org/10.1109/ACCESS.2020.2997710[PB]

41. Ravikumar, N., Maier, A.: SkinNet: a deep learning framework for skin lesion segmentation (2018). ArXiv.Org. http://search.proquest.com/docview/2074059294/

42. Sherif, F., Mohamed, W.A., Mohra, A.S.: Skin lesion analysis toward melanoma detection using deep learning techniques. Int. J. Electron. Telecommun. 65(4), 597–602 (2019). http://ijet.pl/index.php/ijet/article/view/10.24425-ijet.2019.129818%0A

43. Almaraz-Damian, J.A., Ponomaryov, V., Sadovnychiy, S., Castillejos-Fernandez, H.: Melanoma and nevus skin lesion classification using handcraft and deep learning feature fusion via mutual information measures. Entropy 22(4), 484 (2020). https://doi.org/10.3390/e22040484

44. Molina-Molina, E.O., Solorza-Calderón, S., Álvarez-Borrego, J.: Classification of dermoscopy skin lesion color-images using fractal-deep learning features. Appl. Sci. 10(5954), 5954 (2020). https://doi.org/10.3390/app10175954

45. El-Khatib, H., Popescu, D., Ichim, L.: Deep learning-based methods for automatic diagnosis of skin lesions. Sensors 20(6), 1753 (2020). https://doi.org/10.3390/s20061753

46. Goyal, M., Oakley, A., Bansal, P., Dancey, D., Yap, M.H.: Skin lesion segmentation in dermoscopic images with ensemble deep learning methods. IEEE Access 8, 4171–4181 (2020)

47. Song, L., Lin, J., Wang, Z.J., Wang, H.: An end-to-end multi-task deep learning framework for skin lesion analysis. IEEE J. Biomed. Health Inf. **24**(10), 2912–2921 (2020)
48. Ameri, A.: A deep learning approach to skin cancer detection in dermoscopy images. J. Biomed. Phys. Eng. **10**(6), 801–806 (2020). https://doaj.org/article/dd64ab7df19b42938fe73a2ba2ebdd78
49. Harangi, B., Baran, A., Hajdu, A.: Assisted deep learning framework for multi-class skin lesion classification considering a binary classification support. Biomed. Signal Process. Control **62** (2020)
50. Kadampur, M.A., Al Riyaee, S.: Skin cancer detection: applying a deep learning based model driven architecture in the cloud for classifying dermal cell images. Inf. Med. Unlocked **18** (2020). https://doi.org/10.1016/j.imu.2019.100282
51. Olsen, T., et al.: Diagnostic performance of deep learning algorithms applied to three common diagnoses in dermatopathology (Original Article). J. Pathol. Inf. **9**(1), 32 (2018)
52. Jinnai, S., Yamazaki, N., Hirano, Y., Sugawara, Y., Ohe, Y., Hamamoto, R.: The development of a skin cancer classification system for pigmented skin lesions using deep learning. Biomolecules **10**(8) (2020)
53. Zhu, C.-Y., et al.: A deep learning based framework for diagnosing multiple skin diseases in a clinical environment. Front. Med. **8** (2021). https://www.ncbi.nlm.nih.gov/pmc/articles/PMC8085301/
54. Jiang, S., Li, H., Jin, Z.A.: Visually interpretable deep learning framework for histopathological image-based skin cancer diagnosis. IEEE J. Biomed. Health Inf. **25**(5), 1483–1494 (2021)
55. Burlina, P.M., Joshi, N.J., Ng, E., Billings, S.D., Rebman, A.W., Aucott, J.N.: Automated detection of erythema migrans and other confounding skin lesions via deep learning. Comput. Biol. Med. **105**, 151–156 (2019). https://doi.org/10.1016/j.compbiomed.2018.12.007[PB]
56. Premaladha, J., Ravichandran, K.S.: Novel approaches for diagnosing melanoma skin lesions through supervised and deep learning algorithms. J. Med. Syst. **40**(4), 1–12 (2016). https://doi.org/10.1007/s10916-016-0460-2
57. Jafari, M., Nasr-Esfahani, E., Karimi, N., Soroushmehr, S., Samavi, S., Najarian, K.: Extraction of skin lesions from non-dermoscopic images using deep learning. ArXiv.Orghttp://search.proquest.com/docview/2074987175/
58. Bhavani, R., Prakash, V., Kumaresh, R.V, Sundra Srinivasan, R.: Vision-based skin disease identification using deep learning. Int. J. Eng. Adv. Technol. **8**(6), 3784–3788 (2019). https://www.ijeat.org/wp-content/uploads/papers/v8i6/F9391088619.pdf
59. He, K., Zhang, X., Ren, S., Sun, J.: ResNet50 IEEE Conference on Computer Vision and Pattern Recognition (CVPR), pp. 770–778 (2016)
60. Zegedy, C., Ioffe, S., Vanhoucke, V. Alemi, A.A.: Inception-v4, inception-ResNet and the impact of residual connections on learning. In: Thirty-First AAAI Conference on Artificial Intelligence, pp. 4278–4284 (2017)
61. Simonyan, K., Zisserman, A.: Very deep convolutional networks for large-scale image recognition (2014). arXiv preprint arXiv:1409.1556
62. Ronneberger, O., Fischer, P., Brox, T.: U-Net: convolutional networks for biomedical image segmentation. In: Navab, N., Hornegger, J., Wells, W.M., Frangi, A.F. (eds.) MICCAI 2015. LNCS, vol. 9351, pp. 234–241. Springer, Cham (2015). https://doi.org/10.1007/978-3-319-24574-4_28
63. Iandola, F., Moskewicz, M., Karayev, S., Girshick, R., Darrell, T., Keutzer, K.: Densenet: implementing efficient convnet descriptor pyramids (2014). arXiv preprint arXiv:1404.1869

64. Howard, A.G., et al.: Mobilenets: efficient convolutional neural networks for mobile vision applications (2017). arXiv preprint arXiv:1704.04861
65. Minagawa, A., et al.: Dermoscopic diagnostic performance of Japanese dermatologists for skin tumors differs by patient origin: a deep learning convolutional neural network closes the gap. J. Dermatol. (2020). https://doi.org/10.1111/1346-8138.15640

An Expanded Study of the Application of Deep Learning Models in Energy Consumption Prediction

Leonardo Santos Amaral[2(✉)] ⓘ, Gustavo Medeiros de Araújo[2] ⓘ,
Ricardo Moraes[2] ⓘ, and Paula Monteiro de Oliveira Villela[1] ⓘ

[1] Universidade Estadual de Montes Claros - UNIMONTES, Av. Prof. Rui Braga, S/N - Vila Mauriceia, Montes Claros – MG, Brazil
[2] Universidade Federal de Santa Catarina UFSC, R. Eng. Agronômico Andrei Cristian Ferreira, S/N -Trindade, Florianópolis – SC, Brazil
leonardosamaral@hotmail.com, {gustavo.araujo, ricardo.moraes}@ufsc.br

Abstract. The time series of electrical loads are complex, influenced by multiple variables (endogenous and exogenous), display non-linear behavior and have multiple seasonality with daily, weekly and annual cycles. This paper addresses the main aspects of demand forecast modeling from time series and applies machine learning techniques for this type of problem. The results indicate that through an amplified model including the selection of variables, seasonality representation technique selection, appropriate choice of model for database (deep or shallow) and its calibration, it's possible to archive better results with an acceptable computational cost. In the conclusion, suggestions for the continuity of the study are presented.

Keywords: Forecast · Energy · Demand · Deep learning

1 Introduction

Global energy consumption is growing each year, and to satisfy this demand, it is necessary to find ways to make efficient use of this resource and generate more energy. In 2010, global energy consumption was approximately 152 thousand TWh, and this value increased to 173 thousand TWh in 2017, which represents a 13% growth in seven years [10].

At present, the sector is in a transition phase and some changes are happening, such as: increase of the use of renewable sources, increased energy efficiency, modernization of the network infrastructure, consumption patterns changes and deregulation [5]. There is currently greater awareness of the environmental impacts caused by high energy consumption, and despite this increasing consumption, the challenge is to reduce energy production from polluted energy sources such as nuclear and fossil fuels.

A. L. Pinto and R. Arencibia-Jorge (Eds.): DIONE 2022, LNICST 452, pp. 150–162, 2022.
https://doi.org/10.1007/978-3-031-22324-2_12

On a global level, it is essential that the decision makers have information on the energy consumption growth in different countries to meet these challenges. On a local level, this information is also essential due to changes in the sector, such as greater competitiveness, measures to rationalize consumption, and economic interests. The operation of a Smart-Grid network dependent on this information is one example, as it is sensitive to instantaneous load variations, contingencies, and the economic dispatch of loads.

Some energy forecasting models are based purely on statistical methods; however, in the last decades there has been an increase in the use of methods based on machine learning (ML), which make use of the large amount of information currently available to make predictions and obtain more accurate results. Numerous works published in recent decades have addressed demand forecasting, but most do not consider all relevant aspects of it. This work aims to fill this gap by indicating ways to build more complete models.

2   Related Works

Over the last few decades, several demand forecasting techniques have been tested using different strategies to obtain future values of energy consumption. For example, [7] classifies different methods in terms of use; multiple regression or multivariate regression methods are the most used, followed by the ANN (artificial neural network). The most used time series models include ARMA (autoregressive moving average) for stationary series and ARIMA (autoregressive integrated moving average) if the series is non-stationary and requires differentiation. The next in the author's ranking is the SVM (support vector machine) and finally, there are models with small participation at the same level.

In a survey, [11] points out that some models offer advantages over others if the objective is forecasting demand. Multiple regressions provide accuracy in the prediction when the load in time follows a linear behavior. Neural networks are preferred when the time variations are significantly fast. ANN and time series models are often used for STLF (short term load forecasting) when the consumption pattern is more complex. Time series models rely mainly on historical load data, while ANN needs to be trained with the historical load data and the time base. SVM is very similar to ANN, as it also requires parameters as input, but it is faster and has fewer parameters to configure. Evolutionary algorithms run faster and provide better results when used with ANN. Over time, some methods were shown to be ineffective for short-term forecasting demand due to the non-linear relationship between the predicted variables and the predictors, along with the increase in the amount of information.

ML techniques have delivered good results for this type of problem. For example, [8] highlights that, during the last two decades, several ML models for forecasting demands have emerged, because ML offers the best opportunities to search for improvements. Some advantages include the increase in accuracy and robustness, as well as the ability to generalize when creating hybrid models. Among ML techniques, the most promising involve deep learning. In [9], a comparison was made between traditional ML techniques and deep-learning techniques, concluding that the latter leads to better results, although its model preparation presents bigger challenges.

3   Problem and Motivation

When making demand forecasts, some questions arise:

- Which elements of influence should be considered and how? (i.e., seasonality and input variables)
- How should the most relevant variables be selected and the redundant ones eliminated for better computational performance and results?
- Which prediction technique should be used?
- How should the model be calibrated?

There are few publications that attempt to answer all these questions simultaneously, and this fact motivated the development of this study, whose purpose is to build an expanded model that contemplates all these aspects simultaneously.

4   Proposed Model

4.1   Database

The database used in this case study is available at ISO NE (Independent System Operator New England) at http://www.iso-ne.com. It includes the sum of the global electrical load data from several cities in England for the period between January 2017 and December 2019. Altogether, it contains 23 independent variables of the following natures: climate information, economic indicators, and market data.

To better understand demand behavior, Figs. 1, 2, and 3 show its annual, weekly, and daily variation. The concentration of peaks throughout the year appear between the months of June and September, over the week on Mondays, and by day between 6 p.m. and 7 p.m. This behavior reflects the presence of multiple seasonalities.

a) Annual behavior   b) Weekly behavior   c) Daily behavior

Fig. 1. Variation in energy consumption throughout 2017 (Source: the author)

It is very important that the database includes the variables with greatest influence on energy consumption when making predictions. For example, the graphs in Figs. 4, 5, and 6 reproduce the behavior of temperature throughout the day. The temperature variations are shown in the same periods: throughout the year, week, and day.

As shown in Figs. 4, 5, and 6, the temperature peaks from 2017 to 2019 occurred between the months June and October; weekly, they often occur on Wednesdays; and daily, between 5 p.m. and 6 p.m. These data indicate the existence of a correlation between temperature and the target variable, energy consumption.

Fig. 2. Variation in energy consumption throughout 2018 (Source: the author)

Fig. 3. Variation in energy consumption throughout 2019. (Source: the author)

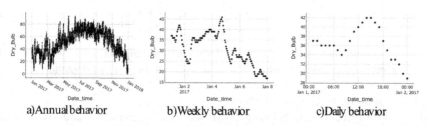

Fig. 4. Dry bulb temperature variation in 2017 (Source: the author)

Fig. 5. Dry bulb temperature variation in 2018 (Source: the author)

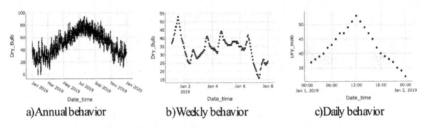

a)Annual behavior   b)Weekly behavior   c)Daily behavior

Fig. 6. Dry bulb temperature variation in 2019 (Source: the author)

4.2 Load Seasonality

As noted in Sect. 4.1, the electrical load has multiple seasonalities. This issue is addressed in [3], which proposes different ways of coding to represent them. They are shown below.

Representation of the Year Period

To encode the variations caused by hot and cold periods throughout the year, a trigonometric function is used that generates a specific value for each day of the year. The expression is shown below:

$$p = [\sin(2\pi \frac{(i+\tau)}{366}) \; \cos(2\pi \frac{(i+\tau)}{366})]. \tag{1}$$

where i represents the current day and τ the prediction range in days. So $i + \tau = 1$, 2,…366 represents the number of the day of the year of the forecast demand.

Representation of the Day of the Week

The day of the week varies between 1 (Monday) and 7 (Sunday), and six different encodings are used to represent them, listed in Table 1. One scales the day of the week between [1 … 1/7]: in this successive encoding, days of the week have successive scaled index values. A trigonometric expression is used to encode the index of the day in the second representation, and the following ones use bits to represent each day of the week.

Table 1. Representation of the day of the week

d	1 d^1	2 d^2	3 d^3	4 d^4	5 d^5	6 d^6
Monday	8/7	$[\sin(2\pi \frac{(8)}{7}) \; \cos(2\pi \frac{(8)}{7})]$	1000000	001	001	00
Tuesday			0100000	010	011	01
Wednesday			0010000	011	010	01
Thursday			0001000	100	110	01
Friday			0000100	101	111	01

(continued)

Table 1. (*continued*)

d	1 d^1	2 d^2		3 d^3	4 d^4	5 d^5	6 d^6
Saturday				0000010	110	101	10
Sunday				0000001	111	100	11

Source: [3]

Representation of the Hour of the Day

The representation of the time of the day is made by five encodings, as shown in Table 2. The first scale is the time of the day [1 ... 24], successive hours of the day having successive scaled index values. The second representation has a trigonometric expression that generates values for each hour of the day, and for representations 3, 4, and 5 bits are used to represent the hour of the day.

Table 2. Representation of the hour of the day

h	1 h^1	2 h^2	3 h^3	4 h^4	5 h^5
Hour 1	$\delta/24$	$[\sin(2\pi t\frac{(\delta)}{24})\ \cos(2\pi t\frac{(\delta)}{24})]$	1000...0	00001	00001
Hour 2			0100...0	00010	00011
Hour 3			0010...0	00011	00010
...			...	...	...
Hour 24			0000...1	11000	10100

Source: [3]

4.3 Consumption Prediction from Time Series

It is possible to make future prediction of H energy values from a univariational time series comprised of T observations [12]. Typically, energy data are characterized by high variance and non-linear behavior between independent and dependent variables.

As pointed out in the cited works in Sect. 2, due to these characteristics, deep-learning techniques have stood out in demand forecastting applications based on time series. For this reason, this work focuses on using deep-learning models to predict energy consumption. According to [1], several steps are necessary to assemble a good model, as shown in Fig. 7.

The preprocessing step is very important, because helps to reduce the database dimensionality while keeping the most relevant information [2]. According to [2], some of the offered advantages are reduced processing time, increased accuracy, and the possibility of a better understanding of the learning model and data. He classifies the variable

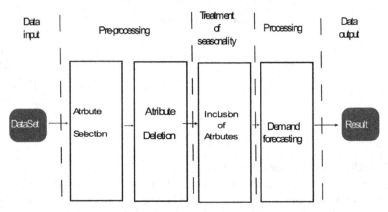

Fig. 7. Framework for energy prediction (Source: Author)

selection methods as: filter, wrapper, and embedded. The next step is the seasonality treatment, which consists of adding attributes to reproduce it.

Due to the advantages exposed in Sect. 2, it was decided to make the predictions using SVM, a classic and widely used ML method, and two deep-learning techniques: the multi layer Perceptron and LSTM (long short-term memory). It will thus be possible to evaluate the potential of the proposed models.

5   Implementation and Results

5.1   Variable Selection and Model Entry

The increase in the database dimensions with a large supply of data exposes the limitations of ML algorithms in terms of learning capacity and processing time. A high number of input variables makes the processing heavy without necessarily delivering better results [6]. For this reason, a preprocessing step is included to remove irrelevant and redundant data. In this step, the whole database is submitted to algorithms capable of identifying the most relevant attributes; then, the result of this selection is submitted to the RFM (recursive feature elimination) algorithm to eliminate redundant attributes.

The database was loaded into the WEKA tool and processed through attribute-selection algorithms. Weka is a free ML tool developed in Java at the University of Waikato, which has the main attribute-selection algorithms implemented and offers easy access. More information about WEKA's variable selection algorithms can be found in its manual.

The algorithms were used in Table 3 to allow a relevance and redundancy analysis on the database attributes. CFS privileges subsets that have less intercorrelation with each other but are highly correlated with the target [4]. The ClassifierAttributeEval checks the value of an attribute used with a specific classifier selected by the user. The main component is used to extract more relevant information from a redundant and noisy dataset. Relief is a well-known method that measures the relevance of attributes close to the target. Mutual information focuses on relevance analysis using the concept of mutual information [6].

Below, Table 3 identifies the selection method and the attributes considered most relevant. The purpose is to reduce the dimensionality of the database, so the main attributes were selected. The results of the pre-processing are shown in Table 3, which identifies the algorithm and the most relevant attributes.

Table 3. Attribute selection

Algorithm	Selection criteria	Stop criterion	Result	Used for	Problem type	Source
CfsSubsetEvail	Subset	**Greedy** Stepwise	RT demand	Eliminate attributes	Nonlinear	WEKA
			DA_CC			
			DA MLC			
			RT MLC			
			Min_5min_RSP			
			Max_5min_RSP			
ClassifierAtributeEvail	Individual	Ranking	Max_5min_RCP	Eliminate attributes	Nonlinear	WEKA
			DA_EC			
			DA_CC			
			RT demand			
			DA LMP			
PrincipalComponentes	Individual	Ranking	RT LMP	Eliminate attributes	Nonlinear	WEKA
			RT_EC			
			DA LMP			
			DA_EC			
			RT MLC			
Relief	Subset	Ranking	RT demand	Eliminate attributes	Nonlinear	WEKA
			DA demand			
			DA_EC			
			DA_LMP			
			Reg_Service_Price			
Mutual information	Individual	Ranking	DA_ MLC	Eliminate attributes	Nonlinear	Python Code
			DA_LMP			
			Min_5 min_RSP			
			DA_EC			
			Dew Point			

Source: Author

It is important to highlight that this step only considered the original attributes of the database, so it did not consider the attributes that will be added due to the reproduction of seasonality of the electrical load.

5.2 Comparison of the Models Results

To test three different energy consumption prediction models, several simulations were performed using the database described in Sect. 4.1. The first model tested used the SVM as the estimator, the second used the multilayer Perceptron, and the third uses the LSTM. As discussed above, these estimators were chosen because they are effective in making estimates from time series. The model using SVM is considered a traditional ML model and was calibrated to solve the problem and be a reference in the comparison with deep neural network models. In Figs. 8 and 9 below, two model variants, one shallow and the other deep, will be considered in the analysis. What distinguishes the two is the number of intermediate layers. Note that shallow models have only one input layer, followed by a dense layer that generates the output values. The deep model has different layers of the relevant class in series and an output dimensionality similar to the shallow model.

Input Layer: Perceptron	Input	456		Input layer: LSTM	Input	(none,1,456)
	Output	8			Output	(none,1,50)

Output layer: Perceptron	Input	8		Output layer: LSTM	Input	(none,1,50)
	Output	24			Output	(none,1,50)

Fig. 8. Shallow models (Source: Author)

Input Layer: Perceptron	Input	456		Input Layer: LSTM	Input	(none,1,456)
	Output	8			Output	(none,1,50)

Middle Layer: Dense	Input	8		Middle Layer: LSTM	Input	(none,1,50)
	Output	8			Output	(none,1,50)

Middle Layer: Dense	Input	8		Middle Layer: LSTM	Input	(none,1,50)
	Output	8			Output	(none,1,50)

Middle Layer: Dense	Input	8		Middle Layer: LSTM	Input	(none,1,50)
	Output	8			Output	(none,1,50)

Output layer: Dense	Input	8		Output layer: Dense	Input	(none,1,50)
	Output	24			Output	(none,1,1)

Fig. 9. Deep models (Source: Author)

In this study, simulations were performed to calibrate the models, and the results are shown in Tables 4, 5 and 6 below. They indicate the values of the main parameters of the models.

The simulations in Table 4 indicate that increasing the value of C and using the RBF kernel increases the accuracy of the model. However, it should be noted that in this condition greater computational effort is required to process the data. For example, when migrating from C = 20 to C = 2000, the processing time increases from 0.6 to 14.4 min.

Table 4. SVM Model processes

C	Epsilon	Rbf		Polynomial	
		MAPE	RMSE	MAPE	RMSE
20	0,01	2,09	869	9,24	1553
	0,1	2,09	869	9,24	1553
200	0,01	1,0	590	7,37	1598
	0,1	1,0	590	7,37	1598
2000	0,01	0,53	374	7,04	1888
	0,1	0,53	374	7,03	1887

Source: Author

Table 5. Perceptron model processes

epoch	Optimizer	Activation Function	Test (%)	Error	
				MAPE	RMSE
50	RMSProp	relu/tanh	20	3,54	617
	RMSProp	relu	20	5,6	932
	RMSProp	relu/tanh	10	2,85	607
	RMSProp	relu	10	4,44	760
	Adam	relu/tanh	10	2,29	500
	Adam	relu	10	4,26	811
100	RMSProp	relu/tanh	20	3,22	741
	RMSProp	relu	20	4,78	1006
	RMSProp	relu/tanh	10	2,71	573
	RMSProp	relu	10	5,03	990
	Adam	relu/tanh	10	2,72	619
	Adam	relu	10	4,28	838

Source: Author

Table 5 shows the simulations performed with the model using Perceptron, with the main Perceptron hyperparameters.

From the results of Table 5, it can be observed that both the RMSprop and Adam optimizers offer satisfactory performance, and that the use of the relu activation function in the intermediate layers and tanh in the output layers also contributed to delivering better results. It is also evident that by increasing the training percentage and the number of epochs, the accuracy of the model improves. Similar to the other cases, Table 6 includes processing performed by varying the main parameters of the LSTM.

Table 6. LSTM model processes

Epoch	Optimizer	Activation function	Loss	Error	
				MAPE	RMSE
50	RMSProp	relu	mse	3,95	519
	RMSProp	relu	mae	3,85	512
	RMSProp	tanh	mse	4,18	549
	RMSProp	tanh	mae	3,84	511
	RMSProp	sigmoid	mse	4,72	613
	Adam	sigmoid	mse	3,85	522
100	RMSProp	relu	mse	4,10	560
	RMSProp	relu	mae	4,19	583
	RMSProp	tanh	mse	3,97	520
	RMSProp	tanh	mae	3,78	504
	Adam	relu	mse	3,95	540

Source: Author

Once again, it was possible to observe that both the Adam and RMSprop optimizers offer good performance and that the use of the tanh activation function also contributes to achieving better results. Error functions do not significantly influence the results.

The next step after calibrating the models is to evaluate their response to different input conditions. Table 7 includes seven different input situations and the respective responses of the models. The first considers all the attributes of the base and disregards seasonality, and the following three consider only the main variables selected by some of the methods indicated in Table 3, also disregarding seasonality. The last three considered the same entries as the previous items with the addition of seasonality variables.

The results in Table 7 indicate that the highest model accuracy was achieved when all independent variables were considered in their modeling (first line of Table 7). The accuracy achieved with the SVR-based model exceeded that obtained with the deep-learning models. This result demonstrates that it is a simpler method to use and may be more useful depending on the database size. When reducing the dimensionality of the database, the accuracy of the models was reduced, although the benefit in terms of computational cost justifies doing so. Regarding the impact of the selection of variables, the best results were obtained in most processing using the CFS.

In some simulations, improvements were observed resulting from the implementation of seasonality, however, the need to test other forms of coding was evident. In this work, only codes using trigonometric expressions were tested. The results indicate that, for this particular database, the shallow models generated better results than deep ones.

Table 7. Simulations with demand prediction models

Selection Attributes (criteria)	Seasonality	SVR		PERCEPTRON				LSTM			
				Shallow		Deep		Shallow		Deep	
		mape	rmse	mape	rmse	mape	rmse	mape	rmse	mape	rmse
100% da base	n	2,09	869	3,26	550	3,36	615	3,76	633	3,97	650
CFS	n	1,63	777	5,41	1017	6,09	1247	3,83	514	3,94	671
Relief	n	1,15	659	5,47	1116	5,60	1100	3,94	669	4,17	727
Mutual information	n	9,58	166	5,43	1091	5,81	1154	3,88	652	4,03	690
CFS	s	2,22	825	5,23	1056	5,66	1150	3,84	654	4,10	718
Relief	s	1,59	728	5,23	10,37	5,4	1054	3,86	653	4,01	696
Mutual information	s	9,74	1674	4,79	965	5,78	1192	3,86	517	4,12	715

Source: Author

6 Conclusion

The main objective of this study was to show the potential of ML techniques to forecast energy demand from time series and illustrate the main challenges in building more complete models. As explained in Sect. 4.3, to overcome the limitations of ML techniques, it is recommended to reduce the database dimensionality, selecting the input variables for the model. The results indicate that, with a reduced number of variables, it is possible to build a model with an accuracy very close to that achieved with a model that uses all the attributes of the database, as shown by the results achieved with the CFS method using the SVR, which generated a map of 2.09 against 1.15, and with LSTM, which generated a map of 3.76 against 3.83.

When comparing the simulations with and without the representation of seasonality, it is possible to observe the improvement in the model response in parts of the simulations. This shows the need to test other forms of coding to expand the benefits of representing this phenomenon in the model. The results also showed that, for the database used, shallow models were more appropriate for modeling, as they required less computational effort and presented better results. However, as the database grows, it is likely that this behavior will change and the accuracy of deep models will exceed the accuracy of shallow ones.

Future work could consider tests with larger databases, using a greater number of exogenous variables (irradiation level, economic indicators and others), new ways of representing seasonality and reflections of electric energy generations distributed.

References

1. Ahmad, W., et al.: Towards short term electricity load forecasting using improved support vector machine and extreme learning machine. Energies **13**, 2907 (2020)

2. Cai, J., Luo, J., Wang, S., Yang, S.: Feature selection in machine learning: a new perspective. Neurocomputing **300**, 70–79 (2018)
3. Dudek, G.: 'Multilayer perceptron for short-term load forecasting: from global to local approach. Neural Comput. Appl. **32**(8), 3695–3707 (2020)
4. Gnanambal, S., Thangaraj, M., Meenatchi, V., Gayathri, V.: Classification algorithms with attribute selection: an evaluation study using WEKA. Int. J. Adv. Netw. Appl. **9**, 3640–3644 (2018)
5. Keitsch, K.A., Bruckner, T.: Input data analysis for optimized short term load forecasts. In: IEEE Innovative Smart Grid Technologies, Asia (ISGT-Asia), Melbourne, VIC, pp. 1–6 (2016)
6. Khalid, S., Khalil, T., Nasreen, S.: A survey of feature selection and feature extraction techniques in machine learning. In: 2014 Science and Information Conference, pp. 372–378 (2014)
7. Kuster, C., Rezgui, Y., Mourshed, M.: Electrical load forecasting models: a critical systematic review. Sustain. Cities Soc. **35**, 257–270 (2017)
8. Mosavi, A., Salimi, M., Ardabili, S.F., Rabczuk, T., Shamshirband, S., Várkonyi-Kóczy, A.R.: State of the art of machine learning models in energy systems, a systematic review. Energies **12**, 1301 (2019)
9. Paterakis, N.G., Mocanu, E., Gibescu, M., Stappers, B., Van Alst, W.: Deep learning versus traditional machine learning methods for aggregated energy demand prediction. In: IEEE PES Innovative Smart Grid Technologies Conference Europe, ISGT-Europe – Proceedings (2017)
10. Smil, V.: Energy Transitions: Global and National Perspectives. ABC-CLIO, , Santa Barbara (2017)
11. Upadhaya, D., Thakur, R., Singh, N.K.: A systematic review on the methods of short-term load forecasting. In: Proceedings of the 2019 2nd International Conference on Power Energy, Environment and Intelligent Control (PEEIC), Greater Noida, India, 18–19 October, pp. 6–11 (2019)
12. Müller, K.-R., Smola, A.J., Rätsch, G., Schölkopf, B., Kohlmorgen, J., Vapnik, V.: Predicting time series with support vector machines. In: Gerstner, W., Germond, A., Hasler, M., Nicoud, J.-D. (eds.) ICANN 1997. LNCS, vol. 1327, pp. 999–1004. Springer, Heidelberg (1997). https://doi.org/10.1007/BFb0020283

Application and Evaluation of a Taxonomy in the Context of Software Requirements Management

Priscila Basto Fagundes[1]([⊠]) [ID], Douglas Dyllon Jeronimo de Macedo[1] [ID],
and António Lucas Soares[2] [ID]

[1] Federal University of Santa Catarina/PPGCIN, Florianópolis, Brazil
`priscila.bfagundes@gmail.com, douglas.macedo@ufsc.br`
[2] INESC Technology and Science and Faculty of Engineering, University of Porto, Porto,
Portugal
`als@fe.up.pt`

Abstract. The requirements of a software are the characteristics of the system,
being identified based on information provided by the users or by experts in the
business; and the effective management of this information is essential to ensure
that the system meets the needs of those who will use it. According to research,
one of the problems that negatively impacts the software development process is
related to the conduction of the project requirements management activity. And in
order to alleviate this problem, we carried out a research to verify if taxonomies,
as tools used by the area of information management, can be applied in the context of requirements management. For this, we developed a taxonomy to meet a
real software project and the results were evaluated in relation to its complexity,
satisfaction, resources involved and adaptability. The present research is characterized in terms of nature as an applied research, aiming at solving real-world
problems; as for the objectives, as exploratory and descriptive; and as for the
approach, mixed methods are used, since it combines qualitative and quantitative
forms of research in the same study. As for the methodological procedures, the
bibliographic research was chosen to understand the concepts related to information management, taxonomies and requirements management. The evaluation
results showed that taxonomies can contribute to the activities of the requirements
management process and consequently increase the chances of project success.

Keywords: Requirements engineering · Software · Information management ·
Requirements management · Taxonomy

1 Introduction

The initial specification activity, in which the software functionalities and restrictions to
its operation are defined, counts on the Requirements Engineering area to support the
discovery, analysis, documentation, validation and management of system requirements

A. L. Pinto and R. Arencibia-Jorge (Eds.): DIONE 2022, LNICST 452, pp. 163–177, 2022.
https://doi.org/10.1007/978-3-031-22324-2_13

[1]. Requirements are conditions or capabilities that a software needs to have in order to meet the needs of its users, being considered a critical factor in projects, because, if not well defined and managed, they directly impact the success of the product that will be delivered.

It is possible to observe in the literature different proposals regarding how Requirements Engineering activities should be carried out, and this definition should consider factors such as the type of software that will be developed, the organizational culture or the resources involved [2]. Authors such as [3–6] propose that one of the activities of Requirements Engineering is related to requirements management, and this activity should manage the identified requirements, defining their relationships, allowing their traceability and facilitating changes when necessary.

Requirements management involves generating and managing considerable amounts of information about system requirements and, like other requirements engineering activities, it demands techniques and tools to assist in their realization. Despite the efforts of Requirements Engineering to propose solutions that help the execution of its activities, it is still possible to observe the need for proposals contemplating new approaches to improve requirements management, an activity considered transversal and in support of the others [5].

Software requirements are based on and also generate information [7, 8]. And it was taking into account that the main object of Requirements Engineering is information, whether as a subsidy for the definition of software requirements or being contained in the different documents generated throughout the process, that it was considered pertinent to investigate how the tools used by the information management area could contribute to the requirements management activity.

This investigation resulted in the proposition of a framework, called FIRMa – Framework based on Information Management to Requirements Engineering, composed of tools used by information management to be applied in the requirements management process with the objective of helping the development of the activities of (i) organization of requirements; (ii) control of the changes suffered by them; (iii) maintenance of traceability between them; and (iv) management of artifacts containing project requirements [9].

Therefore, this article focuses on presenting the application of taxonomies, one of the information management tools contemplated by FIRMa, as well as the results of the evaluation of its application in a real software development process that considered four aspects: complexity in its utilization, satisfaction with results, utilization of resources and adaptability.

The research that resulted in the elaboration of this article is characterized in terms of nature as applied research, aiming at solving real-world problems; as for the objectives as exploratory and descriptive; and as for the approach, mixed methods were used, since it associates forms of qualitative and quantitative research in the same study.

As for the structure of this article, Sect. 2 presents: concepts related to Requirements Engineering, focusing on requirements management activity; taxonomies as a tool used by the information management area to organize and categorize information and; some research has already been developed proposing the application of taxonomies to assist in the requirements management process.

Section 3 presents an analysis of the taxonomies' objectives in relation to the objectives of each of the four requirements management activities, namely: requirements organization; control of the changes suffered by them; maintenance of traceability between them; and management of artifacts containing the requirements. This analysis allowed us to verify that taxonomies can be considered to help all four activities.

Section 4 presents the stages and activities carried out during each one of them for the development of this research.

Section 5 presents the process we used to apply and evaluate taxonomies in a real software project. The criteria defined for the evaluation of taxonomies are exposed in relation to their applicability in the requirements management process and the results obtained with the application and evaluation of the tool are shown. The results showed that taxonomies: present low complexity in terms of understanding, applicability and use; are considered highly satisfactory about their possibility of contributing to requirements management; they do not require large resources and investments for their application and; have a high degree of adaptability, as they can be designed to meet any type of software project.

Finally, Sect. 6 presents the conclusions for this research and proposals for future work.

2 Background

2.1 Requirements Engineering and the Activity of Software Requirements Management

Requirements Engineering is considered a subarea of Software Engineering and belongs to the specification stage in the development process, in which the person responsible for the project's requirements seeks to understand what the real needs of users are with regard to solving the problem that arises.

Regarding the understanding of users' needs, requirements are considered a critical factor in software projects, because, if not well defined, they directly impact the success of the project. In addition, requirements are used to measure the size, complexity and, consequently, the cost of the software. Furthermore, when problems with the identification of requirements are detected late, there is a high cost to correct them.

From the perspective of [10], a software requirement is a condition or a capability that a software needs to have in order to meet the needs of its users. The requirements of a system are the descriptions of what the system must do, the services it offers and the restrictions on its operation and it can be classified as functional and non-functional. Functional requirements are statements of services that the system must provide, of how the system must react to specific inputs, and of how the system must behave in certain situations; and non-functional requirements, unlike functional requirements, do not express any function to be performed by the software, but rather behaviors and constraints that the software must satisfy [1].

According [6], Requirements Engineering involves the process of determining requirements, analyzing them, validating them and managing them throughout the project lifecycle. The requirements management activity can be defined as a systematic approach to managing the requirements of the system, in the same way that it establishes and maintains an agreement between the client and the technical project team about the changes suffered by the requirements [11].

The requirements management process must provide a means for the requirements, which were previously identified, documented and validated, to be carefully controlled, in order to establish a baseline for project management. The artifacts containing the specifications of the software requirements are treated as the central document, being an element that has important relationships with other elements of the project. Problems caused by failures during the requirements management process in the software project are widely recognized and studies show that this is one of the areas with the highest incidence of failure in this type of project [12].

It is possible to find in the literature different proposals on which activities should be performed during the requirements management process. This article considers the activities recommended by [3–6], which suggest the following: (i) organizing the identified requirements; (ii) control the changes suffered by the requirements throughout the project; (iii) maintain traceability between requirements; and (iv) manage artifacts containing information about requirements.

2.2 Taxonomies in the Context of Information Management

The information management comprises a variety of activities and disciplinary areas, each focused on different types of information and management [13, 26]. Information management is composed of elements of a polysemic nature and, as such, is addressed in several areas of knowledge. At the same time that it presents influences from the areas of Administration, Document Management, Librarianship, Computing and Information Science, information management practices can also be applied in different sectors of society.

For [14], information management is an area of interest in Computing with regard to the development of support tools for information management in organizations. Such tools constitute a valuable resource in practically all organizational processes, supporting the identification of information needs, guiding the search and acquisition of information, and constituting the basis of the organization and storage of information, in addition to enabling the elaboration of and the distribution of information products and services.

Among the activities of the information management process are the organization and representation of information and one of the tools used to carry out this activity are taxonomies. A taxonomy can be defined as a classification system that supports access to information, allowing it to classify, allocate, retrieve and communicate information in a logical way. According to [15], a taxonomy organizes information from the most generic to the most specific, using the hierarchical relationship or the gender-species relationship between the terms.

In this context, [16] present four methodological steps to be carried out in the elaboration of a taxonomy: the first consists of surveying the areas of knowledge and the hierarchical relationships of the terms that will compose the first version of the taxonomy; the second is about to analyze the documents and information that will be added to the taxonomy in order to adapt the existing information in the collections to the terminology presented; the third refers to the elaboration of the preliminary version of the taxonomy, including the specification of sub-terms in levels, as necessary; and the fourth concerns the validation of the preliminary version of the taxonomy with the professionals involved.

2.3 Related Works

In order to identify studies already carried out on the use of taxonomies in requirements management, we we realized a systematic literature reviews [25] using the string ("taxonomies" OR "taxonomy") AND ("requirements management" AND "software") in the following databases: Web of Science, Scopus, IEEE Xplore Digital Library (IEEE) and Library, Information Science & Technology Abstracts (LISTA). And we defined as inclusion criteria within the tools of each of the databases studies published between 2000 and 2020; studies that were publications in journals or publications in conference proceedings; studies that went through the peer review process; and studies in Portuguese, English and Spanish.

The results were analyzed and after that, we selected those published in journals and/or events recognized as of quality by the scientific community and those in which it was possible to identify in which or in which requirements management activities the proposed taxonomy was applied. Other factors that were considered in the selection of the study were whether it presented the taxonomy application process, as well as the results obtained with its application. Studies identified according to the defined criteria are presented below.

The paper presented by [17] defines a taxonomy to be used in different software projects in order to help control changes in requirements based on documentation, more specifically in cases containing the requirements. Another study with a similar purpose is presented by [18], in which the proposed taxonomy, based on the types of changes that occur in UML models, is used to identify changes between two different versions of the models, helping the identification of the impact of the changes.

In [19] is propose a taxonomy based on characterizing the factors that influence changes, but focusing on technical aspects (how, when, what, and where), rather than the purpose of the change (why) or the stakeholders interested in it (who). And in [20] pro-pose a taxonomy that considers the source (who) that requested the change, allowing distinctions between the factors that contribute to the uncertainty of the requirements.

Table 1 presents a comparison between the identified works and the study presented in this article. It is presented which requisition management activities are involved in the application of the taxonomy.

As can be seen, we identified that taxonomies have been used to assist the requirements management process, especially in what involves the activities of controlling changes to requirements and managing artifacts. What differentiates this study from those that have already been developed is that it is being proposed that taxonomies be used in the four activities of the requirements management process: organizing the requirements; control changes to requirements; maintain traceability between requirements; and manage artifacts containing information about requirements; and not only in a specific activity of this process.

Table 1. Works identified in the literature X objectives of this article.

Publication	Requirements management activity
[18]	Artifacts management
[19]	Change control
[20]	Change control
[17]	Change control
This work	Organization of requirements; change control; maintenance of traceability, and management of artifacts

3 Research Stages

For the development of this research, the steps presented in Table 2 were followed:

Table 2. Research stages.

Stages	Description
1. Identification of the problem to be solved	Based on the literature, we identified that one of the main factors of failure in software projects is related to the Requirements Engineering process [12]. And considering that requirements are information, we look for an area called information management tools used to assist this process, identifying taxonomies as one of the possible tools to be used in this context
2. Analysis of taxonomies' goals in relation to requirements management goals	In order to verify if the taxonomies were indeed capable of being applied in Software Requirement Engineering, we carried out an analysis of their objectives in relation to the objectives of each of the activities of the requirements management process, and after this analysis we found that the taxonomies could help the activities of: requirements organization; control your changes; maintenance of traceability between them and management of artifacts containing the project requirements
3. Definition of the process for applying taxonomies and criteria for evaluating the results	During this stage, we defined the project in which the taxonomy would be applied. We developed guidelines for applying the taxonomy in the context of requirements management, and defined the criteria for evaluating the results of applying the taxonomy
4. Construction of a taxonomy to meet the requirements management of a project and evaluation of the results obtained	We built a taxonomy to help the requirements management process of a real software, and after its application, it was evaluated and classified considering four aspects of applicability: complexity of use in the context of software development, satisfaction with the results, use of resources and adaptability

4   Analysis of Taxonomies' Objectives in Relation to the Objectives of Requirements Management Activities

To verify if in fact the taxonomies would be candidates to be used in the context of requirements management, we carried out an analysis to identify in which or which of the activities of the requirements management process they could add value to. The analysis was carried out based on the objectives of the taxonomies and the objectives of the requirements organization activities; control your changes; maintenance of traceability between them and management of artifacts containing the project requirements.

According to [15], a taxonomy is defined as a classification system that supports access to information, allowing to classify, allocate, retrieve and communicate information in a logical way, and can be used both for the organization of documents and for the organization of information related to a given context.

Despite having been identified in the literature proposals for the use of taxonomies to support the activities of control of the changes suffered by the requirements, and of management of the artifacts containing the information about the project requirements – as presented above; based on the objectives of this tool, we found that, in addition to assisting in the aforementioned activities, taxonomies can be used in requirements organization activities and also in maintaining traceability between them, through the classification of requirements and also of the documents generated.

5   Application and Assessment of Taxonomies in the Context of Software Requirements Management

To demonstrate that taxonomies can be used in the context of requirements management and meet the four activities of this process, they were applied in a project of a system to meet a need of the Personnel Management Department of a company in southern Brazil called Special License System, whose objective is to automate the process of requesting and authorizing the company's employees to enjoy a special leave, and after its application, the taxonomy created was evaluated in relation to its complexity, satisfaction, resources involved and adaptability.

5.1   Taxonomy Application

The taxonomy application process began at a meeting with those responsible for the Special License System requirements, where we presented the planned steps for the application and evaluation of the tool. Soon after, those responsible for the requirements made available the documentation containing the requirements and other artifacts already prepared. For the Special License System design, the team used the Enterprise Architect tool to document the functional requirements (FR), non-functional requirements (NFR) and business rules (BR); develop use case diagrams; and store images of screen prototypes to meet some of the requirements. And, to represent the most critical functional requirements, the Business Process Model and Notation (BPMN) and the Bizagi Modeler tool were used.

After analyzing the artifacts, we started the construction of the taxonomy based on the identified requirements and their documentation, which followed the four steps suggested in [16]: (i) capture of knowledge related to the taxonomy to be developed; (ii) analysis of the information that will compose the taxonomy; (iii) elaboration of the taxonomic structure; and (iv) validation of the taxonomy created.

To capture knowledge related to the taxonomy, we used all artifacts containing functional requirements, non-functional requirements, business rules, use case diagrams, prototypes and BPNM models prepared by the Special License System project team. It is important to emphasize that, in general, taxonomies are organized based on hierarchical categories, but for [21] this is not the most suitable option for those that aim to meet demands in corporate environments, since, for this purpose, they need to be flexible, pragmatic and coherent. Considering that a taxonomy, to meet the context of software development, has such characteristics, we chose not to use hierarchical categorization, but rather the associative classification, which is more recommended in these cases.

After the first step, we started the process of analyzing the information to compose the taxonomy, giving rise to four main classes: artifacts, business rules, functional requirements and non-functional requirements. Using associative classification, each class was subdivided, generating a structure to assist the requirements management process in its four activities: organizing the requirements, controlling the changes suffered by them, maintaining their traceability and organizing the documents containing the requirements. We classify the functional requirements and business rules according to the modules to which they belong in the Special License System, we classify the non-functional requirements according to the classification suggested by [22] – reliability, usability, performance and supportability – and we classify the artifacts according to the information contained in each of them. Figure 1 presents a part of the elaborated taxonomy.

In addition to the organization of requirements and artifacts, this classification structure enabled the establishment of requirements-requirements, requirements-business rules and requirements-artifacts relationships, allowing better traceability and, consequently, better control of its changes. We used the TemaTres[1] tool to build the taxonomy and the taxonomy created to meet the requirements management process of the Special License System is available in full at https://pbfagundes.com/firma.

---

[1] TemaTres is an open source tool for managing formal representations of knowledge, including thesauri, taxonomies, ontologies and glossaries. It is available for download at: https://www. vocabularyserver.com/.

Fig. 1. Part of the taxonomy elaborated for the Special License System.

5.2 Taxonomy Assessment

After preparing the taxonomy, we started its evaluation and, for that, we defined that the process would be composed of two steps: verifying if in fact the taxonomy meets the objectives of the requirements management activities to which it was related in the analysis carried out and presented in the Sect. 4; and classify the taxonomy in terms of its applicability in the requirements management process.

To classify the taxonomy in relation to its applicability, aspects of complexity, satisfaction, resources and adaptability were considered. These aspects were defined with reference to other research already carried out that addressed evaluation methods in models for Software Engineering and Requirements Engineering, such as those presented in [23–25], who suggest that techniques, tools, instruments, models or processes should be easy to use and understand, adaptable to different application contexts, and its results must satisfy the needs of the interested parties.

A set of questions was defined to evaluate each of the mentioned aspects, which composed an evaluation form where we used dichotomous questions (yes or no) and using a Likert scale from 1 to 4: 1. I totally disagree; 2. Disagree; 3. Agree; and 4. I fully agree.

The taxonomy elaborated was evaluated with the contribution of the professionals involved in the Special License System project. For each question, only one value was assigned, which, depending on the case, was a consensus among all. To arrive at the final classification of each of the aspects evaluated, the same value of the evaluation scale was considered – 1. I totally disagree; 2. Disagree; 3. Agree; and 4. I fully agree – for each of the questions answered, and the arithmetic average calculated, according to the formula presented in Fig. 2.

$$\frac{QV1 + QV2 + ... + QVn}{TI} = FAV$$

QV = question value;
TI = total aspect issues; and
FAV = final aspect value.

Fig. 2. Formula for calculating the final aspect value (FAV)

After calculating the final value of each aspect, which could vary from 1 to 4 in decimal values, it was necessary to define a rounding criterion to transform it into an integer value, which would be assigned to the final classification of the aspect (FCA), presented in Table 3. The description of each FCA for each of the aspects is presented in Table 4.

Table 3. Criteria for the final appearance classification (FAC).

FAV	FAC
If FAV $= 4$	4
If FAV < 4 e $> =3$	3
If FAV < 3 e $> =2$	2
If FAV < 2	1

Table 5 presents the form with the results of the assessment made for the taxonomy designed to help manage the requirements of the Special License System project.

Table 4. Description of the final aspect classification (FAC).

Aspect	Description of Each Final Aspect Classification
Complexity	If FAC = 4 - No complexity If FAC = 3 - Low complexity If FAC = 2 - Medium complexity If FAC = 1 - High complexity
Satisfaction	If FAC = 4 - Highly satisfactory If FAC = 3 - Satisfactory If FAC = 2 - Moderately satisfactory If FAC = 1 - Unsatisfactory
Resources	If FAC = 4 - No need to use specific resources or investments If FAC = 3 - Low need to use specific resources or investments If FAC = 2 - Medium need to use specific resources or investments If FAC = 1 - High need to use specific resources or investments
Adaptability	If FAC = 4 - High degree of adaptability If FAC = 3 - Medium degree of adaptability If FAC = 2 - Low degree of adaptability If FAC = 1 - No adaptability

Table 5. Taxonomy evaluation result.

1. Do you consider that the results obtained with the elaboration of the taxonomy helped the requirements organization activity?			(X) yes ( ) no	
2. Do you consider that the results obtained with the elaboration of the taxonomy helped the control activity in the alterations of the requirements?			(X) yes ( ) no	
3. Do you consider that the results obtained with the elaboration of the taxonomy helped the traceability activity among the requirements?			(X) yes ( ) no	
4. Do you consider that the results obtained with the elaboration of the taxonomy helped the activity of managing the artifacts?			(X) yes ( ) no	

Complexity Aspect	1	2	3	4
1. Guidelines for applying taxonomies are easy to understand.			X	
2. No experience is required for its application in the requirements management process.				X
3. The taxonomy was easy to apply in the context of software development.				X

(continued)

Table 5. (*continued*)

4. The generated artifacts were easy to understand and use by those responsible for the project requirements.				X
FAC - Complexity: 3 (Low complexity)				

Satisfaction Aspect	**1**	**2**	**3**	**4**
1. The resulting artifacts were found to be useful for requirements management.				X
2. The results achieved the objectives of the requirements management activities for which it is proposed.				X
3. The effort required was satisfactory in terms of its contribution to the requirements management process.				X
FAC - Satisfaction: 4 (Highly Satisfactory)				

Resources Aspect	**1**	**2**	**3**	**4**
1. It does not require the use of specific resources for itsapplication in the context of requirements management.			X	
2. It does not require the use of specific resources for the use of artifacts resulting from its application in the context of requirements management.				X
3. It does not require financial investments for its application in the context of requirements management.				X
4. It does not require financial investments for the use of artifacts resulting from its application in the context of requirements management.				X
FAC - Resources: 3 (Low need to use specific resources or investments)				

Adaptability Aspect	**1**	**2**	**3**	**4**
1. Taxonomies can be applied to any type of software development process.				X
2. You can apply taxonomies regardless of project size.				X
3. You can apply taxonomies regardless of the project domain.				X
FAC - Adaptability: 4 (High degree of adaptability)				

5.3 Analysis of Application Results and Assessment of the Taxonomy in the Context of Requirements Management

Regarding their understanding, applicability and use, taxonomies present a low degree of complexity. The evaluation showed that there is no need for previous experience with the instrument itself; however, we believe that a prior knowledge of classification processes on the part of the person responsible for requirements management can help in its elaboration.

The evaluation carried out indicated that the taxonomy elaborated was classified as "highly satisfactory" in terms of its possibility of contributing to the management of the Special License System requirements, as well as in relation to the effort required for its application, since the results obtained reached the objectives of the requirements management activities to which they were related.

Regarding the resources needed for the elaboration of the taxonomy, we found that this tool does not need specific resources or financial investments for its elaboration and use, given that it can be built and visualized from tools available for free. However, we recommend the use of software that helps in the elaboration, maintenance and use of this type of tool, such as, for example, TemaTres.

Taxonomies can be developed to meet any type of software project and do not necessarily need to cover all requirements and/or all artifacts generated for the project. If the person responsible for managing requirements identifies, for example, the need to develop a taxonomy that meets only the artifacts containing the requirements, it can be developed. The important thing to highlight in this case is that those responsible are aware of the real needs involved with the application of this instrument and that the success of its use is directly related to the purpose it seeks to meet.

6   Conclusions

Although there are proposals in the literature involving the use of taxonomies to meet some of the activities of the requirements management process, we found that taxonomies can contribute to the process as a whole, confirming the analysis presented in Sect. 4. Therefore, it can be said that the evaluation showed that this instrument can be considered within the scope of requirements management for:

- organize the requirements, once they have been classified and organized into classes according to specific characteristics previously defined;
- help control the changes suffered by the requirements, because from this organization and classification it was possible to establish relationships between them, so that, if a requirement is changed, it is possible to identify the other requirements related to it;
- maintain traceability between requirements (vertical traceability) and between requirements and their artifacts (horizontal traceability), because from the established relationships it was also possible to define traceability points. However, it should be noted that navigability between them is only possible through a tool that allows this action; and
- enable better management of artifacts, since the artifacts were classified according to their contents and related to the requirements contained in each of them.

We also concluded that the taxonomic structure to be used must meet the objectives defined for the taxonomy, there being no single guideline for its elaboration in the context of requirements management. The definition of the classes and subclasses that will be used in its structure must be based on the needs and objectives of its use in requirements management, and the decision must involve the person responsible for managing the requirements and the users of the taxonomy.

An important issue is the timing of taxonomy construction in the Requirements Engineering process. For the Special License System, it was elaborated after defining the general requirements of the system and after elaborating some technical artifacts; however, we believe that the taxonomy can be structured even before the requirements identification activity. As requirements are identified and artifacts are created, they are associated with classes and subclasses created.

Although we came to the conclusion that taxonomies may contribute to the requirements management process, it was not possible to establish the extent of this contribution. For this, it would be necessary to apply them in different projects and contexts and compare the results obtained. Thus, it is suggested that one of the proposals for future work is the development of studies that can continue this investigation, based on the definition of criteria for the assessment of the impacts of the application of taxonomies in the requirements management process.

References

1. Sommerville, I.: Software Engineering. 10. ed. Pearson, London (2016)
2. Macedo, D.D., Araújo, G.M., Dutra, M.L., Dutra, S.T., Lezana, Á.G.: Toward an efficient healthcare CloudIoT architecture by using a game theoryapproach. Concurr. Eng. **27**(3), 189–200 (2019)
3. Kotonya, G., Sommerville, I.: Requirements Engineering: Processes and Techniques, 1st edn. Wiley, West Sussex (1998)
4. Pressman, R.S.: Software Engineering: A Practitioner's Approach, 8th edn. McGraw-Hill, New York (2014)
5. Pohl, K.: Requirements engineering: fundamentals, principles, and techniques. Springer, New York (2010)
6. O'Regan, G.: Concise Guide to Software Engineering: From Fundamentals to Application Methods. Springer, New York (2017)
7. Goguen, J.A.: Formality and informality in requirements engineering. In: IEEE International Conference on Requirements Engineering. IEEE, Colorado Springs (1996)
8. Jackson, M.: Problems and requirements. In: IEEE International Symposium on Requirements Engineering (RE 1995). IEEE, York (1995)
9. Fagundes, P.B.: FIRMa: Uma proposta baseada nos instrumentos utilizados pela gestão da informação para auxiliar o processo de gestão de requisitos de software. Ph.D (Thesis) Federal University of Santa Catarina - UFSC, Florianópolis (2021)
10. Kruchten, P.: The Rational Unified Process: An Introduction, 3rd edn. Addison-Wesley Professional, Boston (2003)
11. Aurum, A., Wohlin, C.: The fundamental nature of requirements engineering activities as a decision-making process. Inf. Softw. Technol. **45**(14), 945–954 (2003)
12. Fernandez, D.M., et al.: Naming the pain in requirements engineering: contemporary problems, causes, and effects in practice. Empir. Softw. Eng. **22**(5), 2298–2338 (2017)

13. Kahn, R., Blair, B.: Information Nation: Seven Keys To Information Management Compliance, 2nd edn. John Wiley & Sons, Indianapolis (2009)
14. Kettinger, W.J., Marchand, D.A.: Information management practices (IMP) from the senior manager's perspective: an investigation of the IMP construct and its measurement. Inf. Syst. J. 21(5), 385–406 (2011)
15. Hodge, G.M.: Systems of Knowledge Organization for Digital Libraries: Beyond Traditional Authority Files. The Digital Library Federation, Washington (2000)
16. Holgate, L.: Creating and using taxonomies to enhance enterprise search. EContent 27(7–8), S10–S10 (2004)
17. Basirati, M.R., et al.: Understanding changes in use cases: a case study. In: IEEE International Requirements Engineering Conference. IEEE, Ottawa (2015)
18. Briand, L., et al.: Impact analysis and change management of UML models. In: IEEE International Conference on Software Maintenance, ICSM. IEEE, Amsterdam (2003)
19. Buckley, J., et al.: Towards a taxonomy of software change. J. Softw. Maintenance Evol. 17(5), 309–332 (2005)
20. Mcgee, S., Greer, D.: A software requirements change source taxonomy. In: International Conference on Software Engineering Advances, ICSEA, pp. 51–58. IEEE Computer Society (2009)
21. Woods, E.: The corporate taxonomy: creating a new order. KMWorld (2004). https://www.kmworld.com/Articles/Editorial/Features/The-corporate-taxonomy-creating-a-new-order-9566.aspx. Accessed 14 Jan 2022
22. Leffingwell, D.: Agile Software Requirements: Lean Requirements Practices for Teams, Programs, and the Enterprise. Addison-Wesley Professional, Boston (2010)
23. Beecham, S., et al.: Using an expert panel to validate a requirements process improvement model. J. Syst. Softw. 76(3), 251–275 (2005)
24. Keshta, I., et al.: Towards implementation of requirements management specific practices (SP1.3 and SP1.4) for saudi arabian small and medium sized software development organizations. IEEE Access, 5, 24162–24183 (2017)
25. Niazi, M., et al.: A maturity model for the implementation of software process improvement: an empirical study. J. Syst. Softw. 74(2), 155–172 (2005)
26. Silva Júnior, E.M., Dutra, M.L.: A roadmap toward the automatic composition of systematic literature reviews. Iberoamerican J. Sci. Meas. Commun. 1(2), 1–22 (2021). https://doi.org/10.47909/ijsmc.52

Assessment of Heart Patients Dataset Through Regression and Classification Algorithms

Eliane Somavilla$^{(\boxtimes)}$ ⓘ and Gustavo Medeiros de Araujo ⓘ

PGCIN, Federal University of Santa Catarina, Florianópolis, Brazil
eliane.somavilla@gmail.com, gustavo.araujo@ufsc.br

Abstract. This study focused on the survival analysis of patients with heart failure who were admitted to the Institute of Cardiology and Allied Hospital of Faisalabad-Pakistan during April and December 2015. All patients had left ventricular systolic dysfunction, belonging to classes III and IV of the classification carried out by the New York Heart Association. Several Machine Learning algorithms capable of analyzing data through regression and classification techniques were used to predict the mortality rate of future patients with similar problems. Characteristics such as age, ejection fraction, serum creatinine, serum sodium, anemia, platelets, creatinine phosphokinase, blood pressure, diabetes and smoking were considered as potential contributors to mortality. All characteristics were analyzed in order to identify the minimum set of information necessary for a quick and efficient diagnosis of heart failure.

Keywords: Heart patients · Regression algorithms · Classification algorithms · Feature select

1 Introduction

Annually, cardiovascular disease kills millions of people worldwide and manifests itself primarily as myocardial infarctions and heart failure. Heart failure is characterized by the heart's inability to act as a pump, either by a deficit in contraction and/or relaxation, compromising the body's functioning. When untreated, the quality of life is reduced, which can lead to the patient's death [1].

The main cardiovascular risk factors are directly related to factors such as high blood pressure, diabetes, smoking, dyslipidemia (fats in the blood) and sedentary lifestyle. The presence of these factors alone or together in an organism causes the development of coronary disease that can lead to acute myocardial infarction or decreased heart performance [1].

Other causes include diseases that affect the heart valves (degenerative or inflammatory, such as kidney and rheumatic diseases), congenital diseases, genetic diseases, autoimmune, inflammatory (Eg: during peripartum), toxicity (cancer treatment) and also infectious (Eg: AIDS). The abuse of alcoholic beverages and drugs such as cocaine also increases the risk of developing heart disease which is now responsible for 31% of deaths worldwide [1].

© ICST Institute for Computer Sciences, Social Informatics and Telecommunications Engineering 2022
Published by Springer Nature Switzerland AG 2022. All Rights Reserved
A. L. Pinto and R. Arencibia-Jorge (Eds.): DIONE 2022, LNICST 452, pp. 178–190, 2022.
https://doi.org/10.1007/978-3-031-22324-2_14

Diagnosis of heart failure is made clinically by a medical professional specialized in cardiology, through the history told by the patient. The report may include intolerance to exertion, shortness of breath at bedtime, and swelling in the lower limbs and abdomen. The diagnosis usually also considers the physical examination of the accumulation of blood in the lungs and in the body as a whole [1].

Left ventricular systolic involvement is responsible for most cases of chronic heart failure and can be diagnosed echocardiographically by a left ventricular ejection fraction equal to or less than 0.40. Diastolic dysfunction is characterized by symptoms of heart failure with preserved ejection fraction (usually > 0.45) [2].

Heart failure can be established in any age group and its prevalence is estimated at 1 to 2% of the population. In addition, it affects progressively with increasing age, and after 70 years of age, more than 10% of the population is affected. After the age of 55, there is an approximate 30% risk of developing heart failure [1].

Aiming to support health professionals in the diagnosis of their patients, the objective of this study is to estimate the mortality rates due to heart failure and prove its connection with some of the main risk factors pointed out by the Hospital Israelita Albert Einstein in the city of São Paulo/ SP-BR and SCIELO-Brasil, choosing a reliable database for the study and application of Machine Learning algorithms specialized in data analysis through regression and classification techniques.

Also considering that the reality of many hospitals and clinics in Brazil and in several other countries does not contribute to a complete and detailed diagnosis for patients, in this study we assess what are the minimum characteristics that a health professional must have access to make a quick diagnosis and effective with respect to heart failure.

2   Related Work

The original version of the dataset used in this study was collected by Tanvir Ahmad, Assia Munir, Sajjad Haider Bhatti, Muhammad Aftab and Muhammad Ali Raza (Faculty of Government University, Faisalabad, Pakistan) and made available in July 2017. The current version of the dataset was compiled by David Chicco (Krembil Research Institute, Toronto, Canada) and donated to the University of California Machine Learning Repository under the same copyright in January 2020 [3].

In the study published in 2017 by Ahmad, Munir, Bhatti, Aftab and Raza, the collected data were analyzed using the COX regression model. Using the COX regression model, the risk of death of an individual was linked with one or more variables and the significance of these variables was also tested. The results were validated by calculating the calibration slope and the model's discrimination ability via bootstrapping [5].

As a result, it was observed that the chances of death from heart failure increase with increasing age. The risk of death increases by 4% for each additional year of age. Ejection Fraction (EF) was another significant factor, the hazard ratio among patients with EF ≤ 30 was 67% and 59% higher compared to patients with EF 3045 and EF ≥ 45, respectively. Other data observed indicates that the risk of death doubles when serum creatinine is above its normal level. The study shows that an anemic patient is 76% more likely to die compared to a non-anemic one. Increasing serum sodium reduces the risk of death by 6%. Data on sex, smoking, high blood pressure, diabetes, creatinine phosphokinase and platelets were not significant. Through graphs to measure the model's calibration, an accuracy of 77% was proven, considering the death event occurred with an average of 50 days of medical follow-up and 81% when considering the death event occurred with 250 days of treatment doctor. This shows that the Cox model's skill is greater at a longer follow-up time [5].

In 2020 researchers Chicco and Jurman published a new study with this same database using machine learning, whose focus was on the use of the Random Forests algorithm compared to several biostatistics techniques, that is, statistical methods focused on the biological and medical field.. The methods used were the Mann-Whitney U test, the Pearson correlation coefficient and the chi-square test to compare the distribution of each characteristic between the two groups (surviving individuals and dead patients). In addition to the Shapiro-Wilk test to verify the distribution of each resource [4].

As a result, traditional biostatistical analysis selected ejection fraction and serum creatinine as the two most relevant characteristics. The same result was obtained with machine learning. In addition, our approach has shown that machine learning can be used effectively for binary classification of electronic health records from patients with cardiovascular disease [4].

3   Methodology

In this study, we analyzed a database with real information about patients with heart failure using machine learning algorithms. In this way, computers have the ability to earn according to expected responses through associations of different data.

Another benefit achieved refers to the selection of resources, because, through specific functions of the algorithms, it is possible to automatically select the subset of data considered most relevant to define the result of the computational analysis. In this way, we improve computational efficiency and reduce the model's generalization error by removing extraneous data or noise.

In this study we use several Machine Learning algorithms to analyze the result achieved through different perspectives. We made use of the Python programming language and the main library used was sklearn, which offers a set of classification and regression algorithms. Before applying the algorithms, we carry out the initial processing of the database.

3.1   Pre-processing

After initial analysis of the data that make up the dataframe, we divided the database composed of 299 records into two sets, X and y, respectively. The set X corresponds to the independent variables of the dataframe, which are the data from the blood tests and the echocardiogram of each patient. The set corresponds to the dependent variable, y, indicates whether the patient died or not considering the result of the combination of variables independently assigned to each patient (Fig. 1).

Next, we use the SelectKBest resource belonging to the feature_selection module of the sklearn library. This feature removes all variables, except K features with the

	age	anaemia	creatinine_phosphokinase	diabetes	ejection_fraction	high_blood_pressure	platelets	serum_creatinine	serum_sodium	smoking
0	75.0	0	582	0	20	1	2	1.9	130	0
1	55.0	0	7861	0	38	0	2	1.1	136	0
2	65.0	0	146	0	20	0	2	1.3	129	1
3	50.0	1	111	0	20	0	2	1.9	137	0
4	65.0	1	160	1	20	0	2	2.7	116	0

Fig. 1. Fragment of the set X

highest score, where K is a parameter that indicates the number of variables that should be evaluated by the resource used. [11].

The next step was the division of sets X and y in order to properly train the algorithms and perform machine learning. 80% of the data was used for training and 20% of the data was intended for testing in order to verify the behavior of each algorithm when receiving new data and make sure that the algorithm really learned based on the data used during the training.

Afterwards, we use the StandardScaler feature to normalize the values of variables X that will be used for training and testing. This feature transforms the data so that the distribution has a mean value of 0 and a standard deviation of 1 [14].

Finally, we ran the entire pre-processing process 10 times and the algorithms were run with increasingly smaller datasets considering the K most important characteristics pointed out by SelectKBest. The result obtained in each round was recorded for future comparison after applying other similar resources, but more suitable for each algorithm.

3.2 Regression Algorithms

Regression is one of the most used forecasting methods in the statistical field. The main objective is to verify how the variables of interest influence a response variable (y), in addition to creating a mathematical model capable of predicting y values based on new values of predictor variables X [15].

Multivariate linear regression is indicated when the set X includes more than one predictor variable. In our study, initially, 10 variables are considered in set X [16].

Once the pre-processing is executed, the recursive elimination of resources (RFE) is used to evaluate the best characteristics specifically for this algorithm through the RFE function. Given an external estimator that assigns weights to resources (for example, the coefficients of a linear model), the objective of recursive resource elimination (RFE) is to select variables considering smaller and smaller sets. First, the estimator is trained on the initial set of features and the importance of each feature is obtained through any specific attribute (such as coef_ or feature_importance). Then, the less important features are removed from the current set. This procedure is repeated on the remaining set until the desired number of features to be selected is reached [13].

Polynomial regression makes use of polynomials, which are algebraic expressions, used in cases where the model variables do not follow a linear form of data. In this case, the independent variables are expanded by the number of polynomials, as configured. In the present study, the best results for this algorithm were observed using the degree 3 of polynomials [15].

After pre-processing, we again use recursive resource elimination (RFE) to identify the importance of each variable from set X to the model.

The result obtained was expressed through the metric R2_score that calculates the coefficient of determination. This coefficient provides a metric of how well future samples are likely to be predicted by the model. The best possible score is 1.0 and can be negative because the model can be arbitrarily worse. The same metric was used with the Multivariate Linear Regression algorithm to measure the accuracy of the model during the test phase [12].

This entire process was performed 10 times for each of the regression algorithms. Each round considered the best variables according to the resource selection method used. The result obtained in each round was recorded for future comparison after applying similar resources, but more suitable for each algorithm.

3.3 Classification Algorithms

Classification algorithms aim to classify items or samples according to observed characteristics. Through algorithms that implement this method, it is possible to teach the computer to carry out the classification in order to identify which category a given data sample belongs to [15].

KNN (K-Nearest Neighbors) is a classification and regression algorithm whose objective is to determine to which group a sample belongs based on the distance to K neighboring samples [15]. In the present study, considering all the variables of the independent set, the best results for this algorithm were observed through the analysis of the 6 closest neighbors.

After the pre-processing, we use the Direct Sequential Selection through the SequentialFeatureSelector (SFS) function belonging to the feature_selection module of the sklearn library. SFS removes or adds one resource at a time based on the performance of the classifier until the desired K size resource subset is reached [17].

The RFC (Random Forest Classifier) is a classification and regression algorithm whose objective is to determine to which group a given sample belongs based on decision trees created at the time of training [15]. In the present study, considering all the variables of the independent set, the best results for this algorithm were observed through the creation of 7 decision trees. After pre-processing, we use the feature_importances function available to all ensemble algorithms, such as RFC. This method returns a score for each variable. The higher the score, the greater the importance of this variable for the result of the computational analysis [18].

The SVM (Support Vector Machine) is a classification and regression algorithm whose objective is to determine which group a given sample belongs by means of a separation line between two classes. This line is commonly called the Hyperplane. This algorithm has a theory a little more robust compared to other simpler algorithms such as KNN. The SVM can be configured to work with linear problems, using the Linear Kernel, or nonlinear ones, using the RBF Kernel (Radial Basis Function), which performs a mapping to a larger space [10].

After preprocessing the data, we used recursive resource elimination (RFE) to identify the importance of each variable from set X to the model.

In the first tests performed in this study, the Linear kernel reached 75% accuracy considering the entire set of initial independent variables and showed similar accuracy as the resources were recursively eliminated. Kernel RBF reached the same percentage from the moment that set X was made up of 8 variables. We chose to follow the study with the Linear Kernel.

The Logistic Regression, is a classification algorithm considered the most used statistical method to model categorical variables. Logistic Regression and Linear Regression are similar. While in Linear Regression we have a continuous independent variable, in Logistic Regression the response variable is binary [15].

After preprocessing the data, we used recursive resource elimination (RFE) to identify the importance of each variable from set X to the model.

The result obtained for all classification algorithms was expressed through a confusion matrix, which is a comparative table of the values that each algorithm brought as a prediction in relation to the real values that occurred [15]. That is, after training a model and applying the predictions on the separate dataset for testing, the result obtained is expressed in a column with the predictions.

This entire process was performed 10 times for each of the regression algorithms. Each round considered the best variables according to the resource selection method used. The result obtained in each round was recorded for future comparison after applying similar resources, but more suitable for each algorithm.

4 Exploratory Data Analysis

4.1 Dataset

The database used for the study is part of the Machine Learning Repository (UCI) file repository that maintains a collection of databases and data generators used by the community to feed machine learning algorithms. Created in 1987. Since then, it has been widely used by students, educators and researchers around the world as a primary source of machine learning datasets [3].

The data set chosen for the study contains the medical records of 299 patients with heart failure and all patients had left ventricular systolic dysfunction, belonging to classes III and IV of the classification performed by the New York Heart Association. Data collection was carried out during the follow-up period in 2015, specifically between the months of May and December. This data period was the most detailed dataset available at the UCI [3].

Each patient profile has 13 clinical features. Are they:

1. **Age**: patient age (years)
2. **Anemia**: decreased red blood cells or hemoglobin (boolean)
3. **High blood pressure**: if the patient has hypertension (Boolean)
4. **Creatinine phosphokinase (CPK)**: blood CPK enzyme level (mcg / L)
5. **Diabetes**: if the patient has diabetes (Boolean)
6. **Ejection fraction (EF)**: percentage of blood that leaves the heart with each contraction (percentage)
7. **Platelets**: platelets in blood (kilo plates / mL)

8. **Gender:** female or male (binary)
9. **Serum creatinine:** blood serum creatinine level (mg / dL)
10. **Serum sodium:** blood serum sodium level (mEq / L)
11. **Smoking:** whether the patient smokes or not (Boolean)
12. **Time:** follow-up period (4 to 285 days, with an average of 130 days)
13. **Death event:** if the patient died during the follow-up period (Boolean)

4.2 Exploratory Analysis

The current study is based on 299 heart failure patients, 105 women and 194 men. For the quantitative assessment of disease progression, physicians typically use the New York Heart Association (NYHA) functional classification, which determines four classes ranging from the absence of symptoms of normal activity (Class I) to a stage in which any activity causes discomfort and symptoms occur at rest (Class IV) [4].

All patients were between 40 and 95 years old, had left ventricular systolic dysfunction, and had previous heart failure that placed them in class III or IV of the New York Heart Association (NYHA) classification. The disease was diagnosed in patients in this database by echocardiogram report, blood tests or notes written by the physician [4].

Follow-up time ranged from 4 to 285 days, with an average of 130 days. Follow-up time was not considered as an input parameter for this study, as it aimed to focus on data related to the cause of heart failure and not on the length of time the patient was under follow-up and medical treatment. The gender of patients (sex) was also not considered as an input parameter as it is understood that it is only a characteristic used to categorize patients into two distinct groups.

After disregarding the length of follow-up and gender variables, the other characteristics were used as potential variables to explain mortality from heart failure. Platelets were divided into three levels based on medical references per liter of blood [6]: values below 150000 indicate a low index, between 150000 and 450000 indicate a normal index and above 450000 indicate a high index related to the presence of thrombi or blood clotting. Serum creatinine greater than its normal level (1.5) is an indicator of renal dysfunction [4].

Among the 299 patients studied, 96 were smokers, 105 had high blood pressure, 67 had creatinine greater than 1.5, 125 had anemia, 129 had diabetes and 219 had ejection fraction less than or equal to 40, that is, the percentage of blood pumped out of a left ventricle with each heartbeat was up to 40%. A total of 252 patients had a normal platelet count, which means that there was no thrombus or blood clotting. A total of 96 patients died during the study period.

Sodium is a mineral that serves the correct functioning of muscles and nerves. An abnormally low level of sodium in the blood can be caused by heart failure [7]. Sodium is considered low when lower than 136 (mEq / L), and in these cases the patient has hyponatremia, which is the most common electrolyte disturbance in hospitalized patients. The presence of hyponatremia is associated with the need for admission to the intensive care unit, prolonged hospitalization and mortality. It is still unclear whether there is a direct causal relationship or whether hyponatremia is just a marker of underlying disease severity. However, it is known that the inadequate management of a patient with hyponatremia can cause severe neurological damage or death [8]. In the study, a total of 200 patients have normal levels of sodium in the body and 99 have low levels.

Finally, creatinine phosphokinase (CPK) indicates the level of the CPK enzyme in the blood. When muscle tissue, such as the heart and brain, is damaged, CPK flows into the blood. Therefore, high levels of CPK in a patient's blood may indicate heart failure or injury. Reference values for creatine phosphokinase (CPK) are 32 and 294 U/L for men and 33 to 211 U/L for women, but may vary depending on the laboratory where the test is performed [9]. Considering this reference, 91 men and 58 women have an indication of damaged muscle tissue. Graphically, we can see the following percentages (Fig. 2):

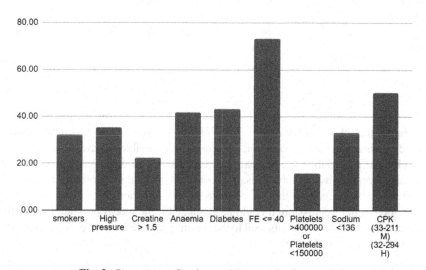

Fig. 2. Percentage of patients with a certain characteristic

5   Results and Discussion

When evaluating the results achieved through the SelectKBest resource, we can observe that the best accuracy was achieved by the classification algorithms, considering a minimum set of 3 to 4 variables for the model.

Among the 4 algorithms evaluated in this category, we observed that the KNN had a notable improvement in the accuracy rate when considering only 3 variables in the model, reaching 77% confidence. The other classification algorithms presented consistent data according to the elimination of variables from the model, obtaining a low variation in the accuracy rate. When considering only 2 variables, the model lost effectiveness for all algorithms (Table 1).

We noticed through this feature that the regression algorithms did not prove to be good options to define whether a patient will die because, in the case of Multivariate Regression, the accuracy of the model obtained a low percentage regardless of the number

Table 1. Result with SelectBest feature for evaluating variables

General Evaluation - Accuracy Using the Resource "SelectBest"

Algorithms	10 Featur.	9 Featur.	8 Featur.	7 Featur.	6 Featur.	5 Featur.	4 Featur.	3 featur.	2 Featur.
KNN	0.65	0.65	0.66	0.66	0.7	0.7	0.65	0.77	0.7
SVM	0.75	0.73	0.72	0.73	0.72	0.73	**0.73**	0.72	0.63
Random forest	0.65	0.73	0.68	0.66	0.7	0.7	0.66	**0.72**	0.66
Logistic regression	0.72	0.73	0.72	0.72	0.7	0.72	0.73	**0.73**	0.65
Polynomial regression	**0.94**	0.32	0.75	0.64	0.49	0.45	0.39	0.33	0.14
Multivariate regression	0.15	0.16	0.17	0.17	0.17	0.17	0.17	0.16	0.06

of variables that made up the model. The Polynomial Regression Algorithm obtained accuracy greater than 90% when considering the 10 variables in the model, however, when eliminating variables the accuracy decreased and we did not verify linearity in the percentage obtained as a result. Thus, it is considered that this algorithm did not show consistency in the same way that we observed in classification algorithms. Specifically for the Polynomial Regression, it could be evaluated if the model presented overfitting, which occurs when the model fits well to the training dataset, but proves to be ineffective to predict new results (Fig. 3).

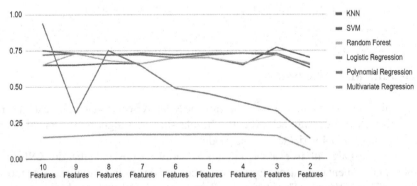

Fig. 3. Accuracy achieved through the SelectBest feature for evaluating variables

5.1   Evaluating Algorithms with Other Resources

When evaluating the results achieved through specific resources used to identify the best variables of each algorithm, we can observe that the best accuracy was achieved by each algorithm with a distinct amount of minimum variables (Table 2).

Table 2. Result with different ways to evaluating variables

General Evaluation - Accuracy Using Different Methods for each Algorithm									
Algorithms	10 Featur.	9 Featur.	8 Featur.	7 Featur.	6 Featur.	5 Featur.	4 Featur.	3 Featur.	2 Featur.
KNN	0.65	0.62	0.65	0.65	0.65	0.65	0.65	**0.68**	0.7
SVM	0.75	0.75	0.75	0.73	**0.75**	0.72	0.72	0.72	0.63
Random Forest	0.65	0.68	0.7	0.66	0.7	0.68	**0.75**	0.66	0.56
Logistic Regression	0.72	0.72	0.72	0.73	0.73	0.75	**0.75**	0.73	0.68
Polynomial Regression	**0.94**	0.72	0.72	0.69	0.57	−0.66	0.34	0.33	0.16
Multivariate Regression	0.1564	0.1548	0.1552	0.1511	0.1655	0.1667	0.1522	0.1598	−0.0077

We note that:

- The **KNN** algorithm, which used the feature_selection feature of the SequentialFeatureSelector function from the mlxtend library, obtained better accuracy when used with a minimum of **2 variables**. However, the algorithm maintained low variation, regardless of using the 10 model variables or only the reduced set of 2 variables.
- The **SVM**, which used the feature_selection feature of the RFE function from the sklearn library, obtained the best result with a minimum of **6 variables**. However, the algorithm kept low variation, regardless of using the 10 model variables or just the reduced set of 3 variables. Its accuracy dropped considerably when only 2 variables were evaluated.
- The **Random Forest Classifier**, which used the feature_importances resource (proper methods of assembly algorithms), obtained the best result with a minimum of **4 variables**. It is observed that as the variables were eliminated from the model, the accuracy increased, however, there was a reduction in the accuracy rate when evaluating the algorithm with a reduced set of 7 or 3 variables. When considering a set of only 2 variables, the accuracy drops considerably.
- The **Logistic Regression**, which used the feature_selection feature of the RFE function from the sklearn library, obtained better accuracy when used with a minimum of **4 variables**. However, the algorithm kept low variation, regardless of using the 10 model variables or just the reduced set of 3 variables. Its accuracy dropped considerably when only 2 variables were evaluated.

- The **Polynomial Regression**, which used the feature_selection feature of the RFE function from the sklearn library, obtained the best result when evaluating the total set of 10 variables. As the variables were eliminated from the model, the accuracy dropped considerably, reaching negative values
- The **Multivariate Regression**, which used the feature_selection feature of the RFE function from the sklearn library, did not present an accuracy higher than 16.5% at any time, even presenting negative values.

Graphically, we clearly observe the variations (Fig. 4):

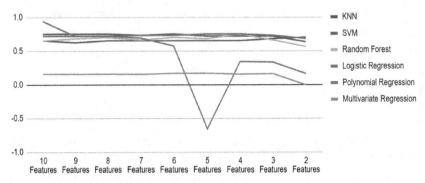

Fig. 4. Accuracy achieved through various variable evaluation features

5.2   Conclusion

All algorithms used to classify the data sample obtained consistent and linear results. Furthermore, it was confirmed that the Polynomial Regression and Multivariate Regression algorithms do not present efficient results to predict the death of a patient.

In general, age, ejection fraction (EF) and serum creatinine were the main variables to predict the mortality rate through classification algorithms. Data about anemia and diabetes, the amount of platelets in the blood and if the patient is a smoker or not were the variables that least influenced the results obtained. Variables related to high blood pressure, sodium and creatinine phosphokinase (CPK) proved to be important contributors but not determinants of the possibility of survival of a patient.

Thus, we can conclude that, through a reduced data set consisting of age, ejection fraction (EF) and serum creatinine, it is possible to predict the probability of death of patients considering an accuracy rate greater than 70% for all algorithms classification used in this study.

Considering the scenario of clinics and hospitals that often do not have all the resources needed to assess the condition of a patient with heart failure, this study directs health professionals to prioritize the data that are most relevant to the probability of survival of a patient.

6 Future Work

Considering the results obtained, a score could be developed to classify the patient's risk of dying, according to the data obtained for the variables studied. Variables that did not have a great influence on the model, such as anemia, diabetes, platelets and whether the patient is a smoker or not, could have a lower weight. On the other hand, Ejection Fraction (EF), age and serum creatinine would have a higher weight. Variables related to high blood pressure, sodium and creatinine phosphokinase (CPK) could have an intermediate weight. In this way, healthcare professionals could rely on a formula to predict the survival rate of patients with heart failure.

During the research studies were found on the influence of quality of life on treatment success for patients with heart failure. According to the Hospital Israelita Albert Einstein (2021), sedentary lifestyle is one of the causes of cardiovascular diseases that can be prevented with physical exercise.

Quality of life is also influenced by culture, income, access to information and location in which each person lives, as these variables can limit access to activities that help prevent cardiovascular disease [1]. If there was a database with information about the quality of life of patients, we could analyze the results of the study considering this reality.

References

1. Einstein, H.I.A.: https://www.einstein.br/especialidades/cardiologia/doencas-sintomas/insufi ciencia-cardiaca. Accessed 03 July 2021
2. Scielo. Tratamento da insuficiência cardíaca -- aspectos atuais. Revista da Associação Médica Brasileira, vol. 44 (2020). https://www.scielo.br/j/ramb/a/npPgV7NzQ99tWdQhvZJvCfs/?lang=pt. Accessed 03 July 2021
3. UCI. Machine Learning Repository. https://archive.ics.uci.edu/ml/datasets/Heart+failure+cli nical+records. Accessed 01 July 2021
4. Chicco, D., Jurman, G.: Machine learning can predict survival of patients with heart failure from serum creatinine and ejection fraction alone. BMC Med. Inf. Decis. Mak. **20**(16) (2020). https://bmcmedinformdecismak.biomedcentral.com/articles/10.1186/s12911-020-1023-5. Accessed 02 July 2021
5. Ahmad, T., Munir, A., Bhatti, S.H., Aftab, M., Raza, M.A.: Survival analysis of heart failure patients: a case study. Plos One (2017). https://doi.org/10.1371/journal.pone.0181001. Accessed 02 July 2021
6. Lemos, M.: https://www.tuasaude.com/plaquetas/. Accessed 03 July 2021
7. Stephens, C.: https://www.healthline.com/health/sodium-urine#purpose. Accessed 17 July 2021
8. Rocha, P.N.: Hiponatremia: conceitos básicos e abordagem prática. Revista da Associação Médica Brasileira (2011). https://www.scielo.br/j/jbn/a/ggcdv7X6mjHSyVRtcY 8fTxS/?lang=pt&format=pdf. Accessed 07 July 2021
9. Lemos, M.: https://www.tuasaude.com/exame-cpk/. Accessed 06 July 2021
10. de Oliveira Júnior, G.M.: Máquina de Vetores Suporte: estudo e análise de parâmetros para otimização de resultado. Trabalho de Conclusão de Curso (Graduação em Ciências da Computação) – Instituto de Matemática e Estatística da Universidade Federal de Pernambuco – Pernambuco (2010). https://www.cin.ufpe.br/~tg/2010-2/gmoj.pdf. Accessed 22 July 2021

11. Santana, R.: https://minerandodados.com.br/aprenda-como-selecionar-features-para-seu-modelo-de-machine-learning/. Accessed 08 July 2021
12. Scikit-Learn. https://scikit-learn.org/stable/modules/generated/sklearn.metrics.r2_score.html?highlight=r2%20score#sklearn.metrics.r2_score. Accessed 17 July 2021
13. Scikit-Learn. https://scikit-learn.org/stable/auto_examples/feature_selection/plot_rfe_digits.html#sphx-glr-auto-examples-feature-selection-plot-rfe-digits-py. Accessed 15 July 2021
14. Scikit-Learn. https://scikit-learn.org/stable/modules/generated/sklearn.preprocessing.StandardScaler.html?highlight=standardscaler#sklearn.preprocessing.StandardScaler.fit_transform. Accessed 17 July 2021
15. dos Santos, H.G.: Comparação da Performance de Algoritmos de Machine Learning para Análise Preditiva em Saúde Pública e Medicina. Tese (Doutorado em Ciências) - Programa de pós Graduação em Epidemiologia da Faculdade de Saúde Pública da Universidade de São Paulo, São Paulo (2018). https://www.teses.usp.br/teses/disponiveis/6/6141/tde-09102018-132826/publico/HellenGeremiasdosSantos_DR_ORIGINAL.pdf. Accessed 20 July 2021
16. Nogueira, F.E.: Modelos de Regressão Multivariada. Dissertação (Mestrado em Ciências) – Instituto de Matemática e Estatística da Universidade de São Paulo – São Paulo (2007). https://teses.usp.br/teses/disponiveis/45/45133/tde-25062007-163150/publico/dissertacao_4.pdf. Accessed 22 July 2021
17. Github. http://rasbt.github.io/mlxtend/user_guide/feature_selection/SequentialFeatureSelector/. Accessed 15 July 2021
18. Brownlee, J.: https://machinelearningmastery.com/calculate-feature-importance-with-python/. Accessed 15 July 2021

Classification Model Based on Chatbot and Unsupervised Algorithms to Determine Psychological Intervention Programs in Peruvian University Students

Baldwin Huamán[1]([⊠]) [iD], Dante Gómez[1] [iD], Danny Lévano[1] [iD],
Miguel Valles-Coral[2] [iD], Jorge Raul Navarro-Cabrera[2] [iD], and Lloy Pinedo[2] [iD]

[1] Escuela de posgrado, Unidad de Posgrado de Ingeniería y Arquitectura, Universidad Peruana Unión, Lima, Perú
baldwin.laban@upeu.edu.pe
[2] Facultad de Ingeniería de Sistemas e Informática, Universidad Nacional de San Martín, Tarapoto, Perú

Abstract. A strategy that supports the student's academic and personal formation is that university consider tutoring as a mechanism that supports with favorable results to fight against the desertion of students. However, there are related problems in performing student segmentation and conducting psychological interventions. The objective was to formulate a classification model for intervention programs in university students based on unsupervised algorithms. For this, we carried out a non-experimental, simple descriptive study on a population of 60 university students; we carried out the data extraction process through a chatbot that applied the BarOn ICE test. After we obtained the data, the unsupervised k-means algorithm was used to group the students into sets determined based on the closest mean value obtained from the psychological test. We built a model for classifying students based on their answers to the BarOn ICE test based on K-means, with which we obtained five groups. The model classifies students by applying a different mathematical method to that used by the models applied by psychologists.

Keywords: Automated classification · Artificial Intelligence · Grouping · K-means · University Tutoring

1 Introduction

The emotional and psychological state of the student is a fundamental element for university academic success [1], in this sense, according to University Law No. 30220 promulgated in July 2014, in Peru the State is the regulatory agent and supervisor of compliance with the basic quality conditions in public and private universities [2]. Thus, the National Superintendence of Higher University Education (SUNEDU), as established in the Law

A. L. Pinto and R. Arencibia-Jorge (Eds.): DIONE 2022, LNICST 452, pp. 191–203, 2022.
https://doi.org/10.1007/978-3-031-22324-2_15

has defined compliance with key processes to be developed to guarantee comprehensive university education [3].

Article 87 of the Law makes it mandatory for universities, through their teachers, to provide tutoring to students to guide them in their academic development and this seeks to identify, prevent and correct various situations of psycho-emotional risk, through monitoring and adequate support to the student's problem [4].

Tutoring constitutes a mechanism that can support with favorable results in the fight against the desertion of students in their university academic activities, in addition this strategy, apart from collaborating with academic training, supports personal training [5]. This process considers the university education of the student and the extracurricular needs that they may have, all developed under a personal accompaniment system, in order to support, guide and advise the student in the academic, professional and personal-social dimensions [6].

Under this premise, university tutoring together with the teaching function provide the essential mechanisms for monitoring the student's training process [7]. In this sense, universities must respond to the challenge of providing comprehensive education, institutionalizing methods and procedures that guarantee the identification of students with academic risks and establish preventive and corrective intervention programs to mitigate the probability of dropout and academic delay [8]. Thus, within universities, the tutoring area is in charge of directing certain key processes related to the psychological care and monitoring of the university student in order to promote professional development and projection [9].

However, there are factors that affect the university tutoring process such as the excessive workload of teachers, making the work they do in the academic field more difficult [10, 11]. The insufficient equipment and technological support services, where the tools used are not innovative and most of the processes are carried out manually, making it difficult to acquire new learning and adequately manage the results of psychological evaluations towards students, also affecting the time to obtain results, and limiting the performance of more periodic tests during the academic semester [12, 13].

Consequently, the difficulties that arise in monitoring the tutoring process are poor academic performance; a very common issue in universities that is related to the psychological aspect of the student [14]. Another consequence is that teachers have difficulties in virtual teaching due to technological aspects (connectivity) and this affects the basic conditions of quality, by not providing an educational service that cares about the needs of the student [15]. That is why information and communications technology (ICT) have become a basic pillar in education today, which favors and facilitates the teaching and learning processes [16, 17]. In this sense, there is a need to incorporate ICT in universities, because it is positive due to its importance in the novelties it brings with it and the employment capacity it possesses [18, 19].

The use of ICT in the field of education has become important [20], since technological tools are linked to students, because these are the ones who use electronic equipment in their related activities in their university academic training [21]. Likewise, ICT in the university context has become an element that adapts to the needs to increase the competitive advantages of universities [22].

ICTs as computer support of the knowledge society help to build innovation capacities in the field of education [19]. Digital inclusion in organizations has allowed the development of technology based on Artificial Intelligence (AI), such as chatbots and autonomous learning systems [16, 23].

That is why AI-based technology has revolutionized the ways of conducting tutoring. This has not been excepted in university tutorials that have applied business intelligence (BI) for decision-making, however, none of these focuses on being able to identify the psychological situation when they enter university [24]. Rules-based models make it easy to create chatbots. Conversational agents or chatbots have the ability to interact with users using natural language and have the capacity for continuous learning in order to expand their knowledge in the field or subject of their programmed specialty [25].

However, it is difficult to create a bot that answers complex queries. Pattern matching is weak and therefore bots based on AIML (Artificial Intelligence Markup Language) suffer when they encounter a sentence that contains no known patterns. Also, it is quite time consuming and requires a lot of effort to write the rules manually [25]. As part of the solution to this problem, unsupervised algorithms are evaluated using various structural indices [26].

The methods used to evaluate the algorithms that solve classification problems change considerably due to the intrinsic characteristics of each type of problem [7, 27]. The main applications of unsupervised learning are related in the grouping or clustering of data [28, 29]. These algorithms are based on the distance between observations. The most used clustering algorithms are k-means clustering and hierarchical clustering [30, 31].

The development of the study considered three principles: first, the disposition of the conversational agent for the effective delivery of messages; second, to control and monitor the responses and behaviors of each student; and finally the personalized interaction with each user [32, 33]. In addition, the significant presence of issues that respond to the socio-psychological dimension is considered important [34].

This study aimed to develop an automated classification model based on the collection of information through a chatbot and the unsupervised learning algorithm application k-means, for the assertive determination of psychological intervention programs for university students carried out during the evaluation process of university tutoring of the universities of Peru.

2   Materials and Methods

2.1   Unit of Analysis

It is a simple descriptive, non-experimental investigation. The study used a sample of 60 students from the Faculty of Engineering and Architecture of the Universidad Peruana Unión, to whom we applied the BarOn ICE test through a chatbot, in order to obtain data on their performance regarding to the different criteria taken into account to evaluate emotional intelligence.

2.2 Chatbot Construction and Data Extraction

We obtained data through a virtual tutoring platform based on chatbot in which a conversation was configured using the BarOn ICE test that was sent to the student's email; containing 60 items that were answered evaluating the responses on a Likert scale of five possibilities [35]. Once we obtained the data, we tabulated and processed according to the logic of the BaronICE test, generating as a result scores valued according to seven dimensions of emotional intelligence.

The chatbot is useful for automating tasks and processes in order to provide a better user experience [25, 36]. The developed chatbot can support different platforms. The prototype construction process included a review phase and an error correction phase.

The construction begins with the design of the entity-relationship model of the database that supports the logic necessary to obtain information on the dimensions of emotional intelligence of each university student. We used Navicat 15 to build the model and we deployed the database in MySQL 8.0.25.

The design of the interfaces took into account the following basic modules: importation of students, data collection instruments, scheduling of mailings, follow-up of responses and a statistical module on the performance of the use of the chatbot.

We developed the chatbot-based virtual tutoring platform in Python version 3, using the Django framework in version 3.2; it consists of the test modules and test types. We design the graphical user interface using Bootstrap 4.

2.3 Data Processing

Once we consolidated and transformed the data into useful information, we take the scores of the scales obtained thanks to the BarOn ICE qualification; we carried out this process for each student, all finally stored in a dataset, for processing.

The data was compiled in the Jupyter Notebook tool using the k-means algorithm, one of the most popular clustering algorithms [37]. This algorithm assigns each data to one of the N clusters [38]. The ideal cluster in k-means is a sphere with the centroid as the center of gravity [39]. The goal in k-means is to minimize the average distance of the data from its cluster centers, where a cluster center is defined as the mean or centroid in a cluster [40, 41]. We summarized the process in Fig. 1.

The process starts with the initialization of the packages and libraries for data processing and subsequent drawing.

We used a library for mathematical calculations, for the manipulation and operationalization of numerical tables, for the generation of graphs based on lists and the one that allows the use of the k-means algorithm.

```
import numpy as np
import pandas as pd
import matplotlib.pyplot as plt
from sklearn.cluster import KMeans
```

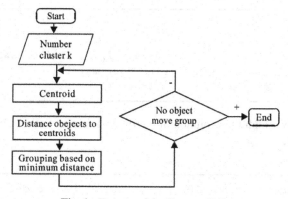

Fig. 1. K-means flow diagram [31].

To import the data, we opened the database contained in the file "BarOn Ice.csv Database" and we eliminated the first column corresponding to the identification of the students.

```
estudiantes = pd.read_csv('/home/gcode/Documentos/Base
de datos BarOn Ice.csv', engine="python")
estudiantes_var = estudiantes.drop(['Alumno'],  axis=1)
```

For data scaling we import the "preprocessing" package from the "sklearn" library for the data normalization process.

```
from sklearn import preprocessing as pp
```

We assigned the normalized data to the variable "data". In addition, we copy the data from in the variable "x" for the search process for the optimal number of clusters.

```
datos_n = pp.Normalizer().fit_transform(estudiantes_var)
```

To find the optimal number of clusters, inertia is the term used to denote the sum of the squared distances of each point with respect to the centroid of its own cluster [42]. Likewise, we execute the k-means algorithm repeatedly, each time giving it a greater number of clusters in its parameters, we measure the inertia obtained in each iteration and add it to the "inertia" list.

```
inercia = []
for i in range(1, 10):
algoritmo = KMeans(n_clusters=i, init='k-means++',
max_iter=300, n_init=10) algoritmo.fit(x)
inercia.append(algoritmo.inertia_)
```

Subsequently, graph the evolution of inertia with respect to the number of clusters in each iteration.

```
plt.figure(figsize=[10,6]) plt.title("Método del codo")
plt.xlabel('N° de Clústeres') plt.ylabel("Inercia")
plt.plot(list(range(1, 10)), inercia, marker='o')
plt.show()
```

Once we established the optimal number of clusters, we execute the algorithm with the initial normalized data set "data_n", and we indicated the number of clusters to generate.

```
algoritmo = KMeans(n_clusters=5, init='k-means++',
max_iter=300, n_init=10)
```

Likewise, we fit the model generated with the normalized data in the variable "x" and assign the attributes "cluster_centers_" and "labels_" to the variables "centroides" and "labels" respectively.

```
algoritmo.fit(x)
KMeans(n_clusters=5)
centroides, etiquetas = algoritmo.cluster_centers_,
algoritmo.labels_
```

As a result, we print each student from the initial data set with a label that identifies the cluster to which we assigned by the algorithm.

```
print(etiquetas)
```

Later, we import the package "decomposition" from the library "sklearn" for the graphical representation of the clusters.

```
from    sklearn.decomposition    import    PCA
modelo_pca = PCA(n_components=3); modelo_pca.fit(x)
pca = modelo_pca.transform(x)
centroides_pca = modelo_pca.transform(centroides)
colores  =  ['red', 'blue', 'green', 'yellow', 'black']
colores_cluster = [colores[etiquetas[i]] for i in
range(len(pca))]
plt.scatter(pca[:,  0],  pca[:,1],  c=colores_cluster,
marker  =  'o',  alpha=0.4)
plt.scatter(centroides_pca[:,  0],  centroides_pca[:,1],
marker  =  'x',  s=100,
linewidths=3, c=colores)
xvector = modelo_pca.components_[0] * max(pca[:, 0])
yvector = modelo_pca.components_[1] * max(pca[:, 1])
columnas = estudiantes_var.columns
```

3   Results

3.1   Chatbot Construction and Data Extraction

Figure 2 shows the virtual tutoring chatbot interface that we built to collect data on emotional intelligence from students. We complemented the tool with different instruments provided by a psychologist; this platform carries out the application of these instruments and collects the answers given by the students. To do this, each student enters a personalized link, which we sent to his or her email address from the tutoring administration platform. As in the study of [25], the university chatbot provides efficient and accurate answers to user questions about university information. In addition, [36] develop a multiplatform chatbot that instantly answers student questions; in addition, the chatbot supports a login system to provide answers according to the different student profiles, becoming a more personalized means of communication.

3.2   Data Processing

As the first result of the k-means execution process in the Jupyter Notebook tool, we obtained a graph for the choice of the optimal number of clusters as shown in Fig. 3. The main idea of k-means and the algorithms Clustering is to minimize the intra-cluster variance and maximize the inter-cluster variance, where each observation must be found as close as possible to its group and as far as possible from another type of group, as stated in their studies [28, 39].

To find the optimal number of clusters, the elbow method was applied, where [33] mention that the elbow method is used to optimize the number of clusters in the k-means algorithm. Also [38] determining the exact number of clusters, in such a way the mean distance of the observations was applied to its centroid, obtaining that the value of k satisfies an increase of k.

Fig. 2. Graphical interface of the chatbot on a mobile device

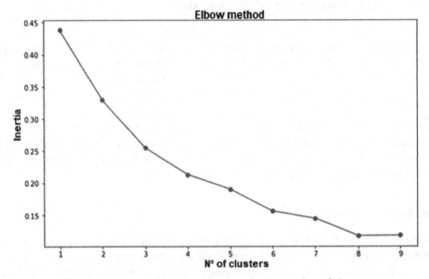

Fig. 3. Evolution of inertia with respect to the number of clusters

After the analysis of the graph of the elbow method Fig. 3, we established the optimal number of clusters and we executed the algorithm with the data set (the consolidated of the responses obtained after applying the BarOn ICE test to the group of students). Indicating the number of clusters that we have to generate and as a result, we obtained the graphical representation of the clusters as shown in Fig. 4. We have to clarify that a psychologist, who would be the commission to develop the intervention programs, as well as the effectiveness, would later analyze the resulting groupings and efficiency of the algorithm represented in the results.

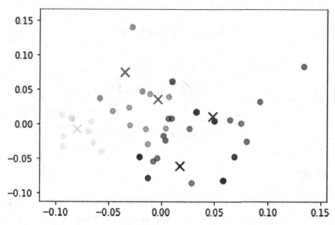

Fig. 4. Graphic representation of the clusters

Based on the results of Fig. 4, we can state that the process of segmenting the individuals of a group based on their behaviors or similar characteristics in the same segment, helps to unravel the hidden patterns in the data for a better decision making [37]. In addition [29, 37] mention that thanks to the help of the unsupervised learning algorithm k-means, the results of the clusters of the data of interest are graphically represented, helping to more optimally determine the density of the clusters, collaborating with the organization of the information generated. Considering that, the visualization tools help the researcher to achieve a better performance in the intermediate tasks of the review of the information, such as identifying main themes, associates and extracts with relevant contributions to the tasks carried out.

The application of the solution allowed generating a segmentation model of university students to determine psychological intervention programs that summarizes all the steps of the intervention carried out as shown in Fig. 5.

In step (0), we show the entities that would participate in the intervention of the process: (1) the selection of a sample of students to whom the psychological test will be applied. (2) A chatbot was the tool built in order to apply the BarOn ICE test for data extraction. (3) Data was stored in a dataset. (4) We carried out the analysis and processing of the data, to transform them into consolidated information, where together with the support of the k-means algorithm we carried out the information segmentation process, obtaining as a result five groups with similar characteristics. (5) The intervention of a psychologist who was in charge of analyzing the final information and being able to carry out psychological intervention programs in university students. In this way, after the application of k-means groupings as in the work of [27], we can be able to identify the factors that lead to the success or failure of a student. This will allow the mentoring area to provide appropriate advice and focus more on those factors.

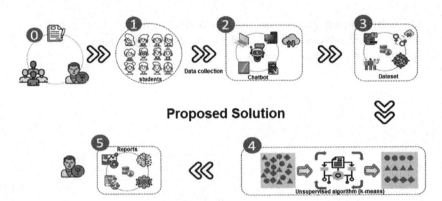

Fig. 5. Student segmentation model

4   Conclusions

The classification model for university students using k-means significantly reduces the work of the psychologist in the data collection and segmentation process. Based on the processing of the responses of the applied test, clusters were obtained that must later be labeled by a qualified professional. The elbow method allows the formation of an optimal number of clusters. Due to its parameterizable characteristics, the model allows for data clustering regardless of the type of psychological test applied. It is only necessary to scale the response to obtain a number of clusters that represent logical groupings allowing covering more dimensions of the psychological field, with the purpose to identify, prevent and correct various situations of psycho-emotional risk that university students may present.

References

1. Acosta, F.P., Clavero, F.H.: La influencia de las emociones sobre el rendimiento académico. Ciencias Psicológicas **11**(1), 29–39 (2017). https://doi.org/10.22235/CP.V11I2.1344
2. del Barrios-Hernández, K.C., Olivero-Vega, E.: Relación universidad-empresa-estado. Un análisis desde las instituciones de educación superior de Barranquilla-Colombia, para el desarrollo de su capacidad de innovación. Formación universitaria **13**(2), 21–28 (2020). https://doi.org/10.4067/S0718-50062020000200021
3. Coronado, D.M.: El rol de las universidades peruanas frente a la investigación y el desarrollo tecnológico. Propósitos y Representaciones **6**(2), 703–737 (2018). https://doi.org/10.20511/PYR2018.V6N2.244
4. Chacon, M.D.: Acción tutorial en el fortalecimiento del perfil profesional universitario: aportes en el desarrollo de competencias a partir de la educación virtual. Espacios **42**(5), 66–77 (2021). https://doi.org/10.48082/espacios-a21v42n05p05
5. Silva, P.A.P., Hernández, M.O.: Proceso de tutoría psicopedagógica. Acercamiento a la Universidad Técnica Estatal de Quevedo, Ecuador **18**(2), 302–314 (2020). https://mendive.upr.edu.cu/index.php/MendiveUPR/article/view/1886
6. Guzmán, S.E.Y., del Marín, G.J.H.: Tutoría en la educación superior: análisis de la percepción de profesionales y estudiantes en una universidad pública. RIDE. Rev. Iberoam. Investig. Desarro. **9**(18), 717–747 (2019). https://doi.org/10.23913/ride.v9i18.443

7. García, J.L.A.: La tutoría universitaria como práctica docente: fundamentos y métodos para el desarrollo de planes de acción tutorial en la universidad. Pro-Posições **30** (2019). https://doi.org/10.1590/1980-6248-2017-0038

8. del Cabezas, P..P.S., Álvarez, H.E.L., Rodríguez del Rey, M.M.L.: La tutoría en la educación superior y su integración en la actividad pedagógica del docente universitario. Conrado **15**(70), 300–305 (2019). https://conrado.ucf.edu.cu/index.php/conrado/article/view/1140

9. Alonso-García, S., Rodríguez-García, A.M., Cáceres-Reche, M.P.: Analysis of the tutorial action and its impact on the overall development of the students: the case of the University of Castilla La Mancha, Spain. Formacion Universitaria **11**(3), 63–72 (2018). https://doi.org/10.4067/S0718-50062018000300063

10. Alvites-Huamaní, C.G.: Estrés docente y factores psicosociales en docentes de Latinoamérica, Norteamérica y Europa. Propósitos y Representaciones **7**(3), 141 (2019). https://doi.org/10.20511/pyr2019.v7n3.393

11. Mascarenhas, H., Rodrigues Dias, T.M., Dias, P.: Academic mobility of doctoral students in Brazil: an analysis based on lattes platform. Iberoamerican J. Sci. Meas. Commun. **1**(3), 1–15 (2021). https://doi.org/10.47909/IJSMC.53

12. Islas Torres, C.: La implicación de las TIC en la educación: Alcances, Limitaciones y Prospectiva. RIDE. Rev. Iberoam. Investig. Desarro. **8**(15), 861–876 (2018). https://doi.org/10.23913/ride.v8i15.324

13. Poveda-Pineda, D.F., Cifuentes-Medina, J.E.: Incorporación de las tecnologías de información y comunicación (TIC) durante el proceso de aprendizaje en la educación superior. Formación universitaria **13**(6), 95–104 (2020). https://doi.org/10.4067/S0718-50062020000600095

14. Rodríguez, L.M.P.: Factores individuales y familiares asociados al bajo rendimiento académico en estudiantes universitarios **24**(80), 173–195 (2019). https://www.comie.org.mx/revista/v2018/rmie/index.php/nrmie/article/view/1242

15. Montenegro Ordoñez, J.: La calidad en la docencia universitaria. Una aproximación desde la percepción de los estudiantes. Educación **29**(56), 116–145 (2020). https://doi.org/10.18800/educacion.202001.006

16. Ocaña-Fernández, Y., Valenzuela-Fernández, L., Morillo-Flores, J.: La competencia digital en el docente universitario. Propósitos y Representaciones **8**(1), e455 (2020). https://doi.org/10.20511/pyr2020.v8n1.455

17. Gontijo, M.C.A., Hamanaka, R.Y., Araujo, R.F. de: Research data management: a bibliometric and altmetric study based on Dimensions. Iberoamerican J. Sci. Meas. Commun. **1**(3), 1–19 (2021). https://doi.org/10.47909/IJSMC.120

18. Vega-Hernández, M.C., Patino-Alonso, M.C., Galindo-Villardón, M.P.: Multivariate characterization of university students using the ICT for learning. Comput. Educ. **121**, 124–130 (2018). https://doi.org/10.1016/j.compedu.2018.03.004

19. Casas-Huamanta, E.R.: Acceso a recursos tecnológicos y rendimiento académico en tiempos de pandemia y aislamiento social obligatorio. Revista científica de sistemas e informática **2**(1), e296 (2022). https://doi.org/10.51252/RCSI.V2I1.296

20. Chen, M., Yan, Z., Meng, C., Huang, M.: The supporting environment evaluation model of ICT in Chinese university teaching. In: Proceedings - 2018 International Symposium on Educational Technology, ISET 2018, pp. 99–103 (2018). https://doi.org/10.1109/ISET.2018.00030

21. del Bárcenas, M.C.M., Morales, U.C.: Herramientas tecnológicas en el proceso de enseñanza-aprendizaje en estudiantes de educación superior. RIDE. Rev. Iberoam. Investig. Desarro. **10**(19), e005 (2019). https://doi.org/10.23913/ride.v10i19.494

22. Gargallo Castel, A.F.: La integración de las TIC en los procesos educativos y organizativos. Educar em Revista. **34**(69), 325–339 (2018). https://doi.org/10.1590/0104-4060.57305

23. Adakawa, M.I.: D-Space, makerspace, and hackerspace in cyberspace: cybersecurity strategies for digital preservation of library resources in the post-Covid-19 pandemic. Adv. Notes Inf. Sci. **1**, 59–89 (2022). https://doi.org/10.47909/ANIS.978-9916-9760-0-5.98

24. Liang, W.: Development trend and thinking of artificial intelligence in education. In: 2020 International Wireless Communications and Mobile Computing, IWCMC 2020, pp. 886–890 (2020). https://doi.org/10.1109/IWCMC48107.2020.9148078

25. Khin, N.N., Soe, K.M.: University Chatbot using artificial intelligence markup language. In: 2020 IEEE Conference on Computer Applications, ICCA 2020, pp. 1–5 (2020). https://doi.org/10.1109/ICCA49400.2020.9022814

26. De-La-Hoz, E.J., De-La-Hoz, E.J., Fontalvo, T.J.: Metodología de Aprendizaje Automático para la Clasificación y Predicción de Usuarios en Ambientes Virtuales de Educación. Información tecnológica. **30**(1), 247–254 (2019). https://doi.org/10.4067/S0718-0764201900010 0247

27. Debao, D., Yinxia, M., Min, Z.: Analysis of big data job requirements based on K-means text clustering in China. PLoS ONE **16**(8), e0255419 (2021). https://doi.org/10.1371/JOURNAL. PONE.0255419

28. Latipa Sari, H., et al.: Integration K-means clustering method and elbow method for identification of the best customer profile cluster. In: IOP Conference Series: Materials Science and Engineering, p. 012017. https://doi.org/10.1088/1757-899X/336/1/012017

29. Marisa, F., Ahmad, S.S.S., Yusof, Z.I.M., Hunaini, F., Aziz, T.M.A.: segmentation model of customer lifetime value in small and medium enterprise (SMEs) using K-means clustering and LRFM model. Int. J. Integr. Eng. **11**(3), 169–180 (2019). https://doi.org/10.30880/ijie. 2019.11.03.018

30. Rodríguez Chávez, M.H.: Sistemas de tutoría inteligente y su aplicación en la educación superior. RIDE. Rev. Iberoam. Investig. Desarro. **11**(22), e175 (2021). https://doi.org/10. 23913/RIDE.V11I22.848

31. Omolewa, O.T., Oladele, A.T., Adeyinka, A.A., Oluwaseun, O.R.: Prediction of student's academic performance using k-means clustering and multiple linear regressions. J. Eng. Appl. Sci. **14** 22), 8254–8260 (2019). https://doi.org/10.36478/JEASCI.2019.8254.8260

32. Song, D., Oh, E.Y., Rice, M.: Interacting with a conversational agent system for educational purposes in online courses. In: Proceedings - 2017 10th International Conference on Human System Interactions, HSI 2017, pp. 78–82 (2017). https://doi.org/10.1109/HSI.2017.8005002

33. Marutho, D., Hendra Handaka, S., Wijaya, E., Muljono: the determination of cluster number at k-mean using elbow method and purity evaluation on headline news. In: Proceedings - 2018 International Seminar on Application for Technology of Information and Communication: Creative Technology for Human Life, iSemantic 2018, pp. 533–538 (2018). https://doi.org/ 10.1109/ISEMANTIC.2018.8549751

34. Hernandez-Cruz, N.: Mapping the thematic evolution in Communication over the first two decades from the 21st century: a longitudinal approach. Iberoamerican J. Sci. Meas. Commun. **1**(3), 1–10 (2021). https://doi.org/10.47909/IJSMC.88

35. Idrogo Zamora, D.I., Asenjo-Alarcón, J.A.: Relación entre inteligencia emocional y rendimiento académico en estudiantes universitarios peruanos. Revista de Investigación Psicológica (26), 69–79 (2021). https://doi.org/10.53287/RYFS1548JS42X

36. Lee, L.K., et al.: Using a multiplatform chatbot as an online tutor in a university course. In: Proceedings - 2020 International Symposium on Educational Technology, ISET 2020, pp. 53–56 (2020). https://doi.org/10.1109/ISET49818.2020.00021

37. Shamrat, F.M.J.M., Tasnim, Z., Mahmud, I., Jahan, N., Nobel, N.I.: Application of k-means clustering algorithm to determine the density of demand of different kinds of jobs. Int. J. Sci. Technol. Res. **9**(2), 2550–2557 (2020)

38. Liu, F., Deng, Y.: Determine the number of unknown targets in open world based on elbow method. IEEE Trans. Fuzzy Syst. **29**(5), 986–995 (2021). https://doi.org/10.1109/TFUZZ. 2020.2966182
39. Yuan, C., Yang, H.: Research on k-value selection method of k-means clustering algorithm. J. Multidisc. Sci. J. **2**(2), 226–235 (2019). https://doi.org/10.3390/J2020016
40. Nainggolan, R., Perangin-Angin, R., Simarmata, E., Tarigan, A.F.: Improved the performance of the k-means cluster using the sum of squared error (SSE) optimized by using the elbow method. In: Journal of Physics: Conference Series, p. 012015 (2019). https://doi.org/10.1088/ 1742-6596/1361/1/012015
41. Br, R.W., Berahmana, S., Mohammed, A., Chairuang, K., Jimbaran, B.: Customer segmentation based on RFM model using K-means, K-medoids, and DBSCAN methods. Lontar Komputer : Jurnal Ilmiah Teknologi Informasi **11**(1), 32–43 (2020). https://doi.org/10.24843/LKJ ITI.2020.V11.I01.P04
42. Kansal, T., Bahuguna, S., Singh, V., Choudhury, T.: Customer segmentation using k-means clustering. In: Proceedings of the International Conference on Computational Techniques, Electronics and Mechanical Systems, CTEMS 2018, pp. 135–139 (2018). https://doi.org/10. 1109/CTEMS.2018.8769171

Comparison of Algorithms for Classification of Financial Intelligence Reports

Roberto Zaina$^{(\boxtimes)}$ ⓘ, Douglas Dyllon Jeronimo de Macedoⓘ, Moisés Lima Dutraⓘ, Vinicius Faria Culmant Ramosⓘ, and Gustavo Medeiros de Araujoⓘ

Federal University of Santa Catarina, Florianópolis, Brazil
rzaina@gmail.com, {douglas.macedo,moises.dutra,v.ramos, gustavo.araujo}@ufsc.br

Abstract. This work shows the application of machine learning algorithms to decide whether Financial Intelligence Reports analyzed by the Brazilian Federal Police should be investigated or archived. We explain how the suspicious financial operations found in the Financial Intelligence Reports are a crucial piece of information to combat money laundering crimes. We depict the processing of such reports, which are often used to initiate a police investigation. When that is not the case, the reports are archived. In this work, we propose using machine learning to analyze these reports. We trained and used three classification algorithms: Decision Tree, Random Forest, and KNN. The results show that most reports should be archived. While Decision Tree and Random Forest indicated that about 2/3 of the reports should be archived, KNN indicated that about 4/5 of them should be archived. In the end, this work shows the feasibility of automating the analysis of the Financial Intelligence Reports by the Brazilian Federal Police, despite the need for more adjustments and tests to improve the accuracy and precision of the models developed.

Keywords: Financial intelligence report · Artificial intelligence · Machine learning

1 Introduction

1.1 Financial Intelligence Report (FIR)

Money laundering is a crime that consists of operations to give a lawful appearance to resources that come from illegal activities [1]. This crime aims to introduce money from criminal activities into the legal, financial circuits, through complex operations that promote the untying of its illicit origin [2]. Such activity harms society in many ways, mainly because of the damage it causes to the economic order and the administration of justice. "Dirty money" in the economy causes distortions in financial markets, causes fluctuations in stock exchanges, and harms legitimate businesses that do not rely on the easy supply of illicit money [3].

© ICST Institute for Computer Sciences, Social Informatics and Telecommunications Engineering 2022
Published by Springer Nature Switzerland AG 2022. All Rights Reserved
A. L. Pinto and R. Arencibia-Jorge (Eds.): DIONE 2022, LNICST 452, pp. 204–217, 2022.
https://doi.org/10.1007/978-3-031-22324-2_16

In money laundering investigations in Brazil, the essential information to be analyzed is financial and patrimonial, such as suspicious financial transactions, banking transactions and tax declarations. Suspicious financial transactions are contained in documents called Financial Intelligence Reports (FIR), produced by the Brazilian Financial Intelligence Unit (FIU) and disseminated mainly to criminal prosecution agencies, such as the Brazilian Judicial Police and Public Prosecutors.

One of the agencies that receive FIR in Brazil is the Federal Police (FP). After an initial analysis by a significant sector, the FP distributes the reports to police stations throughout the country for further analysis, this time with more context and depth. After this second analysis, the action for each FIR is decided. It can be of 4 types: 1) to forward it; 2) to archive it; 3) to investigate it; 4) to keep it under analysis.

To forward means the FIR is sent to another agency because the facts narrated in the report are not the competence of the Federal Police. For example, when it turns out that the suspected operations of the FIR are related to crimes of state competence, such as loan sharking, which the state police should investigate.

The archiving happens when there is insufficient evidence to start a formal investigation by the FIR analysis. The FIR is stored in a database for future access and can be unarchived whenever relevant new information emerges.

To investigate means that the FIR presents evidence of federal crimes. A formal investigation is necessary to be held, which will allow the FP to use other investigative diligence, including those that need judicial authorization.

Finally, keeping the FIR under analysis means that assessing the operations described in the report has not yet been completed. Thus, there is no decision whether the FIR will be forwarded, archived, or whether the FP will start a formal investigation.

It is important to emphasize that the decision of forwarding, archiving, or investigating is complex and laborious. It depends on analyzing many elements related to suspicious financial transactions and the people mentioned in the FIR. Aspects such as the number of people and companies mentioned, the sum of the values of operations, locations, and characteristics of transactions, among others, can be considered. Furthermore, the FIR is usually a very extensive and complex document, which cites dozens of people and companies and contains hundreds or thousands of suspicious financial transactions that involve, in many cases, millions of Reais (The Brazilian currency in suspicious values).

This paper proposes to train machine learning algorithms to assist in the FIR-based decision-making of investigating or archiving. This proposal intends to contribute to the automation of the FIR analysis process and the improvement of the efficiency of the investigation work of money laundering crimes by the Brazilian Federal Police.

2 Background

2.1 Artificial Intelligence and Machine Learning

Artificial intelligence is the ability of machines to solve a particular problem on their own, without any human intervention, that is, that the solutions are not programmed directly in the system, but rather that the data is interpreted by the artificial intelligence tool, which produces a solution by itself [4]. Artificial intelligence is the science and engineering of making intelligent machines, especially intelligent computer programs, and intelligence is the computational ability to achieve goals in the world [5].

Machine learning is a subfield of artificial intelligence that trains a machine with specific data and changes when exposed to new data. According to these authors, machine learning focuses on extracting information from large data sets and then detects and identifies patterns using various statistical measures to improve their ability to interpret new data and produce more effective results. Among the most used statistical measures in machine learning are clustering, association, regression and classification [4].

Since our proposal aims to assist in the FIR-based decision-making of investigating or archiving, we sought efficient algorithms for this purpose. We obtained the results presented in this paper by using the Decision Tree, Random Forest, and K-Nearest Neighbors (KNN) algorithms.

2.2 Decision Tree Algorithm

Decision Tree is a predictive model that can represent classification and regression measures, composed of tree decisions and consequences [6]. Classification trees are used to sort an object in a set of classes based on its variables, as shown in Fig. 1.

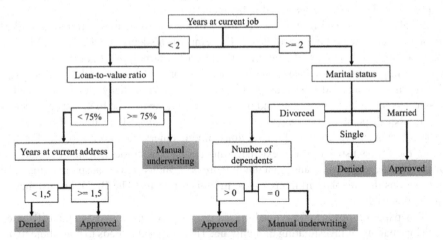

Fig. 1. Example of Decision Tree. Adapted from MAIMON and ROKACH [5]

In this example, a Decision Tree was trained to decide on real estate mortgage lending to choose an "Approved," "Denied," or "Manual underwriting" class. For example, at least two years old in the current job, a married person would have approved his/her mortgage. On the other hand, a person under two years of current employment, with a loan less than 75% of the property's value, with less than 1.5 years of current residence, would have the mortgage denied.

For the present study, Fig. 2 shows, hypothetically, what is expected of applying the Decision Tree algorithm to classify an FIR.

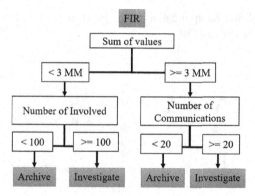

Fig. 2. A hypothetical example of applying Decision Tree to an FIR

In the example above, an FIR with a sum of R$ 3 million with at least 20 communications will be investigated, while one with a sum less than R$ 3 million and less than 100 involved will be archived.

2.3 Random Forest Algorithm

Random Forest consists of tree-structured classifiers, where variables are randomly distributed and identical. Each tree registers a vote to decide the most popular class (most voted) [7]. Random Forest algorithm uses multiple Decision Trees to determine the most votes class, besides having better accuracy compared to a single "tree" [8], as shown in Fig. 3.

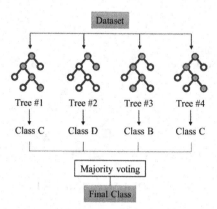

Fig. 3. Random Forest example. Adapted from KIRASICH et al. [7]

In this example, the Random Forest algorithm was trained and processed using 4 Decision Trees, with variables randomly positioned, and each tree (#1, #2, #3, and #4) resulted in a class (C, D, B, and C, respectively). The final class chosen was the one with most of the results, class C.

Figure 4 exemplifies the application of the Random Forest algorithm to determine the action to be taken with an FIR.

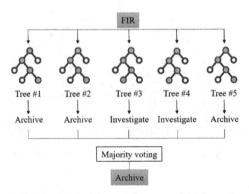

Fig. 4. Hypothetical example of applying Random Forest to a FIR

By Random Forest, defining whether an FIR will be archived or investigated will depend on the decision-making process. In this work, the decision that appeared the most was to "Archive."

2.4 K-Nearest Neighbors (KNN) Algorithm

KNN is based on the closest grouping of elements with the same characteristics and decides the class category in its "k" nearest neighbors [9]. That "k" value depends on the dataset's size and the type of classification problem. Figure 5 below exemplifies the application of KNN.

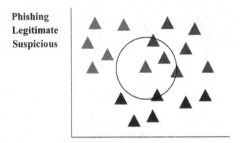

Fig. 5. Example of K-Nearest Neighbors (KNN). Adapted from Altaher [8]

In this example, to sort whether a site (the orange triangle) should be framed as "Phishing," "Legitimate," or "Suspicious," we must check the class type that has the most neighbors nearby. When considering the three nearest neighbors, the site would be set to "Legitimate."

By applying the KNN algorithm to classify an FIR, we expect it to behave as shown in Fig. 6.

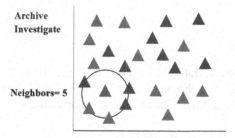

Fig. 6. A hypothetical example of KNN application in an FIR

When using the KNN algorithm to indicate whether an FIR will be archived or inves-tigated, the class with more than "k" nearest neighbors is checked. In this example above, if we consider the nearest five neighbors, the "Investigate" class has more occurrences than the "Archive" class and, therefore, it is chosen.

3   Methodology

The using of Decision Tree, Random Forest, and K-Nearest Neighbors (KNN) algorithms to classify Financial Intelligence Reports as "investigate" or "archive" comprises four tasks (Fig. 7): i) Data Collection; ii) Pre-processing; iii) Learning; and iv) Application.

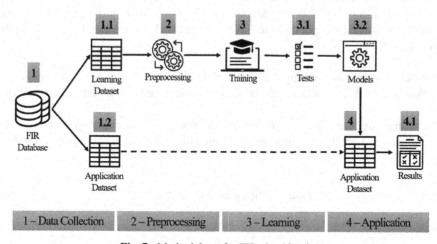

Fig. 7. Methodology for FIR classification

During step 1, we collect the FIR's data from an FP's internal database and store them in two datasets: Learning and Application. In step 2, we process the learning data to eliminate variables with high correspondence and low importance. Next, we run the Decision Tree, Random Forest, and KNN algorithms to train, test, and generate the models (step 3). Finally, in the last step, we apply the models to the Application dataset to get the model's final decision on whether to archive or investigate the FIR.

4   Development

4.1   Data Collection

We accessed a database of 1,427 Financial Intelligence Reports and extracted the following information from each report: "FIR," "NumComm," "SumVal," "NumInvolv," "NumPEPs," "NumEmpl," and "Status." These variables mean:

- FIR: a unique identifier code for the FIR;
- NumComm: number of communications found in the FIR; communication is a set of transactions conveyed to the Financial Intelligence Unit (FIU) by a bank or an investment broker, for example, whenever they identify suspicious financial transactions;
- SumVal: the sum of the values of all operations of the FIR;
- NumInvolv: number of individuals and legal entities involved in the operations of the FIR;
- NumPEPs: number of politically exposed persons involved in FIR operations, such as heads of state or government, politicians, and high-ranking government officeholders;
- NumEmpl: number of government servants involved in the FIR's operations;
- Status: FIR status in the Federal Police, which may be "archived," "investigated," "under analysis," "forwarded," "not registered," etc.

Below, we can check the status of the 1,427 reports collected in the database.

It is worth noticing that the "Status" field is the decision to be predicted by the models, i.e., it is the "target variable." With that in mind, we separated the records into two datasets:

1. FIRs registered as "investigated" or "archived";
2. Application: FIRs "Under analysis" (yet to predict whether to investigate or archive).

We discarded the "Other" FIRs as they did not present relevant information about their progress. After this disposal, we distributed the remaining 1,366 reports according to Table 2:

Table 1. FIR's according to "Situation"

Status	Amount of FIRs
Archived	390
Investigated	183
Under analysis	793
Other	61
Total	1.427

Table 2. 3 Distribution between Learning and Application Tables.

Dataset	Amount of FIRs
Learning	573
Application	793
Total	1.366

4.2 Learning Table Pre-processing

The Learning dataset, composed of 573 FIRs, had the following initial composition of variables (Table 3).

Table 3. Learning dataset variables

Variable	Type
FIR	–
NumComm	Predictor Variable
SumVal	Predictor Variable
NumInvolv	Predictor Variable
NumPEPs	Predictor Variable
NumEmpl	Predictor Variable
Status	Target Variable

The data from the Learning dataset were uploaded and pre-processed. The first processing was verifying the data types and missing data. Then, we applied functions to ascertain the occurrence of variables with high correspondence and variables with low importance, which could negatively affect the learning of the models.

We used the Pearson method to check the correspondence between the predictor variables; Table 4 shows the results.

Table 4. Correspondence between variables (Pearson method)

Variable	NumComm	SumVal	NumInvolv	NumPEPs	NumEmpl
NumComm	–	0,16	0,45	0,47	0,22
SumVal	0,16	–	0,17	0,09	0,09
NumInvolv	0,45	0,17	–	0,59	0,62
NumPEPs	0,47	0,09	0,59	–	0,36
NumEmpl	0,22	0,09	0,62	0,36	–

We cannot see highly matched variables (above 0.9) in the table above, so no variable was dropped from the dataset.

We used two methods to check for low-importance variables: "chi-square" and "f_classif". Table 5 shows the results.

Table 5. Variable Importance

Variable	chi-square	f_classif
NumComm	7015.59	2.10
SumVal	137,654,803,192.23	2.72
NumInvolv	5893.51	3.59
NumPEPs	1.80	0.25
NumEmpl	30.65	1.57

We can notice that in both the "chi-square" and the "f_classif" method, the variables "NumPEPs" and "NumEmpl" are of low importance when compared to the rest. Therefore, we decided to eliminate these variables not to harm the model. Table 6 shows the remaining dataset variables.

Table 6. Learning dataset after preprocessing

Variables	x/y	Type
NumComm	x	Predictive
SumVal	x	Predictive
NumInvolv	x	Predictive
Status	y	Target

4.3 Learning

The Learning process through Decision Tree, Random Forest, and K-Nearest Neighbors algorithms comprise three stages: training, testing, and model generation. Learning data was separated into training (80%) and testing (20%), as shown in Table 7.

We used the following Python-based classification algorithms/APIs during the training stage.

- DecisionTreeClassifier (package sklearn.tree);
- RandomForestClassifier (package sklearn.ensemble);
- KNeighborsClassifier (package sklearn.neighbors).

Table 7. Learning dataset's training and test data

Dataset	Percentage	Amount
Training	80%	458
Test	20%	115

After the training, we tested the models. Decision Tree presented an accuracy of 0.60, Random Forest an accuracy of 0.70, and K-Nearest Neighbors an accuracy of 0.63. Figure 8 shows a comparative chart.

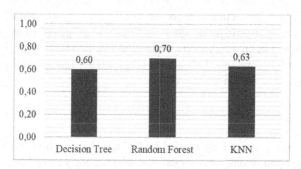

Fig. 8. Accuracy of the tested classification algorithms

In addition to accuracy, another valuable method for evaluating a model training is the confusion matrix, a table generated for a classifier on a data set and used to describe the classifier's performance [10], as shown in Fig. 9.

	Predicted: No	Predicted: Yes
Actual: No	TN	FP
Actual: Yes	FN	TP

Fig. 9. Confusion matrix. MARIA NAVIN and PANKAJA [9]

Description of table terms:

- True Positives (TP) - both prediction and actual are yes.
- True Negatives (TN) - prediction is no, and actual is yes.
- False Positives (FP) - prediction is yes, and actual is no.
- False Negatives (FN) - prediction is no and actual is no.

For the present study, the confusion matrix indicates the "True Investigated," "False Investigated," "True Archived," and "False Archived" FIRs, as shown in Fig. 10.

Decision Tree		Random Forest		KNN	
True Investigated 13	False Archived 20	True Investigated 16	False Archived 17	True Investigated 3	False Archived 30
False Investigated 26	True Archived 56	False Investigated 17	True Archived 65	False Investigated 12	True Archived 70

Fig. 10. Confusion matrix the tested classification algorithms

We can see above that the tested algorithms produced a lot of "True Archived" (bottom right), which shows that they got most of the predictions right when deciding to "archive." However, they also produced many "False Investigated" (bottom left), i.e., the model was wrong in many predictions when deciding to "investigate". Random Forest presented the best performance between hits and misses, reaching almost 80% of the "archived" and half of the "investigated."

4.4 Application

We applied the three adequately trained and tested classification models on the 793 FIRs of the Application dataset to determine whether the FIR should be investigated or archived. The Decision Tree recommended that 291 reports be investigated and 502 archived (Fig. 11).

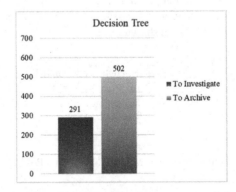

Fig. 11. Decision Tree algorithm recommendation

Random Forest recommended that 271 reports be investigated and 522 archived (Fig. 12).

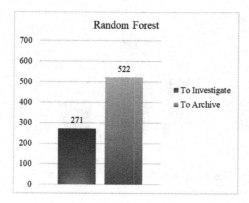

Fig. 12. Random Forest algorithm recommendation

Finally, KNN recommended that 165 reports be investigated and 628 archived (Fig. 13).

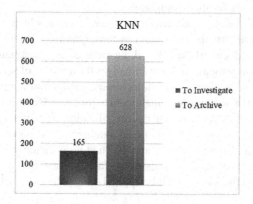

Fig. 13. KNN algorithm recommendation

5 Results

When applying the three algorithms in 793 Financial Intelligence Reports, they recommended that most reports be archived, as shown in Fig. 14.

We can notice that while Decision Tree and Random Forest indicated that about 2/3 of the reports should be archived and 1/3 investigated, KNN recommended that about 4/5 be archived and only 1/5 investigated.

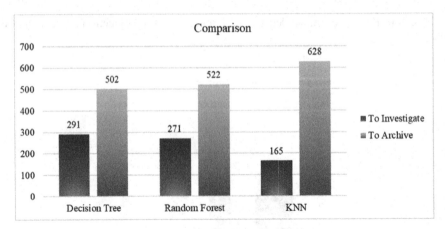

Fig. 14. Comparison of classification models

6 Final Considerations

Money laundering is a crime of complex investigation that usually involves a large set of financial and patrimonial data, including Financial Intelligence Reports (FIR). An FIR is a document generated by the Brazilian Financial Intelligence Unit and disseminated to intelligence agencies for its investigation.

One of those intelligence agencies is the Federal Police, which, after an initial analysis, distributes the reports to police stations throughout the country. Then, they carry out a new analysis to decide if the FIR will be archived or investigated.

This decision to investigate or archive involves the analysis of several variables, such as the number of stakeholders involved, locations, transaction features, etc. This work proposed and applied a machine learning model to process FIRs using the Decision Tree, Random Forest, and K-Nearest Neighbors classification algorithms.

We collected data from 1,427 Financial Intelligence Reports, of which 573 had already been investigated or archived, and 793 had no decision yet. We separate these reports into training and application datasets. In summary, we used the 573 "already labeled" FIRs to train the model and then applied this model to the 793 pending-decision FIRs.

Applying the model in these 793 Financial Intelligence Reports recommended that most of them be archived. While the Decision Tree and Random Forest algorithms recommended that about 2/3 of the reports be archived, the KNN algorithm recommended that 4/5 be archived. As in any statistical analysis, there are advantages and disadvantages in the application of each algorithm, which will vary according to the methodologies used, the computational intensity and complexity of the algorithm [11].

However, these are still early results, which depend on more data, tests, and model calibrations to improve the accuracy and precision of the Learning step. In the next steps of this research, we intend to increase the amount of training data, consider new variables, and test new algorithms, such as Logistic Regression, Support Vector Machine, and Artificial Neural Networks.

References

1. Zaina, R., Ramos, V., Araujo, G.: Triagem Automatizada de Relatórios de Inteligência Financeira. En T.M.R. Dias (Ed.), Informação, Dados e Tecnologia. Advanced Notes in Information Science, volume 2. Tallinn, Estonia: ColNes Publishing, (2022). https://doi.org/10.47909/anis.978-9916-9760-3-6.115
2. Oliveira, T.B.: O bem jurídico-penal no crime de lavagem de dinheiro. Revista Esmat, [S.l.], vol. 4, no. 4, pp. 269–299 (2012)
3. Aras, V.: Sistema nacional de combate à lavagem de dinheiro e de recuperação de ativos. Revista Jus Navigandi, ano 12, no. 1411. Teresina (2007)
4. Das, K., Behera, R.N.: A survey on machine learning: concept, algorithms and applications. Int. J. Innov. Res. Comput. Commun. Eng. 5(2), 1301–1309 (2017)
5. Mccarthy, J.: What is artificial intelligence. Stanford University (2007)
6. Maimon, O.Z., Rokach, L.: Data mining with decision trees: theory and applications. World scientific (2014)
7. Breiman, L.: Random Forests. Machine Learning, 45, 5–32, Kluwer Academic Publishers. Netherlands (2001)
8. Kirasich, K., Smith, T., Sadler, B.: Random Forest vs Logistic Regression: Binary Classification for Heterogeneous Datasets. SMU Data Science Review, vol. 1, No. 3, Article 9 (2018)
9. Altaher, A.: Phishing Websites Classification using Hybrid SVM and KNN Approach. Int. J. Adv. Comput. Sci. Appl. (ijacsa), 8(6) (2017)
10. Maria Navin, J.R., Pankaja, R.: Performance analysis of text classification algorithms using confusion matrix. Int. J. Eng. Tech. Res. (IJETR) 6(4), 75–78 (2016)
11. Daizadeh, I.: Trademark and patent applications are structurally near-identical and cointegrated: implications for studies in innovation. Iberoamerican J. Sci. Measure. Commun. 1(2) (2021). https://doi.org/10.47909/ijsmc.33

Natural Language Processing of Messages from a Social Network for Inflation Analysis

Leonardo Silva Vianna(✉) ⓘ, Lizyane Rosa Antunes ⓘ, Rafael Maia Pinto ⓘ,
and Alexandre Leopoldo Gonçalves ⓘ

Graduate Program in Knowledge Engineering and Management, Federal University of Santa
Catarina, Florianópolis, Brazil
vianna@rocketmail.com

Abstract. Inflation is a progressive increase in the average price of goods and services. It can be measured using different inflation rates, which can vary according to the time, but also according to the region or country. Depending on the variation of product and service prices, users of social networks could discuss and express their private opinions about inflation. We questioned if there is a correlation between the messages transmitted by Twitter© users and the monthly variation of a specific inflation rate. Consequently, this research aims to examine Twitter© messages with content about inflation in Brazil through natural language processing and network analysis. The Twitter© messages from users in Brazil, obtained through the Application Programming Interface of this social network platform, were analyzed. The steps performed included querying the API for data acquisition, processing the messages using Natural Language Processing techniques, and executing a network analysis. We concluded that inflation influences the behavior of social network users and, additionally, natural language processing of Twitter© messages can reveal relevant knowledge for inflation analysis and have potential for prediction purposes.

Keywords: Inflation · Natural language processing · Network analysis

1 Introduction

Inflation is a progressive increase in the average price of goods and services. It can be measured using different inflation rates, which can vary according to the time, but also according to the region or country [1]. Although most economists consider that some inflation is beneficial, it can cause several harmful effects on the economy when it gets out of control. Among these effects, there is the loss of purchasing power, damage in the long-term planning, and the higher cost of public debt, compensating creditors for the value loss of money over time [2].

In Brazil, one of the main objectives of the Central Bank is to maintain inflation under control [3]. In this context, the agency acts through the monetary policy and its efforts are mainly focused in controlling the amount of currency circulating in the economy. This

A. L. Pinto and R. Arencibia-Jorge (Eds.): DIONE 2022, LNICST 452, pp. 218–229, 2022.
https://doi.org/10.1007/978-3-031-22324-2_17

action can generate direct impacts on interactions between economic agents, particularly families, companies, and government. The monetary policy actions result in an effect on market expectations, both short and long term [2]. The standard economic theory state that a tightening in the monetary policy can reduce inflation most of the time, but only for a moment and after a period of time. Pursuing this objective by increasing the public bonds rates leads to a decrease in consumption and, consequently, to a reduction in inflation [4]. Therefore, inflation is a key factor associated with monetary policy, and its control and management require considerable efforts from all related stakeholders.

There are several indexes used to measure the speed at which overall prices change. The national consumer price index (INPC) and the broad national consumer price index (IPCA) – in Portuguese, respectively, *Índice Nacional de Preços ao Consumidor* e *Índice Nacional de Preços ao Consumidor Amplo* – are quantified by the Instituto Brasileiro de Geografia e Estatística (IBGE) in the main metropolitan regions. Likewise, Fundação Getúlio Vargas (FGV) analyzes the prices of different economic sectors (such as the agricultural and industrial sectors), as also collects data in some capitals of the country to generate different general price indexes. Finally, the Fundação Instituto de Pesquisas Econômicas (FIPE) analyzes prices in the city of São Paulo to build a consumer price index [5].

Depending on the variation of product and service prices, users of social networks could discuss and express their private opinions about inflation. Thus, we questioned if there is a correlation between the messages transmitted by Twitter© users and the monthly variation of inflation measured through the IPCA. Consequently, this research aims to examine Twitter© messages with content about inflation in Brazil, with the purpose to identify a correlation between messages and inflation fluctuation.

The evaluation of the aspects related to the price fluctuation linked to inflation could provide understanding of the behavior change in social network users. This knowledge would support data modeling used to develop predictions in different applications, affecting the predictability of the economy behavior. Using data models could also help to improve economic projections, traditionally made by evaluating expert opinion through a heuristic approach.

2 Related Research

Aromi and Martin [6] analyzed the existence of information in Twitter messages that could be applied to predict inflation in Argentina, considering the exchange rate variation between the Argentine peso and the US dollar. For this purpose, they used a corpus of Twitter© messages (tweets) from users located in Argentina to produce an attention indicator that calculated the frequency of the words 'inflation' and 'inflationary' in a specific month, providing a monthly variation rate. The results obtained from a test dataset demonstrated that the models had greater accuracy than a baseline, supporting the claim that social media content could provide valuable information about future inflation levels.

To analyze how the investor behavior characteristics obtained from Twitter© impact the gold price, Kumar, Rao and Srivastava [7] extracted and processed sentiments from tweets and used them for prediction. Likewise, they also applied data from Google

Insights for Search$^©$ to compare predictability with macroeconomic analysis and other factors related to economic stability and indicators of investor fear. Using the data from Twitter$^©$, the sentiments were weekly computed by a Bayesian classifier to calculate a measure of optimism, applying a correlation analysis with the gold price at different lag intervals.

According to Alex [8], Twitter$^©$ messages are dynamic and reflect the opinion of a large sample of the population, allowing to extract useful information about the expected inflation rate. In his research, the author selected some relevant keywords to identify tweets related to current and expected prices of goods and services. Next, he applied the Latent Dirichlet Allocation (LDA) algorithm and a dictionary of bigrams and trigrams to filter the data obtained from Twitter$^©$. Finally, the author computed the daily number of tweets that represented the increase and decrease of inflation expectations, considering them as directional indicators of the inflationary trend.

Kim, Cha and Lee [9] collected real-time information from Twitter$^©$ messages, with an interval of a single day, for evaluation of the daily prediction of price fluctuation of some foods in Indonesia, justified by the fact that governments of developing countries act on food price fluctuations. The authors also evaluated if an additional timestamp for modeling the data led to better results and found that the model was more accurate with a single day lapse. The results obtained by the authors brought to the conclusion that the proposed model accurately predicted food prices and is also resilient, despite the small amount of data. They also stated that the model obtained great short-term accuracy, as there was a tendency for mentions in tweets to increase on the days of the greatest changes in food prices.

Bastida et al. [10] used a hybrid method to analyze the regional Gross Domestic Product (GDP) prediction, applying autoencoder algorithms to learn an intermediate representation associated with tweets and GDP, through three deep learning neural networks: Vanilla autoencoder, convolutional and recurrent. Then, the authors applied Support Vector Regression (SVR) and Random Forest Regressor algorithms in the intermediate representation for GDP prediction. The results of the hybrid method proposed by the authors surpassed those obtained by a baseline (persistence model), a linear regression only on GDP data, or the application of only one autoencoder algorithm.

Techniques for text sentiment analysis were designed primarily for the social media domain, but not for the Economy field. Shapiro, Sudhof and Wilson [11] developed a model for economic sentiment analysis, considering its temporal aspect. The analysis of economic and financial journal articles allowed building a model based on lexical sentiment analysis, combined with some existing lexical models. The authors also performed predictions to estimate the impulse response in some macroeconomic indicators. As a result, they concluded that positive sentiment was related to the increase in consumption, output, and interest rates, as also to the decrease in inflation.

Although the behavior of users in social networks has been analyzed and compared with different inflation rates, to the best of our knowledge, studies about inflation that performed natural language processing to obtain a corpus of text and, thereafter, fulfilled a network analysis have not been published yet.

3 Method

This research consists of the analysis of Twitter© messages (tweets) from users in Brazil, obtained through the Application Programming Interface (API) of this social network platform. The steps performed included querying the API for data acquisition, processing the messages using Natural Language Processing techniques, and executing a network analysis.

The research period was determined by the existence of messages on Twitter© that contained the search terms established for extracting the messages. Although message extraction was defined on the first date available in the API (October 1, 2006), the first extracted tweet had the creation date on October 12, 2010, as shown in the Result Analysis section. Consequently, the first year considered for analysis in the research was 2011.

3.1 Data Acquisition

Tweets were extracted through the Twitter© API using the 'id', 'text', 'created_at', and 'geo.place_id' response fields, as shown in Table 1. A query was built to obtain the messages through the interface, using the standardized operators of the second version of the Twitter© API (Twitter API v2).

Table 1. Response fields applied in the Twitter© API with the data used in the research.

Field	Type	Description
id	String	Unique identifier of each tweet
text	String	Text with the content of the posted tweet
created_at	Date	Tweet creation date in ISO 8601 standard
geo.place_id	String	Tweet postage location identifier, if cataloged by Twitter (despite being collected, the information was not applied in the present research)

The query process used to obtain the tweets was executed in Python language, as also other processes performed in the present research. The search terms instructed in the query were: 'inflacao lang:pt place_country:BR'. Using these settings, the query obtained tweets that contained the term 'inflation' and extracted only messages in Portuguese posted by users located in Brazil. Procedures to query the interface also required to set the start and end dates for data collection, which were repeated on a daily basis. The dataset obtained was stored in a standard comma-separated values (CSV) file for further processing, containing the fields presented in Table 1.

In addition, the IPCA index (considered the official inflation index by the federal government) was acquired from the website of the IBGE [12]. A file containing a historical series with the monthly variation of the IPCA between July 1994 and September 2021 was obtained from the website, further processed and stored in a suitable format for use in the research. In this process, the data with a monthly frequency were restricted to the defined study period.

Thereafter, graphs were generated to assist the interpretation of results obtained with the search conducted in the Twitter© API. These charts provided the comparison between the number of tweets obtained and the IPCA measured in each month, as shown in the Result Analysis section.

3.2 Natural Language Processing

Different techniques were applied for text preprocessing with the purpose to suppress some expressions commonly found in tweets and recurrent in several messages. Therefore, expressions identifying names of users mentioned in the text (preceded by the character '@'), links to other websites (URLs), reposted message tags (retweets), and line break marks (line feeds) were removed.

In the next step, the spaCy© library, available in Python©, was used to construct a corpus of texts. A set of the standard library components was separately performed to each message. The components included functions used to remove stop words and to apply a lemmatization process on the obtained terms, with the objective of inflecting the different forms of each word. In addition to the set of stop words provided by the library, other empty words identified were also suppressed after text processing. Then, the obtained terms were filtered again to eliminate punctuation and spaces, as also keeping only those with alphabetic characters. Finally, the corpus was also normalized to lowercase characters without accents (frequent in the Portuguese language) and then appended to a dataset.

Finally, bigrams of each message were obtained from the processed corpus and stored in a CSV file. The bigrams comprised the connected words from each message, combining a first word with its successor. The file also contained timestamps of the tweet creation dates (field 'created_at'). A structure with the 'source', 'target', and 'time' fields was specifically defined in the file for the network analysis.

3.3 Network Analysis

The Gephi© program was used for the network analysis of the corpus obtained by the natural language processing of the tweets. The previously stored bigrams were interpreted as nodes and edges of a network by the program, additionally with the provided timestamp. When processing this data, the program calculated the weight of each edge, which is the number of existing connections between all the terms of the corpus. Because data only contained bidirectional connections, the program defined the edges as non-directed.

Due to the substantial number of terms and aiming to allow an adequate interpretation of the corpus, only the most significant nodes were used for the network construction. The determined baseline was 5% of the weight of the edge with the highest value – ('inflation', 'high'), with a calculated weight of 2,576. Consequently, only edges with a weight equal to or greater than 128.8 were kept for analysis. Therefore, the edges were grouped by year, enabling an analysis of the temporal evolution of the tweets and identifying the most relevant terms in the posted messages.

Gephi© automatically calculated the centrality measures for the network of words obtained for each year (from 2011 to 2020), which were stored in CSV files. The betweenness centralities were used to analyze the temporal evolution of the network [13], considering only nodes with values greater than zero. A table was built with the concatenated values to present the results and an interactive graph was produced.

Although the terms in the messages posted in 2021 were not used for the analysis of the temporal evolution, due to the lack of complete data at the moment it was extracted, the tweets posted in this year were used for the construction of a graph of words. Therefore, this chart was applied for a non-temporal analysis of the term correlations.

4   Results Analysis

The messages extracting process through the Twitter© API resulted in 60,292 tweets, as shown in Table 2. Figure 1, in turn, presents the number of tweets grouped by the day that the social network users posted the message, according to the search terms applied in the query executed in the interface. It is important to emphasize that this graph contains the results of the entire message acquisition process, including the first messages posted in 2010.

Table 2. Summary of message extraction results through the Twitter© API.

Data characteristic	Result
Number of tweets	60,292
Days with tweets	3,886
First day	2010-10-12
Last day	2021-09-30
Unique geolocations	2,066

Figure 1 represents the number of tweets related to price increases over the months, since 2011. The highest peak of tweets happened in October 2014, the year of federal elections in Brazil. Specifically in these elections, there was a second round of voting on the last Sunday in October. Therefore, possibly, the theme "inflation" was a significant factor of political discussion in electoral campaigns.

The joint representation of the tweets and the inflation rates that actually occurred, expressed in Fig. 2, allows a cross-examination of the issue. In October 2014, the inflation rate was not significantly higher than the average. However, in the months following the elections, resulting in the reelection of the president, inflation rates rose considerably, which may suggest that there was some form of price control by the government for electoral purposes. Nevertheless, it can be noticed that tweets about inflation decreased, because the peak of discussions in October 2014 was not surpassed in other moments. Although, in subsequent months, the average of tweets related to inflation grew when compared to previous periods, which suggests a greater concern of society with post-2014 election inflation.

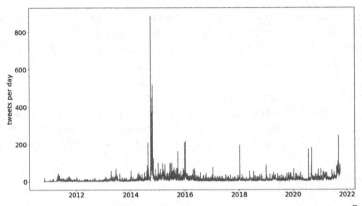

Fig. 1. Number of tweets per day, obtained by the query executed in the Twitter© API.

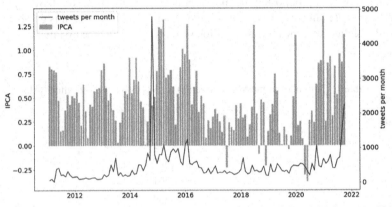

Fig. 2. Number of tweets per month and the monthly variation of the IPCA between 2011 and 2021.

Therefore, Gephi© provided a set of terms that presented at least some betweenness centrality, allowing the identification of the most relevant terms, as shown in Table 3. In the context of temporal analysis, the evolution of the betweenness centrality was examined from 2011 until 2020 because the data was available in all months in these years. We also produced an interactive graph in order to analyze the relevance temporality of the terms contained in the messages, which can be accessed through the electronic address https://public.flourish.studio/visualisation/7900429/.

Table 3 enhances that the term 'inflacao' (inflation) had a high centrality due to its application as a search term. Otherwise, in the first years of the analysis, we identified the terms with the highest centrality related to the demand of maintaining price stability. Among these, the terms 'manter' (to keep), 'real' (Brazilian currency) and 'preco' (price) repeatedly appeared as the most relevant until 2013. After the first years, starting in 2014, other terms acquired greater relevance, demonstrating the persistence of a situation that resulted in an economic crisis. The terms 'alta' (high), 'contas' (accounts), 'desempregado' (unemployed) and 'crise' (crisis) emerged with greater centrality. Thereafter, in

2015 and 2016, the inflation – which increased the price of important products – could be identified by the greater centrality of the terms 'gasolina' (gasoline) and 'gas' (cooking gas).

Table 3. Time evolution of the betweenness centrality from 2011 until 2020.

Term	2011	2012	2013	2014	2015	2016	2017	2018	2019	2020
inflacao	7383.85	7408.67	9862.33	10132.92	11109.95	10138.50	10410.93	11120.92	11554.08	11270.92
real	243.00	243.00	281.00	285.00	299.00	285.00	289.00	299.00	305.00	301.00
manter	243.00	243.00	281.00	285.00	299.00	285.00	289.00	150.00	305.00	301.00
preco	125.95	126.33	284.83	288.83	304.05	147.50	151.03	155.33	310.33	156.33
dilma	122.00	–	141.00	143.00	150.00	143.00	145.00	150.00	153.00	151.00
crise	122.00	122.00	141.00	143.00	150.00	143.00	145.00	150.00	153.00	151.00
aumento	75.93	86.00	86.75	93.58	107.25	94.00	100.77	102.33	108.08	102.33
acima	39.12	2.50	45.00	45.25	46.75	45.25	45.62	46.00	47.83	47.50
salario	36.12	54.17	42.00	42.25	43.75	42.25	42.62	44.50	44.83	44.50
juro	5.20	3.75	5.08	5.08	5.08	2.83	3.42	5.08	5.08	5.08
alto	3.50	3.83	6.92	9.25	8.95	7.33	7.83	7.33	9.00	7.33
subir	2.33	1.17	2.92	2.92	2.78	2.00	2.17	2.33	2.83	2.33
ano	2.00	2.17	3.25	2.00	2.00	2.00	2.00	2.00	2.00	2.00
dolar	1.25	0.33	2.25	1.25	7.92	0.92	2.33	3.75	6.25	1.25
governo	1.00	0.50	2.00	1.00	1.00	1.00	1.00	2.00	1.00	2.00
baixo	0.50	0.50	0.50	0.50	0.50	–	0.50	0.50	0.50	0.50
taxa	0.50	0.50	0.50	0.50	0.50	0.50	0.50	0.50	0.50	0.50
gasolina	0.42	0.58	0.42	0.42	299.87	144.67	288.53	299.67	305.92	301.67
minimo	0.33	–	0.33	0.33	0.33	0.33	0.33	0.33	0.33	0.33
contas	–	122.00	141.00	143.00	150.00	143.00	145.00	150.00	153.00	151.00
passar	–	–	141.00	0.50	0.50	0.50	0.50	0.50	0.50	0.50
fhc	–	–	141.00	0.50	0.50	0.50	–	150.00	–	151.00
alta	–	–	141.00	–	290.28	–	145.00	–	153.00	–
familia	–	–	141.00	143.00	150.00	143.00	145.00	150.00	153.00	151.00
pib	–	–	0.50	0.50	0.50	0.50	0.50	0.50	0.50	0.50
desempregado	–	–	0.42	146.42	153.42	146.42	148.42	153.42	156.42	154.42
dinheiro	–	–	–	143.00	150.00	143.00	145.00	150.00	153.00	151.00
fome	–	–	–	1.00	1.00	1.00	1.00	1.00	1.00	1.00
coxinhas	–	–	–	–	150.00	–	–	–	–	–
gas	–	–	–	–	150.00	–	145.00	150.00	153.00	151.00
pao	–	–	–	–	5.92	–	–	–	–	–
estavel	–	–	–	–	3.20	–	–	–	–	–
democracia	–	–	–	–	–	–	145.00	1008.00	1029.00	1015.00
deputado	–	–	–	–	–	–	4.00	298.00	304.00	300.00
senador	–	–	–	–	–	–	3.00	150.00	153.00	151.00
federal	–	–	–	–	–	–	3.00	444.00	453.00	447.00

(*continued*)

Table 3. (*continued*)

Term	2011	2012	2013	2014	2015	2016	2017	2018	2019	2020
vereador	–	–	–	–	–	–	–	870.00	888.00	876.00
distrito	–	–	–	–	–	–	–	730.00	745.00	735.00
estadual	–	–	–	–	–	–	–	588.00	600.00	592.00

Through the temporal evolution of the network, the term 'democracia' (democracy) emerged as one of the greatest centralities from 2017 onwards. The incidence of this word in the tweets remained high throughout the rest of the analyzed period, demonstrating the concern regarding this sensitive topic in discussions held by the society. In 2018, due to the state and federal elections, the words 'vereador' (city councilor), 'deputado' (congressman), 'estado' (state), 'federal' (federal) and 'distrito' (district) began a period in which they had greater relevance in the corpus of texts, remaining between the most important ones through 2020.

The network of words obtained in 2021 enabled to build a graph containing the most relevant edges, as shown in Fig. 3. The terms connected to inflation have red edges, allowing identification of the word correlations, calculated by the edge weight through Gephi©. The graph indicated that the edges with greater weight (characterized by the thickness of the connection curve) correlate 'inflation' to terms that denotes its increase: ('inflacao', 'alto'): 2,576; ('aumentar', 'inflacao'): 1,704; ('acima', 'inflacao'): 1,508; and ('inflacao', 'subir'): 1,376. Likewise, the edge ('inflacao', 'desempregado') – in English, ('inflation', 'unemployed') –, with a weight of 1,676, enabled to infer that there was a correlation between inflation rate growth and the rise in unemployment in this year.

Furthermore, excluding the bigrams with 'inflation', the edge with the highest weight was ('salario', 'minimo') – in English, ('salary', 'minimum') –, with a weight value of 1,011. Other bigram with the same characteristics were ('banco', 'central') and ('juro', 'alto') – respectively, ('bank', 'central') with 546, and ('interest rate', 'high') with 483 –, indicating the importance of the central bank to carry out the right decisions for controlling high inflation rates.

The monetary policy of a country seems to be a technical aspect restricted to Economists and stock traders. Nevertheless, the achievements brought forward that it was a major concern for users of social networks, even though the words applied in the messages were not specific technical terms used in the Economy. Therefore, the results reflected that social network environments are responsive to the influence of price increase, as it directly impacts everyday life.

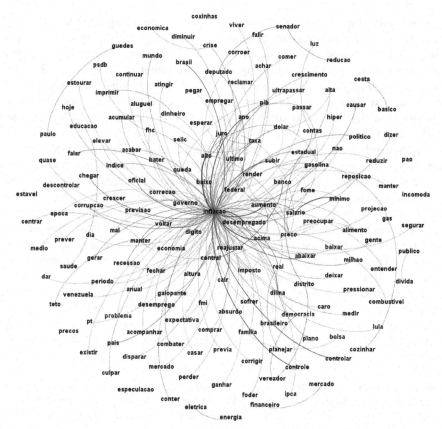

Fig. 3. Graph of the most relevant terms of the network, from the messages of 2021.

5   Final Remarks

Social networks influence people's behavior and, consequently, the economy, in both positive and negative aspects. Considering that inflation is directly linked to the loss of purchasing power, as also to long-term planning and the cost of public debt, deepening studies in this area becomes a central concern to macroeconomics. The use of artificial intelligence as an ally to conduct analysis of the economic scenario is important and can bring the opportunity to apply natural language processing techniques for better understanding the inflationary phenomenon in Brazilian society.

In this study, we suggested the existence of a correlation between the messages transmitted by Twitter© users and the monthly variation of inflation measured through the broad national consumer price index (IPCA) in Brazil. When the inflation rate is high, Twitter© users could discuss and express their private opinions about the general price level more frequently. The use of Twitter© messages to make predictions is well known in the world academy, since the social networks reflect the opinion of a significant sample of the social stratum, and is used to predict inflation [5], to predict the price of goods [7, 8], and to analyze feelings expressed in social network messages [6, 10].

Considering the methods applied in this research, natural language processing provides the ability to process and understand unstructured text, by parsing the meaning of a user content message in an automatized manner [14]. Its main objective is to allow computers to understand human language, which is inherently complex and ambiguous. The task of splitting the words from a corpus of text and rendering in an n-gram format enable the text representation in a low dimension format for a better machine understanding. However, as context-specific interpretation and domain knowledge are some challenges when performing NLP [15].

The network analysis identified prominent bigrams that reflected the price increase with a straight connection with inflation. Although this correlation was expected, terms related with economics difficulties associated with extended periods of inflation and the degradation of the economic scenario were also discovered in the tweets. Likewise, the bigrams without the term 'inflation' also included words associated with the worse circumstances caused by the price increase. Consequently, we concluded that inflation influences the behavior of social network users and, additionally, natural language processing of Twitter© messages can reveal relevant knowledge for inflation analysis and have potential for prediction purposes.

The research results contributed to increase the knowledge for building good data models for predictions in the Economy field. These capabilities should be examined in future research using tweets and could be confronted with other inflationary indices, such as the IGP-M and the INPC, as well as the use of other tools to compile data for analysis.

Acknowledgement. This study was financed in part by the Coordenação de Aperfeiçoamento de Pessoal de Nível Superior – Brasil (CAPES) – Finance Code 001. It was carried out under the Graduate Program in Knowledge Engineering and Management (PPGEGC), at the Federal University of Santa Catarina (UFSC).

References

1. Mankiw, N.G.: Macroeconomics, 3rd edn. Worth Publishers, New York (1996)
2. Akerlof, G.A., Dickens, W.T., Perry, G.L.: Low inflation or no inflation: should the federal reserve pursue complete price stability? Challenge **39**(5), 11–17 (1996)
3. Metas para a inflação: https://www.bcb.gov.br/controleinflacao/metainflacao. Accessed 22 Nov 2021
4. Nakamura, E., Steinsson, J.: High-frequency identification of monetary non-neutrality: the information effect. Q. J. Econ. **133**(3), 1283–1330 (2018)
5. Índices de preços: https://www.bcb.gov.br/controleinflacao/indicepreco. Accessed 09 Sep 2021
6. Aromi, J.D., Martin, L.: Forecasting inflation with twitter. Asociación Argentina de Economía Política (2020)
7. Kumar, J., Rao, T., Srivastava, S.: Economics of gold price movement-forecasting analysis using macro-economic, investor fear and investor behavior features. In: Srinivasa, S., Bhatnagar, V. (eds.) BDA 2012. LNCS, vol. 7678, pp. 111–121. Springer, Heidelberg (2012). https://doi.org/10.1007/978-3-642-35542-4_10
8. Alex, D.: Anchoring of inflation expectations in large emerging economies. J. Econ. Asymmetries **23**, e00202 (2021)

9. Kim, J., Cha, M., Lee, J.G.: Nowcasting commodity prices using social media. PeerJ Comput. Sci. **3**, e126 (2017)
10. Bastida, J.O., Gallego, A.J., Juan, J.R.R., Albarrán, P.: Regional gross domestic product predictions using Twitter deep learning representations. In: 17th International Conference on Applied Computing, pp. 89–96. Lisboa (2020)
11. Shapiro, A.H., Sudhof, M., Wilson, D.J.: Measuring news sentiment. J. Econom. **228**(2), 221–243 (2022)
12. Índice Nacional de Preços ao Consumidor Amplo: https://www.ibge.gov.br/estatisticas/economicas/precos-e-custos/9256-indice-nacional-de-precos-ao-consumidor-amplo.html. Accessed: 10 Oct 2021
13. Freeman, L.C.: A set of measures of centrality based on betweenness. Sociometry **40**(1), 35–41 (1977)
14. Chen, X., Ding, R., Xu, K., Wang, S., Hao, T., Zhou, Y.: A bibliometric review of natural language processing empowered mobile computing. Wirel. Commun. Mob. Comput. **18**, 1–21 (2018)
15. Pouyanfar, S., et al.: A survey on deep learning: algorithms, techniques, and applications. ACM Comput. Surv. **51**(5), 1–36 (2018)

Mining Association Rules in Commuter Feedback Comments from Facebook of Swiss National Railways (SBB) Using Apriori Algorithm

Patrick Blatter[1] and Farshideh Einsele[2]([envelope])

[1] Distance University of Applied Sciences, Zollstrasse 17, 8005 Zurich, Switzerland
[2] Bern University of Applied Sciences, Brückenstrasse 63, 3002 Bern, Switzerland
farshideh.einsele@bfh.ch

Abstract. Nowadays, all kinds of service-based organizations open online feedback possibilities for customers to share their opinion. Swiss National Railways (SBB) uses Facebook to collect commuters' feedback and opinions. These customer feedbacks are highly valuable to make public transportation option more robust and gain trust of the customer. The objective of this study was to find interesting association rules about SBB's commuters pain points. We extracted the publicly available FB visitor comments and applied manual text mining by building categories and subcategories on the extracted data. We then applied Apriori algorithm and built multiple frequent item sets satisfying the minsup criteria. Interesting association rules were found. These rules have shown that late trains during rush hours, deleted but not replaced connections on the timetable due to SBB's timetable optimization, inflexibility of fines due to unsuccessful ticket purchase, led to highly customer discontent. Additionally, a considerable amount of dissatisfaction was related to the policy of SBB during the initial lockdown of the Covid-19 pandemic. Commuters were often complaining about lack of efficient and effective measurements from SBB when other passengers were not following Covid-19 rules like public distancing and were not wearing protective masks. Such rules are extremely useful for SBB to better adjust its service and to be better prepared by future pandemics.

Keywords: Opinion mining · Data mining · Association analysis · Apriori algorithm · Online customer feedback mining · Text mining

1 Introduction

Swiss Federal Railways (SBB) is the national railway company of Switzerland. SBB was founded in 1902 as a government institution, but since 1999 Swiss cantons are participating in its ownership as well. While SBB is ranked first among national European rail systems in 2017 due to its intensity of use, quality, and reliability, it is also suffering from breakdowns and security problems, struggle to keep timetable and overcrowded

A. L. Pinto and R. Arencibia-Jorge (Eds.): DIONE 2022, LNICST 452, pp. 230–241, 2022.
https://doi.org/10.1007/978-3-031-22324-2_18

trains. At the same time the wages in the SBB boardroom have been highly risen. (Handelszeitung 2019). Additionally, the company suffers from outdated rolling stock as well as its dependency on foreign rolling stock.

Like many other companies SBB is on Facebook and has a visitor page, where the commuter can leave their comments. These comments are written in majority in German (approx. 80%) but also French and Italian. Switzerland is a multi-language country, and these are its official written and spoken languages. The idea of this study was to mine association rules in commuter feedback and gain an understanding of their opinion and satisfaction rate in various categories.

Consumer reviews are a reliable source of market response and text mining on these unstructured textual review data which can provide significant insight about consumers opinion. That is why many researchers have used text mining methods in different business contexts to extract meaningful insights and applied association mining to extract association rules to summarize customer opinions. Mining association rules as a method for customer opinion mining has been used by various researchers. The main objective of association mining is to determine rules that are extracted from a specific database by a pre-determined minimum percentage of support and confidence. (Wong 2009) extracts feature and opinion using part-of-speech tagging on each review sentence and applies a-priori algorithm to gain association rules to summarize customer review opinions. Liang et al. (2017) used a set of trivial lexical-part-of-speech patterns to find the optimal number of topics from online feedbacks of Chinese users along with Apriori algorithm and found out strong rules in each topic. Abuleil and Alsamara (2017) has utilized NLP techniques to generate some rules that helps to understand customer opinions and reviews written in the Arabic language. Peska and Vojtas (2017) uses a specific user behavior pattern as implicit feedback, forming binary relations between objects i,e. analyzing rule relations though it is not insignificant to capture the implicit relations and even to make the actionable well-known rules. (Hilage and Kulkarni 2011) describes using association rule mining, rule induction technique and Apriori algorithm to understand the correct buying behavior of the customer. (Huang and Lin 2011) use the relevance feedback mechanism in the collaborative recommendation system and adopt statistical attribute distance method to calculate the customer feedback correlations. They then apply multi-tier granule mining to find association rules to provide customers more relevance information.

Knowledge discovery in Databases (KDD) has been proposed by Fayyad et al. (1996) as a framework to gain relevant knowledge in large and often unstructured databases. The process of knowledge discovery contains 6 steps to obtain knowledge from one or more databases. The process starts with retrieving data from various sources, clean and pre-process them and integrate them into one single database. Apply data mining and finally discover novel and useful knowledge.

In our study, we apply KDD steps. Since in our case data is available in form of textual comments from commuters, we use some manual text mining techniques to gain categories and then build a relational database with each category as a table containing several sub-categories. In data mining step we have chosen Apriori algorithm over FP-growth, due to its simplicity, since our data set was relatively small and Apriori algorithm has proven to be as effective as FP Growth. We have gained interesting association rules that summarize the customer's opinion of SBB for the entire year of 2020. 2020 was a special year driven by Corona pandemic, hence a substantial number of comments were related to Covid-19 pandemic which were combined with different other categories extracted through text mining.

2   Data Selection

Data was extracted using an online extraction tool as a headless browser that programmatically visits a website and follows a sequence of predefined interactions. A linguistic recognition of the individual feedbacks was carried out using Open Refine (Open Refine 2020) to remove all non-German-speaking feedback.

3   Pre-processing

The data was pre-processed with the "Open Refine" tool. Open Refine is a software provided by Google freely available and a part of CS&S (Code for Science & Society 2021)). The messages were cleaned up to the point that all line breaks (tag: \ n) and emojis were removed. See Fig. 1 (removing line break tag) & Fig. 2 (removing emojis).

Expression

```
return value.replace("\n", "");
```

Fig. 1. Removing line break tags

Expression

```
import re

def remove_emojis(data):
    emoj = re.compile("["
        u"\U0001F600-\U0001F64F"  # emoticons
        u"\U0001F300-\U0001F5FF"  # symbols & pictographs
        u"\U0001F680-\U0001F6FF"  # transport & map symbols
        u"\U0001F1E0-\U0001F1FF"  # flags (iOS)
        u"\U00002500-\U00002BEF"  # chinese char
        u"\U00002702-\U000027B0"
        u"\U00002702-\U000027B0"
        u"\U000024C2-\U0001F251"
        u"\U0001f926-\U0001f937"
        u"\U00010000-\U0010ffff"
        u"\u2640-\u2642"
        u"\u2600-\u2B55"
        u"\u200d"
        u"\u23cf"
        u"\u23e9"
        u"\u231a"
        u"\ufe0f"  # dingbats
        u"\u3030"
                      "]+", re.UNICODE)
    return re.sub(emoj, '', data)

return remove_emojis(value)
```

Fig. 2. Removing emojis

Apart from the above removals, further text mining steps were not carried out because the textual data was not automatically processed. Instead, we divided the feedbacks into categories and sub-categories in order not to lose the context of feedbacks. At the same time, an attempt was made to keep the number of categories & their sub-categories as small as possible to avoid a kind of overfitting, which in turn can lead to many non-meaningful association rules. Each feedback is always assigned to at least the overall-impression category. This category records the state of mind of the person who wrote the message. In addition, each feedback is divided into one of the following time groups based on the publication date of the feedback: night (24:00–06:00), rush hour morning (06:00–09:00), marginal time (09:00–11:00 and 2 p.m.–4 p.m.), noon (11 a.m.–2 p.m.), rush hour evening (4 p.m.–7 p.m.) and evening (7 p.m.–midnight), this division was performed automated. Table 1 shows the categories, their sub-categories and number of corresponding feedbacks in percentage. This type of classification is also called {multi-label classification in the machine learning environment. The aim is to assign text fragments such as sentences, sections, or even entire documents to one or more labels (Paperswitchcode 2021).

Table 1. Categories and sub-categories

Category	Sub-category	Number of feedbacks %
Gesamteindruck	Unzufrieden, Neutral, Zufrieden	100.0
Zeitgruppe	Stosszeit Morgen, Mittag, Randzeit, Stosszeit Abend, Abend	100.0
Service	Unternehmen, Kundenservice, Information, Ansage, Frage, Sonstiges, Auskunft, Kritik, Lob, Mitarbeiter	21.03
Corona	Keine Maske, Prävention, Frage, Sonstiges, Fahrplan, Maske, Ticket	19.80
Tickets	Zurücklegen/Rückerstattung, Unverständliche Busse, Preis zu hoch/Preisgestaltung, Kauf nicht möglich, Frage, Sonstiges, GA, Studenten-GA, SwissPass, Sparbillet, Klassenwechsel, Hundepass	17.54
Infrastruktur	Zug defekt, Verbesserungsvorschlag, Temperatur, Zug verkürzt, Behindertengerecht, Frage, Sonstiges, Sauberkeit, WC, Stauplatz, Tür automatisch	15.53
Zuverlässigkeit	Verspätung, Zu früh, Ausfall, Anschluss verpasst, Frage, Sonstiges, Störung	13.61
Sonstiges	Frage zu Baustelle, Diebstahl, Bettler, Frage, Sonstiges	12.4
Fahrplan	Fehlerhaft, Verbesserungsvorschlag, Frage, Sonstiges, Einhaltung, Streichung	7.84
Kapazität	Überfüllt	7.60

(continued)

Table 1. (*continued*)

Category	Sub-category	Number of feedbacks %
App	Störung, Fehlerhaftes Angebot, Frage, Sonstiges, Fahrplan	5.76
Bahnhof	Beschädigt, Vandale, Frage, Sonstiges, Sauberkeit, Infrastruktur	4.54
Mitreisende	Falsches benehmen, Frage, Sonstiges, Korrektes benehmen	4.36
Restaurant	Angebot, Geschlossen, Frage, Sonstiges, Kein Speisewagen, Reservation	1.74

Multiple researcher report of using automatic categorization in their works. Liu et al. (http://arxiv.org/abs/2008.06695) achieved a Micro F1 score of a maximum of 72% in their proposed procedure in a data set consisting of 55,840 samples with a total of 54 possible labels to choose from (Liu et al. 2020). The Micro F1 score describes the quality (correct assignment of artifact and label) of the model used. Ibrohim and Budi achieved an accuracy of 66% in the classification of 5561 tweets that could be assigned to six possible labels (three main categories, three sub-categories) (Ibrohim and Budi 2019). Based on the results of their finding, we decided to take a manual approach because a correct prediction of labels in the range of 66–72% is not satisfying given the small number of data set.

Furthermore, based on the already small total amount of the database (1000 Feedbacks for 2020), we decided that an accuracy of less than 85% cannot be regarded as sufficient due to the falsified results. In addition to this, the poor quality of the feedback itself speaks in favor of manual classification. Spelling errors, Helvetisms (a.k.a Swiss German spoken dialect) and sarcasm as well as the mixing of German and Swiss German were all supplement factors that made it difficult to assign correct categories automatically.

To sum up, to achieve the best possible results from the association analysis, an automated process was therefore withdrawn. The Categories & sub-Categories are therefore intuitive. This means that the classified data can turn out differently depending on the person who performs this task. Figure 3 shows the categories, the sub-categories, and the number of corresponding feedbacks in percentage.

4   Data Transformation

Data has been transformed into a database using a dimensional scheme with the category overall-impression as the fact. The other categories are viewed as dimensions of feedback, as they describe the context of feedback in more detail. These tables contain the associated subcategories as attributes in a binary form (0 = feedback does not belong to this category, 1 = feedback belongs to this category). The fact table represents the feedback in the center of the scheme and uses a binary form to describe the affiliation to the other categories. The fact table includes all main categories as non-optional foreign keys to ensure that every feedback must explicitly describe whether it belongs to a category or not. As a result, the consistency and integrity of the data can be guaranteed as soon as feedback is inserted into the table scheme).

The tables are filled automatically using Python. The categorized data in the original CSV format served as the starting point. For this purpose, the file was read, and the python code was carried out, which fills the DB with the data from the file.

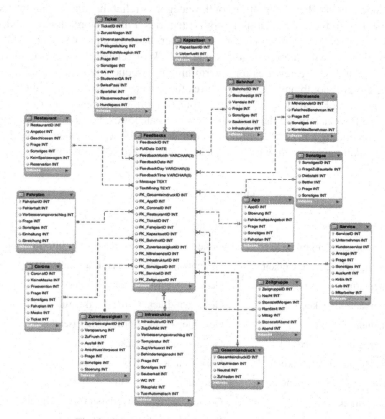

Fig. 3. Dimensional database scheme of feedbacks

5   Data Mining

Due to our relatively small number of feedbacks (1000 feedbacks for 2020) and a relatively small number of assigned categories and sub-categories of the feedback, there is little difference in performance whether to use the a-priori or FP growth algorithm to determine the frequency sets. The rules resulting from the association analysis can in this case be achieved with both algorithms without being able to determine qualitative differences. On this basis, the decision was made to determine the frequent item sets using the a-priori algorithm.

5.1 Building Frequent Item Sets

We have determined the possible combinations of the sub-categories within each category to build the frequent 2, 3, 4 item sets. As an example of this, if selecting the categories to build a frequent 3-item set were overall impression and service, then a possible frequent itemset could consist of the s satisfied, employee, praise. Table 2 shows an overview of the distribution of the categories. It can be seen that numerous combinations are possible with the overall-impression category due to the frequency of this category. At the same time, further observations of the categories reliability and restaurant showed that there was no feedback relating to both categories. Furthermore, it was decided not to consider the category miscellaneous for further analysis, since no meaningful rules could be formed with these categories due to lack of related data. Furthermore, the greater the number of categories for determining the frequent item sets, the fewer possible meaningful combinations of categories there were. This is because there is only a small amount of feedback that includes four or more categories. For example, there is only one feedback in the database that has five categories. For this reason, only sets up to and including a maximum of four frequent item-sets were created. Table 2 shows category combinations from which frequent 2- and 3-item sets were created.

Table 2. Frequent item-sets

Frequent 2-itemsets	Frequent 3-itemsets
Gesamteindruck, Zeitgruppe	Gesamteindruck, Zuverlässigkeit, Infrastruktur
Gesamteindruck, Zuverlässigkeit	Gesamteindruck, Corona, Kapazität
Gesamteindruck, Corona	Gesamteindruck, Corona, Service
Gesamteindruck, Ticket	Gesamteindruck, Corona, Infrastruktur
Gesamteindruck, App	Gesamteindruck, Corona, Mitreisende
Gesamteindruck, Service	Gesamteindruck, Ticket, Service
Gesamteindruck, Infrastruktur	Gesamteindruck, Zuverlässigkeit, Service
Gesamteindruck, Restaurant	Zeitgruppe, Zuverlässigkeit, Infrastruktur
Gesamteindruck Bahnhof	Gesamteindruck, Zuverlässigkeit, Zeitgruppe
Gesamteindruck, Fahrplan	Gesamteindruck, Ticket, Corona
Ticket, Service	Gesamteindruck, Service
Corona, Mitreisende	Gesamteindruck, Corona
Infrastruktur, Kapazität	Service, Zuverlässigkeit
Corona, Ticket	Gesamteindruck, Corona, Fahrplan
Zuverlässigkeit, Service	–

5.2 Building Association Rules

We have built association rules using python as follows: the records (feedbacks) of an itemset combination that are in the database were first loaded into the main memory with a read query. For this purpose, all possible columns in the database were determined for each item set that occurs (without a primary key, as this does not contain any useful information). As soon as these were available, a SQL statement was generated, which linked the column n with a table prefix until all columns to be read appeared in the statement. The statement is completed so that all categories of an item set are linked to the Feedbacks table by means of an inner join. The following parameters were used to create the frequent item sets and the association rules: For the generation of frequent item-sets there was a minimum support given that had to be achieved for it to be considered in the association rule mining process. A parameter defining how many items can occur in total within an association rule was passed along while building up to 4-itemsets and starting from 2. For every found association rule it was further checked if they meet a minimum confidence of 0.7.

6 Results (Association Rules)

We have built a total of 315 association rules, i.e., 75/2-itemsets, 197/3-itemsets and 43/4-itemsets association rules from our 2, 3, 4 frequent item-sets. Below are some examples of the gained rules:

6.1 Overall Impression and Corona

A total of 227 feedbacks belonged to this item set. {Used minimum support: 0.1

1. In 86% of the cases, a missing mask also leads to dissatisfaction. Both occur in 3.75% of all feedback. There is a correlating dependency between premise and conclusion (lift = 1.17)
2. In 84.7% of the cases, the (lack of) prevention leads to dissatisfaction. This occurs in 10.21% of the total amount. There is a correlating dependency between premise and conclusion (lift = 1.15)

6.2 Overall Impression and Ticket

A total of 201 feedbacks belonged to this item set. Minimum support used: 0.1

1. In 96.0% of the cases, the pricing leads to dissatisfaction. This appears in 4.42% of all feedbacks. There is a positive correlation between premise and conclusion (lift = 1.62)
2. If for some reason the purchase of a ticket is not possible, the customer is dissatisfied with the experience in 84.0% of the cases. Both occur in 2.18% of the total amount and there is a positive correlation between premise and conclusion (lift = 1.49)

6.3   Overall Impression, Reliability, Time

A total of 156 feedbacks belonged to this item set. Minimum support used: 0.1

1. In 82.6% of the cases, dissatisfaction at rush hour can be attributed to being late. All occur in 1.66% of the total amount. There is a positive correlation between premise and conclusion (lift = 1.18)
2. A delay in the evening leads to dissatisfaction in all cases. Together, these appear in 1.4% of all feedbacks. There is almost no dependency between premise and conclusion (lift = 1.01)
3. A delay in the morning rush hour leads to dissatisfaction in all cases. Together, these occur in 1.66% of all feedback. There is almost no dependency between premise and conclusion (lift = 1.01)
4. A delay at off-peak times leads to dissatisfaction in all cases. Together, these occur in 1.66% of all feedback. There is almost no dependency between premise and conclusion (lift = 1.01)

7   Knowledge Interpretation

In the following paragraphs, we give a brief interpretation of some of the interesting rules found in our data-mined categories. An overall interpretation was that especially dissatisfied customers left their feedbacks. Rules that contained the item Satisfied very often have not even reached the set minsup and were therefore ignored when generating the rules. In this case, the minimum support should have been set very low, which in turn would have caused the problem of generating too many rules.

7.1   Reliability

As a state-owned company, the main task of SBB is to transport commuters. Hence the commuters were especially dissatisfied when train was not on time or another expectation from their point of view could not be met. Rules found from the areas of reliability and time indicate that traffic is at its peak and is often delayed during rush hours in the morning as well as evening, whereas trains were mostly half full in the remaining hours. SBB should come with a better plan to answer this shortcoming.

7.2   Covid-19

A novel source of dissatisfaction has emerged from the initial lockdown situation in 2020 when commuters didn't wear a protective mask and not complying with Distance rules result from overcrowded trains to prevent the Covid-19 virus. These rules turned out to be very interesting. Through increased train controls by SBB in combination with covid-related fines for commuters who do not wore the protective mask, SBB could have counteracted at least the point regarding non-compliance with the mask requirement. Part of the blame, however, lays in the decision of SBB to shorten train formations. This decision may seem a cost-optimizer and it may be justifiable since the offer was limited, however the actual demand from commuters was greater than anticipated.

In addition, the exemplary behavior of the SBB employees highlighted in relation to the prevention of the Covid-19 virus. Their Action has often led to explicit praise. Another positively correlating rule is dissatisfaction with cleanliness and Hygiene and the resulting inadequate prevention of Covid-19. Commuters wished, among other things, that the train doors would open by themselves, so that they come so little as possible into contact with material from potentially infected persons. SBB could improve the unsatisfied customers with a more transparent communication towards the passengers, to what extent cleaning was carried out.

Lastly, customers who have a relatively expensive yearly ticket (GA travelcard) were often dissatisfied, since it was not possible to receive compensation such as an extension of their subscription due to the reduced SBB offer. With a clear communication policy, it would have been possible to explain to customers even better why it was not possible to compensate.

7.3 Train Ticket

The commuters wished for more goodwill by fines. Many fines were considered incomprehensible from the perspective of the commuters. This led to dissatisfaction and criticism in equal measure. For example, when for uncertain reasons the ticket purchase was not possible, the commuters were dissatisfied, since the commuters had to carry the risk of receiving fines or be delayed.

7.4 SBB APP

The App timetable and the ticket purchase with wrong prices were sources of discontent. Both points have turned out to be interesting rules. In some cases, delays or train cancellations were not apparent. In the worst case, there were even false reports of train connections. It also happened that, for example, certain tickets could be purchased at the wrong price. A fault within the app, on the other hand, which receives most of the feedback within this Category, show almost no dependency, which is why it cannot be said that a disorder leads to dissatisfaction.

7.5 Timetable

The deletion of a connection led often to dissatisfaction with those directly affected. This can be attributed to the fact that these individuals rely on exactly this connection and are now looking for alternatives as a result. Regarding a timetable optimization on the part of the SBB, it is obvious that SBB cannot meet all passenger needs. In this regard, only early information in connection with any reasons for the decision, should be put on place by SBB to minimize this dissatisfaction as much as possible and, if necessary, to make the appeal understandable to the commuters.

8 Conclusion and Future Work

The presented study reports of mining interesting association rules from Facebook-posted commuter feedbacks of Swiss National Railways (SBB). This study is the first public study on commuter feedback of SBB. We have used text mining and datamining specifically association analysis to by applying Apriori algorithm on the data. We have built different categories and built association rules within their different subcategories. Since the data set was very unbalanced, i.e. there were many more dissatisfied entries than satisfied ones, most of the rules were based on factors related to a dissatisfaction. Because of that rules that relate to satisfaction can be valuable as well. However, this is a known phenomenon by customer feedback on a company's online page. This kind of feedback is fundamentally different from the posts where customers write their opinion for other customers like in TripAdvisor and share their good and bad experiences. Notwithstanding, the rules related to passenger's discontent are not any less useful, as they provide insights into the customer's point of view and define specific pain points.

Most unsatisfied comments were found by late train during rush hours, deleted but not replaced connections on the timetable due to SBB's timetable optimization, inflexibility of fines due to unsuccessful ticket purchase. Additionally, a considerable amount of discontent was related to the policy of SBB during the initial lockdown of the Covid-19 pandemic. Commuters were often complaining about lack of efficient and effective measurements from SBB when other passengers were not following Covid-19 rules like public distancing and were not wearing protective masks. Such rules of discontent give a valuable insight into what exactly needs to be done to meet the commuter's expectations.

During the implementation it was shown that some steps of text mining should be performed manually to categorize the data. In practice, this approach does not represent a scalable and efficient method in large data collections, since the process execution is time consuming. For our future work, we intend to perform automatic text categorization while gathering more data.

Another weakness of Apriori algorithm is the definition of a minimum support. It is important to find a mediocrity in order not to have to generate too many uninteresting rules and at the same time not to delete too many potentially interesting rules. This value can only be found by trial and testing.

To be able to address the problem of scalability present in this study, an increase in the accuracy of multi-label classification models would be desirable. This depends on various factors such as the number of labels, the amount of database and their balance. An experiment could be used to research whether a certain degree of accuracy with several labels can be achieved. Among other things, this would be It is also interesting to see which number of labels by the size of the data would lead to the predefined maximum accuracy (between 80%–100%). We intend to consider the above-mentioned improvements in our future work.

References

Handelszeitung (2019). https://www.handelszeitung.ch/unternehmen/si-kemme-am-saggsi-und-geen-am-zwai

Wong: A method for opinion mining of product reviews using association rules. In: Proceedings of the 2nd International Conference on Interaction Sciences: Information Technology, Culture and Human, ICIS 2009, November, pp. 270–274 (2009). https://doi.org/10.1145/1655925.1655973

Liang: Mining Product Problems from Online Feedback of Chinese Users. Emerald Publishing Limited (2017). https://doi.org/10.1108/K-03-2016-0048

Abuleil, S., Alsamara, K.: Using NLP approach for analyzing customer reviews, pp. 117–124 (2017). © Cs & It-Cscp 2017 https://doi.org/10.5121/Csit.2017.70112

Peska, L., Vojtas, P.: Using implicit preference relations to improve recommender systems. J. Data Semant. **6**(1), 15–30 (2017)

Hilage, T., Kulkarni, R.: Application of data mining techniques to a selected business organization with special reference to buying behaviour. Int. J. Database Manag. Syst. **3**(4), 169–181 (2011)

Huang, Y., Lin, S.: Applying multidimensional association rule mining to feedback-based recommendation systems. In: IEEE International Conference on Advances in Social Network Analysis and Mining, ASONAM (2011). https://doi.org/10.1109/ASONAM.2011.29

Fayyad, U., Piatetsky-Shapiro, G., Smyth, P.: Knowledge discovery and data mining: towards a unifying framework. In: Proceedings of the KDD 1996 (1996)

Open Refine (2020). http://www.geobib.fr/blog/2020-04-29-openrefine-detect-lang. Accessed 25 Aug 2021

CS & S, Code for Science & Society (2021). https://codeforscience.org/. Accessed 25 Aug 2021

Paperswitchcode (2021). https://paperswithcode.com/task/multi-label-classification. Accessed 25 Aug 2021

Liu, H., Yuan, C., Wang, X.: Label-wise document pre-training for multi-label text classification. In: Zhu, X., Zhang, M., Hong, Yu., He, R. (eds.) NLPCC 2020. LNCS (LNAI), vol. 12430, pp. 641–653. Springer, Cham (2020). https://doi.org/10.1007/978-3-030-60450-9_51. https://arxiv.org/abs/2008.06695

Ibrohim, M., Budi, I.: Multi-label hate speech and abusive language detection in Indonesian Twitter. In: Proceedings of the Third Workshop on Abusive Language Online, Florence, Italy (2019). https://doi.org/10.18653/v1/W19-3506

Enhancement of Voting Scores with Multiple Attributes Based on VoteRank++ to Identify Influential Nodes in Social Networks

Pham Van Duong[1,3], Tuan Minh Dang[2,3], Le Hoang Son[4], and Pham Van Hai[1(✉)]

[1] School of Information and Communication Technology, Hanoi University of Science and Technology, Hanoi, Vietnam
haipv@soict.edu.vn

[2] Posts and Telecommunications Institute of Technology, Km10, Nguyen Trai Street, Hanoi, Vietnam
tuandm@ptit.edu.vn

[3] CMC Institute of Science Technology, No. 11 Duy Tan Street, Hanoi, Vietnam
dmtuan1@cmc.com.vn

[4] VNU University of Science, Vietnam National University, Hanoi, Vietnam
sonlh@vnu.edu.vn

Abstract. With the prosperity of social networks, Influence maximization is a crucial analysis drawback within the field of network science due to its business value. In this regard, we propose the EAVoteRank++, inspired by VoteRank++, to iteratively select the influential node. It is commonly recognized that degree is a well-known centrality metric for identifying prominent nodes, and neighbors' contributions should also be considered. Furthermore, topological connections between neighbors have an impact on node spreading ability; the more connections between neighbors, the higher the risk of infection. Therefore, EAVoterank++ algorithm identify nodes's voting ability by considering degree, position in network by improve k-shell decomposition and clustering coefficient as well as neighbors. The weights of attribute are calculated by entropy technology. Furthermore, based on VoteRank++, EAVoteRank++ minimizes the voting ability of 2-hop neighbors of the selected nodes to decrease the overlapping of influential regions of spreaders. To demonstrate the effectiveness of the proposed method, we employ both the SIR model and LS model to simulate the spreading progress, then calculate the accuracy of the proposed algorithm, compare with other methods. The experimental results with 2 propagation simulation models on 6 datasets demonstrate the good performance of the proposed method on discrimination capability and accuracy.

Keywords: Influence maximization · Influential node · Social networks · Voting approach · Spreading model · Multiple attribute · Information entropy

1 Introduction

The modalities of communication between individuals and the methods in which information is generated are fast evolving, due to the continued growth of the Internet. In

© ICST Institute for Computer Sciences, Social Informatics and Telecommunications Engineering 2022
Published by Springer Nature Switzerland AG 2022. All Rights Reserved
A. L. Pinto and R. Arencibia-Jorge (Eds.): DIONE 2022, LNICST 452, pp. 242–257, 2022.
https://doi.org/10.1007/978-3-031-22324-2_19

particular, social media platforms like Facebook, Twitter, Tiktok, as well as a burgeoning landscape of microblogs, have aided in the consumption and sharing of information [1]. As a result, studies on social networks have received a lot of interest from academic and industrial groups. Researchers regconized information may be transferred through the links in a social network, potentially causing a chain reaction [2]. Many algorithms have been studied and proposed with different approaches to solve influence maximization. One of these approaches is to rank the nodes in the graph according to their importance to determine the set of important nodes in the network. The researchers employ two methodologies: network embedding and node centrality.

Early approaches for learning node representations mostly relied on matrix decomposition. These solutions, however, come at a high expense in terms of computing. DeepWalk [3] is a pioneer of network embedding methods, which uses word2vec to generate low-dimensional representation vectors of nodes using random walk sequences. Node2vec improves on the DeepWalk algorithm by integrating breadth-first and depth-first search into the random walk sequence generation. Besides, SDNE [4] uses deep neural networks to model the nonlinearity between nodes. For node centrality method, this kind of method usually express the significance of one node with a numerical value and finally outputs a ranking list. Degree centrality [5] (DC) is the simplest method to determine node influence, this metric focuses only on the number of neighbors of the node. In addition, there are CC and BC algorithms, which use the local information of each node to calculate the influence of that node. K-shell and some improved methods are representative methods based on local network topology to determine the importance of nodes according to the position of nodes in the network. Furthermore, algorithms such as eigenvector centrality (EC) [6] and HITS [7] have been explored and proposed to enhance node ranking. Recently, several academics suggested a novel perspective on the influence index of network nodes. Ma et al. [8] suggested two methods based on the law of gravity, which take into account both neighborhood influence information and graph connectivity information.

In general, ranking algorithms assume that a set of important nodes will solve the IM problem, but some problems. These algorithms are likely to choose a set of influential nodes in the same locations, for example. The distances between multiple spreaders have a crucial role in maximizing the impact, according to Kitsak et al. As a result, selecting influential nodes throughout a network is a wise idea. The main concept is to identify a set of influential nodes, known as seed nodes, that are distributed across the network. To identify influential nodes in the network, Zhang et al. [9] presents the VoteRank algorithm, which is based on the voting mechanism. Guo et al. [10], based on the VoteRank algorithm, proposed the EnRenew algorithm, which selects seed nodes based on the information entropy of the nodes and achieves a significant improvement over the original technique. VoteRank is one of these algorithms that has gotten a lot of interest since it gives a quick and easy solution to the IM issue. Then a proposed VoteRank++ [11], an improvement to the VoteRank algorithm. This method is improved in two ways: (1) a node's voting ability is connected to its relevance in the initiation process, and (2) each node can vote for its neighbors differently in the voting process. Also, to reduce the computation time of the algorithm, we update only part of the nodes in each iteration instead of all the nodes. Based on an improved idea inspired by VoteRank++, this paper proposes a new algorithm named EAVoteRank++, which to repeatedly select influential nodes. The influence of neighboring nodes is ignored by the centrality measurements. It is generally recognized that magnitude is a well-known central metric for identifying prominent nodes and that the contributions of neighboring countries should also be considered. Furthermore, topological connections between neighbors have an impact on the propagation capacity of a node. The more connections there are between neighbors, the higher the risk of infection. Therefore, the EAVoterank++ algorithm determines the voting ability of the nodes, considering the degree, the position in the network by improving the k-shell decomposition and clustering coefficient as well as the neighborhoods. Attribute weights are calculated using entropy technology. Furthermore, based on VoteRank++, EAVoteRank++ minimizes the voting capacity of the 2-step neighbors of the selected nodes to reduce the overlap of the affected regions of the spreader. To demonstrate the effectiveness of the proposed method, we use both SIR to simulate the progression of the spread. The test results on 6 datasets prove the good performance of the proposed method in terms of discriminant ability and accuracy.

The rest of this paper is written out as follows. Section 2 discusses the concentration measuring algorithm, whereas Sect. 3 discusses the proposed algorithm and Sect. 4 discusses its performance evolution. Finally, in Sect. 5, we discuss our results and future improvements.

2 Backgrounds

Given a network $G = \langle V, E \rangle$ with G is an undirected and unweighted network, where V and E represent nodes and edges. We denote $A = (a_{ij})_{N \times N}$ is the adjacency matrix of G. If there is an edge between node i and node j then $a_{ij} = 1$, otherwise $a_{ij} = 0$.

2.1 Centrality Measures

Degree Centrality (DC) [4] is defined as the number of edges occurring on a node is known as the number of edges node. $DC(i)$ of node i can be calculated by:

$$DC(i) = k(i) = \sum_j a_{ij} \tag{1}$$

where $k(i)$ is the degree of node i.

K-Shell Decomposition: [12] This approach can be considered as a node degree-based coarse graining sorting algorithm. The following is the specific decomposition procedure: The initial stage in KS is to remove all nodes in the network with a degree of 1 from the network. Then, after one round of removal, it removes nodes with a degree of $k \leq 1$ since this step may cause the degree values to be reduced throughout the removal process. All nodes deleted in this stage generate 1-shell and their k-shell values are equal to one until there are no nodes in the network with degree $k \leq 1$. Then repeat the process to get two shells, three shells, and so on. Finally, all nodes are separated into distinct shells, and each node's k-shell value may be calculated.

Improve K-Shell Decomposition

[13] proposed he improved k-shell index of node i, denoted by $k_s^*(i)$, can be calculated by:

$$k_s^*(i) = k_s(i) + \frac{p(i)}{q(k)+1} \qquad (2)$$

where $p(i)$ is the stage in a k-shell layer decay for which node i is removed from the graph, $q(k)$ is the set of the number of stages in the k-shell decay.

Local Clustering Coefficient: Other measurements can be computed for each node and used to create a distribution function, but the most common is degree. A node's clustering coefficient [14] estimates how many vertices will more often than not be grouped together. There are two types of clustering coefficients, global and local. In this paper, we use the local clustering coefficient. Specifically, given a vertex v and và $d_v = |N_v|$ its degree. The local clustering coefficient C_v of node v can be calculated as follows:

$$C_v = \frac{2.|\{v', v''\} \in E(G) : v', v'' \in N_v|}{d_v(d_v - 1)} \qquad (3)$$

H-Index

The H-index [15] of a node is defined to be the maximum value h such that there exists at least h neighbours of degree no less than h. H is a function that works on a finite number of reals $(x_1, x_2, \ldots, x_n)$ and returns an integer $y = H(x_1, x_2, \ldots, x_n)$, where y is the largest integer such that $(x_1, x_2, \ldots, x_n)$ has at least y items, each of which is greater than y. $x_1, x_2, \ldots, x_n$ is the number of citations to these articles for a scholar with n publications, and $H(x_1, x_2, \ldots, x_n)$ the scholar's H-index.

$$h_i = H(k_{j1}, k_{j2}, \ldots, k_{ji}) \qquad (4)$$

We define $h_i^{(0)} = k_i$ to be the zero-order H-index of node i, and define the n-order H-index iteratively as

$$h_i^{(n)} = H(h_{j1}^{(n-1)}, h_{j2}^{(n-1)}, \ldots, h_{jk_i}^{(n-1)}) \qquad (5)$$

The H-index of node i is equal to the first-order H-index, namely $h_i^{(1)} = h_i$.

MCDE

The MCDE [16] algorithm considers a combination of the indices of the node location in the network, the node's order coefficient, and that node's entropy. This algorithm is used to rank the nodes in the network. MCDE of node v is calculated by the formula

$$MCDE(v) = \alpha KS(v) + \beta DC(v) + \gamma Entropy(v) \qquad (6)$$

$$Entropy(v) = -\sum_{i=0}^{KS_{n\Omega}} (p_i * log_2 p_i) \qquad (7)$$

$$p_i = \frac{the\ number\ of\ neighbors\ of\ node\ v\ in\ the\ i - th\ KS}{DC(v)} \qquad (8)$$

ECRM

The ECRM [17] algorithm is an improved cluster ranking approach presented taking into account the common hierarchy of nodes and their neighborhoods. The influence score of a node in the network applying the ECRM algorithm is calculated as follows:

$$ECRM_i = \sum_{v_j \in N_i} CRM_j \qquad (9)$$

$$CRM_i = \sum_{v_j \in N_i} SCC_j \qquad (10)$$

$$SCC_i = \sum_{v_j \in N_i} \left((2 - C_{i,j}) + \left(2\frac{d_j}{max(d)} + 1 \right) \right) \qquad (11)$$

$$C_{i,j} = \frac{\sum_{k=1}^{f} \left(SV_i^{(k)} - \overline{SV_i} \right) \left(SV_j^{(k)} - \overline{SV_j} \right)}{\sqrt{\sum_{k=1}^{f} \left(SV_i^{(k)} - \overline{SV_i} \right)^2} \sqrt{\sum_{k=1}^{f} \left(SV_j^{(k)} - \overline{SV_j} \right)^2}} \qquad (12)$$

$$SV_i = \left\{ \left| N_i^{(1)} \right|, \left| N_i^{(2)} \right|, \left| N_i^{(3)} \right|, \dots \left| N_i^{(f)} \right| \right\} \qquad (13)$$

where $ECRM_i$ is the influence score of node i calculated by ECRM algorithm, CRM_i is the coefficient of cluster coefficient ranking measure determined by the cascade clustering coefficients of the neighbors SCC_i, $C_{i,j}$ is Pearson's correlation coefficient among class vectors SV_i.

EnRenew

These two concepts are fed into the complex network in order to calculate node importance [10]. The information entropy of any node v can be calculated in

$$E_v = \sum_{u \in \Gamma_v} H_{uv} = \sum_{u \in \Gamma_v} -p_{uv} log p_{uv} \qquad (14)$$

$p_{uv} = \frac{d_u}{\sum_{l \in \Gamma_v} d_l}$, $\sum_{l \in \Gamma_v} p_{lv} = 1$ and Γ_v is the set of neighbors of node v, d_u is the degree centrality of the node u, H_{uv} is the ability to propagate information from node u to node v. After each high impact node is selected, the algorithm improves the information entropy of all nodes in its local range according to the formula

$$H_{u^{l-1}u^l} - = \frac{1}{2^{l-1}} \frac{H_{u^{l-1}u^l}}{E_{\langle k \rangle}} \qquad (15)$$

where $E_{\langle k \rangle} = -\langle k \rangle . \frac{1}{\langle k \rangle} . log \frac{1}{\langle k \rangle}$ where $\langle k \rangle$ is the average of the degree centrality of the entire network, $\frac{1}{2^{l-1}}$ is the coefficient decreases.

VoteRank

VoteRank algorithm [9] used to identify influential nodes in an unweighted network using the idea of voting process. A pair of values (vs_v, va_v) representing each node $v \in V$, where vs_v and va_v correspond to the influence score voted on by the neighbors and the node's voting power score. v. The voted influence score vs_v of a node v is equal to the sum of the voting possibility scores of all its direct neighbors, which is determined by the formula:

$$vs_v = \sum_{u \in \Gamma_v} va_u \tag{16}$$

where Γ_v is the set of neighbors of node v. VoteRank algorithm is divided into 4 main stages.

Initialization: The influence score vs_v of each node v is initialized by default to 0, and the voting ability of each node va_v is set to 1.

Voting: During this phase, voting is conducted. Each node v gets a vote equal to the sum of the voting ability scores of its immediate neighbors. This is considered as the point of influence of that node. The node with the highest influence score will be considered as the node that propagates the influence. Furthermore, the selected node will not be allowed to participate in subsequent voting rounds by setting that node's voting ability score to 0.

Update: TO find influence nodes from different locations in the graph network, thus the voting probability score of the neighbors of a node was chosen to perform influence propagation in the next iteration will be $\delta = 1/\langle k \rangle$, where $\langle k \rangle$ is the average of the degree of the nodes.

Iteration: The voting and update step will be repeated until l influence nodes are selected where l is a predefined constant.

VoteRank++

With the VoteRank++ approach [11], nodes with different degree centrality will have influence scores voted on by different node. Like VoteRank algorithm, VoteRank++ is divided into 4 main stages.

Initialization: The influence score vs_v of each node v is initialized to 0 by default, and the voting ability score of each node va_v is calculated by the formula:

$$va_v = log\left(1 + \frac{k_v}{k_{max}}\right) \tag{17}$$

Voting: During this phase, voting is conducted. Each node v gets a vote equal to the sum of the voting ability scores of its immediate neighbors. This is considered as the score of influence of that node.

$$VP_{uv} = \frac{k_v}{\sum_{w \in \Gamma_u} k_w} \tag{18}$$

$$vs_v = \sqrt{|\Gamma_v| \sum_{u \in \Gamma_v} VP_{uv}.va_u} \tag{19}$$

The node with the highest influence score will be considered as the node that propagates the influence. Furthermore, the selected node will not be allowed to participate in subsequent voting rounds by setting that node's voting ability score to 0.

Update: The VoteRank++ algorithm improves the reduction of the voting ability score to two-hop influence on its neighbors by the fomula:

$$va_v = \begin{cases} \lambda.va_v & v \text{ is a first} - order\ neighbor \\ \sqrt{\lambda}.va_v, & v \text{ is a second} - order\ neighbor \end{cases} \tag{20}$$

Iteration: The voting and update step will be repeated until l influence nodes are selected where l is a predefined constant.

Information Entropy

Information entropy [18] is a well-known notion in information theory. In general, the more unpredictable or random an occurrence is, the more data it contains.

The information entropy is defined as follows:

$$H(X) = H(x_1, x_2, \ldots, x_n) = -\sum_{i=1}^{n} p(x_i) logp(x_i) \tag{21}$$

where $X = \{x_1, x_2, \ldots, x_n\}$ is set of possible events and $p(x_i)$ is the probability of event x_i

One of the most important uses of information entropy in the field of social science is the entropy weighting technique. The entropy weighting approach is frequently used to compute the weights of distinct qualities in multiattribute decision-making situations, as well as to evaluate the relevance of nodes in complex networks, due to its good performance. Assume there are n qualities to take into account. The weight of attribute i abbreviated w_i, is computed as follows:

$$w_i = \frac{1 - H_i}{\sum_1^n (1 - H_i)} \tag{22}$$

where $H_i (i = 1, 2, .., n)$ is the information entropy of each attribute.

2.2 Performances Metrics

Susceptible Infected Recovered (SIR) Model and Susceptible Infected (SI) Model
A classic infectious disease model, the susceptible infected recovered (SIR) [19] model
may also be used to abstractly represent information transmission. The SIR model
assumes all nodes to be susceptible (S) at first, except for the source node, which has
been infected (I). Each infected node has a possibility of infecting its susceptible neighbors with probability β. Each infected node recovers to become a recovered node with
a chance of μ at each time step. The infection process will continue until there are no
more infected nodes [18]. The influence of node i could be calculated using the formula:

$$P(i) = \frac{R(t^*)}{N} \tag{23}$$

where $R(t^*)$ is the number of recovered nodes when the dynamic process achieves steady-
state and N is the total number of nodes in the network. The corresponding epidemic
threshold is:

$$\beta_c \approx \frac{\langle k \rangle}{\langle k^2 \rangle - \langle k \rangle} \tag{24}$$

The susceptible infected (SI) model is a special case of the susceptible infected
(SIR) model. The SI model is based on the SIR model and assumes that the recovery
rate $\mu = 0$, meaning that once a node has been infected, it cannot be recovered. The
number of experiments is K. $F(t)$ represents the average number of infected nodes in
the SI model at time t.

Average Shortest Path Length
L_s Is the average shortest path length of initial infection set S [9]. Usually, with larger
L_s, the initial spreaders are more dispersed and can influence a larger range. This can be
caculated by fomula:

$$L_S = \frac{1}{|S|(|S| - 1)} \sum_{u,v} l_{u,v} \tag{25}$$

where S is the set of spreaders that have been identified, and $l_{u,v}$ denotes the length of
the shortest path from node u to node v. If there is no path between u and v, $l_{u,v} = \delta + 1$,
where δ is the enormous linked component's diameter.

3 Proposed Algorithm

The proposed algorithm, EAVoterank++ researches and improves the VoteRank++ [11] algorithm to determine the set of influential nodes in the graph. Algorithm divided into 4 main steps.

Step 1: Calculate Voting Ability Score
In EAVoterank++, we make the appropriate modifications in the method's voting and update stages. Each node's state is represented as a tuple (vs_v, va_v), where vs_v is the voting score of node v as determined by its neighbors, and va_v is the voting score of node v as determined by its neighbors. We consider that a node's voting ability is proportional to its importance. So, the voting ability score (va_v) is obtained by considering the order coefficient, information about the position of the node in the network is based on the k-shell decomposition as well as the clustering coefficient of the node along with its neighbors. The weight of each index is determined by the entropy information [18]. The voting ability of node v is calculated mathematically as

$$va_v = log\left(1 + \frac{score_v}{score_{max}}\right) \tag{26}$$

with $score_v$ of each node v is caculated by fomula:

$$score_v = w_1 I_{DC}(v) + w_2 I_{KS\_im}(v) + w_3 I_C(v) \tag{27}$$

where $I_{DC}(v)$ indicates the influence of the node's degree and the degree of its neighbors v, respectively, $I_{KS\_im}(v)$ denotes the influence of the node's k-shell and the k-shell of its neighbors v and $I_C(v)$ represents the influence of clustering coefficient and second-level neighbors' clustering coefficient of node v is determined according to the formula (28), (29), (30).

$$I_{DC}(v) = DC(v) + \sum_{u \in \Gamma_v} DC(u) \tag{28}$$

$$I_{KS\_im}(v) = KS\_im(v) + \sum_{u \in \Gamma_v} KS\_im(u) \tag{29}$$

$$I_C(v) = e^{-C_v} \sum_{u \in \Gamma_v^2} C_u \tag{30}$$

w_1, w_2, w_3 are weights corresponding to the index and are calculated using entropy information as follow:

Firstly, set up a decision matrix with the values $I_{DC}(v)$, $I_{KS\_im}(v)$ and $I_C(v)$ with all nodes present in the network

$$D = \begin{bmatrix} I_{DC}(1) & \cdots & I_{DC}(n) \\ I_{KS\_im}(1) & \cdots & I_{KS\_im}(n) \\ I_C(1) & \cdots & I_C(n) \end{bmatrix} \tag{31}$$

The next step is to normalize the multi-attribute decision matrix. Since each index has a different dimension, the matrix D needs to be normalized to a normalized matrix R

$$R = \begin{bmatrix} r_{11} \cdots r_{1n} \\ r_{21} \cdots r_{2n} \\ r_{31} \cdots r_{3n} \end{bmatrix}, \quad r_{ij} = d_{ij} / \sqrt{\sum_{j=1}^{n} (d\_{ij})^2} \tag{32}$$

Then, calculate the information entropy of each rating metric. According to Eq. (21), the information entropy of index j can be calculated by:

$$E_i = -\frac{1}{\ln n} \sum_{j=1}^{n} r_{ij} \ln r_{ij}, \quad i = 1, 2, 3; j = 1, 2, \ldots, n \tag{33}$$

Finally, determining the weight of each metric. According to Eq. (9), the weight of index j can be calculated by:

$$w_i = \frac{1 - E_i}{2 - \sum_{i=1}^{3} E_i}, \quad i = 1, 2, 3 \tag{34}$$

Step 2: Voting
We not only consider neighbor nodes as participating to the vote to elect the source spreader because nodes other than immediate neighbors in the system may play a crucial role in the selection of source spreaders, but also the voting ability of the node itself to determine the influence score. We expanded VoteRank from unweighted networks to weighted networks to determine the voting score of a node, also known as node influence score, and defined the voting score as

$$vs_v = \sqrt{|\Gamma_v|.va_v + \sum_{u \in \Gamma_v} w_{uv}.va_u} \tag{35}$$

where is w_{uv} is the weight between nodes u and v in weighted networks, $w_{uv} = 1$ in unweighted networks and Γ_v is the neighbor set of node v.

If this node was not elected before, the node with the most votes gets elected as an influential node in the current round. The same node will not participate in the voting process in later rounds, and its voting ability will be set to 0.

Step 3: Update
The voting ability of the neighbors of the selected spreaders is inhibited to guarantee that the identified influential nodes are dispersed throughout the network. As a consequence, when a node is voted as a spreader, it could have a two-hop influence on its neighbors. A node's voting ability is reduced by a factor of when it has voted and is up to two hops from the selected spreader. The updated voting ability of the neighbor nodes is represented by the following Eq. 20.

The voting ability of a node's first-order and second-order neighbors is reduced if it is determined as influential. As a result, only nodes with shortest distances of three or less from the selected node need to update their voting scores.

Step 4: Interation
Steps 2 and 3 are iterated until l influential nodes are selected, where l is a constant.

4   Experimental Results

We used complex network datasets of various types and abilities to verify the proposed approach as well as other existing methods. The datasets chosen comprise a variety of graph features displayed by the networks, which may be used to properly assess the algorithms' performance. The following are the brief descriptions for these networks. (1) Jazz: the network of collaborations between a group of jazz musicians. (2) Email: a network of email exchanges among members of the University Rovira I Virgili. (3) USAir: a network of the US air transportation system in 2010. (4) Hamster: a friendship network between users of the website hamsterster.com. (5) Condmat: a co-authorship network of scientists working on Condense Matter Physics. (6) Facebook: an anonymized social network extracted from Facebook consists of 'circles' (or friends lists) from Facebook. Facebook data was collected from survey participants using this Facebook app. Table 1 describes basic features of 6 experimental networks.

The experiment findings of infection scale $F(t)$ against time t are displayed in Fig. 1 using the SIR model. With $\beta = 1.5$ and $\rho = 0.03$ correspondingly the results are averaged across 1000 independent runs.

Table 1. Basic features of 6 experimental networks

Networks	N	M	$\langle k \rangle$	$\langle k_{max} \rangle$
Jazz	198	2,742	27.69	100
Email	1,133	5,451	9.62	71
USAir	1,574	17,215	21.87	314
Hamster	2,426	16,631	13.71	273
Facebook	4,039	88,234	43.69	1045
Condmat	23,133	93,497	25.64	281

The purpose of this experiment is to examine the diffusion rates of various ways after the number of initial spreaders is set. In all 6 experimental networks, EAVoteRank++ may infect a higher number of nodes than baseline approaches with the same number of initial spreaders, as seen in Fig. 1. More specifically, in the stable stage, VoteRank++ outperforms rival algorithms in the the infection scale on 6 experimental networks.

Figure 2 shows the final effect scales $F(t_c)$ for different ratios of infected nodes at the initiation. With an infection rate of $\beta = 1.5$, the results are averaged or 1000 independent experiments. The goal of this experiment is to see how different strategies with different numbers of initial spreaders effect the final ranges. More initial spreaders, without a doubt, reach a larger area. EAVoteRank++ achieves an impressive result on these networks, as evidenced by the fact that its ultimate influence grows under the same ratio of initial spreaders, especially when the ratio is enormous, are always ranked first. When is large, on the other hand, information can flow rapidly across the network.

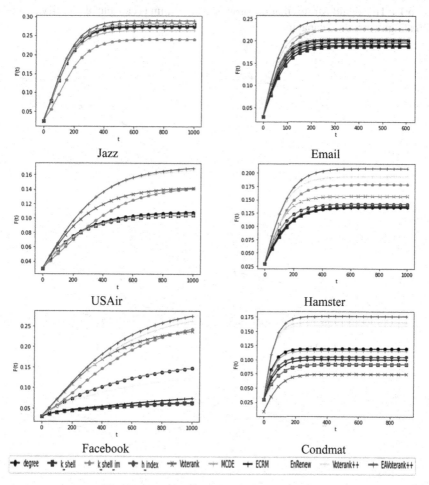

Fig. 1. The infection scales $F(t)$ against time t

Figure 3 shows the final effect scaling $F(t_c)$ for several approaches with varied infection rates. EAVoteRank++ can obtain the maximum or near to the largest spread scale in most situations under varied conditions, as shown in Fig. 3, notably on the Jazz, Email, USAir, Hamster, Facebook and Condmat networks. Based on the results in Fig. 3, we can conclude that EAVoteRank++ has a better generalization ability than baseline approaches.

The distances between spreaders are critical in increasing the impact. On 6 networks, Fig. 4 illustrates the L_s of spreaders found using various approaches. Except for the USAir network, EAVoteRank++ outperforms the baseline approaches because it always has the greatest or near to the largest L_s. In other words, the EAVoteRank++ technique identifies influential nodes that are dispersed over a network. The proposed algorithm outperforms all baseline approaches for the two largest networks, Condmat and Facebook. Implying that the prominent nodes picked by EAVoteRank + + are more decentralized in these networks. This demonstrates that the proposed algorithm is capable of identifying nodes with a high spreading capacity.

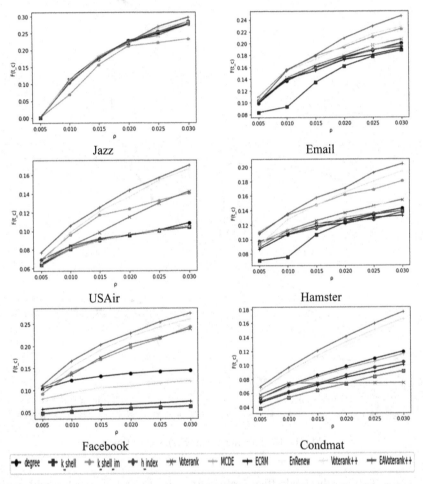

Fig. 2. The final infection scales $F(t_c)$ with different ratio of initial infected nodes ρ

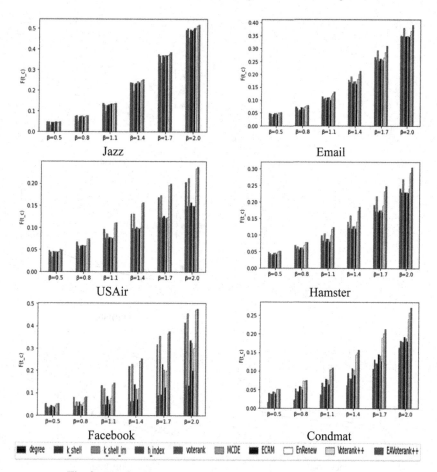

Fig. 3. The final infection scale $F(t_c)$ with different infect rate β

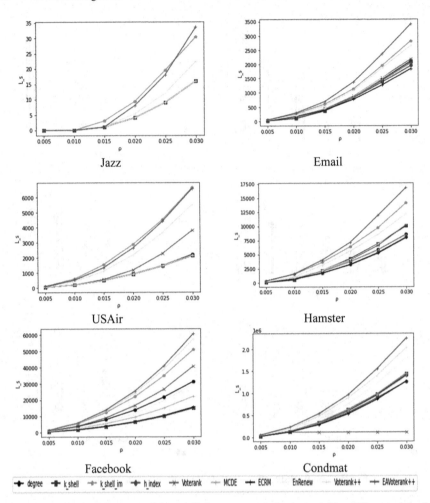

Fig. 4. The average shortest path length L_s between spreaders selected by different methods

5   Conclusions and Future Work

In this paper, we propose EAVoteRank++ for identifying influential nodes in social networks by using nodes's voting ability by considering degree, position in network by improve k-shell decomposition and clustering coefficient as well as neighbors. The weights of attribute are calculated by entropy technology. In experiment, The SIR model is employed to simulate the spreading progress. The experimental results on 6 networks show that in terms of infection scale, in most circumstances, EAVoteRank++ outperforms state-of-the-art baselines. However, there are still certain challenges to overcome in order to improve our work. Firstly, social networks, on the other hand, can evolve dynamically in real life. As a result, we will continue to strive to improve the algorithm's performance and investigate dynamic network features in future study. Firsly, we will consider using network embedding to extract the node feature information in the network, then we can apply Deep Learning model to use these features. Secondary, we will minimize the cost of further operations to accommodate a network of more nodes and relationships.

Acknowledgment. This research is funded by CMC Institute of Science and Technology (CIST), CMC Corporation, Vietnam.

References

1. Bond, R.M., et al.: A 61-million-person experiment in social influence and political mobilization. Nature **489**(7415), 295–298 (2012)
2. Perozzi, B., Al-Rfou, R., Skiena, S.S.: DeepWalk: online learning of social representations. In: ACM SIGKDD International Conference on Knowledge Discovery & Data Mining (2014)
3. Dinh, X.T., Van Pham, H.: Social network analysis based on combining probabilistic models with graph deep learning. In: Sharma, H., Gupta, M.K., Tomar, G.S., Lipo, W. (eds.) Communication and Intelligent Systems. LNNS, vol. 204, pp. 975–986. Springer, Singapore (2021). https://doi.org/10.1007/978-981-16-1089-9_76
4. Wang, D., Cui, P., Zhu, W.W.: Structural deep network embedding. In: Proceedings of the 22nd ACM SIGKDD International Conference on Knowledge Discovery and Data Mining, pp. 1225–1234 (2016)
5. Mikolov, T., Sutskever, I., Chen, K., et al.: Distributed representations of words and phrases and their compositionality. Adv. Neural Inf. Process. Syst. **26**, 3111–3119 (2013)
6. Gao, Y.-C., Fu, C.-J., Cai, S.-M., Yang, C., Eugene Stanley, H.: Repulsive synchroni-zation in complex networks. Chaos **29**, 053130 (2019)
7. Brin, S., Page, L.: Reprint of: the anatomy of a large-scale hypertextual web search engine. Comput. Netw. **56**(18), 3825–3833 (2012)
8. Ma, L.L., Ma, C., Zhang, H.F., Wang, B.H.: Identifying influential spreaders in complex networks based on gravity formula. Phys. A **451**, 205–212 (2016)
9. Zhang, J.-X., Chen, D.-B., Dong, Q., Zhao, Z.-D.: Identifying a set of influential spreaders in complex networks. Sci. Rep. **6**(1), 27823 (2016)
10. Guo, C., Yang, L., Chen, X., Chen, D., Gao, H., Ma, J.: Influential nodes identification in complex networks via information entropy. Entropy **22**(2), 1–19 (2020)
11. Liu, P., et al.: Identifying influential nodes in social networks: a voting approach. Chaos Solitons Fractals **152**, 111309 (2021)
12. Sabidussi, G.: Thee centrality index of a graph. Psychometrika **31**(4), 581–603 (1966)
13. Li, Z., Huang, X.: Identifying influential spreaders in complex networks by an improved gravity model. Sci. Rep. **11**(1), 1–10 (2021)
14. Eguiluz, V.M., Klemm, K.: Epidemic threshold in structured scale-free networks. Phys. Rev. Lett. **89**(10), 108701 (2002)
15. Lü, L., Zhou, T., Zhang, Q.-M., Stanley, H.E.: The H-index of a network node and its relation to degree and coreness. Nat. Commun. **7**(1), 10168 (2016)
16. Sheikhahmadi, A., Nematbakhsh, M.A.: Identification of multi-spreader users in social networks for viral marketing. J. Inf. Sci. **43**(3), 412–423 (2017)
17. Zareie, A., Sheikhahmadi, A., Jalili, M., Fasaei, M.S.K.: Finding influential nodes in social networks based on neighborhood correlation coefficient. Knowl Based Syst **194**, 105580 (2020)
18. Yang, Y., et al.: A novel centrality of influential nodes identification in complex networks. IEEE Access **8**, 58742–58751 (2020)
19. Shulgin, B., Stone, L., Agur, Z.: Pulse vaccination strategy in the SIR epidemic model. Bull. Math. Biol. **60**(6), 1123–1148 (1998)

Identification of the Relationships Between Data Provenance and Blockchain as a Contributing Factor for Health Information Systems

Márcio José Sembay(✉) 🆔, Douglas Dyllon Jeronimo de Macedo🆔, and Alexandre Augusto Gimenes Marquez Filho🆔

Federal University of Santa Catarina, Florianópolis, Brazil
marcio.sembay@posgrad.ufsc.br, douglas.macedo@ufsc.br

Abstract. On the one hand, data provenance provides the history of the origin of data and updates the modification cycle on one side, on the other hand, blockchain offers features that meet these immutability requirements of a version of data. These two technologies have applications and features that, in union, contribute to generate ideal technological structures to the management of data in several organizations. The objective of this study is to present an analysis of the relations between the main applications of data provenance as well as the blockchain features and point out applications in the Health Information Systems (HIS), in addition to a literature review on the theme. In regard to that, an analysis has been made as described in this study methodology, where the following questions were answered: i) What relations are there between data provenance and blockchain? ii) Can data provenance in union with blockchain contribute to applications in the HIS? Soon after, it was possible to prove through some of the studies present in the literature the combined use of data provenance and blockchain in HIS. Based on the relationships found between data provenance and blockchain, it was possible to conclude that these relationships contribute to data management in any organization, including HIS. It was also observed that different data provenance and blockchain methods, techniques, models, and methodologies are intertwined to generate the structures of data management in HIS, especially in Personal Health Record (PHR) and Electronic Health Record (EHR).

Keywords: Data Provenance · Blockchain · Health Information Systems

1 Introduction

The information systems and the Information and Communication Technologies (ICT), provide us with ways of communication that are changing not only our way of living but also the way businesses happens in all sectors [1]. In this context, we understand that these technologies provide the construction of one of the main human health-oriented technological scenarios, as in the case of HIS, defined as "data provenance system, information and knowledge in health care" [2].

© ICST Institute for Computer Sciences, Social Informatics and Telecommunications Engineering 2022
Published by Springer Nature Switzerland AG 2022. All Rights Reserved
A. L. Pinto and R. Arencibia-Jorge (Eds.): DIONE 2022, LNICST 452, pp. 258–272, 2022.
https://doi.org/10.1007/978-3-031-22324-2_20

The world health sectors are characterized by the increase of the production of data related to the patients care demands [3]. This increase in data production includes hospital records, exams results, devices that are part of the Internet of Things (IoT), among other medical data [3]. We face tons of data about varied aspects of our life, especially in health. As well as in any other sector, the health organizations are producing data to a tremendous fee, which results in many advantages and challenges all in one. Technological advances have helped generate a huge amount of data, making it a complex task when ordinal actual technology is utilized, mainly when the structures of IoT devices are geared towards user-centered design [3, 4].

In this sense, the need to manage large volumes of data in HIS meets the use of allied computational strategies that contemplate the historical processing of this data, as is the case of data provenance and blockchain. The tracking of provenance is one of the main usages of blockchain and emphasizes still that blockchain can guarantee the safety of a provenance information database [5]. Data provenance is a process which aims to provide a general view of data utilized by information systems. It focuses on the origin of data, mainly identifying the data sources and the transformations they have undergone throughout time. It is related to different application scenarios, emphasizing here the health field [6]. Data provenance usage in health has been suffering an increase in researches based on the most varied types of scientific experiments. Technologies applied to this area have obtained expressive results [7]. Data provenance is the ground to medical data quality and patients' privacy [8]. When it comes to blockchain technology, to the health field, it stands out as a record technology which is trustworthy and of consensus distributed offering alternatives to the creation of inter-operable systems, audible and safe [9]. Blockchain can be applied to the health field to control the access and distribution of sensitive information, in the transparency and audibility of service provision and data interoperability, among other situations [10].

Thus, this article analyses the main applications of data provenance defined in the work of [11] with the blockchain features presented by [12] identifying the possible existing relations between these two technologies. Eventually the analysis is finalizes with a description of some of the works found in literature which verify the usage of data provenance together with blockchain applied in HIS. Regarding this, we conclude that the analysis presented in this study that identify possible existing relations between the main applications of data provenance and blockchain features, could contribute to new studies involving these two technologies, especially in the HIS field. Therefore, the objective of this article is to present the results to this analysis and promote the use of data provenance together with blockchain in the health field, including the researches involving the prospect of these the technologies in HIS, in addition to a literature review on the theme.

This article is organized in the following manner. Section 2 describes the review of literature, where HIS, data provenance and blockchain are highly regarded. In Sect. 3, the methodology utilized in the analysis is described. Section 4 presents the analysis and identification of relations between the main applications of data provenance with the features of blockchain, and then some of the studies which verify these relations applied specifically in HIS. And finally, in Sect. 5, the conclusions and future work to this study are described.

2 Literature Review

2.1 Health Information Systems

The HIS can also be highly regarded as an information system which composes the collection, the processing, the communication, and the usage of fundamental information to perfect the efficiency of health services by means of the best management in all levels of the health sector. HIS are being implemented in all aspects of healthcare, from administration to clinical decision support systems [13]. This type of system produces relevant and good quality information to support the management and planning of health programs [2, 14]. HIS has been increasingly used around the world to improve hospital efficiency, the quality of service and patients' satisfaction [15]. HIS can also be highly regarded as an information system which integrates the collection, the processing, the communication, and the use of critical information to improve the efficiency of health services by means of a better management in all health sectors. This system produces relevant information and of good quality to support the management and planning of health programs [2, 14]. The HIS fits into two main categories. The first being the recording of individual data and the second, the collection of data for decision making and information management, usually called information management health system [16].

It is important to highlight the fact that HIS allows all the information related to the patients to be computerized, thus providing better and more efficient health services [17]. In this context, HIS is defined as a computerized means of collection, storage and recovery of information about people in health fields. Which includes patients, doctors, nurses and others who collect clinical and administrative data. This process in accomplished regardless of whether in the same or different environment in local or national levels [18–20].

Regarding this, we point out some of the main existing HIS in actuality, which are: Electronic health Record (EHR) [21], Personal Health Record (PHR) [22], Learning Health System (LHS) [23], Healthcare Monitoring System (HMS) [24], Clinical Research Information System (CRIS) [25], Hospital Information System (HIS) [26]. These HIS are utilized in several countries and are responsible for many of the processes executed in relation to the health data, contributing to a much more efficient management.

2.2 Data Provenance

Data provenance is the complementary documentation of a certain data which contains the description as "how", "when", and "why" it's been obtained and by "whom" [27]. Data provenance makes it possible to guarantee the quality and veracity of data, for example, identifying the origin of errors and attributing the sources [8]. Still, data provenance can be defined as information that helps determine the historical derivation of a data product from its origin sources, being it regarded as an essential component to allow result reproducibility, sharing and reuse of knowledge by the scientific community [28]. Now about the operation of data provenance in general, what happens is: when consultations and programs are executed the data in a data bank are moved to another data bank, and thus a description of the involving relations is created [29]. It's important to point out that in a data bank research, provenance helps in the tracking process and also in the signaling of the data origin, as well as its movement between different data sources [11].

In the context of health, the tracking of health data provenance allows the patients to have complete control over the use of all secondary personal data, in other words, creating awareness about where this data is going (for instance, public health consultations, clinical trials, among other controls in the health field) [8]. The actual health systems manage the provenance through complicated methods. These methods provide safety mechanisms that guarantee the sources of data. However, they show huge deficiencies, like depending on trustworthy third parts and vulnerability to semantics interoperability issues due to the registers of different organizations [8]. Thus, to overcome these deficiencies, data provenance models are recommended by World Wide Web Consortium[1] (W3C), named as family PROV [30] for the assistance to management of data provenance in HIS. Data provenance methods, techniques, models and methodologies are associated to different computer technologies, also observed in literature to application in HIS. In this sense, the usage of data provenance, regardless of the model, provides an essential basis for evaluation and authentication of data, offering reliability and reproducibility [31].

Regarding this, we highlight that data provenance can be applied to several scenarios [32, 33] including the health field [7]. Many research efforts in the field of data provenance induced [11] the creation of a taxonomy to categorize the efforts. The work of [11] shows that the provenance systems can be built to operate in different ways, with different characteristics and operations. Thus, we assume in the article that part of the taxonomy [11] is essential for the analysis of the relationships here considered. It also contributes to applications in the context of HIS, as has been summarized by [34]: i) Data quality: the lineage can be used to estimate the data quality and reliability based on the original data and transformation [35]. it can also offer proof declaration in data derivation [36]; ii) Audit trial: provenance can be used to track the audit trail [37], determine the usage [38] and detect mistakes in data generation [39]; iii) Replication recipes: detailed provenance information allows the repetition of data derivation, help maintain actuality [37] and be a recipe to replication [40]; iv) Attribution: pedigree can establish copyright and data propriety, make citation possible [35], and determine the responsibility in the occurrence of incorrect data; and, v) Informational: the generic usage of lineage is to consult based in lineage metadata for the discovery of data. It can also be browsed to provide a context to interpret data.

It is important to highlight that a deeper comprehension of data provenance application combined with other technologies is necessary to identify new ways of exploring its full potential.

2.3 Blockchain

Blockchain is essentially a data structure distributed, also called "public records book", in which all the confirmed transactions are stored by data sets in units called blocks. Each block refers to the previous one in chronological order, thus origination a blockchain.

---

[1] See https://www.w3.org.

This chain gets longer gradually as new transactions are added to the book. A mechanism of asymmetric cryptography has been applied to avoid the edition of previous blocks [41]. Blockchain in an emerging technology that has revolutionized the world scene, it was first launched in 2008 by the publication of white paper "Bitcoin: A Peer-to-Peer Electronic Cash System", when this phenomenon became popular with the creation of cryptocurrency bitcoin by [42]. However, when it comes to blockchain, there's still a certain difficulty in conceptualizing it, making it possible to find several definitions that comprise only certain aspects of this technology.

In this way, three categories are delimited in relation to the evolution of the blockchain [9]: i) Blockchain 1.0: applications in cryptocurrency, like bitcoin; ii) Blockchain 2.0: applications related to contracts of all kinds that go further than money transactions. This kind of application allows for contracts related to stock, loans, mortgage, scrip and smart contracts; and, iii) Blockchain 3.0: this category encloses the applications that go beyond the ones previously mentioned. With emphasis on areas like governmental, health, science, literature, culture, and arts. From a technical point of view, blockchain technologies are used to create a shared digital record, safe and immutable which records the history of transactions between knots in public or private peer-to-peer network. When a transaction is executed, all the knots in the network need to be in concordance about the shared record. The focus of blockchain is accounting functionality decentralized of transactions to be used to register, confirm, and transfer all kinds of contracts and properties with no need of any mediator [9].

It is important to point out that, blockchain has four features [12]: i) Immutable – (permanent and tamper-proof) a blockchain is a permanent record of transactions. Once a block is added it can't be tampered, which creates a reliable transaction record; ii) Decentralized – (networked copies) a blockchain is stored in a file that can be accessed and copied by any knot in the network, which creates decentralization; iii) Consensus Driven – (trust verification) each block in a blockchain is verified independently using consensus models that have certain rules for block validation, and often use a scarce feature (like computer power) to prove that an adequate effort has been made. In bitcoin, this process is known as mining. This mechanism works regardless of a central authority or a proxy agent; and, iv) Transparent – (full transaction history) blockchain is an open file, it can be accessed by any part and audit transactions. Which creates a provenance that makes possible to track the lifespan of actives.

Regarding this, in the health context, the potential of blockchain technology can change the way the health sector shares information, the way the medical data are updated and maintained, the way a patient's medical records are shared and updated, how the population health data are assembled and analyzed and how prescribed medication is tracked and monitored through a supply chain [43]. In the health field, blockchain can be applied to the control of access and distribution of sensitive information, in transparency and audibility of service provision and in the interoperability of data, among other situations [10]. Thus, in the works of [44] e [45], the authors reason potential blockchain contributions for the health field, which are: safety in the sharing of health data, interoperability of health data at national range, tracking of the supply chain and medical devices, tracking of the medication distribution chain, monitoring of drugs prescription, observation of aggregated events (Big Data) with main applications in collective health, patients identification, data sharing for scientific research, implementation of independent structures (e.g., management and controlling of supplementary health insurance).

3   Methodology

As for its nature, this study is considered basic research, for it is a type of research uninterested in application, inserted in a disciplinary and academic atmosphere which contrasts in all analytical aspects [46]. As to the procedures, this research is characterized as a bibliographic study, which can be defined as any research that requires the gathering of information and published material. This material may include traditional resources as books, magazines, periodicals, newspapers, and reports, but can also consist of electronic media like audio, films and video records, on-line resources like sites, blogs, and bibliographical bank data [47]. It can also be characterized, as to the objectives, like exploratory study, often named pilot and viability studies, which are considered fundamental in the evaluation of viability and value of progression for the efficiency of a study. Such studies can provide vital information to support sturdier evaluations, reducing costs and minimizing possible damages to [48]. The study also possesses a qualitative approach, with regard to the comprehension of a certain aspect of social life and its methods of (in general) generate words, instead of numbers, as data to be analyzed [49]. It is also important to point out that some methods of analysis and interpretation to be carried out in this study were based on research by [50, 51].

For the analysis of the main data provenance application relations defined by [11] with the blockchain features presented by [12], the following features have been considered: i) Highly relevant: considering the relations observed by [11] and [12] which has a direct effect on data – represented by the symbol ◉; ii) Relevant: considering the relations defined by [11] and [12] which have an indirect effect on data – represented by the symbol ◉; and, iii) Unidentified: no relation defined by [11] and [12] – represented by the symbol ○.

Also, to prove the existing relationships between data provenance and blockchain based on the studies of [11] and [12], a literature review was carried out where five studies as of 2017 were found that presented relevant contributions to the topic in question. In this sense, the choice of these five studies for sample in this article, was based on the relevance of the existing relationships, included in some way, directly or indirectly, in the studies of [11] and [12]. Thus, for such analyzes the following questions were answered: i) What relations are there between data provenance and blockchain? and, ii) Can data provenance in union with blockchain contribute to applications in the HIS?

These relations were discovered and described in Sect. 4, considering as well the works found in literature which showed the use of data provenance and blockchain combined for the success in HIS applications.

4   Analysis

The analysis that guides this study have been accomplished in this section with the objective of identifying the relations between data provenance and blockchain and also verify through literature the direct and indirect use of such applications in HIS.

4.1 Identification of Relations Between the Main Applications of Data Provenance and Blockchain Features

Based on the works by [11] and [12], Table 1 shows a compassion between the main applications of data provenance with blockchain features in order to verify the technological harmony they both share, identifying their relations. The relations are presented below.

Table 1. Identification of the relations between data provenance and blockchain

		Blockchain characteristics			
		Transparent	Consensus Driven	Decentralized	Immutable
Main applications of Data Provenance	Informational	⊙	⊙	⊙	⊙
	Attribution	⊙	⊙	◎	◎
	Replication recipes	◎	⊙	◎	◎
	Audit trail	◎	◎	◎	○
	Data quality	⊙	⊙	⊙	⊙

◎ Highly relevant: considering the relations observed by [11] and [12] which has a direct effect on data; ⊙ Relevant: considering the relations defined by [11] and [12] which have an indirect effect on data; and, ○ Unidentified: no relation defined by [11] and [12].

As we can observe on Table 1, applications related to informational, identifies relevant relations with all features (transparent, consensus driven, decentralized and immutable). Considering the fact that this application regards data discovery in its purpose, we observe that all blockchain features are relevant when it comes to this application. For application regarding attribution, we observe a relevant relation with the blockchain features (transparent, consensus driven). Considering that this application can establish the author copyright and propriety of data, we observe that these features may contribute to a complete and verified history between data. A highly relevant relation has been identified with the features (decentralized and immutable) for this application, considering that the copied in the network and the manipulation of data must take into account the responsibility in the occurrence of erroneous data. When it comes to replication recipes with the feature (consensus driven), the identified relation is relevant, seeing as the replication of data provenance takes into account trust verification, thus allowing the guarantee of data replication for new experiments. A highly relevant relation has been identified with the features (transparent, decentralized, and immutable) for this application, considering that replication of data provenance depends on blocks which compose an immutable history record of each transaction since its origin date in a transparent and decentralized data storage. For the audit trial application, a highly relevant relation has been observed with the features (transparent, consensus driven and decentralized), considering that provenance may operate as a means of audit for data and production process, the guarantee of data audit depends on their transparency and reliability in the most diverse computer networks. There hasn't been any relation observed with the feature (immutable). Regarding application of data quality, relevant relations have been identified with all features (transparent, consensus driven, decentralized and immutable), considering that provenance can be used to obtain data quality, these data must obey certain important requirements of data provenance related to transparency and immutability of a version of data in reliable and decentralized sources. It has been observed in the analysis that audit trial applications and recipes replications both stand out relevantly with most of the features. The concentration of these applications is shown by the reasons data provenance can contribute to the guarantee, safety, confidentiality, integrity, and quality of data in several areas of knowledge.

4.2 Some of the Studies Which Verify the Relations Between Data Provenance and Blockchain Applied in HIS

In this subsection some of the studies are described that ensure and contemplate somehow the relations found in Table 1 for the health field, specifically applied to HIS.

Thus, we begin highlighting the first study, entitled *"Integrating blockchain for data sharing and collaboration in mobile healthcare applications"* [52]. The authors proposed an innovative user-centric health data sharing solution based on mobile user-controlled blockchain for cloud data sharing in a PHR. They used algorithm-based provenance data collection techniques using blockchain technologies. As a result, their solution featured an algorithm capable of managing mHealth provenance data while preserving integrity and privacy. In this study, comparing with the existing relationships in Table 1, the applications of data provenance (audit trail and data quality) with the characteristics of the blockchain (transparent, decentralized, and immutable) were the relationships that, in fact, were presented in this study. The second study is entitled *"Using PROV and Blockchain to Achieve Health Data Provenance"* [53]. The authors propose to solve the problem of managing health care data in EHR systems based on decentralized blockchain technologies and the W3C PROV model. As a result, the proposal presented by the authors was based on existing international standards ensuring interoperability between health data. The use of open systems and blockchain technology combined with the W3C PROV model together promoted the security and immutability of health records. Comparing with the existing relationships in Table 1, the applications of data provenance (informational, replication recipes, audit trail, and data quality) with blockchain characteristics (consensus driven, decentralized, and immutable) were the relationships present in this study. For the third study entitled *"Research on Personal Health data provenance and Right Confirmation with Smart Contract"* [54], to solve the leakage phenomenon, abuse, and illegal acquisition of personal health data, the authors propose a data provenance model named PROV-Chain based on blockchain technologies and Open Provenance Model (OPM). It was introduced seeking PHR applications for an IoT scenario device. As a result, the model's assessments not only guarantee the traceability of personal health data but also identified their right to personal use, guaranteeing security. In this study, comparing with the existing relationships in Table 1, the applications of data provenance (informational and attribution) with the characteristics of the blockchain (transparent, consensus driven, decentralized, and immutable) were the ones that stood out. In the fourth study entitled *"Secure and Provenance Enhanced Internet of Health Things Framework: A Blockchain Managed Federated Learning Approach"* [55], takes place in a scenario of Internet of Health Things (IoHT). For IoHT data to be acceptable to stakeholders, applications that embody IoHT must contain data accuracy, security, integrity and quality. In this sense, the authors present a hybrid federated learning model in which the intelligent blockchain contracts manage the training plan. To support the complete privacy and anonymity of IoHT data, the model has been tested with several learning applications designed for clinical trials with COVID-19[2] patients. As a result, the model in the use of applications demonstrated a strong potential for broader adoption of IoHT-based PHR health management. Comparing with the existing relationships in Table 1, the applications of data provenance (informational, audit trail, and data quality) with blockchain characteristics (consensus driven, decentralized, and immutable) were the relationships highlighted in this study. In the fifth study entitled *"Decentralised provenance for healthcare data"* [8] presents a platform for managing the provenance EHR, which can be implemented in already functioning EHR systems. The authors use blockchain technology as a basis, in addition to the Fast Healthcare Interoperability Resources (FHIR) to represent EHRs. A proxy transparently intercepts the EHRs' modifications and then triggers a smart contract[3] to perform provenance annotations using the W3C PROV language. The resulting PROV documents stored in a Hyperledger Fabric blockchain[4]. In this study, comparing with the existing relationships in Table 1, the applications of data provenance (informational, replication recipes, audit trail, and data quality) with blockchain characteristics (transparent, consensus driven, decentralized, and immutable) are highlighted.

Thus, Table 2 summarizes the studies described in this subsection, referring to the combined use of data provenance and blockchain applied in HIS.

As observed in Table 2, the technologies concerning data provenance are divided between the models (W3C PROV and OPM) and techniques of algorithm and data provenance applied to HIS. W3C PROV defines a model of data provenance to support the inter operable interchange of provenance in heterogeneous environments like the network. The PROV structure is based on the definitions of entities, activity and agents involved in data production or of something and how they are related. Thus, defining the four following types of property: *wasGeneratedBy, wasAssociatedBy, wasAttributedTo* and *used* [30]. Now considering OPM, it defines as model of open provenance that aims to characterize provenance in any "thing", material or immaterial. It seeks to show the causal relationship between events that affect objects (digital or non-digital) and describes this relation using an acyclic info graph oriented [56, 57]. It is important to highlight that the model OPM has already been overlaid by PROV. When it comes to blockchain technologies, the usage of applications is led by smart contract, followed by Hyperledger Fabric Blockchain, decentralized blockchain and health data sharing based

---

[2] See https://www.who.int/health-topics/coronavirus#tab=tab_1.

[3] See https://ethereum.org/en/developers/docs/smart-contracts/.

[4] See https://www.hyperledger.org/use/fabric.

Table 2. Summary of studies that combine data provenance and blockchain in HIS.

Ref.	Authors /Years	Data Provenance Technologies	Blockchain Technologies	Types of HIS	Identification of the relationships between Data Provenance and Blockchain
[8]	Margheri et al. (2020)	W3C PROV	Smart Contract and Hyperledger Fabric blockchain	EHR	Data Provenance (informational, replication recipes, audit trail, and data quality) with Blockchain (transparent, consensus driven, decentralized, and immutable)
[55]	Rayhman et al. (2020)	Algorithms based on Data Provenance	Smart Contract	PHR	Data Provenance (informational, audit trail, and data quality) with Blockchain (consensus driven, decentralized, and immutable)
[54]	Gong, Lin and Li (2019)	PROV-Chain based on the OPM	Smart Contract	PHR	Data Provenance (informational and attribution) with Blockchain (transparent, consensus driven, decentralized, and immutable)
[53]	Massi et al. (2018)	W3C PROV	Blockchain decentralized	EHR	Data Provenance (informational, replication recipes, audit trail, and data quality) with Blockchain (consensus driven, decentralized, and immutable)
[52]	Liang et al. (2017)	Algorithms based on Data Provenance	Data sharing based on blockchain	PHR	Data Provenance (audit trail and data quality) with Blockchain (transparent, decentralized, and immutable)

on blockchain. Considering now the types of HIS, the applications are directed in their most part to PHR, followed by EHR. In PHR the records are often created and monitored by the patients themselves. They can be based on desktop, internet, or smartphone devices (for example, entirely located in a cellphone or portable storage device) [22]. In EHR, collection is embracing, inter institutional and longitudinal of patients' health data. It includes, therefore, data that are not only particularly relevant for medical evaluation of one's treatment, but also for the person's health in general [21]. It is important to note that in Table 2, the relationships found between data provenance and blockchain in the five studies presented here are the same as those shown in Table 1, following the same order of relevance. It is also observed that studies show the upward growth in relation to the use of data provenance and blockchain applied in HIS, in fact contributing to the management of health data. However, it is important to highlight that, the studies here shown are limited to the technologies combined between data provenance and blockchain applied in HIS comprising the focus of the article. Other studies in the literature may bring other combined technologies in addition to those presented here, also reflecting on other successful paths applied in different health scenarios, such as the studies by [58–60].

5 Conclusions and Future Work

Data provenance applications combined with blockchain have become a challenge in HIS. The relations identified in Table 1 have concluded that there is a technological link between the main applications of data provenance combined with blockchain features in HIS. In fact, these relationships promote challenges that can help HIS, allowing to identify in each application the data provenance with the blockchain resources, which depend on the implementation or improvement of principles to obtain the expected success. Concerning this, the applications of data provenance combined with blockchain were highlighted and described in Table 2 through studies found in the literature, where we could verify that this approach applied specifically to HIS allows health organizations to store provenance records that are to be shared and tracked by the blockchain structure, thus avoiding the tampering of data. It causes to reduce the complexity of HIS which faces huge amounts of health data that depend on a safe and reliable management. Still in Table 2, it was possible to conclude through the studies described in literature, that the data provenance and blockchain technologies intertwine in methods, techniques, models, and methodologies aiming the generation of an ideal structure for the management of data in HIS. It was also possible to identify the relationships between data provenance and blockchain for each study presented in Table 2, based on the relationships in Table 1, which in fact proves the growth in the use of these two associated technologies in HIS. It has also been possible to conclude that, according to Table 2, the mainly highlighted HIS in the studies are: PHR and EHR. It being so because PHR is more convenient for patients and health workers that can monitor health data remotely by using mobile devices, especially when going through a pandemic, as is the case of the actual COVID-19. And EHR, for its use as standard medical record and being utilized in several countries in their respective HIS.

As a suggestion for future work, it is proposed the realization of a more detailed study, in the case of a systematic review of literature that might generate results of other data provenance and blockchain, beyond the ones described in this study. Furthermore, present also the main methods, techniques, models and methodologies applied in union with data provenance and blockchain used in different HIS to identify which actions could be taken to adapt technological structures ideal for these systems.

References

1. World Health Organization (WHO). Framework and standards for country health information systems. 2. ed. Geneva: WHO, (2008). ISBN 9789241595940. https://www.who.int/health info/country_monitoring_evaluation/who-hmn-framework-standards-chi.pdf. Accessed 15 Jan 2022
2. Haux, R.: Health information systems-past, present, future. Int. J. Med. Inf. **75**, 268–281 (2006). https://doi.org/10.1016/j.ijmedinf.2005.08.002
3. Dash, S., Shakyawar, S.K., Sharma, M., Kaushik, S.: Big data in healthcare: management, analysis and future prospects. J. Big Data **6**(1), 1–25 (2019). https://doi.org/10.1186/s40537-019-0217-0
4. Samuel, A.M., Garcia-Constantino, M.: User-centred prototype to support wellbeing and isolation of software developers using smartwatches. Adv. Notes Inf. Sci. **1**, 140–151 (2022). https://doi.org/10.47909/anis.978-9916-9760-0-5.125
5. Greenspan, G.: Four genuine blockchain use cases. Technical report (2016). https://www.mul tichain.com/blog/2016/05/
6. Sembay, M.J., Macedo, D.D., Dutra, M.L.: A method for collecting provenance data: a case study in a Brazilian hemotherapy center. In: Proceedings of the 1st EAI International Conference on Data and Information in Online Environments, DIONE 2020, Florianopolis, Brazil, pp. 1–14 (2020)
7. Sembay, M.J., de Macedo, D.D.J., Dutra, M.L.: A proposed approach for provenance data gathering. Mob. Netw. Appl. **26**(1), 304–318 (2020). https://doi.org/10.1007/s11036-020-016 48-7
8. Margheri, A., Massi, M., Miladi, A., Sassone, V., Rosenzweig, A.J.: Decentralised provenance for healthcare data. Int. J. Med. Inf. **141**, 1–21 (2020). https://doi.org/10.1016/j.ijmedinf.2020.104197
9. Swan, M.: Blockchain: Blueprint for a New Economy. O'Reilly Media, Newton (2015)
10. Monteil, C.: Blockchain and health. In: Digital Medicine, pp. 41–47. Springer, Cham (2019)
11. Simmhan, Y.L., Plale, B., Gannon, D.: A survey of data provenance techniques. In: Technical Report TR-618: Computer Science Department, Indiana University (2005)
12. Sultan, K., Ruhi, U., Lakhani, R.: Conceptualizing blockchains: characteristics & applications (2018). https://arxiv.org/abs/1806.03693
13. Sembay, M.J., Macedo, D.D.J.: Sistemas de informação em saúde: proposta de um método de gerenciamento de dados de proveniência no instanciamento do modelo W3C PROV-DM. Adv. Notes Inf. Sci. v. 2, Tallinn, Estonia: ColNes Publishing (2022). https://doi.org/10.47909/anis. 978-9916-9760-3-6.101
14. World Health Organization (WHO). Developing Health Management Information Systems: a practical for developing countries. Manila: Regional Office for the Western Pacific (2004). https://iris.wpro.who.int/handle/10665.1/5498. Accessed 20 Nov 2021
15. Cesnik, B., Kidd, M.R.: History of health informatics: a global perspective. Stud. Health Technol. Inf. **151**, 3–8 (2010). https://doi.org/10.3233/978-1-60750-476-4-3
16. Dehnavieh, R., et al.: The district health information system (DHIS2): a literature review and meta-synthesis of its strengths and operational challenges based on the experiences of 11 countries. Health Inf. Manag. J. **48**(2) (2018). https://doi.org/10.1177/1833358318777713
17. Al Jarullah, A., El-Masri, S.: Proposal of an architecture for the national integration of electronic health records: a semi-centralized approach. Stud. Health Technol. Inf. **180**, 917–921 (2012). https://doi.org/10.3233/978-1-61499-101-4-917
18. Sligo, J., Gauld, R., Roberts, V., Villac, L.: A literature review for large-scale health information system project planning, implementation and evaluation. Int. J. Med. Inf. **97**, 86–97 (2017). https://doi.org/10.1016/j.ijmedinf.2016.09.007

19. Andargolia, A.E., Scheepers, H., Rajendran, D., Sohal, A.: Health information systems evaluation frameworks: a systematic review. Int. J. Med. Inf. **97**, 195–209 (2017). https://doi.org/10.1016/j.ijmedinf.2016.10.008

20. Robertson, A., et al.: Implementation and adoption of nationwide electronic health records in secondary care in England: qualitative analysis of interim results from a prospective national evaluation. BMJ **341**, c4564 (2010). https://doi.org/10.1136/bmj.c4564

21. Hoerbst, A., Ammenwerth, E.: Electronic health records. Meth. Inf. Med. **49**(04), 320–336 (2010). https://doi.org/10.3414/me10-01-0038

22. Liu, L.S., Shih, P.C, Hayes, G. Barriers to the adoption and use of personal health record systems. In: Proceedings of the iConference, pp. 363–370 (2011)

23. Friedman, C., et al.: Toward a science of learning systems: a research agenda for the high-functioning learning health system. J. Am. Med. Inform. Assoc. **22**(1), 43–50 (2014). https://doi.org/10.1136/amiajnl-2014-002977

24. Korhonen, I., Pärkkä, J., van Gils, M.: Health monitoring in the home of the future. IEEE Eng. Med. Biol. Magazine **22**(3), 66–73 (2003)

25. Nadkarni, P.M., Marenco, L.N., Brandt, C.A.: Clinical research information systems. Health Inf., 135–154 (2012). https://doi.org/10.1007/978-1-84882-448-5_8

26. Ismail, A., et al.: The implementation of Hospital Information System (HIS) in tertiary hospitals in Malaysia: a qualitative study Malays. J. Public Health Med. **10**(2), 16–24 (2010)

27. Buneman, P., Khanna, S., Wang-Chiew, T.: Why and where: a characterization of data provenance. In: Van den Bussche, J., Vianu, V. (eds.) ICDT 2001. LNCS, vol. 1973, pp. 316–330. Springer, Heidelberg (2001). https://doi.org/10.1007/3-540-44503-X_20

28. Freire, J., et al.: Provenance for computational tasks: a survey. J. Comput. Sci. Eng. **10**(3), 11–21 (2008). ISSN 15219615. Accessed 24 Dec 2021

29. Tan, W.C.: Provenance in databases: past, current and future. IEEE Data Eng. Bull **30**(4), 3–12 (2008). Accessed 24 May 2018

30. Gil, Y., Miles, S.: PROV Model Primer: W3C Working Draft 30 April 2013 (2013). http://www.w3.org/TR/prov-primer/

31. Moreau L., Growth, P.: Provenance: an introduction to PROV (Synthesis lectures on the semantic web: theory and technology) **3**(4), 1129 (2013). https://doi.org/10.2200/S00528ED1V01Y201308WBE007

32. Pearson, D.: Presentation on grid data requirements scoping metadata & provenance. In: Workshop on Data Derivation and Provenance, Chicago (2002)

33. Cameron, G.: Provenance and pragmatics. In: Workshop on Data Provenance and Annotation, Edinburgh (2003)

34. Goble, C.: Position statement: musings on provenance, workflow and (Semantic Web) annotations for bioinformatics. In: Workshop on Data Derivation and Provenance, Chicago (2002)

35. Jagadish, H.V., Olken, F.: Database management for life sciences research. SIGMOD Rec. **33**(2), 15–20 (2004). https://doi.org/10.1145/1024694.1024697

36. Silva, P.P. da, Silva, D., McGuinness, D.L., McCool, R.: Knowledge provenance infrastructure. In: IEEE Data Engineering Bulletin, vol. 26, pp. 26–32 (2003)

37. Miles, S., Groth, P., Branco, M., Moreau, L.: The requirements of recording and using provenance in eScience experiments. In: Technical Report, Electronics and Computer Science, University of Southampton (2005)

38. Greenwood, M., et al.: Provenance of e-science experiments: experience from bioinformatics. In: Proceedings of the UK OST e-Science second All Hands Meeting (2003)

39. Galhardas, H., Florescu, D., Shasha, D., Simon, E., Saita, C.A.: Improving data cleaning quality using a data lineage facility. DMDW, pp. 1–13 (2001). https://citeseerx.ist.psu.edu/viewdoc/download?doi=10.1.1.22.8651&rep=rep1&type=pdf

40. Foster, I.T., Vöckler, I.S., Wilde, M., Zhao, Y.: The virtual data grid: a new model and architecture for data-intensive collaboration. In: 15th International Conference on Scientific and Statistical Database Management (2003)

41. Tian, F.: An agri-food supply chain traceability system for China based on RFID & blockchain technology. In: International Conference on IEEE Service Systems and Service Management (ICSSSM), vol. 13, pp. 1–6 (2016)

42. Nakamoto, S., et al.: Bitcoin: a peer-to-peer electronic cash system. In: Disruptive Civil Technologies: Six Technologies with Potential Impacts on Us Interests Out to 2025. NIC (National Intelligence Council) (2008). https://fas.org/irp/nic/disruptive.pdf. Accessed 28 Jan 2020

43. EY. Blockchain in health: How distributed ledgers can improve provider data management and support interoperability, p. 12 (2016). https://www.hyperledger.org/wp-content/uploads/2016/10/ey-blockchain-in-health.pdf. Accessed 10 Jan 2022

44. Bell, L., et al.: Applications of blockchain within healthcare. Blockchain Healthc. Today (2018). https://doi.org/10.30953/bhty.v1.8. Disponível em. https://blockchainhealthcaretoday.com/index.php/journal/article/view/8/40. Accessed 25 Oct 2019

45. Zhang, P., et al.: Blockchain technology use cases in healthcare. Adv. Comput. (2017). https://doi.org/10.1016/bs.adcom.2018.03.006

46. Schauz, D.: What is basic research? Insights Hist. Semant. Minerva **52**(3), 273–328 (2014)

47. Allen, M.: Bibliographic research. In: The SAGE Encyclopedia of Communication Research Methods. https://doi.org/10.4135/9781483381411.n37(2017)

48. Hallingberg, B., Turley, R., Segrott, J., et al.: Exploratory studies to decide whether and how to proceed with full-scale evaluations of public health interventions: a systematic review of guidance. Pilot Feasibility Stud. **4**, 104 (2018). https://doi.org/10.1186/s40814-018-0290-8

49. McCusker, K., Gunaydin, S.: Research using qualitative, quantitative or mixed methods and choice based on the research. Perfusio **30**, 537–542 (2015)

50. Coimbra, F.S., Dias, T.M.R.: Use of open data to analyze the publication of articles in scientific events. Iberoamerican J. Sci. Measur. Commun. **1**(3), 1–13 (2021). https://doi.org/10.47909/ijsmc.123

51. Gontijo, M.C.A., Hamanaka, R.Y., de Araujo, R.F.: Research data management: a bibliometric and altmetric study based on Dimensions. Iberoamerican J. Sci. Measur. Commun. **1**(3), 1–19 (2021). https://doi.org/10.47909/ijsmc.120

52. Liang, X., Zhao, J., Shetty, S., Liu, J., Li, D.: Integrating blockchain for data sharing and collaboration in mobile healthcare applications. In: IEEE 28th Annual International Symposium on Personal, Indoor, and Mobile Radio Communications (PIMRC), Montreal, Qc, Canada, pp. 1–25 (2017)

53. Massi, M., Miladi, A., Margheri, A., Sassone, V., Rosenzweig, J.: Using PROV and Blockchain to Achieve Health Data Provenance. Technical report (2018)

54. Gong, J., Lin, S., Li, J.: Research on personal health data provenance and right confirmation with smart contract. In: IEEE 4th Advanced Information Technology, Electronic and Automation Control Conference (IAEAC) (2019). https://doi.org/10.1109/iaeac47372.2019.8997930

55. Rayhman, M.A., Hossain, M.S., Islam, M.S., Alrajeh, N.A., Muhammad, G.: Secure and provenance enhanced internet of health things framework: a blockchain managed federated learning approach. IEEE **8**, 205071–205087 (2020). https://doi.org/10.1109/ACCESS.2020.3037474

56. Moreau, L., Kwasnikowska, N., Van den Bussche, J.: The foundations of the open provenance model (2009). https://eprints.soton.ac.uk/267282/1/fopm.pdf

57. Open Provenance Model (OPM) (2010). https://openprovenance.org/opm/old-index.html

58. Macedo, D.D., de Araújo, G.M., de Dutra, M.L., Dutra, S.T., Lezana, Á.G. Toward an efficient healthcare CloudIoT architecture by using a game theory approach. Concurrent Eng. **27**(3), 189–200 (2019)

59. Puel, A., Wangenheim, A.V., Meurer, M.I., de Macedo, D.D.J.: BUCOMAX: collaborative multimedia platform for real time manipulation and visualization of bucomaxillofacial diagnostic images. In: IEEE 27th International Symposium on Computer-Based Medical Systems, pp.392–395 (2014). https://doi.org/10.1109/CBMS.2014.12

60. Macedo, D.D.J., de Von Wangenheim, A., de Dantas, M.A.R.: A data storage approach for large-scale distributed medical systems. In: 2015 Ninth International Conference on Complex, Intelligent, and Software Intensive Systems, pp. 486–490 (2015). https://doi.org/10.1109/CISIS.2015.88

Author Index

Printed in the United States
by Baker & Taylor Publisher Services